Death and the Americar

This rich collection of original essays illuminates the causes and consequences of the South's defining experiences with death. Employing a wide range of perspectives while concentrating on discrete episodes in the region's past, the authors explore topics from the seventeenth century to the present, from the death traps that emerged during colonization to the bloody backlash against emancipation and civil rights to recent canny efforts to commemorate – and capitalize on – the region's deadly past. Some authors capture their subjects in the most intimate of moments: killing and dying, grieving and remembering, believing and despairing. Others uncover the intentional efforts of Southerners to publicly commemorate their losses through death rituals and memorialization campaigns. Together, these poignantly told southern stories reveal profound truths about the past of a region marked by death and unable – perhaps unwilling – to escape the ghosts of its history.

Craig Thompson Friend is professor of history and director of public history at North Carolina State University.

Lorri Glover is the John Francis Bannon Endowed Chair in the department of history at Saint Louis University.

Cambridge Studies on the American South

Series Editors

Mark M. Smith, *University of South Carolina, Columbia*
David Moltke-Hansen, *Center for the Study of the American South, University of North Carolina at Chapel Hill*

Interdisciplinary in its scope and intent, this series builds upon and extends Cambridge University Press's long-standing commitment to studies on the American South. The series not only will offer the best new work on the South's distinctive institutional, social, economic, and cultural history but will also feature works in a national, comparative, and transnational perspective.

Titles in the Series

Robert E. Bonner, *Mastering America: Southern Slaveholders and the Crisis of American Nationhood*
Ras Michael Brown, *African-Atlantic Cultures and the South Carolina Lowcountry*
Christopher Michael Curtis, *Jefferson's Freeholders and the Politics of Ownership in the Old Dominion*
Louis A. Ferleger and John D. Metz, *Cultivating Success in the South: Farm Households in Postbellum Georgia*
Luke E. Harlow, *Religion, Race, and the Making of Confederate Kentucky, 1830–1880*
Ari Helo, *Thomas Jefferson's Ethics and the Politics of Human Progress: The Morality of a Slaveholder*
Susanna Michele Lee, *Claiming the Union: Citizenship in the Post–Civil War South*
Scott P. Marler, *The Merchants' Capital: New Orleans and the Political Economy of the Nineteenth-Century South*
Peter McCandless, *Slavery, Disease, and Suffering in the Southern Lowcountry*
Barton A. Myers, *Rebels against the Confederacy: North Carolina's Unionists*
Johanna Nicol Shields, *Freedom in a Slave Society: Stories from the Antebellum South*
Brian Steele, *Thomas Jefferson and American Nationhood*
Jonathan Daniel Wells, *Women Writers and Journalists in the Nineteenth-Century South*

Death and the American South

Edited by

CRAIG THOMPSON FRIEND

North Carolina State University

LORRI GLOVER

Saint Louis University

CAMBRIDGE
UNIVERSITY PRESS

University Printing House, Cambridge CB2 8BS, United Kingdom

One Liberty Plaza, 20th Floor, New York, NY 10006, USA

477 Williamstown Road, Port Melbourne, VIC 3207, Australia

4843/24, 2nd Floor, Ansari Road, Daryaganj, Delhi - 110002, India

79 Anson Road, #06-04/06, Singapore 079906

Cambridge University Press is part of the University of Cambridge.

It furthers the University's mission by disseminating knowledge in the pursuit of education, learning and research at the highest international levels of excellence.

www.cambridge.org
Information on this title: www.cambridge.org/9781107446038

First published 2015
First paperback edition 2017

A catalogue record for this publication is available from the British Library

ISBN 978-1-107-08420-9 Hardback
ISBN 978-1-107-44603-8 Paperback

Contents

Illustrations

Contributors

Andrew Denson is associate professor of history at Western Carolina University and author of *Demanding the Cherokee Nation: Indian Autonomy and American Culture, 1830–1900* (2004).

Craig Thompson Friend is professor of history and director of public history at North Carolina State University, author of *Kentucke's Frontiers* (2010) and *Along the Maysville Road: The Early American Republic in the Trans-Appalachian West* (2005), co-editor with Lorri Glover of *Southern Manhood: Perspectives on Masculinity in the Old South* (2004), co-editor with Anya Jabour of *Family Values in the Old South* (2010), and editor of *Southern Masculinity: Perspectives on Manhood in the South since Reconstruction* (2009) and *The Buzzel about Kentuck: Settling the Promised Land* (1999).

Lorri Glover is John Francis Bannon, S. J., Professor of History at Saint Louis University and the author of *Founders as Fathers: The Private Lives and Politics of the American Revolutionaries* (2014), *Southern Sons: Becoming Men in the New Nation* (2007), and *All Our Relations: Blood Ties and Emotional Bonds among the Early South Carolina Gentry* (2000); co-author with Daniel Blake Smith of *The Shipwreck that Saved Jamestown: The* Sea Venture *Castaways and the Fate of America* (2008); and co-editor with Craig Thompson Friend of *Southern Manhood: Perspectives on Masculinity in the Old South* (2004).

Donald G. Mathews is professor emeritus of history at the University of North Carolina at Chapel Hill; author of *Religion in the Old South* (1977) and *Slavery and Methodism: A Chapter in American Morality, 1780–1845*

(1965); co-author of *Sex, Gender, and the Politics of ERA: A State and the Nation* (1990); and co-editor of *Religion in the American South: Protestants and Others in History and Culture* (2004).

Kristine M. McCusker is professor of history at Middle Tennessee State University, author of *Lonesome Cowgirls and Honky-Tonk Angels: The Women of Barn Dance Radio* (2008), and co-editor with Diane Pecknold of *A Boy Named Sue: Gender and Country Music* (2004) and *A Boy Named Sue, Too: New Essays in Gender and Country Music* (2014).

Peter N. Moore is associate professor of history at Texas A&M University at Corpus Christi; author of *World of Toil and Strife: Community Transformation in Backcountry South Carolina, 1750–1805* (2007); and editor of *The South Carolina Diary of Reverend Archibald Simpson* (2012).

Diane Miller Sommerville is associate professor of history at Binghamton University and author of *Rape and Race in the Nineteenth-Century South* (2004).

Jewel Spangler is associate professor of history at the University of Calgary and author of *Virginians Reborn: Anglican Monopoly, Evangelical Dissent, and the Rise of the Baptists in the Late Eighteenth Century* (2008).

Jeff Strickland is associate professor of history at Montclair State University and author of *Unequal Freedoms: Ethnicity, Race, and White Supremacy in Civil War Era Charleston* (2014).

Jason Morgan Ward is associate professor of history at Mississippi State University and author of *Defending White Democracy: The Making of a Segregationist Movement and the Remaking of Racial Politics, 1936–1965* (2011).

Jamie Warren is assistant professor of history at Borough of Manhattan Community College, CUNY.

Introduction: Death and the American South

Craig Thompson Friend and Lorri Glover

As her family carried her in a coffin for burial in Jefferson, Mississippi, Addie Bundren remembered how "My father said that the reason for living is getting ready to stay dead. I knew at last what he meant and that he could not have known what he meant himself, because a man cannot know anything about cleaning up the house afterward." William Faulkner's *As I Lay Dying* ranks consistently among the twentieth century's finest novels, and much of that esteem derives from Faulkner's brilliant engagement of one of the most difficult of human topics: death. The novel relates the story of Addie Bundren and her family's odyssey to respect her wishes and bury her some distance from their home, on the other end of Yoknapatawpha County. But each of her kin has his or her own reason to undertake the quest, beyond and despite Addie's burial. The story introduced thousands of readers to the peculiarities of southern life – and southern death.[1]

How has death framed southern history? That is the essential question behind this book, which began as a conference in April 2011 titled "'Death! 'Tis a Melancholy Day': Death, Mourning, and Memory in the American South," underwritten by the Department of History at North Carolina State University. Scholars presented papers on a rich variety of subjects relating to individual and community experiences with death between the seventeenth and twentieth centuries. The strength of those

[1] William Faulkner, *As I Lay Dying: The Corrected Text* (New York: Vintage International, 1985), 175–76.

works and others solicited in this emergent field convinced us that a volume on death would enrich southern history.[2]

Death and the American South explores the intimate relationship between death and southern history, but we are not making a generalizing case for the uniqueness of southern death and deathways. In some of the authors' stories, deathways appear patently southern: demographics, physical environments, religion, race and gender values, and politics often shaped many regional rituals of and attitudes toward death. But the history of death in the South took shape within larger contexts – European empires, plantation colonies, the United States, the Western world – that make futile any argument for consistently unique southern ways of death.

Instead, these scholars explore what we consider a more interesting and significant question: what were the causes and implications of the South's defining experiences with death? Taking a wide range of perspectives while concentrating on discrete episodes in the region's past, the authors of these essays tease out shifting, complex relationships between death and the American South. While many of the essays connect to the violent biracial history of the region, others remind readers of the continued influence of Native Americans. Several essays reveal the power of religion in shaping attitudes toward death and mourning. Demographics drive some scholars' interpretations, while others emphasize cultural changes apart from – even at odds with – mortality rates. Several authors illuminate the fact that death is at once deeply intimate and a powerful public site. The history of death takes many forms, and the authors consider killing and suicide, disease and decay, corpse preparations and mourning traditions, filiopietism and memorialization, the mourners and the dead.

Death's grim and constant presence in the American South began with the region's earliest manifestation. Roanoke colonists in the 1580s witnessed around them the ghastly consequences of the epidemic disease they unwittingly transmitted to local Indians. And, like later voyagers to southern outposts, they paid for their American folly with their lives. When war prevented the English from resupplying the Roanoke colony until 1590, the colonists disappeared. Many Englishmen preferred to believe they had starved or been killed: the possibility that they had been assimilated into

[2] We thank Jonathan Ocko and the Department of History at North Carolina State University for funding the conference that initiated this project.

the Indian populations was a "social death," a degeneration into savagery that few Europeans wanted to acknowledge.[3]

Roanoke was just the start. From their earliest colonial foundations, all the southern colonies struggled with forbidding environments. During Jamestown's "starving times" of 1609–10, only 60 of the 240 colonists at the fort survived the winter. Some survivors resorted to cannibalism, and several of the dying dug their own graves, hoping to keep their bodies from being ravaged by wild animals – and fellow colonists. Within a few years of the colony's founding, one seventeenth-century Englishman observed that "in steed of a Plantacion," colonial Virginia deserved "the name of a Slaughterhouse." And mortality rates in the Chesapeake only mildly improved over the next century. South Carolina's Lowcounty was even more dangerous than the Chesapeake, and deadlier still for African slaves than English colonists. In the autumn of 1711, several simultaneous epidemics killed 250 whites and nearly 400 blacks. Wealthier whites abandoned the Lowcounty seasonally to avoid disease, leaving behind susceptible slaves. Death was so pervasive among the colony's slave populations that those communities did not reproduce through natural increase until the turn of the nineteenth century. Farther south, the Spanish colony of Florida witnessed its own share of epidemics, deprivation, and bloodshed. Unlike the English colonies to the north, the Spanish widely used Native Americans as laborers. In the mid-seventeenth century, however, when three waves of smallpox and measles killed more than ten thousand Guales, Timucuas, and Apalachees living and laboring in the Spanish missions, the Spanish began to import African slaves.[4]

Those Native Americans who died in the Florida missions were symptomatic of a larger carnage underway within Southeastern Indian nations. While European colonists faced inhospitable environments, they also brought diseases and intercultural violence that made environments equally

[3] Erik R. Seeman, *Death in the New World: Cross-Cultural Encounters, 1492–1800* (Philadelphia: University of Pennsylvania Press, 2010), 67–77; James Horn, *A Kingdom Strange: The Brief and Tragic History of the Lost Colony of Roanoke* (New York: Basic Books, 2010).

[4] Nathaniel Butler, "The Unmasked Face of Our Colony in Virginia" (1623), excerpted in "The Virginia Planters' Answer to Captain Butler, 1632" in *Narratives of Early Virginia, 1606–1625*, ed. Lyon Gardiner Tyler (New York: Charles Scribner Sons, 1907), 417; Martha McCartney, "The Starving Time," Encyclopedia Virginia, www.encyclopediavirginia.org, January 1, 2014; John H. Hann, "Demographic Patterns and Changes in Mid-Seventeenth Century Timucua and Appalachee," *Florida Historical Quarterly* 64 (April 1986): 380–81; Peter McCandless, *Slavery, Disease, and Suffering in the Southern Lowcountry* (New York: Cambridge University Press, 2011).

unfriendly to Native Americans, who suffered far greater population losses in the early South. Traveling among the Sewees and Congarees of the Carolina backcountry in 1701, John Lawson related how, "The Small-Pox has been fatal to them; they do not often escape, when they are seiz'd with that Distemper, which is a contrary Fever to what they ever knew." Lawson did not understand how the disease was transmitted, but its consequences were devastatingly clear: "it destroy'd whole Towns, without leaving one *Indian* alive in the Village. ... The Small-Pox and Rum have made such a Destruction amongst them, that, on good grounds, I do believe, there is not the sixth Savage living within two hundred Miles of all our Settlements, as there were fifty Years ago."[5]

War, too, devastated Indians and their cultures, particularly because Europeans had more advanced weaponry. More than one thousand Tuscaroras died during the Tuscarora War, almost half of them in one incident in 1713 when colonial forces burned Tuscarora men, women, and children alive in Fort Neoheroka. Two years later, the Yamasees led a confederation of several Indian nations against South Carolina. Hundreds of European colonists were killed, but when the Cherokee decided to support the Carolinians over the Yamasees, the tide turned, hundreds of Yamasees died, and the survivors fled to Spanish Florida for refuge. Fourteen years later, the Natchez rebelled against French colonists at Fort Rosalie, killing more than two hundred and holding the fort for months before French-allied Choctaws besieged and captured the fort, murdering at least one hundred of the Natchez. Natchez peoples tried to take refuge among the Chickasaws, and when the French demanded the refugees be handed over, the Chickasaw War erupted, costing hundreds of Chickasaw lives and destroying their villages and culture.[6]

Death defined the character of southern provinces even before there was a self-conscious South, distinguishing the southern colonies from other North American ventures. Jamestown, the Carolina Lowcounty, St. Augustine and the Spanish missions of Appalachee and Timucua, the French settlements of the lower Mississippi valley – all starkly contrasted to New England, the mid-Atlantic, and New France's northern colonies

[5] John Lawson, *A New Voyage to Carolina*, ed. Hugh Talmage Lefler (Chapel Hill: University of North Carolina Press, 1967), 231–32.

[6] Paul Kelton, "The Great Southeastern Smallpox Epidemic, 1696–1700: The Region's First Major Epidemic?" in *The Transformation of the Southeastern Indians, 1540–1760*, ed. Robbie Ethridge and Charles Hudson (Jackson: University Press of Mississippi, 1998), 21–38; John H. Hann, "St. Augustine's Fallout from the Yamasee War," *Florida Historical Quarterly* 68 (October 1989): 180–200.

where death rates fell dramatically and consistently after the first years of settlement. The deaths of tens of thousands of Native Americans through disease and war facilitated European expansion, opening up acreage for staple crop production. But death played an even greater role in determining the rhythms of southern life during the region's formative decades: white Southerners' obsession with land and slaves was born out of death. Losses of both African and Native American laborers pushed Europeans to import greater numbers of Africans, binding southern agriculture more tightly to the international slave trade. By driving eighteenth-century importation patterns, demographic patterns, and family life, death also shaped the emergence of divergent African-American cultures in the southern colonies.[7]

So, too, was the white South's suspicion of the dark "Other" established during the death throes of the colonial era. More than 150 Carolina settlers died in the opening days of the Tuscarora War of 1711–13. During the Yamasee War of 1715, nearly 7 percent of South Carolina's white population died, a higher percentage and number of deaths than that suffered by New Englanders during King Philip's War. The Stono Rebellion of 1739 witnessed the death of thirty white colonists and forty-four insurgent African slaves, provoking strict slave codes that framed white-black relationships through the decades of slavery and Jim Crow and convincing white colonists that African slaves, no less than Indians, posed a constant threat to their very existence. As Craig Thompson Friend explores in "Mutilated Bodies, Living Specters: Scalpings and Beheadings in the Early South," Indians, whites, and blacks used mutilation of the dead to create scenes of terror and send political messages to those who came upon such scenes. Violence against corpses became as ubiquitous in the early South as violence against the living. As two forms of bodily mutilations, scalpings and beheadings earned a particularly visible role in the development of the early South.[8]

The colonial South's oppressive mortality also framed family life. Children died young and in large numbers; those who survived often found themselves orphaned by widespread parental death. War, epidemic and endemic disease, and famine meant that most people did not live to be

[7] Philip Morgan, *Slave Counterpoint: Black Culture in the Eighteenth-Century Chesapeake and Lowcountry* (Chapel Hill: University of North Carolina Press, 1998).

[8] William L. Ramsey, *The Yamasee War: A Study of Culture, Economy, and Conflict in the Colonial South* (Lincoln: University of Nebraska Press, 2008); Peter H. Wood, *Black Majority: Negroes in Colonial South Carolina from 1670 through the Stono Rebellion* (New York: W.W. Norton, 1974).

grandparents, leaving the care of children to aunts, uncles, and extended kin networks. In the near absence of an elderly, established population, patriarchy was weak, forcing young men to compete for wealth and power early in life, consequently marrying and beginning families at early ages. Throughout the seventeenth and early eighteenth centuries, these patterns crossed racial and ethnic lines.[9] The colonial South's peculiar intersection of racial interactions, persistently high mortality rates, and familial instability contributed to evolving ideas about death and the afterlife.

A larger cultural shift was under way in Western cultures that sought to soften the intensity of death's role in daily life, the final result of which was rejection of the medieval idea of the deathbed scene as a battlefield where good and evil fought over the soul of the dying. In its place emerged a more humanist vision of the "good death" and the anticipation of familial reconciliation in Heaven. The South had its own regional manifestation of this cultural transformation. West African cosmology emphasized life after death as one of ancestral guides and eternal life with forefathers. As African slaves became Christianized, they blended their traditions with European beliefs in a Great God and single Heaven for all believers. The intimacy of white and black lives and deaths in the colonial South accelerated the sharing of these ideas. Christian ministers, particularly during the First Great Awakening, tapped into the South's blended theology and the more emotive demonstrations that accompanied it, employing the vision of afterlife to draw in converts.[10] In "The Usable Death: Evangelicals, Anglicans, and the Politics of Dying in the Late-Colonial Lowcountry," Peter N. Moore examines how evangelical leaders reacted to these shifts in deathways by encouraging followers to die according to Reformed evangelical ideas of the "good death," curbing excessive grief even over the tragic loss of children and spouses. Moore also uncovers the interplay between

[9] Daniel Blake Smith, "Mortality and the Family in the Colonial Chesapeake," *Journal of Interdisciplinary History* 8 (winter 1978): 403–27; Carville V. Earle, "Environment, Disease, and Mortality in Early Virginia," in *The Chesapeake in the Seventeenth Century: Essays on Anglo-American Society and Politics*, ed. Thad W. Tate and David L. Ammerman (Chapel Hill: University of North Carolina Press, 1979), 96–125; Lorena S. Walsh and Russell R. Menard, "Death in the Chesapeake: Two Life Tables for Men in Early Colonial Maryland," *Maryland Historical Magazine* 69 (summer 1974): 211–27; Darrett B. and Anita H. Rutman, "'Now-Wives and Sons-in-Law': Parental Death in a Seventeenth-Century Virginia County," in Tate and Ammerman, eds., *The Chesapeake in the Seventeenth Century*, 153–82.

[10] Philippe Ariès, *The Hour of Our Death* (New York: Oxford University Press, 1981), esp. 297–321; Michel Sobel, *The World They Made Together: Black and White Values in Eighteenth-Century Virginia* (Princeton: Princeton University Press, 1987), esp. 214–25.

proper death accounts and political power – a theme that other authors show continued to mark the South into the modern era.

By the 1770s, as second- and third-generation Southerners acclimated to endemic and epidemic diseases, death rates began to fall, families and communities became more stable, and the notion of the South as a self-consciously distinct region began to emerge. In some ways, the American Revolution not only served to create a new nation but contributed to the South's regional formation. In the new republic, men who had participated in the creation of the United States became mythologized as "founders," specifically in the public commemorations of their deaths over the following decades. As Founding Fathers, they became the divinities in an American civic religion intended to legitimize the nation. Simultaneously, they lived as southern aristocrats on vast estates, surrounded by slaves and all of the amenities that patriarchy afforded gentlemen. As Lorri Glover relates in "When 'History Becomes Fable Instead of Fact': The Deaths and Resurrections of Virginia's Leading Revolutionaries," the apotheoses of George Washington, Thomas Jefferson, and James Madison were more than public affairs: nationwide veneration went hand-in-hand with relatives' efforts to frame deathbed narratives and the public's memory. By creating laudable death narratives, descendants resurrected their famous ancestors as paragons of republican virtue, the American founding, and southern patriarchy.[11]

Before arguments over the morality of slavery began to rend apart the nation, then, the South played an important role in defining what was "American." The democratic impulses set in motion by the American Revolution, however, extended public mourning beyond the deaths of Founding Fathers. In "American Mourning: Catastrophe, Public Grief, and the Making of Civic Identity in the Early National South," Jewel Spangler demonstrates how memorialization of the deceased following 1807's *Chesapeake* affair and a devastating fire in 1811 Richmond, Virginia, inspired a "national" form of mourning that we still employ today. In contrast to commemoration of great men, the episodes in Virginia made possible more egalitarian remembrances, reflecting in public rituals of grief the democratization of the early American republic.

[11] Andrew Burstein, "Immortalizing the Founding Fathers: The Excesses of Public Eulogy," in *Mortal Remains: Death in Early America*, ed. Nancy Isenberg and Andrew Burstein (Philadelphia: University of Pennsylvania Press, 2003), 91–107; Gerald Kahler, *The Long Farewell: Americans Mourn the Death of George Washington* (Charlottesville: University of Virginia Press, 2008).

By the 1840s, however, self-defined southern men, in thrall of a culture of honor and determined to perform their manhood, turned the South into a killing field with sadistically romanticized duels, vicious exploitation of slaves, and, ultimately, the overwhelming carnage of the Civil War. Death remained a powerful shaper of southern values, and as attitudes toward the afterlife and deathbed evolved, so, too, did attitudes toward the corpse. The ways in which people treat dead bodies have always signaled their cultural values, and in the Old South, not all corpses were treated equally. Jamie Warren's "To Claim One's Own: Death and the Body in the Daily Politics of Antebellum Slavery" explores issues of power and ownership under slavery. By following the corpse from deathbed to the grave (or lack thereof), Warren reveals how, in taking care of corpses and preparing them for burial, slaves found ways to reclaim autonomy as they asserted authority over the anatomies of their kin. Race, then, became a significant factor in the treatment of corpses, which in turn reinforced racial distinctions and racial contests over power in the plantation South.[12]

So, too, did death contribute to identity formations in antebellum southern cities. As immigrants filled places like New Orleans, Savannah, and Charleston, most did not have the means to escape the seasonal epidemics as plantation families had since the colonial era. In "Nativists and Strangers: Yellow Fever and Immigrant Mortality in Charleston, South Carolina," Jeff Strickland exposes how nativism manifested among native-born white Charlestonians who often blamed yellow fever epidemics on German and Irish immigrants, even as they argued that epidemics were useful for thinning out immigrant populations. Death, then, became an accomplice in making "southern" a synonym for whiteness and contributing to emerging racial ideals about the innate inferiority of blacks, unassimilated immigrants, and other "Others."

The terror and destruction of yellow fever epidemics were soon surpassed by the horrors of war. The carnage of the Civil War left a self-inflicted scar on the South that would not mend for generations. By 1865, southern white family life, the plantation economy, and the foundations of the region's long-standing social order crumbled under the weight of 260,000 Confederate corpses – lives squandered in a failed bid

[12] Mark S. Schantz, *Awaiting the Heavenly Country: The Civil War and America's Culture of Death* (Ithaca: Cornell University Press, 2008), chap. 5; Seeman, *Death in the New World*, 1–10; Stephanie Smallwood, *Saltwater Slavery: A Middle Passage from African to American Diaspora* (Cambridge: Harvard University Press, 2008), esp. chap. 7.

to deny freedom to 4,000,000 African Americans.[13] Confederates faced a social death as well: their soldiers had physically died, but when the war ended, the larger American nation did not bereave their deaths or recognize their sacrifices. Between Fort Sumter and Appomattox, the meaning of war had shifted so that President Lincoln could proclaim at Gettysburg "that this nation, under God, shall have a new birth of freedom." There was no rebirth for the Confederacy, however: it died, and with it everything for which it had stood. In the aftermath of the war, former Confederate soldiers dealt with a disenfranchised grief, mourning friends and family who had died while they had survived. Their losses, although publicly mourned in the South, were celebrated in the North.[14]

The depth of white Southerners' loss and despair during and after the war resulted in many considering suicide and many more reconsidering its morality. In "'Cumberer of the Earth': Suffering and Suicide among the Faithful in the Civil War South," Diane Miller Sommerville analyzes how changing religious considerations reshaped ideas about suicide among southern white men and women of faith who either contemplated suicide or responded to loved ones who took their own lives. As witnesses to unprecedented suffering, many Southerners gradually tempered their longstanding and intractable theological condemnation of suicide as an affront to God as they developed a more compassionate response, one that considered self-murder tragic but understandable given the dire conditions of war's aftermath.

As Reconstruction ended and the South was "redeemed," white Southerners undertook a variety of new ways to escape the world they had inherited – and to resurrect the world they had lost. The struggle to restore southern men's sense of value and manliness resulted in white women's massive memorial efforts, which recast Civil War deaths into

[13] Drew Gilpin Faust, *This Republic of Suffering: Death and the American Civil War* (New York: Knopf, 2008); Franny Nudelman, *John Brown's Body: Slavery, Violence, & the Culture of War* (Chapel Hill: University of North Carolina Press, 2004), chaps. 3 and 4; Gary Laderman, *The Sacred Remains: American Attitudes toward Death, 1799–1883* (New Haven: Yale University Press, 1996), pt. II.

[14] Abraham Lincoln, "The Gettysburg Address," November 19, 1863, Gettysburg, Pennsylvania; David W. Blight, *Race and Reunion: The Civil War in American Memory* (Cambridge: Harvard University Press, 2001); Therese A. Rando, *How To Go On Living When Someone You Love Dies* (New York: Bantam Books, 1991), 57–60; Kenneth J. Doka, ed., *Disenfranchised Grief: Recognizing Hidden Sorrow* (New York: Lexington Books, 1989), 4.

narratives of honor and sacrifice.[15] At the same time, the fight to ensure white prerogative manifested in Jim Crow segregation and macabre lynch mobs policing the color line through racially motivated murder.[16]

One of the main subjects in Donald G. Mathews's essay, Corra White Harris embodied these two impulses, recasting her husband's suicide as martyrdom while defending racial violence as essential. In both instances, sex intersected with race. In 1899, Harris penned an editorial defending the lynching of Sam Hose, an African American accused of murdering a white farmer and raping his wife. Not coincidentally, Harris's husband, the Reverend Lundy Harris, had confessed to sexual interludes with African-American women. As was typical in the New South, white male predations on black women got perversely twisted into the inverse: stereotypes of black male sexual aggression against white women.[17] Corra Harris condemned black men's rape of white women – a ubiquitous rumor but exceedingly rare crime – as an affliction on "respectable" society. But when Lundy Harris later committed suicide, Corra insisted that he was ultimately not to blame for his sexual transgressions or even his self-murder. In "The 'Translation' of Lundy Harris: Interpreting Death out of the Confusion of Sexuality, Violence, and Religion in the New South," Mathews examines this family saga to reveal the hypocrisies of interracial sex and racialized violence.

Just as the demographics of death had framed the development of the early South – from settlement patterns to the importation of greater numbers of African slaves – so, too, did it have a hand in shaping the New South. Widespread poverty, a paucity of medical professionals, and persistent ruralism conspired to make the New little changed from the Old South in the most universal of ways: Southerners white and black still had shorter life expectancies and higher mortality rates than the rest of the

[15] Karen L. Cox, *Dixie's Daughters: The United Daughters of the Confederacy and the Preservation of Confederate Culture* (Gainesville: University Press of Florida, 2004); Gaines M. Foster, *Ghosts of the Confederacy: Defeat, the Lost Cause, and the Emergence of the New South, 1865–1913* (New York: Oxford University Press, 1987); Caroline E. Janney, *Burying the Dead but Not the Past: Ladies' Memorial Associations and the Lost Cause* (Chapel Hill: University of North Carolina Press, 2007).

[16] See, for example, W. Fitzhugh Brundage, *Lynching in the New South: Georgia and Virginia, 1880–1930* (Urbana: University of Illinois Press, 1993); Claude A. Clegg, *Troubled Ground: A Tale of Murder, Lynching, and Reckoning in the New South* (Urbana: University of Illinois Press, 2010).

[17] Danielle McGuire, *At the Dark End of the Street: Black Women, Rape, and Resistance – A New History of the Civil Rights Movement from Rosa Parks to the Rise of Black Power* (New York: Knopf, 2010).

nation. Perceptions of the South in the early twentieth century echoed the three-century-old portrayal of the region as a slaughterhouse. By the late 1930s, Billie Holiday sang of how "Southern trees bear a strange fruit, blood on the leaves and blood on the root" and Blind Willie McTell lyricized that "don't a man feel bad, when his baby's on the coolin' board?"[18] Lynchings and other homicides, deaths resulting from malnutrition and poor health care, and newer causes of death from automobile and train travel, mill work, mining accidents, and the trials of the Great Depression – all reinforced characterizations of the South as peripheral to the modern world.

Still, in subtle ways, the South was modernizing, and this was nowhere more evident than in the funeral industry. Casket companies arose, replacing the artisan tradition that had long produced coffins. Chemical manufacturers developed new ways of embalming. Undertakers became professionalized as funeral directors, reigning over the new institution of the funeral home. The dead no longer relied on family and friends to be prepared for the grave; the funeral home performed those necessary and unpleasant preparations. And as southern white funeral directors rejected black corpses, Jim Crow ironically ensured black funeral directors a steady stream of customers, strengthening not only their businesses but their political influence as well.[19]

The condolence industry also flourished in the early twentieth century. When etiquette guru Emily Post heartily encouraged readers to send letters of condolence upon receiving word of a death, her advice was eagerly adopted by Southerners who used the practice to both reinforce and redefine social place in southern society. An emergent middle-class person could, for example, write to a grieving social better, claiming for herself a place once reserved for the elite and educated few. As Kristine M. McCusker reveals in "'He's Only Away': Condolence Literature and the Emergence of a Modern South," a new consumerism emerged around death by the 1940s, manifesting in the sale of preprinted cards that included messages of solace (and very little mention of death) and shifting

[18] Blind Willie McTell, *Cooling Board Blues* (1935), from *Blind Willie McTell – Statesboro Blues: The Early Years 1927–1935*, Documents Records GBENE0501598, 2005, compact disc; Billie Holiday, *Strange Fruit* (1939), from *Billy Holiday: All or Nothing at All*, Rovi Music MW0000311353, 1955, LP album.

[19] Suzanne E. Smith, *To Serve the Living: Funeral Directors and the African American Way of Death* (Cambridge: Harvard University Press, 2010), chaps. 1 and 2; Gary Laderman, *Rest in Peace: A Cultural History of Death and the Funeral Home in Twentieth-Century America* (New York: Oxford University Press, 2003), chap. 1.

attention away from the apocalyptic biblical allusions used to console the grieving in the 1910s and 1920s.

So long as Jim Crow was in place, however, the South could never really escape its nineteenth-century past. A centerpiece of southern literature and lore was white women's vulnerability and the rapaciousness of black male sexuality as justification for vigilantism. Lynchings – unofficial executions performed by self-appointed mobs who, without due process, captured and killed alleged suspects – flourished across the South between the end of Reconstruction and the 1960s. In "'A Monument to Judge Lynch': Racial Violence, Symbolic Death, and Black Resistance in Jim Crow Mississippi," Jason Morgan Ward details how African Americans made meaning from racial violence and brutalized bodies. Following lynchings at Mississippi's infamous "hanging bridge," first in 1918 and again in 1942, local African Americans refused to follow the white script for these sadistic rituals. They sacrificed cherished death customs by refusing to accept the victims' bodies for burial, keeping alive stories of black resistance. Coinciding with both world wars, reactions to the lynchings became part of the coalescing civil rights activism that would result in the mass movement of the 1950s and 1960s.[20]

Spectacles of racial brutality like the ones at the "hanging bridge" hardly depended on vigilantism in the New South; the law afforded ample opportunity for white power to be inflicted on black bodies. Mississippi's notorious Parchman Farm created in an ostensible prison system a deadly workplace that one prominent historian characterized as "Worse than Slavery." Prisoners, many detained under vagrancy laws expressly designed to reduce African Americans to peonage, served what often turned out to be life terms; men were worked to death or even murdered by guards.[21] Likewise, the death penalty was, in its application in southern courts, patently racist. In the same era in which lynchings flourished, more than five thousand legal executions took place in the South, with four of every five executed criminals being black. Hangmen's nooses no longer provide

[20] Karla FC Holloway, *Passed On: African American Mourning Stories* (Durham: Duke University Press, 2003); John Egerton, *Speak Now against the Day: The Generation before the Civil Rights Movement in the South* (New York: Knopf, 1994); Glenda Elizabeth Gilmore, *Defying Dixie: The Radical Roots of Civil Rights, 1919–1950* (New York: W.W. Norton, 2008).

[21] David M. Oshinsky, *Worse than Slavery: Parchman Farm and the Ordeal of Jim Crow Justice* (New York: Free Press, 1996). See also Wilbert Rideau, *In the Place of Justice: A Story of Punishment and Deliverance* (New York: Knopf, 2010); Michelle Alexander, *The New Jim Crow: Mass Incarceration in the Age of Colorblindness* (New York: New Press, 2010).

the symbolic link between lynchings and capital punishment, but modern-day capital punishment in the South cannot be divorced from the unequal punishments meted out to slaves and the legal and extralegal punishments of the Jim Crow era. Since the United States Supreme Court lifted the ban on death sentences in 1976, nearly 80 percent of all American executions have taken place in the South.[22]

As southern business and community leaders sought to distance their cities from the region's dark and bloody past, death found a new place in the South's cultural tourism industry. The ghost tours of Savannah; Andersonville National Historic Site in Georgia; the cemetery tours of New Orleans; the death site of Ma Barker in Oklawaha, Florida; and the Kentucky and Missouri grave sites of Cherokees pushed westward during the Trail of Tears – Southerners have appropriated death to draw in tourism dollars. In the 1830s, when the United States forcibly removed Cherokee from their homelands, more than four thousand died of starvation and exposure. In the modern South, those removal-era Cherokee graves became significant sites of commemoration that demonstrate the power of the dead to fix particular historical memories on the landscape – and attract tourist dollars. Andrew Denson explores these memories in "Reframing the Indian Dead: Removal-Era Cherokee Graves and the Changing Landscape of Southern Memory." Denson finds that local identity is often inspired by the commemoration associated with such sites, whether their histories are factual or imagined. Although memorials, they also serve as tourist attractions and define for visitors the history of the Trail of Tears. Death's association with southern memory, history, and identity has thus become an important component of the region's heritage tourism, blending the past with the present.

Death has played a central role in defining the South, from the earliest intercultural contacts to plantation slavery to the evolution of southern whiteness and the Lost Cause to the emergence of the New South and the conflicts of the Civil Rights era. And death continues to occupy a central place in Southerners' public memory and image: from the assassinations of John F. Kennedy in Dallas, Texas, Medgar Evers in Jackson, Mississippi,

[22] Howard W. Allen and Jerome M. Clubb, *Race, Class, and the Death Penalty: Capital Punishment in American History* (Albany: State University of New York Press, 2008); Stuart Banner, "Traces of Slavery: Race and Death Penalty in Historical Perspective," in *From Lynch Mobs to the Killing State: Race and the Death Penalty in America*, ed. Charles J. Ogletree and Austin Sarat (New York: New York University Press, 2006); Michael Fraser, "Crime for Crime: Racism and the Death Penalty in the American South," *Social Sciences Journal* 10 (2010): 1, online journal, www.repository.wcsu.edu/ssj.

and Martin Luther King Jr. in Memphis, Tennessee; to the haunting imagery of John Berendt's *Midnight in the Garden of Good and Evil* and HBO's *True Blood*; to the outrage over (and indifference to) Hurricane Katrina and Trayvon Martin.

But is that not what the South is: a region where the past has always bled into the present, where the dead continue to haunt the living? Or, as Faulkner wrote in another of his luminous novels, a place where "the past is never dead. It's not even past"?[23] The contributors to this collection capture their subjects in intimate moments of killing and dying, grief and remembrance, faith and despair. The deceased continue to live on, though, because individuals, families, and communities felt compelled to render their passings public – and now they have been written into history. Together, these stories about southern ways of death tell profound truths about the past of a region marked by death and unable, perhaps unwilling, to escape the ghosts of its own history.

[23] William Faulkner, *Requiem for a Nun* (1951; reprint, New York: Random House, 1994), 77.

1

Mutilated Bodies, Living Specters: Scalpings and Beheadings in the Early South

Craig Thompson Friend

"Can human nature bear the horror of the sight! See yonder! the hairy scalps clotted with gore! the mangled limbs! Women ripped up! the heart and bowels still palpitating with life, and smoking on the ground!" boomed the fiery evangelical preacher Samuel Davies in mid-August 1755; "See the savages swilling their blood, and imbibing a more outrageous fury with the inhuman draught! Sure these are not men; they are not beasts of prey; they are something worse; they must be infernal furies in human shape." One can imagine the reception by his audience, a company of Virginia volunteers preparing to engage the French and their Indian allies: some recoiling in horror at the imagery, others tearing up as they recalled the deaths of loved ones, and still others salivating at the thought of blood revenge. Dead bodies – or rather pieces thereof – haunted Davies's world, and he shared the call of the dead with the men before him: "And have we tamely looked on, and suffered them to exercise these hellish barbarities upon our fellow-men, our fellow-subjects, our brethren! Alas! with what horror must we look upon ourselves, as being little better than accessaries to their blood!" The dead did not cry out for vengeance; they demanded penance and restitution.[1]

Corpses as victims of war, enslavement, famine, and disease haunted the early South. There were corpses, too, in New England and the Mid-Atlantic, New France, and New Spain similarly speaking to the living through memories and words that were often put in their mouths by relations, friends, and preachers. Corpses communicated corporeally as well through

[1] *Sermons by the Reverend Samuel Davies*, 3 vols. (Philadelphia: Presbyterian Board of Publication, 1864), 3: 96.

the ways in which they were displayed, manipulated, and desecrated. Those messages, too, were not their own but imposed upon them.[2]

But this is a story of the early South, where particular intersections of red, white, and black among the dead as well as the living were laden with symbolism. As three peoples came together in the early South, two forms of death took a prominent place on the landscape: scalpings and beheadings. The latter were an instrument of governments and plantations to lay claim to slaves and their bodies. Occasionally, beheadings were appropriated by Africans to invert colonial justice, but most often they was employed by whites to reinforce that system, first under European flags and then in the new American nation. Scalping was an equally powerful instrument of Native American cultures, which used it as a "national act" to protect their own political and cultural structures from the European threat. Over the course of the seventeenth and eighteenth centuries, European Americans imagined that they mitigated scalping by pushing Indians westward and opening the South for plantations and yeoman farmers. Europeans portrayed scalpings as barbarous acts, but their own use of beheadings was no less violent or savage.

Both beheadings and scalpings targeted the head as a site of spiritual and cultural significance, and both relied on the corporeal materiality of the head for its power. Flesh and bones are critical to the dead's symbolic effectiveness: their presence and reconstitution into the earth lay claim to a place as a distinct locale or homeland. "This land is mine because this is where my ancestors rest" was a common sentiment among Southerners, red and white. Final resting places asserted ownership, and Southerners related to their homeland thusly. In contrast, blacks viewed the early South as foreign precisely because it was not the land where their ancestors lay buried. Through folklore and song, they harkened to Africa as the final repose of their fathers, their "home" where their own souls would eventually rest. For all, burial of the deceased placed that person among the ancestors.[3]

[2] Katherine Verdery, *The Political Lives of Dead Bodies: Reburial and Postsocialist Change* (New York: Columbia University Press, 1999), 27–29; Michael Meranze, "Major André's Exhumation," in *Mortal Remains: Death in Early America*, ed. Nancy Isenberg and Andrew Burstein (Philadelphia: University of Pennsylvania Press, 2003), 123–35; Peter Silver, *Our Savage Neighbors: How Indian War Transformed Early America* (New York: W. W. Norton, 2008), 227–60.

[3] Robert Hertz, "Contribution à une Étude sur la Représentation Collective de la Mort," *L'Année Sociologique* 10 (1907): 48–137; Mechel Sobel, *The World They Made Together: Black and White Values in Eighteenth-Century Virginia* (Princeton: Princeton University

Death also had the power to remake political geographies: the living employed the dead not only to demarcate homeland but to assert the political order appropriate to that homeland. As historian Nancy Isenberg has demonstrated, in eighteenth-century satirical prints, death – specifically through dismemberment – was a powerful metaphor for imperial decay. During the American Revolutionary era specifically, political cartoonists severed arms and legs from female representations of Britannia.[4]

Such engravings, however, were examples of art imitating life. Real-life dismemberment, particularly scalpings and beheadings, were also often used to symbolize political transformations. For example, the decapitation of enemies and the display of their heads in eighteenth-century Dahomey legitimated monarchical authority in the West African kingdom as its "founder" Wegbaja sought to abandon traditional concepts of kingdom-building based on consanguinity and inheritance. In an effort to destroy British economic influence in 1752, Ottawas and Chippewas joined their French allies in attacking Pickawilly (a Miami village and major trading post in the Ohio River valley) and torturing British ally Chief Memeskia, eventually ripping his heart out, boiling it, and ritualistically consuming the broth before the village. In 1793, throngs of revolutionaries watched Louis XVI's head roll from the guillotine, crowding to dip their handkerchiefs in the pool of blood even as they celebrated the end of French monarchism. In these cases, the mere death of an enemy was insufficient as a political statement: public mutilation and display to signify a new political order were required. Bodily mutilations were performed in the process of killing, making the desecration of the corpse the final ritualistic act.[5]

Beheadings were usually quick (although the guillotine apparently did not kill Louis XVI on its first blow), but even in those instances, there was an intermediary stage between living and dead: dying. The dying are liminal; not yet dead, neither are they quite alive. Their corporeality reminds us of

Press, 1987), 214–25; Craig Thompson Friend, "Little Eva's Last Breath: Childhood Death and Parental Mourning in 'Our Family, White and Black,'" in *Family Values in the Old South*, ed. Craig Thompson Friend and Anya Jabour (Gainesville: University Press of Florida, 2010), 62–85; Verdery, *Political Lives of Dead Bodies*, 105.

[4] Nancy Isenberg, "Death and Satire: Dismembering the Body Politic," in Isenberg and Burstein, eds., *Mortal Remains*, 71–90.

[5] Verdery, *Political Lives of Dead Bodies*, 28; Robin Law, "'My Head Belongs to the King': On the Political and Ritual Significance of Decapitation in Pre-Colonial Dahomey," *Journal of African History* 30 (1989): 399–400; Craig Thompson Friend, *Kentucke's Frontiers* (Bloomington: Indiana University Press, 2010), 22–23; William Doyle, "The Execution of Louis XVI and the End of the French Monarchy," *History Review* 36 (March 2000): 21–25; Thomas S. Abler, "Scalping, Torture, Cannibalism and Rape: An Ethnohistorical Analysis of Conflicting Cultural Values in War," *Anthropologica* 34 (1992): 6.

ourselves as living beings, but as J. Hector St. John de Crèvecoeur expressed in 1782, they are not living as we are. In what became his celebrated *Letters from an American Farmer*, Crèvecoeur described a visit to a South Carolina plantation where, with the owner's encouragement, he wandered the property and came upon a cage on which roosted dozens of birds that scattered at his approach. And then,

> horrid to think and painful to repeat, I perceived a negro, suspended in the cage, and left there to expire! I shudder when I recollect that the birds had already picked out his eyes, his cheek bones were bare; his arms had been attacked in several places, and his body seemed covered with a multitude of wounds. From the edges of the hollow sockets and from the lacerations with which he was disfigured, the blood slowly dropped, and tinged the ground beneath. No sooner were the birds flown, than swarms of insects covered the whole body of this unfortunate wretch, eager to feed on his mangled flesh and to drink his blood. I found myself suddenly arrested by the power of affright and terror; my nerves were convulsed; I trembled, I stood motionless, involuntarily contemplating the fate of this negro, in all its dismal latitude.

Here was a "living spectre," as Crèvecoeur labeled him, alive yet already decomposing, an apparition of his living self. He had killed the overseer and now served as a display of the plantation owner's "justice," meant to terrorize the other slaves into docility and immobility, an effect it seemingly also had on Crèvecoeur. The slave's blood "tinged the ground beneath," consecrating the property for slave labor, reaffirming patriarchy and enslavement as the plantation's political order.[6]

Crèvecoeur's description of the dying slave served as his critique of slavery, in contrast to the principles he thought defined American identity – opportunity, self-determination, ingenuity, and diversity founded upon ethnic, religious, and cultural differences. He situated the story in a chapter entitled "American Savagery," conflating the violence of white southern "civilization" with his audience's expectation that savagery was a Native American quality. "Sure these are not men; they are not beasts of prey; they are something worse," Samuel Davies had pronounced the Native American "savage"; Crèvecoeur and most certainly the dying slave thought similarly of white slaveowners.[7]

From the liminality of the dying, it was only one small step to attribute animation and power to the recently dead as well. In most cultures, the

[6] Verdery, *Political Lives of Dead Bodies*, 31; J. Hector St. John de Crèvecoeur, *Letters from an American Farmer* (New York: Fox, Duffield & Co., 1904), 243–44.

[7] Ian Haywood, *Bloody Romanticism: Spectacular Violence and the Politics of Representation, 1776–1832* (New York: Palgrave Macmillan, 2006), 141.

recently dead were assumed to be in transition. The living occasionally assisted the deceased by providing food and supplies, as one American slave father did for his young son, burying the boy with "a small bow and several arrows; a little bag of parched meal; a miniature canoe, about a foot long, and a little paddle (with which he said it would cross the ocean to his own country), ... and a piece of white muslin, with several curious and strange figures painted on it in blue and red, by which, he said, his relations and countrymen would know the infant to be his son, and would receive it accordingly, on its arrival amongst them." Other cultures sewed bodily orifices shut to keep evil spirits from interfering or covered mirrors so that the deceased would not become trapped in them. Beyond the transitional state of the spirit, however, the body, too, remained liminal. Recall Samuel Davies's exclamation of "Women ripped up! the heart and bowels still palpitating with life, and smoking on the ground!" So, too, would scalps and decapitated heads appear alive. The recently dead were "living spectres," too: corpses that remained animated, serving as mediators between the living and the dead.[8]

Mutilation of the dying and recently dead had a long history in the early South. During Hernando de Soto's 1540 expedition through west Florida, two of his men were captured by Apalachees. One, Simón Rodríguez, attempted to climb a tree but three arrows brought him to the ground. He "had hardly fallen when they removed his head, or rather the entire helmet (one doesn't know the skill with which it is removed and with the greatest ease), and then took it as proof of the deed." Twenty years later, another Spanish expedition led by Tristán de Luna y Arellano joined Creeks from Coosa in invading their rivals' village at Napoche where they came upon a tree "full of hair from the Coosans." The Native Americans "screamed rabidly, mourning the death of their relatives and friends. Many tears were shed there for the lack of the bodies of the dead and for the reproach of the living." They cut down the tree, taking the scalps in order to bury them with "proper ceremony."[9]

8 Charles Ball, *Fifty Years in Chains; or, The Life of an American Slave* (New York: H. Dayton, 1859), 197–98; William May, "Attitudes toward the Newly Dead," *Hastings Center Studies* 1 (1973): 9; Ruth Richardson, *Death, Dissection and the Destitute* (London: Penguin Books, 1988), 14–15. Lawrence R. Schehr, "Foucault's Body" *Bulletin de la Société Américaine de Philosophie de Langue Française* 6 (spring 1994): 60.

9 Garcilaso de la Vega, *La Florida del Inca*, ed. Emma Susana Speratti (Mexico City: Fondo de Cultura Económica, 1956), 181–82; Agustín Dávila Padilla, *Historia de la fundación y discurso de la provincia de Santiago de México de la Orden de Predicadores*, 2nd ed. (Brussels: Ivan de Meerbeque, 1625; facsimile Mexico City: Editorial Academia Literaria, 1955), 260. I am indebted to James McConnell for his translations.

Agustín Dávila Padilla, who described this episode of the Luna expedition, interpreted the Coosans' grief as resulting from the absence of corpses – "the lack of the bodies" – without which burial and the "good death" were problematic. His own perspective mattered, however: within European culture, particularly Padilla's Roman Catholic tradition, a good death required a calm deathbed scene that solemnized the transition from earthly body to Heavenly spirit. The ideal deathbed scene, then, helped to ease the dying's anxiety about his judgement by contextualizing his demise within the collective rites of death. Padilla and Europeans struggled with sudden and violent death – the *mors improvisa* – precisely because it disrupted the good death. Indeed, without the security of collective rites, there was no certainty about the salvation of victims of *mors improvisa*.[10]

The threat of *mors improvisa* in the Americas was made visual for Europeans in the 1590s when Theodorus de Bry interpreted the paintings of Jacques Le Moyne de Morgues, one of the few survivors of Fort Caroline, a French colony in northeastern Florida conquered in 1565 when the Spanish executed 140 colonists for their Protestantism. Among de Bry's engravings was "How Outina's Men Treated the Slain of the Enemy," picturing an actual scalping, the drying of scalps, and their attachment to poles then carried back to the victors' village for display. Europeans were well-practiced in the atrocities of war: throughout early modern Europe, dismemberment (including the occasional decapitation) was used as punishment for wartime enemies. When such episodes occurred in European warfare, they were excused as civilized warriors overwhelmed by the fervor of battle. When Europeans read about and saw images of Native American scalping (Figure 1), however, they interpreted it as indicative of the character of "savage" warfare, consequently justifying violence against Native Americans by portraying the enemies' behavior as deviant. This opinion of savage warfare permeated European thought for centuries, and the belief persisted that it could only be tempered by "civilization," as evidenced in British naturalist John Lawson's parenthetical comment about Florida Indians in 1709: "when they take any Prisoners, (if the *English* be not near to prevent it) [they] sculp them, that is, to take their Hair and

10 Philippe Ariès, *Western Attitudes toward Death: From the Middle Ages to the Present*, trans. Patricia M. Ranum (Baltimore: Johns Hopkins University Press, 1974), 37, 47; idem, *The Hour of Our Death*, trans. Helen Weaver (New York: Oxford University Press, 1981), 108, 118.

FIGURE 1. Europeans framed ideas about Native American "savagery" partially from sketches of scalping created in the Americas.

Source: Theodor de Bry, "How Outina's Men Treated the Slain of the Enemy" (1591), based on watercolors by Jacques Le Moyne de Morgues. Courtesy of the State Archives of Florida, Florida Memory, http://floridamemory.com/items/show/254226

Skin of their Heads, which they often flea away, whilst the Wretch is alive."[11]

It is simple to understand why Europeans considered scalping a savage act. A Frenchman observed during the French and Indian War that

> When he has struck two or three blows, the savage quickly seizes his knife, and makes an incision around the hair from the upper part of the forehead to the back of the neck. Then he puts his foot on the shoulder of the victim, whom he has turned over face down, and pulls the hair off with both hands, from back to front... When a savage has taken a scalp, and is not afraid he is being pursued, he stops and scrapes the skin to remove the blood and fibres on it. He makes a hoop of green

11 James Axtell and William C. Sturtevant, "The Unkindest Cut, or Who Invented Scalping," *William and Mary Quarterly* 37 (July 1980): 466; Theodor de Bry, "How Outina's Men Treated the Slain of the Enemy," 1591, State Archives of Florida, *Florida Memory*, www.floridamemory.com; Abler, "Scalping, Torture, Cannibalism and Rape," 4; John Lawson, *A New Voyage to Carolina*, ed. Hugh Talmage Lefler (Chapel Hill: University of North Carolina Press, 1967), 10.

wood, stretches the skin over it like a tambourine, and puts it in the sun to dry a little.

In contrast to European means of wartime killing, scalping – the slicing, ripping, and scraping – was far more intimate a relationship between killer and the victim's flesh. The sword, ax, and guillotine separated bodies from their heads from a distance, if only a few feet. Scalping, in contrast, demanded interpersonal contact: the executioner grasped the hair and jerked viciously, tearing the flesh from the skull, depriving the victim of a good death.[12]

Native Americans counted on such an interpretation of scalping. Many believed that the scalp and hair incarnated the spirit and identity of the individual. Loss of one's scalp, then, shamed the victim through social death and condemned the victim to spiritual death while transferring power to the holder. The Creeks, for example, camped on the right side of paths, leaving the left wayside clear for the "Ghosts of their departed Heroes who have either unfortunately lost their scalps, or remain unburied." Without a scalp, the spirit could not be admitted into the "Mansion of Bliss" but instead was "sentenced to take up its invisible and darksome Abode, in the dreary Caverns of the Wilderness" until a scalp was taken from the enemy to satisfy the spirit. Consequently, when scalps were taken, they were displayed with pride, sometimes on a pole or tree in the village, sometimes on a warrior's belt, sometimes in his home or that of a clan member to satisfy a request to replace a lost relative. Because they contained the spirits of victims, scalps were powerful tokens to be venerated and even feared. As German cartographer William Gerard de Brahm explained of the Cherokee: "No Woman, Girl, or Boy can be prevailed upon to go near the Town House at Night, they say, among the Scalps wander the Spirits of the killed." In this manner, the recently dead continued to live.[13]

[12] Sylvester K. Stevens et al., eds., *Travels in New France by J. C. B.* (Harrisburg: Pennsylvania Historical Commission, 1941), 68.

[13] Axtell and Sturtvant, "The Unkindest Cut, or Who Invented Scalping," 451–72; John Pope, *A Tour through the Southern and Western Territories of the United States of North-America: A Facsimile Reproduction of the 1792 Edition*, ed. Barton Starr (Gainesville: University Press of Florida, 1979), 63–64; Louis De Vorsey Jr., ed., *DeBrahm's Report of the General Survey in the Southern District of North America* (Columbia: University of South Carolina Press, 1971), 111; Christina Snyder, *Slavery in Indian Country: The Changing Face of Captivity in Early America* (Cambridge: Harvard University Press, 2010), 82–83.

Although an occasional victim survived scalping, Native Americans tried to assure the death of their victims so that the scalp would fully embody the victim's spirit and identity. De Brahm noted that Cherokees "strike a Tomahawk (Hatchet) anywhere in the Body, wherewith they leave him, after having taken off his Scalp." It was critical that the victim die so that the scalp became a spiritual relic fully imbued with the deceased's energy, deserving of reverence and ritualistic care. When Cherokee Chief Warhatchie met with Maryland officials in 1757, he rejected the colonials' demand that his people abide by a law requiring them to exchange scalps for rewards. "It was the Indians custom to preserve as Trophies the Hair of the Enemies that they killed in Battle and to carry them home to their own People," explained one diplomat, "as it procured them most Honour among their own People." Once purchased by colonials, scalps were destroyed to avoid fraudulent resubmission for rewards. The Cherokees did not want the scalps destroyed "in such a manner as the Act Directs" because it would desecrate the spiritual symbolism of the scalps.[14]

Beyond its ritualistic role, however, scalping also was politically symbolic. Europeans who interpreted scalping as unwarranted savagery misread the act. William Johnson, Britain's Superintendent for Indian Affairs in the Northern Colonies, explained in a 1772 deposition that Native Americans considered scalping "a National Act and Declaration of War." Although they did not live in "nations" as Europeans imagined the concept, Native Americans performed scalping only in the context of wars approved by a majority of war chiefs in their cultural groups. As a military tactic, then, scalping was an action of the nation upon its enemies.[15]

Consequently, the display of scalps served as political warnings. Near Jamestown, in 1608, Powhatan Indians of Virginia surprised a nearby Payankatank settlement, killing twenty-four men and capturing the women and children. They scalped the men's corpses: "the long haire of the one side of their heads, with the skinne cased off with shells or reeds, they brought away." When he visited Powhatan's village, John Smith saw

[14] James Axtell, "Scalping: The Ethnohistory of a Moral Question," in *The European and the Indian: Essays in the Ethnohistory of Colonial North America* (New York: Oxford University Press, 1981), 214; Vorsey, ed., *DeBrahm's Report*, 109; Daniel Wolstenholme to Governor Horatio Sharpe, May 25, 1757, in *Archives of Maryland* 6 (1888): 558.

[15] *Proceedings and Transactions of Royal Society of Canada*, 3rd Series, 36 vols. (Ottawa, Canada: Jas. Hope & Son, 1910), 13: 116.

"the lockes of haire with their skinnes, hanged on a line betwixt two trees" and suspected that the chief not only "made ostentation of his triumph at Weowocomoco" but "intended to have done as much to me and my company." Powhatan may have wanted to add the English colonists' scalps to his collection, but the display had served its purpose: warning Smith of the Native Americans' intentions to dominate local populations, including the one at Jamestown.[16]

In the European mind, scalping epitomized savage warfare and the *mors improvisa*. In Europe, such acts of supplice – torture for the purpose of torment and death, usually in a public forum – were rationally designed. Executions were performances in which the criminal's body was burned, tarred, hanged, drawn and quartered, beheaded, or any combination thereof. Executioners often performed their gruesome work on an elevated stage, so that the criminal became an object of public spectacle before which he was neither living nor dead (or conceivably *both* living and dead, like the slave for whom Crèvecoeur lamented). His spirit already condemned to Hell, all that remained was the corruptible body, the corporeal remnant of the human's *being*. Among Europeans, the tortured criminal became both the object and target of power as he lay subject to the gaze of his audience and the power of the state. His death and dismemberment concluded both his corporeal and spiritual existence. In contrast, Europeans thought scalping irrational and lawless, but it was quite similar to their own versions of supplice. The tortured victim, too, lay subject to the gaze of an audience as the object and target of power, but that audience was most often the victims' family, friends, and acquaintances, many of whom soon became victims themselves.[17]

Although death concluded the victim's corporeal life, however, the corpse – in the form of a scalp with hair – retained the victim's spiritual being. To Native Americans, apparently, it was the hair and not the flesh that mattered, and this was because hair was central to the scalp's animation as a living specter. Contrary to conventional wisdom, hair does not continue to grow after death. Still, hair lengthens on a corpse because, as the skin desiccates, it draws back around the hair, giving the appearance of continued animation. Whereas drying scalps by a fire preserved them for use, it also caused hair to seemingly lengthen and testified to the scalp as

[16] John Smith, *Travels: History of Virginia* (New York: Cambridge University Press, 1908), 124.

[17] Michael Foucault, *Discipline and Punishment: The Birth of the Prison* (New York: Random House, 1995), 3–7, 135–36; Schehr, "Foucault's Body," 60–61.

spiritually alive. Consequently, the display of scalps was significant for they seemingly evinced spiritual power through corporeal animation.[18]

Even for Europeans who imbued them with less spiritual purpose, scalps were tangible symbols, and hair was central to that interpretation. By the late 1700s, when William Blake's "Europe Supported by Africa and Asia" – a prefect allegorical engraving of England's imperial ambitions – went to print, Europeans had employed hair as a marker of ethnic difference for more than two centuries, distinguishing their coiffured forms from the coarseness of African hair and the strange cuts of Native American hair. Additionally, to Europeans, the beardlessness and sparse body hair of Native American men implied femininity and weakness. While Africans and Native Americans employed hair to mark the body's passage through different stages of life, over the late seventeenth century and across the eighteenth century, European Americans became absolutely obsessed with hair as a marker of distinction between not only the stages of life, gender, and classes, but also between themselves and the conquered ethnicities of their empires as well. Consequently, European-American descriptions of scalpings very often related the color, length, and even the coiffure of the hair as indicators of gender, status, and race. When, in 1784, Keturah Leitch Moss arrived in Kentucky as an eleven-year-old, she witnessed the horrors of scalping. Coming on the scene of an Indian attack, her sisters and she saw hanging from a tree limb a scalp with beautiful blonde ringlets, indicating not only the race of the deceased but something of her status and age as well – an image that remained with Moss throughout her life. Because European Americans viewed the hair and scalp as representations rather than embodiments of the spirit, they did not empower scalps as sources of life and animation; scalps were pieces of the dead that could be objectified and even commodified.[19] See Figure 2.

And commodify, they did. Colonial assemblies passed laws offering handsome rewards for scalps, and many Native Americans adjusted their own understanding of scalps to take advantage of the bounties. In 1733,

[18] Angela Rosenthal, "Raising Hair," *Eighteenth-Century Studies* 38 (fall 2004): 1–16.

[19] Karen Ordahl Kupperman, *Indians & English: Facing Off in Early America* (Ithaca, NY: Cornell University Press, 2000), 55–56; Rosenthal, "Raising Hair," 2; Margaret K. Powell and Joseph Roach, "Big Hair," *Eighteenth-Century Studies* 38 (fall 2004): 83; Snyder, *Slavery in Indian* Country, 17; W. H. Perrin et al., *Kentucky: A History of the State* (Louisville: F. A. Battey and Co., 1887), 896; William Blake, "Europe Supported By Africa and America," in *Engravings for J. G. Stedman, Narrative, of a five year's expedition, against the Revolted Negroes of Surinam, in Guinea, on the Wild Coast of South America; from the year 1772, to 1777* (London, 1796).

FIGURE 2. Among Europeans, hair became a primary distinguishing feature of ethnicity and "civilization." The targeting of hair through scalping, therefore, stripped victims of civilized identity and led to social death.
Source: William Blake, "Europe Supported by Africa and America," in John Gabriel Stedman, Narrative of a Five Years' Expedition against the Revolted Negroes of Surinam (London: J. Johnson and J. Edwards, 1796), plate 16.

General James Oglethorpe led an expedition to establish Fort Fredrica to protect the new colony of Georgia from Spanish Florida. During an incursion against Fort Diego, a Spanish bastion some twenty miles north of St. Augustine, an English ranger witnessed the accompanying Yamacraw Indians kill "one Negroe as he was going into Diego Fort and brought his Scalp to the Genl. Who rewarded them very well." Apparently, the Yamacraws willingly sacrificed the spiritual essence of the scalp for trade goods (which provided another type of status in their village). Europeans learned to employ scalping for their own aggrandizement. "We have killed Eight of the Yamases, on[e] of which is the huspaw kings head Warriour and have Brought off all thir Scalps," wrote an Englishman; "We have likewise Taken nine of them a Live, Together with Several Guns, Some Cloth, and Some plunder Out of there Churches, Which you will See When the Warriours Come in." Like guns, cloth, and plunder, scalps were possessions to be stolen or sold, no different from deer skins. In fact, in 1746, a Frenchman observed a transaction between a merchant and a Creek: "not only would he pay him for the scalp, in consideration of his zeal and attachment, but that he would also trade with him for his skins." Add to this commodification of scalps the European trade goods that made scalping easier: a gun to take down the enemy, a metal knife to remove the scalp. In the earliest stages of contact, scalping had been a way with which to terrorize colonists and hold their cultural influences at bay. As European Americans incorporated scalping into their mercantile system over the eighteenth century, and as Native Americans bought into the scalp trade, the spiritual purpose for scalping eroded, and natives became immersed in those economic networks.[20]

As many Native Americans succumbed to the temptations of the market and conceded the spiritual symbolism of scalps, many European Americans became particularly attuned to scalping as a symbolic action, although they interpreted that symbolism somewhat differently. Throughout the Middle Ages, the body had been viewed negatively, as corruptible and consequently an enemy to the purity of the spirit. The Renaissance had introduced new aesthetics of the body as beautiful, fragile, and good. In particular, the head and the hands came to symbolize a person's identity and life force. During the Reformation, Protestants often targeted Catholic statuary as decadent, breaking off heads and hands to "mutilate" the identity of the memorialized. The association of bodily mutilation with political statements evolved into new ideas of the body and led to new

[20] "A Ranger's Report of Travels with General Oglethorpe in Georgia and Florida, 1739–1742," in *Travels in the American Colonies*, ed. Newton Dennison Mereness (New York: Macmillan Co., 1916), 233; "Journal of Captain Tobias Fitch's Mission from Charleston to the Creeks, 1726," in Mereness, ed., *Travels in the American Colonies*, 205; "Journal of Beauchamp's Journey from Mobile to the Choctaws, 1746," in Mereness, ed., *Travels in the American Colonies*, 286; Greg O'Brien, *Choctaws in a Revolutionary Age, 1750–1830* (Lincoln: University of Nebraska Press, 2006), 43; Joyce E. Chaplin, *Subject Matter: Technology, the Body, and Science on the Anglo-American Frontier, 1500–1676* (Cambridge: Harvard University Press, 2001), 114–15.

political language as to the authority of the "head" of household and the "head" of state. Throughout colonial America, patriarchy was the foundation for social, political, economic, familial, and religious developments. The "head" was central to the security and stability of the family, the community, the colony, and the empire.[21]

So, too, were the hands critical to the advancement of patriarchal empire. It is no coincidence that words like "commend" (to commit into one's hands), "command" (to give into one's hands), and "comprehend" (to lay hold of, to seize, to grasp) joined the English language during the Renaissance. Rooted in the Latin *manus*, which means "hand," the words evidenced new ways in which Europeans understood the relationship of information to power. As organs of performance and perception, the hands communicated and built patriarchal empire – and the hands of Others threatened to destroy those efforts. Scalpings held particular political symbolism for Europeans, then, drawing on the head as metaphor for authority and the hands as metaphor for action. Scalpings were a moment of performance between the European head and Native American hands, a moment in which empire and patriarchal rule were threatened.[22]

Moreover, Europeans' new obsession with hair contributed to the power of the metaphor. The act of scalping not only attacked the head as a site of authority, but also removed the hair as a symbol of European identity, replacing it with marks of savagery. Europeans feared death at the hands of Native Americans, and they also feared captivity because it threatened a social death, replacing their cultural identities with assimilation into Indian culture. Scalping conjoined these two threats, literally stripping a victim of his European identity as perpetrators laid claim to the body.

Europeans were familiar with the symbolism and practice of destroying identity through bodily mutilation. Although not common, beheadings were not unknown in Europe and were used to make political statements. The practice arrived in the early South with the first English colonists in 1586. Almost immediately, the Roanoke colonists faced a food shortage.

[21] Richardson, *Death, Dissection, and the Destitute*, 13; Ariès, *The Hour of Our Death*; Anthony Synnott, "Tomb, Temple, Machine and Self: The Social Construction of the Body," *British Journal of Sociology* 43 (March 1992): 90; C. Pamela Graves, "From an Archaeology of Iconoclasm to an Anthropology of the Body: Images, Punishment, and Personhood in England, 1500–1660," *Current Anthropology* 49 (February 2008): 41–43.

[22] Ethel J. Alpenfels, "The Anthropology and Social Significance of the Human Hand," *Artificial Limbs: A Review of Current Developments* 2 (May 1955): 4–21. All etymology is drawn from the Oxford English Dictionary.

A summer storm had wrecked a supply ship, and with only three weeks of sustenance remaining, they abandoned their settlement to seek out security. When the colonists returned to the village, however, it appeared to have been pillaged, and they quickly cast accusations toward their allies, the Aquascogoc Algonquians. The English attacked and burned the Aquascogoc village, then, recognizing their own vulnerability, turned to the Secotans for food and security. But paranoia was high, and Governor Ralph Lane, fearing that Secotan Chief Wingina would eradicate the English, preemptively struck the Secotans. Wingina was beheaded in the ensuing chaos, and his head placed on a pike.[23]

Of course, Wingina's beheading evidenced the horror of intercultural violence. An Englishman had chased Wingina into the woods and killed the Secotan in a moment of anger. In such episodes of callous fear, little thought was given to the symbolism of heads. In 1740, one of James Oglethorpe's rangers, trying to secure better relations with the region's natives, came on a scene where "the Spaniards had been upon the Island of Amelia and had killed two of the Trustees Servts and Cut of their Heads." They were not displayed, just left lying in the sand. Even if the Spanish had intended a message by leaving decapitated bodies and heads to be found, it was lost on the ranger who interpreted instead that the Spanish were "so terrified for fear of the English coming upon them that they Ran away leaving a Hatchet and Knife behind them." Still, in contrast, Wingina's beheading was something more than a moment of horrific violence and mere decapitation: it was punishment for treason. In supposedly planning to attack the governor, Wingina conspired to commit violence against the Crown and its colonization enterprise.[24]

The French similarly dealt with threats to their empire-building but were less inclined to categorize those threats as treason. In 1729, Natchez Indians attacked Fort Rosalie, killing more than two hundred French men, women, and children. French allies among the Choctaws and Tunicas retaliated, killing more than one hundred Natchez who had taken residence in the fort and taking dozens of captives, among whom was the wife of Chief La Farine. She had ordered the torture and deaths of three Frenchmen during the attack, and the Tunica Indians now gifted her to Louisiana governor Etiénne de Périer for justice. Périer rejected the gift, authorizing the Tunicas

[23] Seeman, *Death in the New World*, 76–77; David Beers Quinn, ed., *The Roanoke Voyages, 1584–1590*, 2 vols. (London: Hakluyt Society, 1955), 1: 285–88.

[24] "A Ranger's Report of Travels with General Oglethorpe in Georgia and Florida, 1739–1742," 224.

to torture and burn the woman on a bluff visible to the residents of New Orleans. After preparing the stage for execution, the Tunicas arrived at the jail to collect their victim, finding her "fixing a ribbon to her braided hair." On tying her to the scaffold, they scalped her, hanged the scalp on a pike visible to all, and then ritualistically burned her – body part by body part. As she died, the French women who had suffered at Fort Rosalie pierced her body with flaming canes, and one French officer cut a chunk from her flesh and consumed it.[25]

Still, the French governor categorized her not as treasonous but as criminal. The application of treason to threats to the colonial system seemingly applied primarily to Britain's empire. On the plantations of England's Caribbean colonies, as historian Vincent Brown has shown, "Dead bodies, dismembered and disfigured as they were, would be symbols of the power and dominion of slave masters. In their view, the severed heads standing sentry over the plantation landscape conveyed a warning to potential rebels and reassurance to supporters of the social order." Given the difficulties with which Europeans struggled to establish footholds in the colonial South and Caribbean (and the lingering high mortality rates that accompanied those struggles), any threat to the patriarchal structure of plantations and empire was a threat to social order and security. In 1730, a Virginia slave named James died in custody while awaiting trial for killing his master's daughter. Probably evidencing the eventual verdict, the judges ordered him quartered and beheaded, with each bodily part displayed (or gibbeted) at locations throughout the county – the typical penalty for high treason against the empire. Although the other four body sections most certainly terrorized black and whites alike, the display of his head linked his individual identity to his crime against the emerging southern social order.[26]

James probably would not have fared better had he faced trial. English law had been consistent since 1352 that "if any servant kill his Master, any woman kill her husband, or any secular or religious person kill his Prelate to whom he owes Obedience, this is treason," or more specifically, petty

[25] James F. Barnett Jr., *The Natchez Indians: A History to 1735* (Jackson: University Press of Mississippi, 2007), 118–19; Sophie White, "Massacre, Mardi Gras, and Torture in Early New Orleans," *William and Mary Quarterly* 70 (July 2013): 519–30 (Marc-Antoine Caillot, quoted on 524).

[26] Vincent Brown, *The Reaper's Garden: Death and Power in the World of Atlantic Slavery* (Cambridge: Harvard University Press, 2008), 136; Peter Charles Hoffer and William Scott, eds., *Criminal Proceedings in Colonial Virginia* (Athens: University of Georgia Press, 1984), 133–34; Philip J. Schwarz, *Twice Condemned: Slaves and the Criminal Laws of Virginia, 1705–1865* (Baton Rouge: Louisiana State University, 1988), 81.

treason. The murder of a master's wife or daughter was considered an attack on him and petty treason as well. In contrast, a man who killed his wife or servant would have been accused of murder. To highlight this further, the penalty for murder was public hanging and display of the body. The penalty for petty treason, however, was the same as for high treason: some combination of dismemberment, disembowelment, decapitation, and burning at the stake. The distinction is clear: petty treason was more than an attack on a person, it was an assault on the patriarchal order. In the southern colonies, white women and black slaves may have faced charges of petty treason, but they were judged and punished as traitors against the empire as represented through white patriarchy.[27]

In the early South, this overt protection of patriarchy was reinforced by the dual system of justice that attended to intercultural conflict: the empire had its laws, and the plantation had its justice. The slow starvation of a slave hanging in a cage was nowhere allowed by law, but the planter aristocracy expected dominance over their slaves and exerted extralegal authority to enforce it. Punishment, therefore, did not always fit the crime, at least according to English statutes. In many cases, slaveholders employed decapitation solely and specifically to send a message: like the King over his empire, as sovereigns over their own plantations, they had the authority to punish what they deemed treasonous.[28]

Decapitation was almost a rule for treasonous slaves who threatened the sociopolitical order of England's colonies. Severed heads stared at onlookers from Jamaica to South Carolina. Yet, although planters hoped to control the political message, the heads carried their own symbolism. In 1734, when a slave named Quash was executed for burglary in Charles Town, he was hanged and then his "Head was sever'd from his Body, and fixed upon the Gallows" as a warning. Still, Quash's fate most certainly angered some slaves and turned them into potential rebels who would find a forum in which to express their anger five years later. In September 1739, the Stono Rebellion convulsed the South Carolina Lowcounty. More than eighty slaves rebelled against the plantation system, killing some

[27] 25 Edward III, stat. 5, cap. 2, quoted in Frances E. Dolan, "The Subordinate('s) Plot: Petty Treason and Forms of Domestic Rebellion," *Shakespeare Quarterly* 42 (autumn 1992): 317. On the evolution of petty treason law in early America, see Kathryn Preyer, "Crime, the Criminal Law, and Reform in Post-Revolutionary Virginia," *Law and History Review* 1 (spring 1983): 53–85.

[28] Michael Stephen Hindus, *Prison and Plantation: Crime, Justice, and Authority in Massachusetts and South Carolina, 1767–1878* (Chapel Hill: University of North Carolina Press, 1980), 130–32; Dolan, "The Subordinate('s) Plot," 318.

twenty-five whites before being confronted by a militia. The ensuing battle resulted in another twenty white deaths. More than half of the slaves, forty-four, were killed: "some shot, some hang'd, and some Gibbeted alive." Colonists decapitated the dead slaves, posting their heads atop poles along well-traveled roads between the rebels' home plantations.[29]

As pieces of a corpse, each head went through three stages of decomposition: fresh decay, bloating, and putrefaction. When posted, the decapitated heads had already begun their fresh decay. Enzymes, which had once been held in check by living cells, began to attack those same cells, breaking down their structural integrity and leaking the liquid inside. The liquid oozed between layers of skin and began to loosen them, leading to skin sloughage. While the individuals' identities remained, the skin began to sag, distorting the faces. Even in these early hours of decomposition, flies laid their eggs in points of entry: the eyes, mouth, ears. Thousands of maggots that emerged from the eggs moved beneath the skin, eating away particularly at fatty tissues. Their movements animated the flesh in eerie ways. Bloating arrived as bacteria began to feast, and around the bacteria-filled mouths, the lips swelled and the tongues enlarged so that they protruded. The eyes liquefied and disappeared from the faces. Again, the decapitated heads appeared animated. Typically, the bloat stage of decomposition takes about a week, but given the Lowcounty's heat, humidity, and swarms of insects, the decomposing faces of the Stono rebels remained identifiable for only four or five days.[30]

As the maggots and bacteria ate away at the decapitated heads, putrefaction set in. For about two to three weeks, the bacteria moved through the palates and attacked the brains, soft organs that quickly liquefied, turned yellow with bacteria, oozed through the mouths and ears, and dripped to the ground, killing any vegetation around the bases of the posts. In the meantime, birds and meat-eating beetles ravaged muscle and flesh. If any tissues remained, they were consumed by bacteria so that, within six weeks

[29] Michael Craton, *Testing the Chains: Resistance to Slavery in the British West Indies* (Ithaca: Cornell University Press, 1982), 100; Brown, *The Reaper's Garden*, 135–37; Donald D. Wax, "'The Great Risque We Run': The Aftermath of Slave Rebellion at Stono, South Carolina, 1739–1745," *Journal of Negro History* 67 (summer 1982): 138–39; *South Carolina Gazette*, 6 April 1734; Peter H. Wood, *Black Majority: Negroes in Colonial South Carolina from 1670 through the Stono Rebellion* (New York: W. W. Norton, 1974), 314–17; Mark M. Smith, ed., *Stono: Documenting and Interpreting a Southern Slave Revolt* (Columbia: University of South Carolina Press, 2008), xiii; *Boston Weekly News-Letter*, 8 November 1739.

[30] Mary Roach, *Stiff: The Curious Lives of Human Cadavers* (New York: W. W. Norton, 2003), chap. 3.

of decapitation, the heads were nearly skeletonized. Some dry skin and cartilage remained on the skulls as they began to dry and bleach. And then the skulls began to disappear: without muscle and sinew to keep them on the posts, they fell off or rattled about in the wind. Souvenir collectors grabbed some; others went to mischievous pranksters or individuals who no longer wanted to view the displays; and maybe some were taken and buried by sympathetic friends and families. Through their stages of decay, their animations, and their final states as skulls, the decapitated heads of the Stono rebels had their greatest impact: reminding whites of the terror among them. Not coincidentally, white Carolinians remained suspicious and kept their militias on patrol for the next two months, corresponding roughly with the time it took for the heads to decompose into skulls and begin to disappear from the posts.

There were two other beheadings during the Stono Rebellion worthy of attention. In the community of Stono Bridge, the rebels killed two white shopkeepers – Robert Bathurst and Mr. Gibbs – by cutting off their heads and leaving them displayed on the store's front steps. A nearby tavern keeper was spared "for he was a good man and kind to his slaves," which historian Peter Wood interpreted as "even in the midst of the most desperate revolt, slave violence was by no means haphazard." This is true as well for the deaths of the shopkeepers. Dozens of other whites died at the hands of the rebels, but these two alone were decapitated. Beheadings were not unfamiliar to Africans, neither in their homelands, previous enslavements on Caribbean plantations, nor in the South Carolina Lowcounty. The shopkeepers represented the plantation economy, the export of rice, and the commercial networks prohibited to slaves. By ritually inverting its patterns of discipline and punishment, the rebels' decision to behead Bathurst and Gibbs was an assault against the colonial economy and the planation system that sustained it.[31]

The plantation system and its own form of justice was very much at the heart of decapitation practices. One might attribute colonial white Southerners' use of decapitation and display to the British treason laws under which they lived, statutes that were broadly defined so that resisting the enactment of laws, armed insurrection against local plantations, and even some acts of political opposition were considered attacks on the king.

[31] Wood, *Black Majority*, 315 n 27; "Account of the Negroe Insurrection in South Carolina," in Smith, ed., *Stono*, 14; Edward A. Pearson, "'A Countryside Full of Flames': A Reconsideration of the Stono Rebellion and Slave Rebelliousness in the Early Eighteenth-Century South Carolina Lowcountry," *Slavery and Abolition* 17 (August 1996): 22–50.

With the American Revolution, ideas about treason evolved in the new states. As constitutional historian Bradley Chapin explained, "The problems were to construct a law that could protect the state from disloyal acts involving a betrayal of allegiance, to limit that law so precisely that it could not be used to destroy normal political opposition, and to protect the rights of the individual accused in times of high political excitement." The result was that, during the war, jurors proved extremely reluctant to find a man guilty of treason, and in those few cases of guilt, the sentence was execution by simple hanging. There was no quartering, beheading, or gibbeting. The definition of treason was narrowed to that written into the Constitution of 1787.[32]

The use of decapitation persisted in the early national South, however, because it was directed toward slaves who were, of course, noncitizen Others. In 1754, a British slaver wrote that "many blacks believe that if they are put to death and not dismembered, they shall return again to their own country." The beheading of a slave, then, prohibited the deceased from returning to the African motherland, much as the scalping of a Native American inhibited his entry into the Mansion of Bliss. Southern whites certainly believed that, whether as omens of punishment or to interfere with the journeys of the dead, decapitated heads needed to be displayed. In 1780s and 1790s Virginia, courts ordered the display of black decapitated heads on twenty-six occasions, but never once a white head.[33]

The early national South's most notorious decapitation episode was in January 1811, when several hundred slaves organized an uprising against plantations on Louisiana's German Coast. The rebels moved along the Mississippi River toward New Orleans some thirty miles away, burning and looting, but in the end killing only two whites. Finally, a white militia confronted the rebels, killing more than sixty insurgents and capturing twenty-one who were quickly tried by a parish tribunal and executed. Most were shot. The justices declared "the heads of the executed shall be cut off and placed atop a pole on the spot where all can see the punishment

[32] Bradley Chapin, "Colonial and Revolutionary Origins of the American Law of Treason," *William and Mary Quarterly* 17 (January 1960): 3–21.

[33] Quoted in Sylvia R. Frey and Betty Wood, *Come Shouting to Zion: African American Protestantism in the American South and British Caribbean to 1830* (Chapel Hill: University of North Carolina Press, 1998), 39; Seeman, *Death in the New World*, 196; Hindus, *Prison and Plantation*, 131; Douglas R. Egerton, "A Peculiar Mark of Infamy: Dismemberment, Burials, and Rebelliousness in Slave Societies," in Isenberg and Burstein, eds., *Mortal Remains*, 153–54; Stuart Banner, *The Death Penalty: An American History* (Cambridge: Harvard University Press, 2002), 137–43.

meted out for such crimes, also as a terrible example to all who would disturb the public tranquility in the future." As tribunals judged more suspected insurgents over the following weeks, more heads on poles stared across the Mississippi River; by the end of January, they numbered almost one hundred. "They were brung here for the sake of their Heads, which decorate our Levee, all the way up the coast," noted naval officer Samuel Hambleton; "They look like crows sitting on long poles." Unlike crows, however, the heads would never fly away. They would decay, forsaking their collective message as they deteriorated in the Louisiana climate.[34]

Corpses – in particular their heads – symbolized the culture of death that underlay the emergence of the South, both in its colonial manifestations and as it became part of the new United States. In the era of European colonization, they became weapons in the struggle for dominance: Native Americans used scalps to carve out their own hegemony and ward off European colonists; Europeans and European Americans employed beheadings to claim the land in response to native scalpings and in the name of colonization and plantations; and when they did behead others, African Americans reacted to the plantation system that sustained European colonization. In the new nation, the political messages of scalpings and beheadings remained the same. Whatever the original intent of posting heads on posts in Louisiana or South Carolina or of hanging scalps in Virginia or Alabama, the historical message is that the early South evolved in an atmosphere of interracial violence not only against the living but against the dying and the dead.

[34] W. C. C. Claiborne to Secretary of State, January 9, 1811, in *Official Letter Books of W. C. C. Claiborne, 1801–1816*, ed. Dunbar Rowland, 6 vols. (Jackson: State Department of Archives and History, 1917), 95; Glenn R. Conrad, *The German Coast: Abstracts of the Civil Records of St. Charles and St. John the Baptist Parishes, 1804–1812* (Lafayette: University of Southwestern Louisiana, 1981), 101–102; Daniel Rasmussen, *American Uprising: The Untold Story of America's Largest Slave Revolt* (New York: HarperCollins, 2011), chap. 12; Samuel Hambleton to David Porter, January 15, 1811, in *Slavery*, ed. Stanley Engerman, Seymour Drescher, and Robert Paquette (New York: Oxford University Press, 2001), 326.

2

The Usable Death: Evangelicals, Anglicans, and the Politics of Dying in the Late-Colonial Lowcountry

Peter N. Moore

On June 16, 1770, Archibald Simpson seemed to be dying. Three days earlier, Simpson, whose fourteen-year tenure at Stoney Creek Independent Church had made him one of the longest-lived ministers in the South Carolina Lowcountry, had contracted a sore throat which, by Friday, had developed into a "dangerous quinsy." Never one to shrink from medical treatment, Simpson used all available means – vomits, purges, bleeding, even gargling a cocktail of anther water, Peruvian bark, and snake root – yet still his tongue and palate swelled, his throat closed, and he was beset by fever, delirium, and an excruciating pain in his left ear. On Saturday, the doctor identified three large ulcers deep in his throat and prescribed camphor and sucking "the steam of hot vinegar through a funnel" – all to no avail.

As the neighbors gathered, Simpson set about the important business of dying, a prospect he welcomed with "a most joyful frame of soul." He ordered his will to be drawn up. He comforted his distraught friends and said tearful goodbyes to his two motherless girls, making them promise to "love God and Christ, to pray, to read their books, [and] to be good children." Barely able to open his mouth and racked with convulsions every time he swallowed, Simpson expected a hard death, "either of hunger, or in strong fits." Knowing well that his enemies "might think & call it a Judgment like Death," he assured his people he was willing to die as God saw fit. Most importantly, "I told them that I freely forgave all my Enemies ... that so innocent was I of all their vile charges, that I had never yet seen any one thing, from which I had to ask forgiveness from the Searcher of hearts before whose awful tribunal I expected in a few hours to appear." As night came on and the neighbors went home, Simpson, good eighteenth-century man that he was, remembered to wind the clock though in "unexpressible agony." After winding the clock, he "turned round & said with great difficulty, I believe I am now near done with all time things, I expect my Eternity, a glorious Eternity will begin, & before this clock needs again to be wound up, I expect to be putrifying in my grave."[1]

Rarely do historians of the early South get such a detailed account of someone preparing for death, especially when that account is left by the dying person himself. Fortunately, Simpson survived this ordeal and recorded the entire episode in his diary. As he ordered his final hours, he also left a record of what finally mattered, a to-do list of sorts for the dying man: settle estate, give spiritual advice to children, publicly forgive enemies, make a joyful exit. (Significantly, Simpson did not summon his slaves to his dying bed, a southern convention that did not reach its full expression until the nineteenth century.)[2] These priorities are not particularly surprising for eighteenth-century evangelicals. Nor does the scene itself, with its desperate medicines and anxious neighbors, change what we know about death in the eighteenth-century South. What does stand out, however, is Simpson's concern about the manner of his death. Knowing that the throat distemper might bring a hard death, and certain that his enemies would exploit it as a sign from God, a judgment against his person, his ministry, perhaps even the gospel itself, Simpson went to great lengths to make an orderly ending, disarm his enemies, and control the narrative of his death. Not in the least concerned about dying itself, Simpson was very anxious about the stories people would tell of how he died. Despite the ravages of a "dangerous quinsy," Simpson would wind his clock and die carefully, trusting in God.

Simpson's concern reminds us that dying in the eighteenth-century South was as much a social and political as a personal and spiritual act. Dying, in short, was enormously complicated. Historians have largely overlooked these multiple dimensions of early modern death, and not without reason. Such concerns are difficult to locate in the traditional sources, which tend to gloss over the messy, tangled politics of dying. Epitaphs and printed funeral sermons, for example, alternately praised the dead and warned the living; rarely if ever did they peek behind the curtain, where neighbors dared speak ill of the dead as they jockeyed for

1 Peter N. Moore, ed., *The South Carolina Diary of Reverend Archibald Simpson: Part 2, April 1770–March 1784* (Columbia: University of South Carolina Press, 2012), 32–36.

2 Randy J. Sparks, "The Southern Way of Death: The Meaning of Death in Antebellum White Evangelical Culture," *Southern Quarterly* 44 (October 2006): 38–39.

position or looked to avenge old wrongs. The prescriptive literature on dying is also problematic. Examples of the "good death," the *artes moriandi* of the eighteenth century, filled the pages of evangelical magazines and crowned the biographies of pious men and women, creating a standard death narrative that placed a premium on surrender, assurance, peace, and even joy in dying. Such exemplary "evangelical endings" served as powerful models that shaped the way evangelicals believed they ought to die. But they were ideal types, drawn mainly from biographies, and they had a stylized quality that real dying people often found hard to follow. This standard narrative speaks well to the aspirations of eighteenth-century Southerners, evangelicals and nonevangelicals alike, but it says little about why they found it so important to die well and what happened when they did not.[3]

This essay complicates historical understanding of dying in the early South by emphasizing its local context. The setting is Simpson's two Lowcountry parishes, Indian Land (also called Stoney Creek) and Saltcatcher, circa 1770. The source is Simpson's diary, which transports us beyond the platitudes of epitaphs, eulogies, and printed death narratives and into his parishioner's households, beside their deathbeds, and to their graveside services. In Simpson's small world, every relationship and

[3] Given the rich literature on the early history of evangelicalism, surprisingly few historians have recognized the importance of death and dying to the evangelical movement and evangelical identity. Indeed, the most recent major studies of early southern evangelicalism say almost nothing about death, dying, and mortuary ritual, although they offer thick description and analysis of nearly every other evangelical ritual, belief, and practice. For a sampling, see Leigh Eric Schmidt, *Holy Fairs: Scotland and the Making of American Revivalism*, 2nd ed. (Grand Rapids: Eerdmans, 2001); Christine Leigh Heyrman, *Southern Cross: The Beginnings of the Bible Belt* (New York: Alfred A. Knopf, 1998); Cynthia Lynn Lyerly, *Methodism and the Southern Mind, 1770–1810* (New York: Oxford University Press, 1998); Philip N. Mulder, *A Controversial Spirit: Evangelical Awakenings in the South* (New York: Oxford University Press, 2002); Janet Moore Lindman, *Bodies of Belief: Baptist Community in Early America* (Philadelphia: University of Pennsylvania Press, 2008). The broadest treatment is Sparks, "Southern Way of Death," which is rather more concerned with evangelicals in general than with Southerners in particular. For somewhat more focused studies, see Richard J. Bell, "'Our people die well': Deathbed Scenes in John Wesley's *Arminian* Magazine," *Mortality* 10 (August 2005): 210–23; Henry D. Rack, "Evangelical Endings: Death-Beds in Evangelical Biography," *Bulletin of the John Rylands University Library of Manchester* 74 (spring 1992): 39–56; D. Bruce Hindmarsh, *The Evangelical Conversion Narrative: Spiritual Autobiography in Early Modern England* (New York: Oxford University Press, 2005), 255–60. Bell, Rack, and Hindmarsh recognize the stylized quality of evangelical death narratives, but none moves beyond to examine death on the ground. On the problems with traditional sources for studying the history of death, see Ralph A. Houlbrooke, *Death, Religion, and the Family in England, 1480–1750* (New York: Oxford University Press, 1998), 4.

encounter was freighted with a history of family rivalries, religious disputes, personal hatreds, competing loyalties, outstanding debts, and interlocking social and political agendas. In such a highly charged context, nearly every aspect of death was contested, first at the deathbed, then at the more public funeral service, and finally in the shaping of the death narrative. At the semiprivate scene around the deathbed, Simpson labored under the watchful eyes of family and neighbors to bring the experience of dying in line with the cultural model of the good death. This was no small task. As Simpson knew, the art of dying was difficult business, and few mastered it. Some died well, while others died suddenly or alone, clinging to life or raging against the world, or out of their minds and ravaged by fever.[4] In the very public setting of the funeral service, Anglican and evangelical practices frequently clashed, exposing some of the deepest fault lines in the community. In the much broader social network that shaped the death narrative, friends and enemies seized upon good and bad deaths alike, telling and contesting the stories of how people died, since such stories were potent weapons neighbors deployed in their factional struggles to control the church and the community. The politics of dying made it vitally important to craft and control these stories in order to block or advance personal, social, and political agendas.

Archibald Simpson was no stranger to death. By the time he contracted the throat distemper in the summer of 1770, he had survived numerous near-fatal illnesses, not to mention a childhood marked by chronic respiratory disorders, all of which heightened his expectations of an early death (expectations that were repeatedly disappointed, since his lived into his sixties). Born in Glasgow in 1734, Simpson attached himself at an early age to the evangelical wing of the Church of Scotland. Like their counterparts throughout the British Atlantic world, Scottish evangelicals were distinguished by their emphasis on "experimental" Christianity or religious experience. Evangelicals insisted that right belief and pious living were not the sole marks of authentic Christianity and that true Christians were those who had passed through a conversion experience in which they attained a deep sense of their own sinfulness and unworthiness and became dependent on God's grace to save them and make them holy. Theirs was an intense, Christ-centered version of Christianity that was perfectly suited to

[4] Philippe Ariés stresses the mastery of dying on the early modern deathbed, not unlike the evangelicals studied by Bell, Rack, and Hindmarsh; see "The Reversal of Death: Changes in Attitudes toward Death in Western Societies," in *Death in America*, ed. David E. Stannard (Philadelphia: University of Pennsylvania Press, 1975), 138.

a serious, Christ-haunted young man like Simpson.[5] Religion permeated every aspect of his life; he attended services as frequently as he could, spent his spare moments praying in the fields or "greens" on the edge of Glasgow, and kept his diary religiously. His youthful entries were almost entirely introspective, and their alternately self-loathing and quasi-mystical passages expressed the great spiritual war he waged with his soul.

The religious culture of Glasgow, which stood at the epicenter of Scotland's mid-century evangelical revivalism, groomed young Archibald for the ministry. He carried with him strict attitudes toward sin, worldliness, and complacent Christianity. Evangelicals placed great emphasis on preaching and pastoral care, both of which were means of awakening sinners to their need for Christ and correcting believers who had grown worldly or spiritually lukewarm. Presbyterians held that such important work required extensive training, and they ordained only men with university educations. Simpson accordingly entered the University of Glasgow in 1750, and, after completing his studies in 1753, he married and embarked for Georgia to serve as tutor at Savannah's Bethesda Orphanage. His time at Bethesda was short and disastrous. He soon made enemies and was driven out, he declared, by the "dreadful threatenings ... of a mad Enthusiastick woman." By April 1754, he was in South Carolina, courting the presbytery in Charleston and preaching to congregations at Pon Pon and Wilton along the Edisto River. That experience, too, ended badly, thanks in part to the young minister's zeal for admonishing sinners, one of whom was a leading Wilton trustee who locked Simpson out of the meeting house. In 1756, he took charge of the congregation at Indian Land, where he lowered his expectations and finally learned to navigate the treacherous social terrain of the lower South. There he remained, despite losing his wife and three of his children to fevers, until his return to Scotland in 1772.[6]

5 On his near-fatal illnesses, see Archibald Simpson, Journals and Sermons, 1748–1784, 11 vols., Charleston Library Society, Charleston, SC, 5: 192; *Diary of Reverend Archibald Simpson, Part* 2, 222–23. Simpson's expectations of an early death were a regular feature of his annual birthday lament; for an example, see *Diary of Reverend Archibald Simpson, Part* 2, 19. For a good working definition of evangelicalism, see D. W. Bebbington, *Evangelicalism in Modern Britain: A History from the 1730s to the 1980s* (London: Unwin Hyman, 1989), 3–5.

6 Peter N. Moore, ed., *The South Carolina Diary of Reverend Archibald Simpson, Part 1: May 1754–April 1770* (Columbia: University of South Carolina Press, 2012), 11. Simpson died in Scotland in 1795. For a fuller description of his life, see introduction to Part 1, esp. xi–xix. On the Presbyterian ministry in the eighteenth century, see E. Brooks Holifield, *God's Ambassadors: A History of Christian Clergy in America* (Grand Rapids:

Like Simpson, the congregation at Indian Land was a product of the Great Awakening – a controversial series of transatlantic religious revivals in the 1730s and 1740s. Situated on the Pocataligo River about sixty miles west of Charleston, the church was established as Stoney Creek Independent congregation in 1743 by a group of George Whitefield's followers. Whitefield, an itinerant Anglican minister who preached to vast crowds up and down the eastern seaboard in and after 1739, was a magnetic preacher whose sermons frequently challenged the values of the ruling elite and the smugness of local religious authorities. Doctrinally, Indian Land was Reformed and evangelical, subscribing to basic Calvinist principles of sin, grace, and election (or predestination), but it distinguished itself from similar Presbyterian churches by its independent, congregational polity and its ecumenical spirit. Racially integrated from its inception, Stoney Creek practiced a level of spiritual-racial equality nearly unknown among colonial churches in the lower South. Despite such charismatic beginnings, by 1770 (indeed, much earlier), Stoney Creek's revival had gone cold, its founding members were long dead, and its vision of a Protestant Christian community that was blind to sectarian and racial differences had faded. The congregation was fractured and declining, and it was unable to adequately support a settled minister on its own. As a remedy, in 1766, Simpson organized a new, strictly Presbyterian congregation on the east side of the Saltcatcher River and extended the reach of his parish to both sides of the lower Saltcatcher-Combahee basin.[7]

Part of what led to Indian Land's demise was its unfortunate location: it was perched on the edge of a rice field, and both the church and its people inhabited the malaria-infested, marshy lowlands of the coastal plain. It has become commonplace to say that "death was everywhere" in the early South; this was certainly true for the eighteenth-century Lowcountry, not least of all for Indian Land and similar low-lying neighborhoods where the mortality rate was appalling. In some Lowcountry parishes, only one in seven whites born before 1760 lived beyond the age of twenty and less than

Eerdmans, 2007), 88–92. On similar problems caused by young, overzealous evangelical ministers in the early South, see Heyrman, *Southern Cross*, 88–99.

7 Much has been written on the early, radical phase of Stoney Creek's history and the antics of its sometime prophet, Hugh Bryan. For a recent, short summary, see Thomas S. Kidd, *The Great Awakening: The Roots of Evangelical Christianity in Colonial America* (New Haven: Yale University Press, 2007), 217–19, 253–54. On the founding of Saltcatcher, see George Howe, *History of the Presbyterian Church in South Carolina*, 2 vols. (Columbia: Duffie & Chapman, 1870), 1: 326–27. Stoney Creek's racial egalitarianism extended to the Lord's Supper, where black and white communicants sat together at the same tables. This practice ended abruptly in 1770; see *Diary of Reverend Archibald Simpson, Part 2*, 115–16.

5 percent beyond the age of fifty. Even in the late colonial period, when life expectancy began to increase, sickness was a constant companion, and death was frequently close at hand. Simpson was himself sick much of the time, sometimes seriously ill, as were many of his people who suffered from malaria, influenza, smallpox, scarlet fever, and a whole host of less perilous respiratory and digestive disorders. The Indian Land parish was especially vulnerable. In 1755, it was visited by a "dreadful distemper" that carried off many of the "old standards of the church," and it was subject to annual visitations of malaria in the fall. This was indeed a land of widows and orphans, for few families escaped the loss of a parent, sibling, or child, and most experienced such losses early and often. If colonial South Carolina was not "*only* good for doctors & ministers," as one distressed settler quipped of Virginia, it certainly provided ample opportunities for them to pursue their callings.[8]

Death was also culturally "everywhere" and enjoyed an especially prominent place in evangelical communities like Indian Land. Catechisms, midweek lectures, Sunday sermons, pastoral visits, and funeral services reminded the living that their days on earth were short, and their most pressing business in life was to prepare for its ending. In baptism, they ritually died to the world, and in the Lord's Supper, they feasted on the sufferings and death of Christ, mourned for their sins, and fixed their hopes on the world to come.[9] As worshippers passed through the churchyard on

[8] *Diary of Reverend Archibald Simpson, Part 1*, 91; John Duffy, *Epidemics in Colonial America* (Baton Rouge: Louisiana State University Press, 1953), 208 (emphasis added). The ubiquity of death is a central theme in Sparks, "Southern Way of Death," and it derives largely from Ariés's attention to the public dimensions of dying, summarized nicely in "The Reversal of Death," 138–50. On the unhealthiness of South Carolina, see Peter A. Coclanis, *The Shadow of a Dream: Economic Life and Death in the South Carolina Low Country, 1670–1920* (New York: Oxford University Press, 1989), 42–43. Coclanis's impressive data do not extend to the second half of the eighteenth century, and there is little evidence to locate precisely when mortality rates improved. George D. Terry, "'Champagne Country': A Social History of an Eighteenth Century Lowcountry Parish in South Carolina, St. Johns Berkeley County" (PhD diss., University of South Carolina, 1981), 94–99, indicates that life expectancy increased considerably after 1760, especially among people living beyond twenty, although these effects might not have been evident by 1770. Indeed, there is reason to speculate that South Carolina may have become *more* and not less malarial in this period, especially as land came under rice cultivation; see Duffy, *Epidemics in Colonial America*, 212–13; Gerald L. Cates, "'The Seasoning': Disease and Death Among the First Colonists of Georgia," *Georgia Historical Quarterly* 63 (summer 1980): 146–58. The absence of quantitative data notwithstanding, late-colonial South Carolina remained an unhealthy place, as Simpson's diary amply attests.

[9] The *Westminster Larger Catechism*, question 165, describes baptism as an ingrafting onto Christ. This botanical metaphor of death and life was less overt than the death and rebirth

their way to meeting, they were greeted by the dead whose headstones often beckoned them to the glories beyond the grave. Inscriptions that warned the living to "Prepare for death, and follow me" were common by the last quarter of the century, as were more forward-looking declarations such as Hugh Bryan's 1753 stone that declared "My flesh shall also rest in hope," anticipating the Second Coming when the bones of dead Christians will "put on flesh anew."[10] Thus, church itself was a vivid reminder of the transience of life, the inevitably of death, the horror of the grave, and the hope of the final resurrection. Such an emphasis cannot be dismissed as mere manipulation on the part of ambitious ministers. Rather, it was the logical outgrowth of a culture all too familiar with the sudden onset of incurable illness and the constant, palpable presence of death. Death was to be both feared and welcomed. Like conversion, it stood at the center of evangelical identity: theirs was a gospel of death preached to dying people in a dying world.[11]

Evangelical obsession with death stemmed from authentic concerns about Heaven, Hell, and the eternal prospects of the dying person, but it was also continuous with an ancient Christian worldview in which life on earth was fleeting, a worldview that ennobled suffering and death and traced its roots through centuries of martyrs back to the triumphant death of Christ himself. Yet, death was never a purely private or theological matter. More broadly (and more mundanely), it was connected to the political and social position of evangelicals in the eighteenth-century British Atlantic world. Politically, Presbyterians, Baptists, Methodists, and Independents together made up a militant, embattled minority; they were religious dissenters from the established Anglican Church, and their futures were none too certain. South Carolina was no exception, for the

symbolized by the dunking of adults in Baptist practice. On death and the Lord's Supper, see Schmidt, *Holy Fairs*, 86.

10 On the evangelical function of the church cemetery, see Richard Morris, *Sinners, Lovers, and Heroes: An Essay on Memorializing in Three American Cultures* (Albany: State University of New York Press, 1997), 63–65, which stresses how eighteenth-century memorials "draw attention to death rather than to the dead" (68). On "prospective" grave markers in general, see Robert V. Wells, *Facing the King of Terrors: Death and Society in an American Community, 1750–1990* (New York: Cambridge University Press, 2000), 5–6. Bryan's inscription is recorded in Mabel Runette, "Inscriptions from the Grave-Stones at Stoney Creek Cemetery near Yamassee, Beaufort County, SC," *South Carolina Historical and Genealogical Magazine* 37 (July 1936): 106.

11 Wells, *King of Terrors*, 6. Many historians of evangelicalism have viewed death primarily as a corollary to conversion, the central feature of evangelical Protestantism, stressing the way preachers deployed it as a sermonic tool to manipulate and awaken sinners; see, for example, Mulder, *Controversial Spirit*, 28, and Hindmarsh, *The Evangelical Conversion Narrative*, 255–56.

Church Act of 1706 was still in force. Dissenters were tolerated, but only the Church of England enjoyed public funding and only Anglican clergy could perform official marriages.[12] Sectarian tensions were especially acute at the local level, where factional strife left evangelicals continually on their guard, protecting their reputations and struggling to maintain respectability.[13] In this context, a good death bolstered legitimacy and respectability. It was no consolation to most dying people (Simpson notwithstanding), but how one died meant a great deal to the living. The good death, in short, was a usable death with lasting practical implications.

To understand what evangelicals sought in a good death, it is instructive to contrast the last moments of two of Simpson's Saltcatcher neighbors, Mrs. Lambright and Mr. Jordan. Simpson described Mrs. Lambright's death as "remarkable." Although she was a "hidden" Christian, "timorous and fearful," bashful to a fault, she died exuberantly, constantly "speaking to all about her in the praises of God, of Christ, & religion," exhorting her children, even insisting that her friends and family usher her out of the world by singing psalms. When the medicines failed, she was overcome with joy "as she had repeatedly expressed her fears, of being brought back to health, & to continue in the world." She "Died without pain," Simpson reported, "with joy unspeakable and full of glory ... triumphed over all fears of Death ... & continued speaking & praising till the very last breath." Mr. Jordan, in contrast, had been an active and energetic Christian, a trustee of the Saltcatcher congregation and a pillar of the church. But he made a disappointing exit. His last years had been trying: his only daughter eloped, which tarnished his honor and dashed his hopes for her future, and he subsequently cut her out of his will, remarried a much younger woman, and stopped attending meeting (although he did show up drunk one Sunday, armed with pistols and threatening to kill the "wretched beggarly" man who stole his daughter). Simpson spent two hours in close conversation and prayer with his dying friend but had nothing to show for it. Unlike Mrs. Lambright, Mr. Jordan was generally inattentive, mumbling "Some broken Sentences of Scripture and hymns" but otherwise remaining "stupid & insensible." It was a disheartening visit. "Was concerned," Simpson wrote, "that so great a professor of religion should not

[12] Robert Weir, *Colonial South Carolina: A History* (Columbia: University of South Carolina Press, 1983), 80; *Diary of Reverend Archibald Simpson, Part 2*, 285.

[13] Alexander Hewatt, *An Historical Account of the Rise and Progress of the Colonies of South Carolina and Georgia*, 2 vols. (London: Alexander Donaldson, 1779), 2: 52–53. Dissenters were not able to unify to advance the "dissenting interest," either at the intercolonial or provincial levels; see Howe, *Presbyterian Church*, 1: 379–80.

bear a greater testimony to it on his dying bed, should appear so attached to a present life, so much taken up with his worldly concerns."[14]

To be sure, Simpson's primary role as pastor was to shepherd the souls of the dying into the next world.[15] This was a delicate and difficult process, even with seasoned Christians like Mr. Jordan. It required owning one's sin, bemoaning missed opportunities, detaching from the world, and, in good Calvinist fashion, throwing oneself on the mercy of God. Then, and only then, could one greet death like Mrs. Lambright, hungrily and with "joy unspeakable." This was the evangelical good death. And yet there was much more at stake beside the deathbed than the soul of the deceased. Dying was a shared experience, a fundamentally social event, and, for evangelicals in particular, it was a medium for propagating their faith. Like a catechism, sermon, or conversion narrative, a good death was instructive, a means of grace through which God's word was affirmed. As a quasi-public act, dying was therefore performative. So, Simpson's secondary role was to direct the performance so that it conformed as much as possible to the evangelical script, to fashion a usable death that functioned to advance the kingdom of God. Mrs. Lambright's joyful death fit this model perfectly; it was literally an act of worship that engaged those around the deathbed in singing and praise. In the days that followed, Simpson shared Lambright's story with their neighbors. Seven months later, he still referred to her house as "the place where good old Mrs. Lambright died," so that even her home took on the identity of her remarkable death. Mr. Jordan's mediocre death, by contrast, bore no religious testimony: it was useless.[16]

Few of Simpson's people died as effortlessly or greeted death as gladly as Mrs. Lambright. Rather, most shared the center of the continuum with Mr. Jordan. For example, when young Charles Palmer fell ill with a nervous fever in October 1769, he was "very unwilling to think of dying, and very afraid of Death." Like many of the "ignorant and prophane," he mistook the purpose of the deathbed and looked to the pastor's prayers to save him from death, not prepare him for it. Mrs. Brailsford was likewise "shocked and affected" to learn that her complicated pregnancy would

[14] *Diary of Reverend Archibald Simpson, Part 2*, 23, 62, 239.

[15] On pastoral care, see Peter N. Moore, "Archibald Simpson and the Care of Souls in Lowcountry South Carolina: Sustaining Evangelical Communities between Awakenings," *Journal of Presbyterian History* 90 (fall/winter 2012): 60–71; E. Brooks Holifield, *A History of Pastoral Care in America: From Salvation to Self-Realization* (Eugene: Wipf & Stock, 1983), 67–82.

[16] Sparks, "Southern Way of Death," 36–37; *Diary of Reverend Archibald Simpson, Part 2*, 24, 132.

end in death. Although brought up in a religious way, she had grown worldly and distracted from spiritual matters since her very favorable marriage a year earlier. Now she "lamented her family neglects" and was in "great agony & distress," trapped between denial and surrender, struggling "to place her trust in the Redeemers Infinite righteousness and mercy." Even old, bedridden William Wilkins clung to life. Wilkins had long been one of the most generous contributors to the Saltcatcher church, although he gave "no great evidences of much of a Christian temper & behaviour." Despite his old age and infirmity – "a constant shaking in his nerves ... all over bloated, his feet swelled as with a violent dropsy, his legs & thighs like a skeleton & much grieved" – Wilkins "would not hear of Death" and rebuffed Simpson's ministrations. Skilled and seasoned pastor though he was, Simpson could do little in such cases. "Careless living," as he once noted, "makes poor dying."[17]

Careful living, however, did not necessarily make dying any easier. Dying well was difficult work, and most good deaths, like that of an unnamed "person of Consideration," were hard-earned. When Simpson visited her on the previous day, the unnamed woman was in denial. Although a seasoned Christian, she had "something of a legal frame in her soul," that is, she relied on her own righteousness to justify her before God. Such self-righteousness was the ironic fruit of pious and careful living. Consequently, she approached death casually and overconfidently, "seemingly insencеble of her dangerous Condition." In such cases, it was Simpson's duty as pastor to instruct and awaken; he prayed with her and left. This remedy did its work, and the following day he found her "in great distress of soul," filled with doubt and regret "lest she should not have a real Interest in Christ and the everlasting Covenant," lamenting her wasted time and missed opportunities. "She was under great and sharp Convictions," Simpson noted, and "had strong strugglings in her soul betwext faith and unbelief .... Endeavoured to bring her over intirely to rest wholly on the Lord Jesus Christ and a Covenant of absolutely free mercy and grace, after laboring very earnestly with her, and prayed repeatedly, her soul seemed to fly off from every thing, and cleave most ardently to the Lord Jesus Christ and a free salvation, after this was more composed and had something of peace in believing."[18]

[17] *Diary of Reverend Archibald Simpson, Part 1*, 158, 174, 279; *Part 2*, 111. On life as preparation for death in Puritan New England, see Charles Hambrick-Stowe, *The Practice of Piety: Puritan Devotional Disciplines in Seventeenth-Century New England* (Chapel Hill: University of North Carolina Press, 1982), 219, 229.

[18] *Diary of Reverend Archibald Simpson, Part 1*, 160.

This kind of crisis of faith at the deathbed was a common trope in printed evangelical death narratives and with good reason: at the heart of Reformed attitudes toward death lay a cruel paradox.[19] Dying well required living well, but careful living, as the unnamed woman learned, could also be a snare to good dying because it so easily led to overconfidence, or what Calvinists termed self-righteousness or self-justification: the sense that God "owed" salvation to sinful people because of their good works. In good Reformed fashion, the unnamed woman did not rest on the laurels of a life well-lived, although she was tempted to do so. Instead, she embraced self-doubt and re-experienced her conversion anxiety, which were prerequisites for throwing herself on the mercy of Christ in the hour of her death. In the end, she passed the test and died in comfort, composure, and peace, like Mrs. Lambright (albeit without the exuberance). Yet, unlike Mrs. Lambright, the unnamed woman had to pass through fire to get there, confront the limits of her own meager religiosity, and experience the terrifying humility of re-encountering the God of her conversion who saved by his mercy, not by her good works.

Such deaths bore witness to the virtues of evangelicalism, as the good death of Captain Joseph Miles demonstrates. Miles was a planter of considerable means and equally considerable debt who lived on the edge of the Saltcatcher parish in Ashepoo, about thirteen miles from Simpson's plantation. Miles was not a member of Simpson's congregation – in fact, he was an Anglican – but like many Anglicans in the rural Lowcountry where qualified clergy were hard to find and harder to keep, he turned to Simpson for pastoral care. In 1770, he was in the prime of life with a house full of dependents when he contracted pleurisy. It turned "very bad" some ten days later, and he sent for Simpson, being "much affected with the thoughts of Death, Judgment & Eternity" and "very desirous for instruction." Simpson obliged, speaking to him at length on original sin, "the Gospel Method of Salvation," regeneration, and not least of all Miles's own "shortcomings of duty" and "need of a Saviour." Most Anglican gentlemen would have shuddered at the prospect of spending their final hours taking a crash course on Reformed belief and practice, but Miles "seemed to drink it in with greediness," and he begged Simpson to come as often as possible.[20]

Miles slipped into delirium the next day and never fully regained his senses. He died "unsensible" and in "violent convulsions" three days later. Although hardly exemplary, there are several features of Miles's death that

19 Bell, "'Our people die well,'" 217; Rack, "Evangelical Endings," 48.

20 *Diary of Reverend Archibald Simpson, Part 2*, 123.

evangelicals would have found remarkable and that point to the social and political dimensions of the deathbed. He was eager to die well, hungry for pastoral care, and open to the evangelical way of death. Although alternately in and out of his mind, he was "perfectly Sensible" of Simpson's ministrations and was "very earnest" to join in prayer, after which he "immediately fell into the same raving way as before." Simpson sat up with him all night, and although Miles often failed to recognize his family, even his wife, "he always perfectly knowed me," Simpson noted, "and behaved with that decorum he thought my presence required." Most importantly, Miles's struggle profoundly affected the friends and family gathered around his deathbed. "All were in tears" during the prayer, and when Simpson "came to pray for his wife and three small children, the room echoed, with groans & tears, sobs and cries" as the space itself seemed to evince a divine, "extraordinary influence." In the deathbed narrative Simpson wove, Joseph Miles died well – although Miles himself faded into the background soon after losing his senses. Instead, God was the hero, Simpson was his instrument, and the grieving onlookers comprised a kind of chorus affirming Simpson's pastoral skills and Miles's good death. Thus, in the shared space of the dying room, Simpson, acutely aware of his elite Anglican audience, wrung from Miles's weak performance a perfectly usable death: supernatural, Reformed, and evangelical.[21]

Anglicans like Miles also depended on Simpson to perform funerals, and here, too, the politics of death came into play. Unlike the semiprivacy of the deathbed, the funeral was very much a public event where a family's reputation, status, religious identity, and neighborhood loyalties were on display. Given the institutional realities of Lowcountry communities like Indian Land and Saltcatcher – where religious options were few, and congregations from competing traditions were intermixed and interdependent – markers of familial and communal identity and status were often lost amid Anglican–evangelical disagreements over the very purpose of the funeral.

Although evangelical and Anglican funerals had some common rituals and drew from many of the same scriptural texts, the similarities ended there. Evangelical funerals featured extemporaneous prayer, singing, a brief burying ritual at the graveside, and a sermon or "discourse," in eighteenth-century parlance. The discourse was the centerpiece of the service, and it seemed to have a dual function: to reprove sinners and to elicit grief. At one level, the discourse functioned as a sermon that reminded

[21] Ibid., 127, 128, 130. Miles's role contrasts sharply with the generic ideal described by Ariés, "Reversal of Death," 138.

mourners of their own mortality, urged them to prepare for death, and strove to warn and awaken the unconverted. It was designed, in short, to make its audience *un*comfortable. A sampling of Simpson's texts underscores this point: the time is short (1 Corinthians 7:29), all men must die and face judgment (Hebrews 9:27, Job 30:23), so seek God now (John 7:37). Such sermons had their intended effect. At the funeral of young John Splat, "there was a great weeping" as Simpson preached from Ecclesiastes 12:1 ("Remember your creator in the days of your youth"), which he directed primarily at the young people gathered at the grave. Yet, alongside these sermonic attributes, the funeral discourse paradoxically functioned to comfort the afflicted and elicit sympathy from the mourners. Thus, while the text at Mrs. Brailsford's service was thoroughly evangelical – "Unto you, O men, I call" (Proverbs 8:4) – the real object of the discourse was the grieving mother, Mrs. McPherson, whom Simpson addressed directly, reminding her "that God, who had been her Support in former troubles, would be her Support still, for he never leaves nor utterly forsakes." Simpson had personalized the discourse and shifted the emphasis from judgment to comfort, and the result was predictable: it was "the most weeping auditory I ever Saw," Simpson declared, "all were melted down, Men & women into floods of tears." Unlike the printed funeral sermon that eulogized the dead and delivered a generic, even blunt evangelical message, the funeral discourse was pointed and flexible. It was embedded in the highly personal, lived connections between the mourners, and it could improvise and play upon the swell of emotions in the moment. It was both evangelical and cathartic.[22]

Anglicans, in contrast, emphasized decorum and adherence to a strict liturgy. Although Anglican clergy published hundreds of funeral sermons in the seventeenth century, they began to abandon the practice after 1700 and had completely rejected it by mid-century, at least partly in response to the evangelical challenge. They also frowned on singing at funerals or even eulogizing the deceased. Instead, Anglicans centered their services exclusively on the Order for the Burial of the Dead in the *Book of Common Prayer*.[23] The prayer book service opened on a hopeful note: although

22 Simpson, Journals and Sermons, 7: 155; *Diary of Reverend Archibald Simpson, Part 2*, 18, 133, 155, 158, 241. Simpson described the "typical" evangelical funeral in *Diary of Reverend Archibald Simpson, Part 2*, 192. On the differing purposes of church and nonconformist funerals in Britain, see Houlbrooke, *Death, Religion, and the Family*, 305.

23 Houlbrooke, *Death, Religion, and the Family*, 305, attributes Anglican rejection of the funeral sermon to creeping rationalism. Nicholas M. Beasley, *Christian Ritual and the Creation of British Slave Societies, 1650–1780* (Athens: University of Georgia Press,

dead, those who believe shall live forever, put on flesh anew, and see God with their own eyes. To be sure, the prayer book put life on earth in eternal perspective – our lives are like the grass, our strength soon passes, "and we are gone" – but it muted the theme of judgment and foregrounded hope, stressing Christ's victory over death, the incorruptible bodies of the final resurrection, and the ultimate destruction of death itself. Its gentle reminders to live godly lives and its prayers for God's mercy to sustain the faithful throughout their lives anticipated a glorious resurrection, not the fires of Hell. Its promises, predictability, and familiar cadences provided comfort and hope and enabled mourners to contain their grief.[24]

In an ideal world, Anglican and evangelical ministers conducted their own services for their own people, and all was well. But the rural Lowcountry was far from ideal. To begin with, the parishes were understaffed. Although neighboring St. Bartholomew's and St. Helena's parishes enjoyed a steady stream of Anglican clergy, Prince William's parish (Simpson's Indian Land) was consistently destitute, despite boasting one of the finest chapels in the province. From its inception in 1745 until the end of the colonial period, the parish had just one rector, Robert Cooper, who settled in 1758 and left for Charleston the following year. Neighboring clergy visited periodically to conduct worship, but they could not provide pastoral care.[25] The situation at Saltcatcher was not much better. Officially, this neighborhood belonged to St. Bartholomew's parish, which never lacked a settled minister, but it was at the edge of the parish some twenty-five miles from the chapel at Pon Pon. In both neighborhoods, Anglicans and evangelicals attended Sabbath services at the Reformed meeting house, occasionally joined together to celebrate communion, and relied on Simpson for pastoral care and funeral services.

2009), 128, suggests that Anglicans may have disparaged singing and reading resumés because they associated such practices with slave funerals. Neither argument is fully satisfying, and, given the bold mid-century challenge to moderates and rationalists from low-church Anglicans and evangelicals, it is more probable that Anglicans sought to distance themselves from their threatening and highly visible religious adversaries. Interestingly, Beasley also sees a convergence in mortuary rituals in Charleston as French Huguenot and Lutheran practices gradually conformed to the dominant Anglican practices. The evidence from Simpson's diary clearly shows that Anglican hegemony did not extend into evangelical communities in the countryside. Rather, evangelical forms dominated, and Anglicans adapted.

24 Simpson never failed to comment on the decency and decorum of the Anglican funerals he performed; see *Diary of Reverend Archibald Simpson, Part 1*, 261; *Part 2*, 104, 132.

25 Frederick Dalcho, *An Historical Account of the Protestant Episcopal Church in South Carolina* (Charleston: E. Thayer, 1820), 358; Frederick Lewis Weis, *The Colonial Clergy of Virginia, North Carolina, and South Carolina* (Baltimore: Genealogical Publishing Company, 1976), 71–95.

In many cases, religious differences could be patched over with compromises. At least in the South Carolina countryside, Anglican and evangelical tastes tended to converge: low-church Anglicans moved to the religious center alongside genteel Presbyterians and Independents who sought respectability and distanced themselves from more unrefined Baptists. This was certainly true for the Saltcatcher congregation, which consisted mostly of "church people" who had initially resisted dissenting from the establishment until two Presbyterian families moved into the neighborhood from the adjoining parish. Likewise, at St. Bartholomew's in 1771, the Anglican vestry invited Edward Ellington, an evangelical Anglican and associate of Whitefield with no formal ministerial training, to be the parish priest. He was enthusiastically embraced by the dissenters at Pon Pon, whose Presbyterian pulpit had been vacant since their minister died in 1766. Such routine mixing helped to smooth over the different expectations for funerals and made it easier for dying people and their families to embrace different mortuary practices. Joseph Miles, for example, gave "very particular directions about his funeral," which included adding a discourse and prayer – but not singing – to the prayer book service. When Mrs. Blair was buried in the churchyard at Stoney Creek meeting house, Simpson read the prayer book service but "pronounced the blessing extemporary ... according to the Dissenters Method of burying," which "gave great Satisfaction" to all. Simpson preferred this kind of hybrid service when performing Anglican funerals – indeed, he wrote, it was his "firm determination" to combine the two services, whether in the churchyard or elsewhere, "as *I* may see proper."[26]

That he had to be firmly determined, however, indicates that Anglicans sometimes contested the blended funeral service. Certainly, some of his Anglican neighbors resented the dissenting method, perhaps seeing it as an attempt to exploit the dead and manipulate the bereaved, and they pushed back. At Indian Land, Charles Brown and his wife were displeased with Simpson's discourse at their child's funeral, as Simpson later learned indirectly "by many insinuations" from acquaintances. As a result, when their second child died in 1771, Simpson adhered strictly to the prayer book "without adding a Single word after it," although Brown had asked him to perform the service "in what way was most agreeable to myself." He also omitted the discourse when Mrs. Brown herself died just three

[26] Howe, *Presbyterian Church*, 1: 322, 326–27; *Diary of Reverend Archibald Simpson, Part 2*, 114 (emphasis added), 123, 140–41. Presbyterians, Philip Mulder points out, were centrists by profession, models of "balance and moderation"; *Controversial Spirit*, 21.

months later. These were delicate negotiations: publicly, Brown gave polite directions that respected Simpson's preferences, but privately he complained to friends who let Simpson know it by insinuation. Simpson got the message. Despite his firm determination to blend the two services and use the funeral evangelically to warn the living, comfort the mourners, draw out their grief, and promote the gospel, he would not risk censure by offending Brown again.[27]

The difference between Brown's displeasure with and Miles's openness to the evangelical way was more than a matter of personal taste: it also involved parish politics. Unlike Miles, Brown was connected to the anti-evangelical faction at Indian Land, whose malice toward Simpson and the Stoney Creek evangelicals had deep, complicated roots. As elsewhere in British North America, the politics in Simpson's parish was a tangle of family histories, ethnic origins, personal hatreds, and religious traditions. In general, however, there were two factions. One party, headed by Stephen Bull of Sheldon, was tied to the established church and connected to one of the most powerful families in the province. Bull was the nephew of Lieutenant Governor William Bull, and his grandfather, William Bull Sr., was the moving force behind the building of the Prince William's parish church, which adjoined the five-thousand-acre Sheldon plantation. The other faction lacked a single leader, although it was more evangelically inclined and gravitated toward Simpson and his supporters. As in many pre-Revolutionary communities, the meeting house was a key battleground where these conflicts played out. Although the leading vestryman at the Sheldon church and a steadfast enemy of evangelicalism, Bull "pretend[ed] to be a Trustee" of the Stoney Creek congregation. He and his neighbor William Main exploited Simpson's occasional dissatisfaction with Indian Land and tried to undermine his standing among the parishioners. In Simpson's view, Main's agenda was strictly personal, seeking only to "hurt and ruin" Simpson while Bull, a much more formidable foe, aimed at "destroying the Dissenting interest" itself. Toward this end, in 1771, Bull harbored a fugitive slave who belonged to the Stoney Creek congregation. His goal in doing so was to undermine the congregation's trustees, discredit the evangelical party, gain control of the parsonage slaves who were hired out to support the congregation, and seize control of church affairs. Simpson was "shocked and amazed" at such a "black design," which was in his view obviously intended to "Overthrow the

[27] *Diary of Reverend Archibald Simpson, Part 2*, 59, 104.

Gospel." Such were the dangerous intrigues at Indian Land, where Simpson had to care for the living and bury the dead from both parties.[28]

This context demanded the utmost sensitivity in negotiating funeral arrangements. In most cases, Anglican and evangelical convergence and interdependence made room for compromise, but not in all cases. For at funerals, Simpson and his neighbors publicly declared their loyalties, displayed their status, and watched one another carefully. Community politics spilled over into death, and funerals were shaped not only by received religious identities and adherence to traditional practices, but in the moment, by the push and pull of very peculiar social undercurrents.

Nowhere was the politics of death and dying more conspicuous than in the death narrative. This, after all, was why the good death was so important: because it bore witness to the Christian life and was useful for advancing the gospel and frustrating the designs of God's enemies. Like the funeral service, the death narrative was influenced by the social and political dynamics of the community, but it was less discreet. Neighbors were more than willing to speak ill of the dead, and telling stories of how people died was a safe, coded way to do so. It was also a malleable genre, for dying was subject to interpretation and stories were subject to editing or even to wholesale revision.

Simpson and his neighbors viewed dying in providential terms – that is, it was God's doing, as mysterious as it may seem – and this created a complicated tension in how to interpret it. Especially for Reformed evangelicals, God ordered all things, not least of all the manner of death. Careful preparation and good pastoral care might allow for some individual agency, but the conditions of one's death – whether it was sudden or slow, painful or comfortable, quiet or hard – were determined by divine will. If a good death could be used to strengthen the gospel, a "Judgment like" death could be used to weaken it. Such deaths needed to be rationalized. Early evangelicals became skilled at shaping death narratives to bring providence in line with their expectations.[29]

[28] On the Bull family, Sheldon plantation, and Prince William's church, see Lawrence S. Rowland, Alexander Moore, and George C. Rogers, Jr., *The History of Beaufort County, South Carolina: Volume 1, 1514–1861* (Columbia: University of South Carolina Press, 1996), 114, 117–18. Simpson discusses the enmity of Main and Bull, including details of this plot, in *Diary of Reverend Archibald Simpson, Part 2*, 138–39.

[29] This argument builds on David Hall's treatment of the politics of providentialism in Puritan New England; see *Worlds of Wonder, Days of Judgment: Popular Religious Belief in Early New England* (Cambridge: Harvard University Press, 1989), 94–110.

In some cases, little skill was required. Consider, for example, the death of Elijah Prioleau, a notorious backslider and "desperate reprobate" who died suddenly of a "violent Bilious disorder" in 1769. "I have often heard him," Simpson smugly recalled, "in a very wild, fearful desperate manner, wish for a Sudden Death, and he has got it." Or, take the even more obviously providential death of Mr. Haskins, a freethinker, tavern keeper, and horse trader who opened a race track in Simpson's parish in 1771. For weeks, Haskins desecrated the Sabbath and cursed the rainy weather, even as his health declined, and it appeared he would not live to see the races. He died on the very day the track opened, yet the races went on, and Haskins's family continued to serve liquor and take bets "notwithstanding the Death that was before them, and the Corpse of the principal manager, was in their Sight." Simpson saw Haskins's death as certain evidence that God, like the evangelical community, opposed the race track, "but the Circumstance of Carrying it on notwithstanding the hand of providence ... has grieved & terrified many, and is such a daring piece of wickedness as cannot be sufficiently mourned for."[30]

It is not difficult to imagine Simpson and his neighbors constructing this narrative as the details of Mr. Haskins's death emerged and confirmed their feelings about the race track. Given his personal reputation, the nature of his business, and the timing and circumstances of his demise, Haskins was an easy target for the evangelicals. It proved much more difficult, however, to explain away the judgment-like deaths of good people, like the "sober, well inclined youth" who was killed by lightning in 1770. Simpson had performed his wedding just a week earlier. On the previous Sabbath, the unnamed young man was "much affected" by the sermon and showed signs of a spiritual awakening. Three days later, while going about his "lawful & necessary business," he sheltered himself under an oak tree during a storm and was struck by lightning, instantly killing both him and his horse. Simpson now faced a theological problem – why do bad deaths happen to good people? He rose to the occasion, preaching a funeral sermon aimed at both explaining the providence and drawing a useful lesson from it:

> I discoursed on this melancholy occasion, with a view to these two texts of Scripture, all things come alike to all etc. and, Think ye that those eighteen, upon whom the tower in Siloam fell & a slew them, that they were sinners above all men, that dwelt in Jerusalem. I showed them, that the manner of his Death, was not to be looked upon as a Judgment, that we were not to apply providences in that manner

[30] *Diary of Reverend Archibald Simpson, Part 1*, 227; *Part 2*, 161.

to others, that nothing was to be known of a persons state, by the manner of their Death, that it was a very wrong notion of many, that if people died easy, quietly and willingly, that they were happy, showed them the folly of such a notion, and how contrary it was to the Scripture, which says, that in life the wicked are not plagued as other men, & in Death they have no lands ... concluded with telling something of the nature of the Electricity fire, and showing them that in thunderstorms there was the greatest danger in going under trees.

Clearly, the young man's death was problematic. He died suddenly and alone, both of which were dreaded in the mid-eighteenth century.[31]

As a result, his death was neither shared nor particularly usable. Getting struck by lightning, moreover, lent itself to a providential interpretation. As an adherent at Indian Land who was under Simpson's pastoral care and showing evidence of religious awakening, his judgment-like death undermined the evangelical interest, and it had to be addressed aggressively. Accordingly, Simpson went to great lengths to shape the death narrative: the youth was "sober and well inclined," his business was "lawful and necessary," his soul was drawn to God, and his death, while tragic, was no stroke from God. Lightning was a natural phenomenon, not a supernatural one. Unlike Mr. Haskins's providential death, which clearly signaled God's displeasure at the race track, the young man's death narrative carried a more mundane if equally unambiguous moral: do not stand under a tree during a thunderstorm.

A final example, the death of Mary Cater, shows just how contested these narratives could be when the stakes were high. Cater was connected to the Anglican faction at Indian Land through her guardian, William Main. Some time around 1769, Simpson, in his fourth year of widowhood, proposed marriage to Cater. Perhaps he hoped to bridge the divisions within his parish, or he may have been physically attracted to the young, unmarried Miss Cater, who was about fourteen years his junior, or perhaps he had an eye on her estate and family status. We can only conjecture, since the diary from this period is missing. Whatever his motive, the proposal fell through, and Main made Simpson's private letters to Cater public, hoping to ruin his name. These were the "vile charges" to which Simpson alluded a year or more later in what he assumed were his dying hours.

In 1769, Cater married Charles Dupont, a wealthy planter. In July 1770, she died in childbirth. Her death "was the most melancholy I ever heard,"

[31] *Diary of Reverend Archibald Simpson, Part* 2, 16–18. On fears of dying alone, see Sparks, "Southern Way of Death," 36–37.

Simpson wrote, "She had many fits, was for several days in the most raving distracted condition, full of terror, and in the most fearful despair." Although overwhelmed with emotion at news of her "dismal end," Simpson nonetheless felt vindicated by it, seeing her death as a "chastening" from God for her "vile usage" of him "that she might not be condemned" in the afterlife. Within a week, however, a much different story of Mrs. Dupont's death was circulating, apparently at the hand of Simpson's enemy William Main: she died "a quiet, easy, comfortable Death." Rarely did Simpson express the kind of explosive anger as when these rumors reached him. This story was "false as hell," he declared, "for her Death was the most horrid & terrible, almost, beyond anything on record in history." As to the people who crafted this new narrative, Simpson spared no adjectives in describing them. They were "artful, conniving," self-interested, "smooth fawning, hypocritical, deceitful" wretches.[32]

To be sure, Simpson's indignation was personal: Mrs. Dupont had slandered him, God had vindicated him, and now his enemies were whitewashing her death to tarnish Simpson's reputation. Yet, there is a larger significance rooted in the two very different stories the people of Indian Land told about Dupont's death. Because of her connections with Main, Bull, and Simpson, Mary Cater Dupont stood at the storm center of local politics, the complicated intersection of honor, courtship, neighborhood, kinship, and religion. The story of her death was inseparable from this context, and it served as a powerful weapon to strengthen one party and weaken the other. For Simpson, more than his honor was at stake, for his name was tied to the evangelical party, the dissenting interest, and, in his view, to the cause of true religion. Likewise, the anti-evangelical faction surely sought more than to protect the virtue of Mary Dupont. By shaping the narrative of her death, they could discredit Simpson, strengthen their hand in their struggle to control congregational affairs at Indian Land, and, by extension, gain leverage against religious dissenters at the provincial level. In this context, the way people died mattered, and it mattered enough to lie about, even to make up death narratives out of whole cloth.

Dying was a political act. To fully see its political import, we must look at the local social contexts in which people died, and tease the politics of dying out of nontraditional sources such as letters, diaries, wills, and

[32] On the Duponts, see Louise Bailey and Elizabeth Ivey Cooper, eds., *Biographical Directory of the South Carolina House of Representatives* (Columbia: University of South Carolina Press, 1981), 2: 204–05. Simpson describes Dupont's death in *Diary of Reverend Archibald Simpson, Part 2*, 49; he discusses the contested death narrative in *Part 2*, 87–88.

chancery court records. We must also bear in mind that eighteenth-century evangelicals looked at the world through a providential lens, seeing the hand of God in daily occurrences. In this light, a good death like Mrs. Lambright's comforted believers and confirmed the gospel. Such deaths were models for the evangelical script. A sudden, suspicious death like that of the young man killed by lightning was problematic, and evangelicals went to great lengths to rationalize it. Likewise, when so-called enemies of the gospel died angry or raving deaths, like Mr. Haskins and Mrs. Dupont, Simpson and his neighbors felt vindicated, even as his enemies contested the accounts. Thus, evangelicals fashioned, told, embellished, and defended stories of how people died, with urgency and not a little relish. In the context of a strong Anglican establishment and an embattled evangelical movement, death narratives were just as important to legitimating their religion as stories of remarkable conversions and spectacular revivals.

Death was indeed "everywhere" in the late-colonial Lowcountry: alternately denied, resisted, feared, and welcomed beside every family's sick bed; proclaimed in Sabbath sermons; embedded in religious rituals; carried as news along the paths from plantation to plantation; and inscribed on the landscape in churchyards and the houses of people whose providential deaths their neighbors remembered. As evangelicals carried their deathways with them as they swept across the South after 1800, they transformed the South. Whatever else might account for the extraordinary success of their movement – their openness to intense religious experiences and controversial forms of worship, their willingness to innovate, their egalitarianism, their institutional elasticity, their compatibility with patriarchy and slavery – evangelicals' commitment to the good death spoke to deep and universal anxieties and heightened their appeal. With each pastoral visit and funeral sermon, as with the countless stories of good and bad deaths that passed from ear to ear across the antebellum South, evangelicals taught Southerners how to die, leaving a deep imprint on the region's deathways and laying the foundation for a southern way of death.

3

When "History Becomes Fable Instead of Fact": The Deaths and Resurrections of Virginia's Leading Revolutionaries

Lorri Glover

Death began to claim them in the 1790s. Benjamin Franklin, among the eldest in the pantheon of revolutionary heroes, died first, in the spring of 1790. George Mason, John Hancock, and Roger Sherman passed away in the middle of the 1790s. The greatest orator of the Revolutionary Age, Patrick Henry, was silenced in the summer of 1799. And then, in the last month of the last year of the eighteenth century, the "father of his country" was laid to rest at his beloved Mount Vernon. In the first two decades of the nineteenth century, Americans mourned the demise of a host of luminaries, including Sam Adams, Edmund Randolph, and Gouverneur Morris. By the time Thomas Jefferson and John Adams died on the 4th of July, 1826, the fiftieth anniversary of the Declaration of Independence, few of their cohort remained. James Madison's death in 1836 marked the end of the generation; he was the last survivor among the signers of the Constitution and the last of the delegates to the Continental Congress. Near the end of his life, Madison knowingly remarked "having outlived so many of my contemporaries . . . I may be thought to have outlived myself."[1]

As they faced their own mortality, leading members of the founding generation took great pride in the past even as they feared for the future.

[1] James Madison to Jared Sparks, June 1, 1831, in *The Writings of James Madison*, ed. Galliard Hunt, 9 vols. (New York: G. P. Putnam's Sons, 1900–1910), 9: 460. Many Americans saw the simultaneous deaths of Thomas Jefferson and John Adams, on July 4, 1826, as the end of this era; see, for example, Andrew Burstein, *America's Jubilee: A Generation Remembers the Revolution after 50 Years of Independence* (New York: Random House, 2001), chap. 11; idem, "Immortalizing the Founding Fathers: The Excesses of Public Eulogy," in *Mortal Remains: Death in Early America*, ed. Nancy Isenberg and Andrew Burstein (Philadelphia: University of Pennsylvania Press, 2003), 98–100.

They knew that they had secured the Revolution and achieved immortal fame – that we would celebrate their lives. At the same time, they understood that their fragile American Republic would endure only so long as subsequent generations of Americans followed their example and dedicated their lives to its preservation. The founders, as Franklin famously quipped, had given American citizens "a republic, if you can keep it." Or, as President Washington explained in his first inaugural address: "The preservation of the sacred fire of liberty, and the destiny of the republican model of government, are justly considered as *deeply*, perhaps as *finally* staked, on the experiment entrusted to the hands of the American people."[2]

By the turn of the nineteenth century, those Americans responsible for the "destiny of the republican model of government" could not ignore the sad reality that they were quickly losing, as one Southerner put it, "our venerable men, the remains of the revolution – By degrees they are removed, and a new generation occupy the stage of life."[3] The deaths of revolutionary luminaries grieved the nation, even when these men died peacefully and in old age, for their passing signaled the loss not simply of remarkable individuals but of a unique age. Americans suspected that the rising generation would never be able to live up to the standards set by the founders and so feared that the republic would perish with them. High on their list of concerns was the spread of sectionalism, which was fast turning Americans into Southerners and Northerners, pulled into a mortal conflict over the West. In the last years of his life, as he witnessed the Missouri Crisis, even the typically optimistic Thomas Jefferson worried "that I am now to die in the belief that the useless sacrifice of themselves by the generation of 1776, to acquire self-government and happiness to their country, is to be thrown away by the unwise and unworthy passions of their sons."[4]

[2] Max Farrand, ed., *The Records of the Federal Convention of 1787*, 4 vols. (New Haven: Yale University Press, 1966), 3: 85; George Washington, First Inaugural Address, April 30, 1789. For the importance of fame, see Douglass Adair, "Fame and the Founding Fathers," in *Fame and the Founding Fathers: Essays by Douglass Adair*, ed. Trevor Colbourn (Indianapolis: Liberty Fund, 1998), 3–36.

[3] Henry DeSaussure to Ezekiel Pickens, October 27, 1805, Henry William DeSaussure Papers, South Caroliniana Library. For the generational shift, see Joyce Appleby, *Inheriting the Revolution: The First Generation of Americans* (Cambridge: Harvard University Press, 2000); Burstein, *America's Jubilee*; Lorri Glover, *Southern Sons: Becoming Men in the New Nation* (Baltimore: Johns Hopkins University Press, 2007); Steven Watts, *The Republic Reborn: War and the Making of Liberal America, 1790–1820* (Baltimore: Johns Hopkins University Press, 1987).

[4] Thomas Jefferson to John Holmes, April 22, 1820, in *The Writings of Thomas Jefferson*, ed. Paul L. Ford, 10 vols. (New York: G. P. Putnam's Sons, 1899), 10: 157.

But death, it turned out, would not deny the Revolutionaries the ability to continue to guide posterity toward a bright future. Because they understood the fragile nature of republican governments and the historical significance of their actions, many revolutionary leaders self-consciously groomed their behavior to offer to history a transcendent example of republican character. The parts of their lives that men like George Washington revealed to their countrymen were, to a great degree, public performances effected to convey republican values such as independence, self-restraint, dignity, and sacrifice. They imbedded those same themes in their prodigious, carefully maintained writings. In sum, they intentionally created for the future a record of themselves and the Revolution. After they died, their families followed that same script: the deathbed scenes that relatives of fallen revolutionaries shared with an anxious American public offered up examples of republican virtue and manly character that helped the founders transcend the grave and speak to the needs of future generations.

This essay investigates the deaths of the South's greatest revolutionary-era leaders: George Washington, Thomas Jefferson, and James Madison. While other men worked alongside these three Virginians, none played a longer or greater shaping role in the creation of the American Republic. As commander of the Continental Army, Washington brought the very concept of an American nation into existence. Jefferson captured that country's creed in the Declaration of Independence. And Madison laid out the design of its government with the Constitution. As presidents, these three men led the federal government for twenty-four of its first twenty-eight years. Although it is both fashionable among historians and appropriate to explore the wider social foundations of the revolutionary movement – to tell the stories of the artisans, farmers, mothers, and slaves who contributed to the American Revolution – it remains a simple fact that a relatively small group of men, led by an even smaller cohort of Virginians, created the military, intellectual, and constitutional foundations of the United States.[5]

[5] For Virginia culture, see especially Edmund S. Morgan, *American Slavery, American Freedom: The Ordeal of Colonial Virginia* (New York: W. W. Norton, 1975); Rhys Isaac, *The Transformation of Virginia, 1740–1790* (Chapel Hill: University of North Carolina Press, 1982); T. H. Breen, *Tobacco Culture: The Mentality of the Great Tidewater Planters on the Eve of Revolution* (Princeton: Princeton University Press, 1985); Charles Sydnor, *Gentlemen Freeholders: Political Practices in Washington's Virginia* (Chapel Hill: University of North Carolina Press, 1952). For nonelites in the Revolution, see, for example, Woody Holton, "American Revolution and Early Republic," in *American History Now*, ed. Eric Foner and Lisa McGirr (Philadelphia: Temple University Press, 2011), 24–51; Gary Nash, *The Unknown American Revolution: The Unruly Birth of Democracy and the Struggle to Create America* (New York: Viking, 2005). For explorations of the limits of elite control within revolutionary

But Washington, Jefferson, and Madison were not only revolutionary leaders; they were planter-patriarchs, too. All three came of age in the same Virginia gentry culture that prized independence and landownership predicated on mastery of slaves. Although not yet self-conscious, their southern roots profoundly influenced their outlooks on life and their long political careers. After each man left the presidency, he retired to his plantation to, as they often put it, "live like a patriarch of old."[6] Their deaths occurred in this distinctive national/regional/gentry context, which indelibly marked the stories recounted by witnesses to their last days. And those death narratives, in the telling and retelling, helped cement the historic reputation of these revolutionaries as southern gentlemen and American heroes.

First, we begin with the stories. December 12, 1799, seemed a thoroughly unexceptional day in George Washington's life. He left on horseback in the morning to survey his estate and plan improvements. An innovative planter, Washington was in his cups at Mount Vernon and still quite vigorous at age sixty-seven. He was undeterred when rain turned to sleet, and he did not head home until the afternoon. Although he had gotten wet and "the snow was hanging upon his hair," Washington saw that dinner was waiting. Not wishing to delay his family and guests longer, he sat down to eat without changing his clothes. On the morning of Friday the 13th, Washington's throat hurt, but still he attended to his business, insisting on going out in the snow to mark trees he wanted removed. His step-grandson George Washington Parke Custis (who Washington raised as his own son) recalled that, as usual, Washington tended to his own affairs: "he carried his own compass, noted his observations, and marked out the ground." Although hoarse that evening, "he made light of it" and visited cheerfully with Tobias Lear, his personal secretary who, as the husband of Martha Washington's niece, also lived at Mount Vernon. That night, George worked late in his library. When Martha chided him, he reminded her "that through a long life, it has been my unvaried rule, never to put off till the morrow the duties which should be preformed to-day."[7]

Virginia, see Woody Holton, *Forced Founders: Indians, Debtors, Slaves, and the Making of the American Revolution in Virginia* (Chapel Hill: University of North Carolina Press, 1999); Michael A. McDonnell, *The Politics of War: Race, Class, and Conflict in Revolutionary Virginia* (Chapel Hill: University of North Carolina Press, 2007).

[6] Thomas Jefferson to Maria Cosway, December 27, 1820, in *The Domestic Life of Thomas Jefferson*, ed. Sarah N. Randolph (New York: Harper and Brothers, 1871), 374.

[7] Tobias Lear Diary, December 14, 1799, in Tobias Lear, *Letters and Recollections of George Washington* (London: Archibald Constable and Company, 1906), 129, 130; George

Between two and three o'clock in the morning on Saturday the 14th, Washington woke his wife and told her that he felt "very unwell." She wanted to summon help, but he would not let her get up, fearing she might take cold herself. Being "a manly sufferer," he waited for the sunrise and "uttered no complaint."[8] At dawn, a slave woman named Caroline came in to start a fire, and Martha sent her to get help. An overseer, Mr. Rawlins, came, and Washington asked to be bled. (Eighteenth-century Americans thought that through deliberate cuts their bodies would expel disease.) Rawlins appeared nervous about cutting the clearly ailing former president, so Washington reassured him: "*Don't be afraid.*" Washington's longtime friend and personal physician, Dr. Craik, soon arrived, joined by two other doctors. Multiple rounds of bleeding and blistering ensued, and purgatives were administered. Even after Washington asked his doctors to "let me go off quietly," they blistered his legs and feet and throat. Washington saw before his physicians did that he would not survive. "He was fully impressed at the beginning of his complaint, as well as through every succeeding stage of it," his doctors later explained, "that its conclusion would be mortal; submitting to the several exertions made for his recovery, rather as a duty, than from any expectation of their efficacy."[9]

Fully aware that he was at the end of his life, Washington asked Tobias Lear if he "recollected anything which it was essential for him to do." When confident that he left nothing undone, George gave Martha his will and talked to Tobias about his political papers and burial wishes. He promised everyone present that "*I am not afraid to go.*" And then, without any anguish or regret, he quietly slipped away. As one close relative described it, the father of his country "expired with his characteristic firmness."[10] See Figure 3.

Washington Park Custis Recollections, in *Recollections and Private Memoirs of Washington, by His Adopted Son, George Washington Parke Custis, with A Memoir of the Author, by his Daughter; and Illustrative and Explanatory Notes*, ed. Benson J. Lossing (1860; reprint, Bridgewater: American Foundation Publications, 1999), 472–73, 474.

[8] Tobias Lear Diary, December 14, 1799, in Lear, *Letters and Recollections of George Washington*, 130; George Washington Park Custis Recollections, in Lossing, ed., *Recollections and Private Memoirs of Washington*, 474.

[9] Tobias Lear Diary, December 14, 1799, in Lear, *Letters and Recollections of George Washington*, 129–34; James Craik and Elisha Dick, Account of Washington's Death, December 21, 1799, *Virginia Herald*, December 31, 1799, www.gwpapers.virginia.edu/project/exhibit/mourning/craik.html.

[10] Tobias Lear Diary, December 14, 1799, in Lear, *Letters and Recollections of George Washington*, 133; Thomas Law to Mrs. Barry, December 15, 1799, www.gwpapers.virginia.edu/project/exhibit/mourning. For a thoughtful, thorough exploration of Washington's death, see Peter R. Henriques, "The Final Struggle between George Washington and the Grim King: Washington's Attitudes toward Death and an Afterlife," *Virginia Magazine of History and Biography* 107 (winter 1999): 73–97.

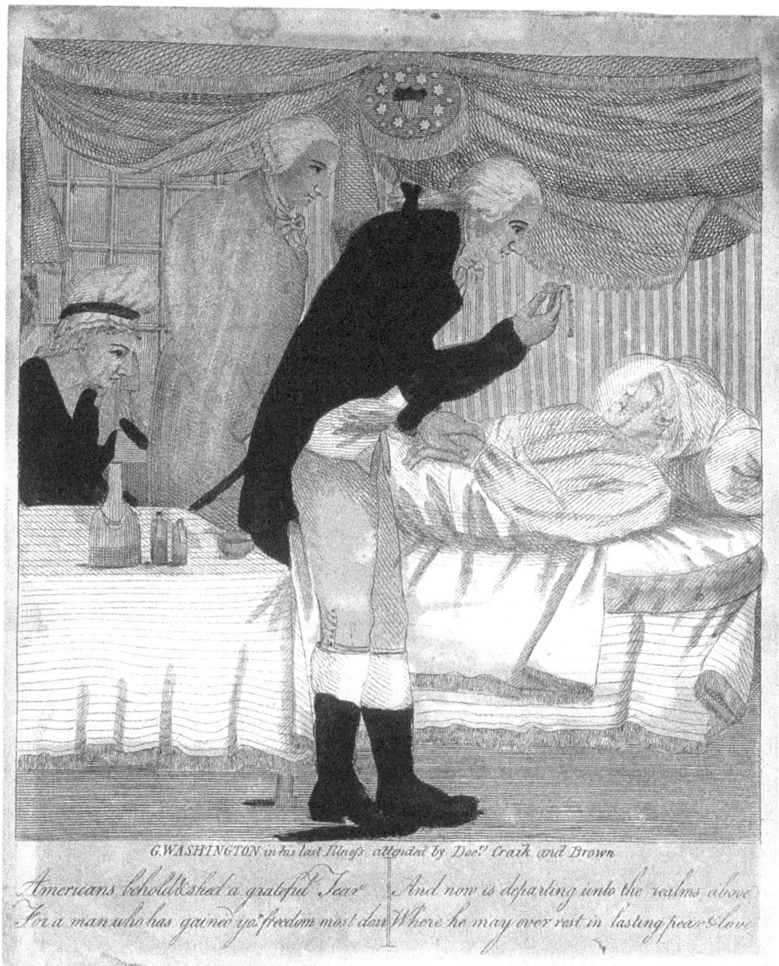

FIGURE 3. Washington's deathbed scene, with Martha Washington seated at the foot of the bed. The caption reads, "Americans behold & shed a grateful Tear/For a man who has gained yo'r freedom most dear/And now is departing unto the realms above/Where he may ever rest in lasting peace & love."
Source: "Washington in his last illness attended by Docrs. Craik and Brown," colored engraving (Philadelphia: Edward Pember and James Luzarder, 1800). Courtesy of The Library Company of Philadelphia.

A quarter century passed between the death of George Washington and that of Thomas Jefferson. Washington's demise came in a matter of hours, whereas Jefferson suffered for months. In fact, he had endured on-and-off health problems for years, "worn down," he told James Madison, "by sickness as well as old age."[11] In 1818, Jefferson had visited a spring where he caught an infection and consequently suffered from terrible boils on his buttocks. In his last years, he was often afflicted with severe diarrhea as well as arthritic pain and urinary tract or kidney problems. His physician prescribed the insertion of tubes up his urethra to try and relieve the blockage. But 1826 was the most trying of times. In January, Jefferson complained that a combination of ailments left him "required to be constantly recumbent." In the months that followed, he sometimes rebounded but never fully recovered. In the last few weeks of his life, he was bedfast. It remains impossible to precisely diagnose the cause of Jefferson's death, but scholars reasonably deduce the eighty-three-year-old could have succumbed to any of a number of problems likely afflicting him: chronic diarrhea, a kidney infection, pneumonia, and prostate cancer.[12] So, Thomas Jefferson lived to be sixteen years older than George Washington, and he died from totally different causes, mostly linked to old age.

But the stories told by Jefferson's relatives of his death sound strikingly similar to the ones that came out of Mount Vernon nearly three decades before. Jefferson's daughter, Martha Jefferson Randolph, and other devoted relatives never left his side. His personal physician, Dr. Dunglison, also remained at Monticello during the last week of Jefferson's life, although he could do little for his dying patient. Jefferson's granddaughter Virginia Trist recalled that although he was the one suffering, it was Jefferson who comforted his kin. Like Washington, Jefferson "resigned himself completely into the doctor's hands" despite wisely perceiving that death was unavoidable.[13]

Knowing the end was near, Thomas composed a poem for Martha, a final token of his abiding love: "Then farewell, my dear, my lov'd daughter, Adieu! The last pang of life is in parting from you!" He spoke with his grandchildren, who recalled that "His parting interview with the different members of his family was calm and composed." Jefferson also took time to reflect on his past, with his political contributions at the center of his

[11] Thomas Jefferson to James Madison, October 18, 1825, in *The Republic of Letters: The Correspondence between Thomas Jefferson and James Madison, 1776–1826*, ed. James Morton Smith, 3 vols. (New York: W. W. Norton, 1995), 3: 1942.

[12] Thomas Jefferson to William Gordon, January 1, 1826, Thomas Jefferson Papers, Library of Congress. See also, "Jefferson's Cause of Death," monticello.org.

[13] Virginia Randolph Trist to Cornelia Randolph, June 20, 1826, Family Letters Digital Archive, Thomas Jefferson Foundation, Inc., www.monticello.org/familyletters. For Martha Jefferson Randolph, see Cynthia A. Kierner, *Martha Jefferson Randolph, Daughter of Monticello: Her Life and Times* (Chapel Hill: University of North Carolina Press, 2012).

memories: "He remarked on the tendency of his mind to recur back to the scenes of the Revolution." Through it all, Jefferson "suffered no pain, but gradually sank from debility. His mind was always clear – it never wandered." Like Washington, Jefferson accepted death with the strength, perspective, and fearlessness that had defined his life: "His manner was that of a person going on a necessary journey – evincing neither satisfaction nor regret."[14]

During the last two days of his ordeal, Jefferson slipped in and out of consciousness. He awoke in the early morning hours of the 4th of July 1826 and asked about the date. Reassured by Dr. Dunglison and his grandson, Thomas Jefferson "Jeff" Randolph, that his final wish had come true, he closed his eyes for the last time. Thomas Jefferson died just before 1:00 in the afternoon, at the same time he had presented the Declaration of Independence to the Continental Congress exactly fifty years before.[15] See Figure 4.

While Washington's death came in a matter of hours and Jefferson's final decline took a few months, James Madison's painful debilitation ran on for years. In March 1832, more than four years before he died, Dolley Madison wrote a friend that "My dear Husband is still confined to his bed – In addition to a disabling Rheumatism throughout the winter, he has had a bilious fever, which has reduced him so that he can only walk from one bed to another." Dolley seldom left James's side for more than a few minutes, and she said she had not ventured beyond "the enclosure around our house for the last eight months, on account of his continued disposition." Two years later, James remained "in very bad health" and "still confined to the house with feebleness – resulting from a painful and diffusive Rheumatism."[16]

Despite his agonizing physical decline – his niece said that in the last years of his life he "was a martyr to rheumatism" – James Madison never lost his prodigious intellectual gifts or his strong spirit. Madison told James Monroe in 1831 that the more his disease progressed the slower his steps and smaller his penmanship became. But he persisted with good humor in

[14] Thomas Jefferson poem for Martha Jefferson Randolph and Thomas Jefferson Randolph Reminiscence, both in Randolph, ed., *Domestic Life of Thomas Jefferson*, 426–27, 429.

[15] Dr. Dunglison and Thomas Jefferson Randolph Reminiscences, both in Randolph, ed., *Domestic Life of Thomas Jefferson*, 424–29.

[16] Dolley Madison to Frances D. Lear, March 1832, and Dolley Madison to Mary Allen, February 25, 1834, both in *The Selected Letters of Dolley Payne Madison*, ed. David B. Mattern and Holly C. Shulman (Charlottesville: University of Virginia Press, 2003), 294, 304.

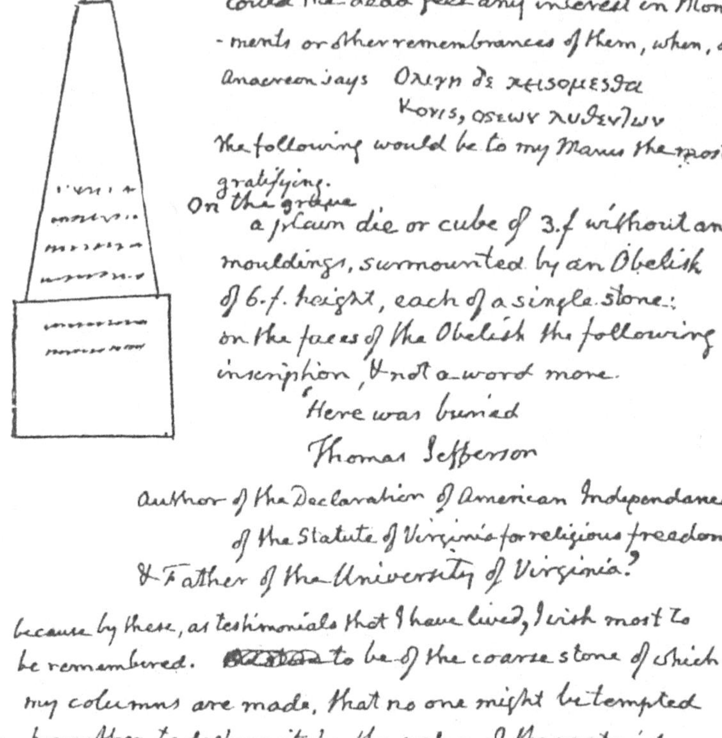
could the dead feel any interest in Monu-
-ments or other remembrances of them, when, as
Anacreon says Ὀλίγη δὲ κεισόμεσθα
Κόνις, ὀστέων λυθέντων
the following would be to my Manes the most
gratifying.
On the grave
a plain die or cube of 3.f without any
mouldings, surmounted by an Obelisk
of 6.f. height, each of a single stone:
on the faces of the Obelisk the following
inscription, & not a word more
'Here was buried
Thomas Jefferson
Author of the Declaration of American Independance
of the Statute of Virginia for religious freedom
& Father of the University of Virginia.'
because by these, as testimonials that I have lived, I wish most to
be remembered. [illegible] to be of the coarse stone of which
my columns are made, that no one might be tempted
hereafter to destroy it for the value of the materials.
my bust by Ciracchi, with the pedestal and truncated
column on which it stands, might be given to the University
if they would place it in the Dome room of the Rotunda.
on the Die of the Obelisk might be engraved
Born Apr. 2. 1743. O.S.
Died ——

FIGURE 4. Probably when he prepared and signed his final will in March 1826, Thomas Jefferson designed his own gravestone and prepared the text to be engraved on it: "Here was buried Thomas Jefferson Author of the Declaration of American Independence of the Statute of Virginia for religious freedom & Father of the University of Virginia."
Source: Thomas Jefferson, Epitaph. c. March 1826, illustrated manuscript. Courtesy of the Library of Congress, Washington DC.

that "microscopic writing" and those "fatiguing" steps. His personal slave or "body servant," Paul Jennings, insisted that even after Madison was confined to bed, "his mind was bright, and with his numerous visitors he talked with as much animation and strength of voice as I ever heard him in his best days." The years took a grievous toll on his body, but just days before Madison's death a visitor likewise found his mind "still bright and sun-like as ever."[17]

In late June 1836, doctors came to Montpelier to attend to the gravely ill Madison. Knowing the sixtieth anniversary of the Declaration of Independence was days away, they offered to try using drugs to try to keep him alive. But Madison declined. He preferred to die "in the full possession of all his noble faculties." Although he did not share a death date with his best friend Thomas Jefferson, James Madison also "died without pain and without fear."[18] Madison, like Washington and Jefferson before him, met death as he had lived. Paul Jennings and James's niece Nelly Willis sat with him that last morning, spelling Dolley. As usual, James appeared serene and self-possessed. Sukey the maid had brought his breakfast, but James could not swallow, and Nelly asked what was wrong. An intellectual to the end, Madison calmly replied, "Nothing more than a change of *mind*, my dear." And then, Paul Jennings said, he was gone: "His head instantly dropped, and he ceased breathing as quietly as the snuff of a candle goes out."[19]

Three deaths, arising from very different circumstances, spanning more than thirty years, yet the stories sound so similar. In fact, the connections are not coincidental, for parts of the tales are simply not credible. The most plausible modern medical theory about Washington's death was that he succumbed to acute epiglottitis, an infection that causes swelling around the windpipe. Today, doctors understand this would have been an agonizing way to die: the patient would have felt himself gradually strangled by his own throat tissue. Jefferson suffered from chronic diarrhea, boils, and a urinary obstruction – any one of which would have been excruciating in its own way. He developed a growing dependence on laudanum and, although his doctor followed best practices of the era, like Washington, Jefferson was subjected to counterproductive treatments. Surviving records reveal less about Madison's ailments, but we do know that for years he

[17] Mary Cutts Memoir, in *The Queen of America: Mary Cutts's Life of Dolley Madison*, ed. Catherine Allgor (Charlottesville: University of Virginia Press, 2012), 177; James Madison to James Monroe, April 21, 1831, in Hunt, ed., *Writings of James Madison*, 9: 458–59; Paul Jennings, *A Colored Man's Reminiscences of James Madison* (Brooklyn: George C. Beadle, 1865), 20; *Richmond Enquirer*, July 1, 1836, quoted in Drew R. McCoy, *The Last of the Fathers: James Madison and the Republican Legacy* (Cambridge: Harvard University Press, 1989), xiii.

[18] Mary Cutts Memoir, in Allgor, ed., *The Queen of America*, 177; Ralph L. Ketcham, ed., "An Unpublished Sketch of James Madison by James K. Paulding," *Virginia Magazine of History and Biography* 67 (October 1959): 437.

[19] Jennings, *A Colored Man's Reminiscences of James Madison*, 20–21.

endured crippling arthritis that eventually left him unable to walk or even write much more than his name. His pain would have been constant. Yet all the eyewitness accounts insist that none of the three gave voice to pain or fear or sorrow. Instead, those keeping vigil emphasized each man's self-possession, intellectual prowess, foresight, selfless concern for others, courage, and dutifulness.

Far from unvarnished reports, these narratives are also too similar to simply reflect the tendency of surviving family members to only speak well of the dead. Rather, the accounts should be read as commentaries on the qualities prized in civic leaders and southern gentlemen. People who watched Washington, Jefferson, and Madison die told tales that cloaked truths about these men's passing in a veil of southern gentry and republican ideals and made them, in death, what they worked toward in life: inspirational icons who could live on in American memory.[20]

Washington's, Jefferson's, and Madison's deathbed scenes also reflected the fact that all three lived as refined and independent planters, at the heads of dutiful white families and vast slave communities, and on picturesque estates. They spent considerable energy positioning themselves as patriarchs over Mount Vernon, Monticello, and Montpelier, and that was how they made their final exits. Although none of these men self-identified as southern (rather, they imagined themselves as Americans and as Virginians), their passages showed the distinct markings of Virginia culture, blended with their class identity, which anticipated some of the most familiar qualities that historians associate with planters in the Old South.[21]

Death remained a decidedly familial matter in the late eighteenth and early nineteenth centuries, especially among planter elites. The professionalization of end-of-life care and funerals still lay decades in the future, and even then, Southerners lagged behind their northern and urban contemporaries. So, all three men died at home, attended to by members of their households, both white relatives and African-American slaves. And they

[20] For crafting a reputation for posterity, see Paul K. Longmore, *The Invention of George Washington* (Berkeley: University of California Press, 1988); Francis D. Cogliano, *Thomas Jefferson: Reputation and Legacy* (Charlottesville: University of Virginia Press, 2006); Andrew Burstein, *Jefferson's Secrets: Death and Desire at Monticello* (New York: Basic Books, 2005). For character and reputation, see Gordon S. Wood, *Revolutionary Characters: What Made the Founders Different* (New York: Penguin, 2006); Adair, "Fame and the Founding Fathers."

[21] For southern culture, see Bertram Wyatt-Brown, *Southern Honor: Ethics and Behavior in the Old South* (New York: Oxford University Press, 1982); Steven M. Stowe, *Intimacy and Power in the Old South: Ritual in the Lives of the Planters* (Baltimore: Johns Hopkins University Press, 1987).

were buried on their own estates. Each of the three men had always planned to make his plantation his final resting place, where he would, as Washington put it, "sleep with my Fathers." It was simply a given that Madison's grave site would be at Montpelier. "Where should it be," his niece Mary Cutts rhetorically asked, "but by the side of his father, mother, brothers, and sisters and other relatives, in the old family burying ground." Jefferson planned precisely where he would be placed in his family cemetery at Monticello: between his wife, Martha, and his daughter Maria Jefferson Eppes. Martha Jefferson Randolph was later buried across the heads of the graves of her mother, father, and sister (Martha's disappointing husband was laid at their feet).[22]

The circumstances of the last days of all three befitted their social standing as patriarchs. Round-the-clock care by private physicians spoke to these men's wealth and the relative isolation of plantations. Exhaustive medical procedures – even to include efforts to extend life to coincide with the 4th of July – reveal their status. The witnesses reflect the capacious nature of southern families. Madison's niece, Jefferson's grandson-in-law, and Washington's niece's husband were considered such close members of their families that they sat vigil with these patriarchs.

In ways their relatives both intended and just reflexively revealed, each of these planters' deaths showcased his lifelong mastery of and dependence on African Americans. Washington, Jefferson, and Madison (typical of their generation of slaveholders) said they considered slavery a necessary evil – antithetical to their republican values, undermining of economic prosperity, and corruptive to the character of whites. Unlike their self-consciously pro-slavery descendants in the mid-nineteenth century, who proudly proclaimed slavery a positive good, members of the revolutionary generation were generally embarrassed about perpetuating what they themselves understood to be an immoral and cruel system of labor. Still, they did nearly nothing to end slavery, either politically or in their households. In

[22] George Washington to Lafayette, February 1, 1784, in *The Papers of George Washington* Confederation Series, ed. W. W. Abbot, 6 vols. (Charlottesville: University Press of Virginia, 1992–1997), 1: 87–88; Mary Cutts Memoir, in Allgor, ed., *The Queen of America*, 179. For family and eighteenth-century Virginians' death traditions, see Daniel Blake Smith, *Inside the Great House: Planter Family Life in Eighteenth-Century Chesapeake Society* (Ithaca: Cornell University Press, 1980), chap. 7; Jan Lewis, *The Pursuit of Happiness: Family and Values in Jefferson's Virginia* (New York: Cambridge University Press, 1983), chap. 3. For later changes, see Gary Laderman, *The Sacred Remains: American Attitudes toward Death, 1799–1883* (New Haven: Yale University Press, 1996); Peter N. Stearns, *Revolution in Sorrow: The American Experience of Death in Global Perspective* (Boulder: Paradigm Publishers, 2007).

fact, Mount Vernon, Monticello, and Montpelier would not have existed and Washington, Jefferson, and Madison could not have lived as they did without slave labor. These men were dependent throughout their lives on racial slavery: for their identity, wealth, lifestyle, and even their political ideas and service.[23]

Death scenes played out against a backdrop of that slaveholding tradition. Accounts of the deaths of Madison, Washington, and Jefferson all placed their "body servants" – the personal slaves who attended to their most intimate needs – at center stage. In Madison's case, Paul Jennings wrote the only eyewitness account of his passing. Burwell Colbert, who was owned by Thomas Jefferson, and Christopher Sheels, Washington's personal slave, similarly looked after their dying owners, perceiving things the white relatives could not. In Jefferson's final moments of semiconsciousness, he tried to tell his grandson something, but Jeff Randolph could not understand. Burwell Colbert did: he knew Jefferson wanted to be raised higher on his pillow, so he made the adjustment for him. Christopher Sheels remained "in the room through the day" that Washington died. More thoughtful and composed than Washington's personal secretary, Sheels reminded Tobias Lear to collect Washington's keys from the late president's pockets.[24]

In the telling of their deaths, not only "body servants" but the larger slave community was mobilized. When Washington first fell ill, Caroline, a slave woman who came to his bedroom to start a fire, was sent to summon Tobias Lear. Lear then sent two other slaves to bring the overseer Rawlins and Dr. Craik. The slave woman Sukey brought James Madison his final meal, and Paul Jennings tended to James's bodily needs the last morning of his life. The work continued into the funerals. At Mount Vernon, slave

[23] For attitudes about slavery, see David Waldstreicher, *Slavery's Constitution: From Revolution to Ratification* (New York: Hill and Wang, 2009); Philip D. Morgan, "'To Get Quit of Negroes': George Washington and Slavery," *Journal of American Studies* 39 (December 2005): 403–29; Lucia Stanton, "'Those Who Labor for My Happiness': Thomas Jefferson and His Slaves," and Paul Finkelman, "Jefferson and Slavery: 'Treason Against the Hopes of the World,'" both in *Jeffersonian Legacies*, ed. Peter S. Onuf (Charlottesville: University Press of Virginia, 1993), 147–80, 181–224; Elizabeth Dowling Taylor, *A Slave in the White House: Paul Jennings and the Madisons* (New York: Palgrave Macmillan, 2012). For the power of slaveholding within Virginia's gentry, see Morgan, *American Slavery, American Freedom*; Kathleen M. Brown, *Good Wives, Nasty Wenches, Anxious Patriarchs: Gender, Race, and Power in Colonial Virginia* (Chapel Hill: University of North Carolina Press, 1996).

[24] Thomas Jefferson Randolph Reminiscence, in Randolph, ed., *Domestic Life of Thomas Jefferson*, 428; Tobias Lear, "Occurrences not noted in the preceding narrative," in Lear, *Letters and Recollections of George Washington*, 135.

men and women prepared Washington's body, the burial site, and all the food for white mourners. After all the white guests departed, their leftovers were "distributed among the blacks." Slaves dug Thomas Jefferson's grave and made his coffin. And James Madison was likewise carried to his grave "by an immense procession of white and colored people."[25]

Stories told by white witnesses about these men's deaths proclaimed their benevolence as slave masters and insisted that, consequently, their slaves were loyal and adoring – an ideal expected of successful planter-patriarchs. In Tobias Lear's account of Washington's death, Christopher Sheels stood faithfully by his master until Washington, worried about Sheels's comfort, invited him to sit. Thomas Jefferson, "anxious to the last" that he pose no undue burden on his slaves, initially refused to allow any of them to sit overnight with him. When "he became so weak as to be forced to yield his consent," he made sure that Burwell Colbert had "a pallet in his room that he might rest during the night." Mary Cutts claimed that as Paul Jennings watched James Madison's remains being lowered into the grave, he was overcome with "sobs and sighs" that "showed how severely he felt his bereavement in the loss of a kind and indulgent master." Jennings was not the only African American weeping at Madison's grave: "the hundred slaves gave vent to their lamentations in one violent outburst that rent the air."[26]

Such sentimentalized, dubious stories could then conveniently be read backward in time. The behavior of slaves at Washington's, Jefferson's, and Madison's deaths appeared to prove how kindly these masters had acted toward those slaves during their lives, thus erasing the fact that all three men used violence and intimidation to maintain their lifestyles and that they enjoyed the benefits of that brutalization until the days they died.

In sharing romanticized stories about dying masters and their "faithful" slaves, white relatives took the opportunity to vindicate these men's lifelong ownership of slaves and, by extension, defend the South's "peculiar institution." Neither Madison nor Washington would have disagreed with

[25] Tobias Lear Diary, December 18, 1799, in Lear, *Letters and Recollections of George Washington*, 141; Annette Gordon-Reed, *The Hemingses of Monticello: An American Family* (New York: W. W. Norton, 2008), 651–52; Jennings, *A Colored Man's Reminiscences of James Madison*, 22. While in other parts of America corpse care and mourning rituals tended to be gendered female, on southern plantations slaves typically did this work. For Philadelphia, see Susan M. Stabile, *Memory's Daughters: The Material Culture of Remembrance in Eighteenth-Century America* (Ithaca: Cornell University Press, 2004), chap. 4.

[26] Dr. Dunglison Reminiscence, in Randolph, ed., *Domestic Life of Thomas Jefferson*, 425; Mary Cutts Memoir, in Allgor, ed., *The Queen of America*, 178.

Jefferson's characterization of slavery as "the perpetual exercise of the most boisterous passions" and an unjust and corrosive institution built on "unremitting despotism."[27] But, in the tales of their deaths, Washington, Jefferson, and Madison were cast as exceptions to these rules: benevolent to their slaves and beloved by them. So, by their purported exceptional mastery, these founders escaped the corruptive influences of slaveholding and won the love and loyalty of their slaves. It remained possible, then, for white Americans, increasingly divided over the place of slavery in the antebellum era, to celebrate these men as both models of the humanity of slave mastery and exceptions to its characteristically vile consequences.

In time, these southern roots became less romantic; Americans preferred to see these men as national heroes rather than as southern planters, and public memory shifted accordingly. The best example of obscuring a founder's southern slaveholding roots is the long-standing trope about George Washington freeing his slaves. While the gradual emancipatory program laid out in his will was surely more in line with republican principles than either Jefferson or Madison chose to be, it is usually forgotten that Washington did not commence that program. He immediately freed only William Lee. The other 123 slaves he personally owned would, according to his will, continue to labor at Mount Vernon until Martha's death. She, not George, emancipated his slaves, and not because of civic ideals but because she feared for her life once they knew her death was their only obstacle to freedom.[28]

Far less controversial and longer-lived were the parts of these men's death stories that illuminated quintessential American values. The Revolution had prized a particular kind of republican character: sacrifice for the greater civic good, dutifulness and perseverance against tremendous odds, self-determination, and independence. Each man – in the eyes of his closest relatives – retained to the last day of his life the character and wisdom that had made him a great leader. During their careers, Washington, Jefferson, and Madison saw what most men could not: that the British would be vanquished, that men could govern themselves, that the Constitution did

[27] Thomas Jefferson, *Notes on the State of Virginia*, ed. William Peden (New York: W. W. Norton, 1972), 162.

[28] George Washington Park Custis Recollections, in Lossing, ed., *Recollections and Private Memoirs of Washington*, 158. For Washington and slavery, see François Furstenberg, *In the Name of the Father: Washington's Legacy, Slavery, and the Making of a Nation* (New York: Penguin, 2006); Philip J. Schwarz, ed., *Slavery at the Home of George Washington* (Mount Vernon Ladies Association, 2001); Morgan, "'To Get Quit of Negroes': George Washington and Slavery."

create a "more perfect union." Such prescience did not betray them as they faced death. Washington readied his relatives for the outcome that he anticipated even before his physicians. He told Tobias Lear and his doctors that he was dying – in fact, he said he had known it from the outset of the illness. "*I find I am going*," he told Lear, "*my breath can not last long. I believed from the first that the disorder would prove fatal.*" Likewise, from Jefferson's bedside on the morning of the 4th, his grandson-in-law, Nicholas Trist, wrote a relative that "From the first, he considered his case desperate – he knew the truth, that the machine was *worn out* in some of its essential parts, and therefore could not go on." And Madison reassured his niece that he understood and did not fear the "change of *mind*" that ended his life.[29]

Indeed, every element of the republican character these men idealized was fulfilled in their deaths – or more accurately in the stories about their passing, which took on a life of their own. In these accounts, the dying men were dutiful and self-sacrificing, submitting to ordeals despite their own desires and to fulfill the hopes of others. Washington was "always endeavouring (from a sense of duty as it appeared) to take what was offered him, and to do as he was desired by the Physicians." And Jefferson decided "for the satisfaction of his family ... from the beginning, to do every thing & any thing the Dr recommended." They did not show weakness. They thought first of others. They were fully in command of themselves and their situation. They took care of settling their affairs. They comforted others. They were resolute, courageous, selfless, and peaceful. David Humphreys, a favorite protégé of Washington, may not have offered an honest assessment of Washington's demise, but he certainly captured his (and his generation's) highest aspirations: "it may be said of him ... that his whole existence was of a piece & that he died as he lived, for the good of mankind."[30]

Age was not allowed to rob these men of their singular talents. Throughout his military career, Washington's physicality had always been extremely important. Men and women routinely marveled at his masculine vigor; he looked better in the saddle than any man of his era, and he

[29] Tobias Lear Diary, December 14, 1799, in Lear, *Letters and Recollections of George Washington*, 133; Nicholas Trist to Joseph Coolidge, July 4, 1826, Family Letters Digital Archive; Jennings, *A Colored Man's Reminiscences of James Madison*, 20.

[30] Tobias Lear, "Occurrences not noted in the preceding narrative," in Lear, *Letters and Recollections of George Washington*, 136; Nicholas Trist to Joseph Coolidge, July 4, 1826, Family Letters Digital Archive; David Humphreys to Martha Washington, July 5, 1800, in *"Worthy Partner": The Papers of Martha Washington*, ed. Joseph E. Fields (Westport: Greenwood Press, 1994), 388–89.

physically commanded any room he entered. "To a stature lofty and commanding," his grandson bragged, "he united a form of the manliest proportions, limbs cast in Nature's finest mould, and a carriage the most dignified, graceful, and imposing." And he maintained that manly prowess until the end of his life: "his step was firm and his carriage noble and commanding, long after the time when the physical properties of man are supposed to be in the wane." So eager were relatives to promote the image of General Washington as paragon of masculinity that they measured his corpse, and, not surprisingly, Washington Custis proudly pronounced it "measured precisely six feet when attired for the grave."[31]

The real crux of the American Revolution had not been fought on the battlefields of the War for Independence, though. The most significant contests in that age were over ideas: the rights and responsibilities of citizens, the nature of just government, and the political structures to fulfill civic ideals. Washington stood alone among this cohort as a classic military hero. Far more important for Jefferson and Madison – and important to Washington, too – was mental strength. In the revolutionary era, what a man knew and accomplished for society mattered more than how he looked. So, the often sickly Madison did not care if visitors saw his crippled body. And as he grew frail, Jefferson was disappointed to have to give up daily walks and horseback-rides, but not embarrassed about his physical decline.

Aging revolutionary heroes worried far more about senility than debility. Jefferson said he "dreaded a doting old age." He and John Adams took pity on a mutual friend in his nineties who, Jefferson said, was "chearful, slender as a grasshopper, and so much without memory that he scarcely recognizes the members of his household." "It is at most," Jefferson concluded, "but life as a cabbage, surely not worth a wish." At age seventy-nine, Jefferson wondered, "When all our faculties have left us, or are leaving us, one by one, sight, hearing, memory, every avenue of pleasing sensation is closed ... when the friends of our youth are all gone, and a generation is risen around us whom we know not, is death an evil?"[32] To lose to old age the intellectual strength that had enabled them to design the American Republic was the worst possible outcome for Washington, Jefferson, and Madison.

[31] George Washington Park Custis Recollections, in Lossing, ed., *Recollections and Private Memoirs of Washington*, 489, 482.

[32] Thomas Jefferson to John Adams, June 1, 1822, in *The Adams-Jefferson Letters: The Complete Correspondence Between Thomas Jefferson and Abigail and John Adams*, ed. Lester J. Cappon (New York: Simon and Schuster, 1971), 577–78.

Not coincidentally, the stories that friends and kin recorded for history uniformly insisted that each man died in full control of his remarkable intelligence. Even at the end, Madison's "sun-like" mind remained as impressive as it had been "in his best days." Washington always "retained the faculties of his mind to the last moment." And Jefferson never lost his "vigorous and unfaded intellect."[33]

The most revered of all of the great revolutionary leaders offers the fullest evidence of the eliding of the truth of death for national and historical purposes. When Americans learned that George Washington had died, they responded with nationwide mourning on an unprecedented scale. Hundreds of eulogies, mock funerals, and commemorations ran across the United States and all the way from the week of his death in December 1799 through his birthday the following February 22. In fact, Congress passed a resolution encouraging towns and communities to plan public ceremonies on that day.[34]

Although Washington died an excruciating death, his heirs, both the familial and national varieties, needed his demise to match his life. And so, in the telling of his death, Washington accepted what he alone saw was coming "with perfect resignation" and "without complaining." Tobias Lear ended his initial account of Washington's death by stating "he expired without a struggle or a sigh!" Lear elaborated on that soon-to-be ubiquitous trope in a later addendum. "His patience, fortitude, & resignation," Lear insisted, "never forsook him for a moment. In his distress he uttered not a sigh, nor a complaint."[35] Given the nature of Washington's affliction and the doctors' gruesome treatments, such stoicism would have been improbable. But if anguish was inevitable, a proper story was essential,

[33] Jennings, *A Colored Man's Reminiscences of James Madison*, 20; Elizabeth Powel to Martha Washington, December 24, 1799, in Fields, ed., *"Worthy Partner": The Papers of Martha Washington*, 325; Dr. Dunglison Reminiscence, in Randolph, ed., *Domestic Life of Thomas Jefferson*, 424.

[34] For reactions to Washington's death, see Gerald Kahler, *The Long Farewell: Americans Mourn the Death of George Washington* (Charlottesville: University of Virginia Press, 2008); Longmore, *The Invention of George Washington*, esp. chap. 17; Catherine L. Albanese, *Sons of the Fathers: The Civil Religion of the American Revolution* (Philadelphia: Temple University Press, 1976) chap. 5; Edward G. Lengel, *Inventing George Washington: America's Founder, in Myth and Memory* (New York: Harper Collins, 2011).

[35] Tobias Lear Diary, December 14, 1799, and Tobias Lear, "Occurrences not noted in the preceding narrative," both in Lear, *Letters and Recollections of George Washington*, 133–35, 135–36. See also Henriques, "The Final Struggle between George Washington and the Grim King."

and so Lear published a death account worthy of the life of Washington. In that story, told not to report facts but to secure a reputation, Lear gave a hero's death to Washington and a patriotic lesson for posterity.

In his published recollection of his grandfather's death, Washington Custis echoed Tobias Lear's implausible story of prescience and serenity. Washington's demise was, like his life, marked by self-control: "With surprising self-possession he prepared to die. Composing his form at length, and folding his arms on his bosom, without a sigh, without a groan, the Father of his Country died. No pang or struggle told when the noble spirit took its noiseless flight, while so tranquil appeared the manly features in the repose of death, that some moments had passed ere those around could believe that the patriarch was no more." In his famous funeral oration, Henry "Light-Horse Harry" Lee repeated this myth and even some of the same language: "His last scene comported with the whole tenor of his life. Although in extreme pain, not a sigh, not a groan escaped him; and with undisturbed serenity he closed his well-spent life." Lee, Custis, and Lear worked off the same script. In a letter to President Adams, Lear said again: "His last scene corresponded with the whole tenor of his life. Not a groan nor complaint escaped him. ... With perfect resignation and a full possession of his reason, he closed his well spent life." And Washington's doctors bolstered this legend, although they employed original phrasing. "During the short period of his illness," they explained, "he economized his time, in the arrangement of such few concerns as required his attention, with the utmost serenity; and anticipated his approaching dissolution with every demonstration of that equanimity for which his whole life has been so uniformly and singularly conspicuous."[36]

It simply would not do for these revolutionary heroes to have endured anything other than a "good death." Their passing needed to be defined by the clear-headedness, resolve, and selflessness that had marked their careers. They deserved to – and their audiences needed them to – go gently. The founders believed that the future of the republic depended on subsequent generations of Americans properly remembering the past and following the example of the founders. George Washington knew that people would scrutinize his death – as they had done his life – for a lesson. Thankfully, he did not have to achieve his last heroic act alone: he had

[36] George Washington Park Custis Recollections and Henry Lee Funeral Oration, December 16, 1799, both in Lossing, ed., *Recollections and Private Memoirs of Washington*, 476–77, 622; Tobias Lear to John Adams, quoted in Kahler, *The Long Farewell*, 3; Craik and Dick, Account of Washington's Death, December 21, 1799.

Washington Custis and Tobias Lear to give him a helping hand, which they did by putting pen to paper, by telling a story from the past for the future.

This relationship between the past and the future was made all the more complicated because George Washington, Thomas Jefferson, and James Madison bridged two very different eras. By the time of Washington's demise, and certainly long before the deaths of Jefferson and Madison, the age these men made (and that made these men) had passed. James Madison's speculation that he might "be thought to have outlived myself" was not simply a commentary on his age, but also on sweeping changes in the decades after the Revolution. The republican ideals of the revolutionary generation were increasingly subsumed by the competitive and market-driven democratic spirit of the early nineteenth century and undermined by intensifying sectionalism. The founders were generally unnerved by the restless rush for money and rank, and what historian Gordon Wood called the "steady vulgarization of eighteenth-century gentility." Many of the generation of 1776 were appalled at the rise to national prominence of rough men like Andrew Jackson and grieved over sectional tensions. The spread of evangelical Christian revivalism also caught these Enlightenment men off guard. By the mid-nineteenth century, evangelicalism and romanticism were generally recasting emotional life and with it American culture. The rise of romantic love, religious enthusiasm, and emotional expressiveness collectively marked the antebellum United States as culturally distinct from the eighteenth century. Although Jefferson and Madison lived well into the nineteenth century, they were, like Washington, quintessential eighteenth-century men. Their idea about how respectable men conducted themselves was a throwback to an earlier age, but their attitudes also marked them as noble examples for a changing country.[37]

These eighteenth-century men believed that emotions, including grief over death, should be restrained. Washington, Jefferson, and Madison thought that both the dying and their mourners should accept death as a natural part of life. Anguish could be felt but should not be revealed. When, for example, George Washington learned in 1797 that his sister Betty Lewis had died, he wrote her widower, George Lewis, capturing eighteenth-century ideals of managed grief. The news, he began by saying, "has filled me with inexpressible concern." But death was a "debt of nature" that "sooner or later must be paid by us all." The "separation

[37] See Gordon S. Wood, *The Radicalism of the American Revolution* (New York: Knopf, 1992), 349 and pt. 3. For shifts in emotional life, see Lewis, *The Pursuit of Happiness*; Smith, *Inside the Great House*.

from our nearest relatives," Washington continued, "is a heart rending circumstance." But, he concluded, "reason religion & Philosophy, teach us to bear it with resignation."[38] Jefferson urged the same acceptance when, in 1818, he learned of the passing of his friend Abigail Adams. He wrote John Adams to share his sympathy and offer the only counsel he could, from dearly bought experience: "Tried myself, in the school of affliction, by the loss of every form of connection which can rive the human heart, I know well, and feel what you have lost." Jefferson believed that, in the face of such losses, "time and silence are the only medicines." He wrote no more because "words are vain."[39]

They did not always live up to those ideals, to be certain. For example, Thomas Jefferson could not control his grief when his wife Martha Wayles Jefferson died in 1782. When the end came, "he was led from the room in a state of insensibility by his sister, Mrs. Carr, who, with great difficulty, got him into the library." He then fainted and "remained so long insensible" the family feared "he never would revive." Decades later, his daughter Martha Jefferson Randolph could only hint at what she witnessed: "the violence of his emotion ... to this day, I dare not describe to myself." Similarly, George Washington cradled his dying stepdaughter in his arms when she succumbed to a seizure, and he and Martha fell into "the lowest ebb of Misery."[40] Such shows of grief appear with increasingly frequency in letters and diaries from the late eighteenth and early nineteenth centuries, especially when it came to the untimely passing of an especially close family member. The sudden loss of a young mother or adored child was a dreadful thing, and relatives did not always control their sorrow. But such

38 George Washington to George Lewis, April 9, 1797, in *The Papers of George Washington* Retirement Series, ed. W.W. Abbot et al., 4 vols. (Charlottesville: University Press of Virginia, 1998–1999), 1: 90.

39 Thomas Jefferson to John Adams, November 13, 1818, in Cappon, ed., *The Adams-Jefferson Letters*, 529; James Madison to Isaac Hite, December 6, 1802, in *The Papers of James Madison* Secretary of State Series, ed. Robert J. Brugger et al., 8 vols. (Charlottesville: University Press of Virginia/University of Virginia Press, 1986–present), 4: 180.

40 Martha Jefferson Randolph Reminiscence, in Randolph, ed., *Domestic Life of Thomas Jefferson*, 63; George Washington to Burwell Bassett, June 20, 1773, in *The Papers of George Washington* Colonial Series, ed. W.W. Abbot et al., 10 vols. (Charlottesville: University Press of Virginia, 1983–1995), 9: 243–44. For Jefferson's reaction to the death of his daughter Maria Jefferson Eppes, see Thomas Jefferson to Governor Page, June 1804, in Randolph, ed., *Domestic Life of Thomas Jefferson*, 302–03. See also Jon Kukla, *Mr. Jefferson's Women* (New York: Knopf, 2007), 82–85; Virginia Scharff, *The Women Jefferson Loved* (New York, Harper Collins, 2010), 148–56.

displays were still usually imagined as exceptions to the restraint idealized by and expected of eighteenth-century elites, men in particular.[41]

Those eighteenth-century attitudes fit the ambitions of nineteenth-century Americans who, although more in thrall themselves of romantic expressiveness, wanted to celebrate the founding fathers' exceptional courage and fortitude. The stoic acceptance of death by Washington, Jefferson, and Madison conveniently reified those ideals – and helped to cement their place in history.

Other parts of these men's eighteenth-century worldview did not stand the test of time, especially their attitudes toward religion. As much as some within later generations wanted – and want still – to see the founding fathers as evangelical Christians, neither their lives nor their deaths support those claims. Their writings indicate that all three men – products of the Enlightenment – believed in providence but at no time in their lives did any of the three write much, if at all, about God or Christ. None gave voice to religious conviction or seemed to think very much about the afterlife. Jefferson wrote more than the other two about his skepticism of miracles and his deistic views, and Washington said the least, remaining essentially silent about religion. Their actions at the point of death help fill in the blanks. It seems logical that if any of the three held strong convictions about an afterlife in heaven that they would have invoked that faith as they lay dying. All three had the time to ponder their demise. But nothing in their conduct in the last days of their lives indicated any particular denominational affiliation or deep religiosity. None of the three sought special prayers on their deathbeds or called for a cleric. In fact, Jefferson was clear that he "did not desire the attendance of a clergyman." When he thought he was being visited by a local minister, he told Jeff Randolph that he "had no objection to see him" provided the man came not as a member of the clergy but "as a kind and good neighbor."[42]

These eighteenth-century sensibilities did not suit some nineteenth-century audiences. So, some descendants decided they needed to alter the historical evidence and public memory by inserting religion into the death narratives of their ancestor. In 1850, Mary Cutts pronounced James Madison's death God's plan: God "watched over the flickering existence of this star, which had so long and so faithfully performed the duties which

[41] See Smith, *Inside the Great House*, esp. chap. 7.

[42] Thomas Jefferson Randolph Reminiscence, in Randolph, ed., *Domestic Life of Thomas Jefferson*, 427. For historical contests over Washington's religious views, see Lengel, *Inventing George Washington*, chap. 4.

He had assigned to him during so lengthened a life."[43] Washington Custis's recollections of his grandfather's death similarly show how thoroughly the politics of religion had shifted between the last year of the eighteenth century, when George Washington died, and the middle years of the nineteenth century, when Custis's writings were published. Custis actually asked the question on evangelicals' minds: "Why was the ministry of religion wanting to shed its peaceful and benign luster upon the last hours of Washington?" His answer met his contemporaries' expectations. He first insisted that "observations of sacred things were ever primary duties" throughout Washington's life – an assertion that Washington's writings clearly do not support. In life, George Washington did attend church, but he did not take communion or kneel at those services, and he never wrote or publicly spoke the name of Jesus Christ. Custis then explained that "circumstances did not permit" any bedside "ministry of religion." There was, he maintained, no time to call for a preacher or undertake Christian rituals. But this, too, does not bear up to scrutiny. Three doctors, an overseer, and relatives were called in. And there was time for Washington to discuss his papers project and burial plans. Rather than an accurate description of events in 1799, Custis's question and answer speaks to his increasingly evangelical audience a generation later.[44]

Despite nineteenth-century changes to the scripts of their deaths, it is clear that the resurrection these men desired was decidedly secular: to serve a political and historical purpose. In death, Washington, Jefferson, and Madison did not seek first the kind of immortality in the next world promised by nineteenth-century evangelical preachers. They wanted transcendent fame, historical renown as men of talent and character, in this world and for generations yet to come. While nineteenth-century Americans decided to see Thomas Jefferson's death on the fiftieth anniversary of the Declaration of Independence as divinely inspired, he had hoped it would provide a civics lesson. He "anxiously desired that his death should be hallowed by the Anniversary of Independence." In the last days of his life, he roused himself several times to inquire about the date. Dr. Dunglison offered palliative care with an eye on the clock. The poetry, then, was planned, not providential. "At fifteen minutes before twelve" on the night of July 3rd, Jeff Randolph recalled, "we stood noting the minute-hand of

[43] Mary Cutts Memoir, in Allgor, ed., *The Queen of America*, 177.

[44] George Washington Park Custis Recollections, in Lossing, ed., *Recollections and Private Memoirs of Washington*, 477. See also, Kahler, *The Long Farewell*, 59–60; Burstein, "Immortalizing the Founding Fathers," 94–97; Henriques, "The Final Struggle between George Washington and the Grim King," 90–91.

the watch, hoping a few minutes of prolonged life." Randolph's brother-in-law Nicholas Trist stood nervously beside him. On the morning of the 4th, Trist reported, "'till *twelve* o'clock last night, we were in momentary fear that he would not live, as he desired, to see his own glorious fourth." "It has come at last," a gratified Trist continued, "and he is still alive."[45]

Even as they sat vigil, then, the heirs of these founders were thinking about the future, about the secular resurrection these famous men sought, and how their images might live on. Tobias Lear saw with perfect clarity that he needed to immediately write down his account of Washington's death. The day, he knew, would "be memorable in the History of America and perhaps of the World."[46]

The deathbed stories that witnesses told were part of a larger history project, commenced by Washington, Jefferson, and Madison and continued by their descendants. Anxious about inspiring future generations, Washington, Jefferson, and Madison actually began working on their postmortem images during the Revolution. They intuited that material reminders would be essential to promoting the kind of national memory that would ensure their fame and the survival of their political experiment. Each man worried about preserving evidence, because, as Jefferson explained, in the hands of the wrong writers, "history becomes fable instead of fact."[47]

These men pursued a number of projects to ensure that history would remember them in the right way. Washington gathered artifacts of his military and political achievements, which he showed to the countless visitors who made pilgrimages to Mount Vernon. Jefferson and Madison likewise welcomed travelers into their homes with their historical legacies in mind. They all sat for paintings and sculptures so that their images could endure across time. In fact, one of James Madison's last acts was to pose for an artist. All three men cooperated with editors compiling documents from the revolutionary era and with hagiographic biographers who chronicled (and embellished) their exploits. Thomas Jefferson created the University of Virginia and Washington and Madison left bequests in their wills to support educational institutions, all in hopes of shaping at once the

[45] Thomas Jefferson Randolph Reminiscence, in Randolph, ed., *Domestic Life of Thomas Jefferson*, 428; Nicolas Trist to Joseph Coolidge, July 4, 1826, Family Letters Digital Archive.

[46] Tobias Lear Diary, December 14, 1799, in Lear, *Letters and Recollections of George Washington*, 129.

[47] Thomas Jefferson to William Wirt, August 14, 1814, in Stan V. Henkels, ed., "Jefferson's Recollections of Patrick Henry," *Pennsylvania Magazine of History and Biography* 34 (1910): 402.

character of young men for generations to come and their own reputations in history. In all these efforts, it was clear that Washington, Jefferson, and Madison wanted to be *remembered* in very particular ways, *celebrated* for their civic achievements, and *emulated* by subsequent generations of Americans.[48]

The centerpiece of each man's campaign to live on in the memories of later generations was his writings. When Washington left the presidency, his grandson recalled that "one of the first employments of his retirement as a private citizen was to arrange certain letters and papers for posthumous publication." Washington had actually begun the project during the Revolutionary War, and he was still at work on it at the end of his life. He was very clear about his motivations: he understood his writings to be an essential and lasting guide for Americans to understand the Revolution and his roles in the creation of the republic. Washington believed that "nothing should be left undone to give to his country and the world a fair and just estimate of his life and actions."[49]

Jefferson also explicitly said that it was "the duty of every good citizen to use all the opportunities which occur to him, for preserving documents relating to the history of our country." Throughout his long career and for years during his retirement, Jefferson systematically organized his letters. Ever curious about inventions, he adopted first a copy press and later a machine of parallel pens to make duplicates of his letters, which ran to the tens of thousands.[50]

Madison heartily agreed with Jefferson and Washington. He began preserving his correspondence in the 1780s, when he also started collecting primary sources from the prior decade, and he never stopped writing and cataloging. In his retirement, Madison's papers project often consumed him. Dolley worked alongside him, although the undertaking sometimes left her exhausted. In February 1820, she confided to a friend, "This is the

[48] Ketcham, ed., "An Unpublished Sketch of James Madison by James K. Paulding," 434. For hagiographic biographies, see Lengel, *Inventing George Washington*, chap. 2. For their campaigns for history, see Longmore, *The Invention of George Washington*; Cogliano, *Thomas Jefferson: Reputation and Legacy*. And for the importance of material objects to public memory, see Stabile, *Memory's Daughters*, 3.

[49] George Washington Park Custis Recollections, in Lossing, ed., *Recollections and Private Memoirs of Washington*, 436–37. See also W. W. Abbott, "An Uncommon Awareness of Self: The Papers of George Washington," in *George Washington Reconsidered*, ed. Don Higginbotham (Charlottesville: University of Virginia Press, 2001), 275–86.

[50] Thomas Jefferson, quoted in Dumas Malone, *Jefferson and His Times: The Sage of Monticello* (Boston: Little, Brown and Company, 1970), 214. For the Jefferson papers, see Cogliano, *Thomas Jefferson: Reputation and Legacy*, chap. 3.

third winter in which he has been engaged in the arrangement of papers, and the business appears to accumulate as he proceeds." The enterprise was, she complained, "out-lasting my patience." In his will, Madison planned for the long-awaited publication of the Constitutional Convention debates. (He had promised to wait until all the delegates were deceased and then found himself the last survivor.) "Considering the peculiarity and magnitude of the occasion," he believed the revelation of those conversations would "be particularly gratifying to the people of the United States and to all who take an interest in the progress of political science and the cause of true liberty."[51]

Each man expected his papers project to survive long after his death, becoming an enduring representation of his life. The projects, in fact, continue today, keeping vibrant the carefully crafted images of these men. Teams of scholars are working right now on multiple series of dozens of volumes of the Madison, Jefferson, and Washington papers – and they will continue for years to come. Editors of the current Jefferson project hope that they will be able to finish their work by 2026, which would be the 250th anniversary of the Declaration of Independence and *eighty-two years* after the series began.

All three accurately perceived their writings as precious and enduring legacies, and each named in his will a specially selected relative to shepherd this vital historical responsibility. George Washington turned to his nephew, Bushrod Washington; Jefferson left his writings to Jeff Randolph; and Madison trusted his wife Dolley, in whom he had "entire confidence in her discreet and proper use of them."[52]

Beneficiaries of their writings understood the profundity of their duty, and most undertook editing and publication with a zeal the founders would have admired. Once, when Dolley Madison's house caught fire, "as soon as she became conscious of the danger, she said 'the papers, the papers first'" and refused to leave until she knew the treasured inheritance was secure.[53] Jeff Randolph and his sisters and their mother labored for

[51] Dolley Madison to Sarah Coles Stevenson, ca. February 1820, in Mattern and Shulman, eds., *Selected Letters of Dolley Payne Madison*, 238–39; Will of James Madison, April 15, 1835.

[52] Will of James Madison, April 15, 1835.

[53] Mary Cutts Memoir in Allgor, ed., *The Queen of America*, 189; Ralph Ketcham, *The Madisons of Montpelier: Reflections on the Founding Couple* (Charlottesville: University of Virginia Press, 2009), 180. For Dolley Madison's efforts, see Holly C. Shulman, "'A Constant Attention': Dolley Madison and the Publication of the Papers of James Madison, 1836–1837," *Virginia Magazine of History and Biography* 118 (2010): 40–70.

years editing Thomas Jefferson's papers for publication. Many of the copied letters were, Martha Jefferson Randolph said, "so faded as to be almost entirely obliterated." When the sun was at its brightest, the women could use magnifying glasses to study the backs of those letters, "where alone the impressions shews; a few lines will sometimes cost as many days." They worked sometimes eight hours a day, readying transcriptions for Jeff Randolph, the lead editor.[54] Although no one earned as much money as they had hoped from the sale of these papers, all three families eventually secured the public distribution of their founders' writings and, more importantly, the immortality that came with the undertakings.

Heirs were so intent on resurrecting their famous ancestors as paragons of republican virtue and southern manhood that some went beyond preserving into manicuring the historical record. They encouraged hagiographic biographies, gave flattering interviews to journalists, and published celebratory "recollections" of events. And they sometimes tried to purge from their ancestor's writings and image unbecoming parts of his personal life, most notably the Randolph siblings' denial of their grandfather's second family with Sally Hemings.[55] By the efforts of their devoted kin, then, these men could be reborn again and again as "The Founders" – larger, better than life.

The Father of the Constitution, the Father of Democracy, and the Father of his Country live on, more or less, in popular imagination (if not historical scholarship) as they and their closest kin had hoped they might. They still represent Americans' highest aspirations and surest foundation. Twenty-first-century Americans continue the tradition commenced in the early nineteenth century of visiting these men's graves to honor their lives and seek guidance for our future. Every March 16 – James Madison's birthday – a wreath is laid at his Montpelier tomb to venerate the architect of a living Constitution. Travelers still visit

[54] Martha Jefferson Randolph, quoted in Cogliano, *Thomas Jefferson: Reputation and Legacy*, 82. Bushrod Washington was considerably less conscientious, and he even gave away some Washington letters as souvenirs. See Lengel, *Inventing George Washington*, 14–18.

[55] For example, see Ellen Randolph Coolidge to Joseph Coolidge, October 24, 1858, Family Letters Digital Archive. For the Hemings family and historical debates over the Jefferson-Hemings relationship, see Annette Gordon-Reed, *Thomas Jefferson and Sally Hemings: An American Controversy* (Charlottesville: University Press of Virginia, 1997); idem, *Hemingses of Monticello*; Jan Ellen Lewis and Peter S. Onuf, eds., *Sally Hemings and Thomas Jefferson: History, Memory, and Civic Culture* (Charlottesville: University of Virginia Press, 1999); Clarence E. Walker, *Mongrel Nation: The America Begotten by Thomas Jefferson and Sally Hemings* (Charlottesville: University of Virginia Press, 2009).

Monticello to honor, as one group of early twentieth-century Missourians said, "the Father of Democracy, who, being dead, yet lives in every heart that beats for liberty." Visitors to Jefferson's and Madison's graves find the same thing that Caroline Moore, who went to Mount Vernon in the nineteenth century, found there: an edifice to a man who achieved exactly the kind of immortality he hoped for. "Nothing was left of Washington," Moore realized at his crypt, except what mattered most: "his imperishable name, and the glorious example he has left to posterity."[56]

The deaths of George Washington, Thomas Jefferson, and James Madison were inevitable facts of life. But their resurrections – as paragons of American character – were far from destined. Rather, a careful design of their own making, deftly executed by their descendants, keeps their images alive and well, even now, one hundred and seventy-seven years after the last of Virginia's great founders was ushered to the grave.

[56] *The Pilgrimage to Monticello, The Home and Tomb of Thomas Jefferson, by the Jefferson Club of Saint Louis, Missouri, October 10 to 14, 1901* (St. Louis: Curran Printing Company, 1902), 65; Caroline Moore Journal, April 30, 1833, in *Experiencing Mount Vernon: Eyewitness Accounts, 1784–1865*, ed. Jean B. Lee (Charlottesville: University of Virginia Press, 2006), 142.

4

American Mourning: Catastrophe, Public Grief, and the Making of Civic Identity in the Early National South

Jewel Spangler

Americans are well versed in the art of public mourning. Every year, the nation pauses to recognize collective losses on such occasions as Memorial Day, Patriot Day, and National Day of Service and Remembrance (September 11). The deaths of high-profile public servants are marked by lowering flags to half-staff, while citizens gather along streets and around screens to observe funeral processions, ceremonies, and burials. All too often, the country also comes together, at least figuratively, to grieve over catastrophic events that seem to demand that Americans express collective pain: so it was with the space shuttle *Challenger* disaster; the Oklahoma City bombing; shootings in Columbine, Aurora, and Newtown; and Hurricanes Katrina and Sandy. The deaths of well-known figures, even if apolitical, can also sometimes capture the national imagination. The spontaneous public outpouring of sadness after performer Michael Jackson's unexpected passing in 2009 and his massive, televised memorial service is just one case in point.

Although such contemporary moments of remembrance reflect a fairly coherent, although not uncontested, sense of national identity, it was not always so. During and immediately after the Civil War, mourning and memorialization reflected two conflicting views of the nation and tended toward dividing rather than uniting Americans. Particularly among white Southerners, memorial days and decoration days, which were typically held

The author thanks the Social Sciences and Humanities Research Council of Canada, which provided the primary funding for this project, the staffs of the Library of Virginia and the Virginia Historical Society who made the archival work possible (and pleasant), and many colleagues who generously offered the benefit of their insights, especially Frank Towers.

in rural family cemeteries to honor kinfolk, became catalysts for sustained loyalty to the Confederacy. African Americans, not surprisingly, held different attitudes toward commemorating wartime death. Black Charlestonians, for example, appropriated the Decoration Day tradition in May 1865 when they cleaned up and landscaped the Charleston Race Course where at least 257 Union prisoners of war had died and were buried. In so doing, they committed themselves to the Union's version of the United States even while standing on former Confederate soil. During Reconstruction, white women in the South turned Memorial Day – inaugurated on May, 5, 1866, in Waterloo, New York – into a pro-Confederate commemoration. All over the former Confederacy, Ladies' Memorial Associations established and attended to permanent cemeteries, organized reburials and funeral ceremonies, and built monuments of remembrance for the Confederate dead. Their efforts to keep alive the idea of the Confederate nation shifted over the next quarter century, as southern Memorial Day observances turned from merely honoring the dead to also promoting their cause – the "Lost Cause" – reflecting a larger shift toward cultural renewal and conservatism in the South.[1]

Such contests between southern and national values in public mourning should not be read too far back into southern history, however. In the early national era, tragedies in the South could just as well make the region seem quintessentially American as distinctly southern. In the early republic, participation in processions, funerals, and displays of mourning symbols for figures considered "public," and the use of language of mourning in a range of elegiac writing for such persons, were part of a process of constructing a nascent collective national identity, a process in which Southerners actively contributed.[2] At the same time, the postrevolutionary

[1] Gaines M. Foster, *Ghosts of the Confederacy: Defeat, the Lost Cause and the Emergence of the New South, 1865–1913* (New York: Oxford University Press, 1988), 36–46; Alan Jabbour and Karen Singer Jabbour, *Decoration Day in the Mountains: Traditions of Cemetery Decoration in the Southern Appalachians* (Chapel Hill: University of North Carolina Press; 2010); David W. Blight, *Race and Reunion: The Civil War in American Memory* (Cambridge: Harvard University Press, 2001), 64–97, esp. 67–70, 295; Caroline E. Janney, *Burying the Dead but Not the Past: Ladies' Memorial Associations and the Lost Cause* (Chapel Hill: University of North Carolina Press, 2008). For the origins of Memorial Day, see Lyndon Johnson, "Presidential Proclamation 3727," The American Presidency Project, www.presidency.ucsb.edu; "Flowers for Jennie," National Park Service, www.nps.gov/ande/historyculture/flowersforjennie.htm.

[2] Public celebration is a much-studied part of the development of the early American republic. A robust literature on the processions and fêtes that enlivened public spaces has illustrated how these performances of "Americanness" brought people together and how an emerging print culture transformed local celebrations into widely disseminated stories that allowed

period witnessed an important adaptation process that transformed traditional, British systems of public mourning into something distinctly American.

This essay considers rituals and language of public grief in North America between 1760 and 1812. It begins with traditions of public mourning that Americans inherited from Britain and examines their employment in service to the founding of the United States. A transatlantic "mourning culture" informed public performances of grief all along the eastern seaboard, but in the revolutionary era such communal displays began to center on North American deaths and to invoke and contribute to a nascent "American" identity. The essay then examines two occasions in the early nineteenth century when deaths in the South became national news and the objects of public mourning outside the region: the attack on the *Chesapeake* by the HMS *Leopard* shortly after it left Norfolk, Virginia, in June 1807, and the devastating Richmond Theatre Fire of December 1811, which killed more than seventy people. Responses to these events illustrate some crucial developments in the formation of a distinctively American type of public mourning, and, at the same time, they capture vividly a time when the South had clearly found its place in an emerging republic, long before it lost its way. These performances of mourning effectively subverted regional divisions in service to the more pressing narrative of national unity. And together they illustrate coalescence around a "republican" process of public mourning, one that emphasized the "citizenship" of both the dead and the mourners.

Displays of public mourning as expressions of national feeling were, of course, part of the fabric of life in British North America long before independence, particularly in urban centers. These rituals fit into a larger, state-driven system of holidays and remembrances that fostered political connectedness in Britain's transatlantic first empire. Government promoted and prescribed these performances of support for the crown and Parliament in eighteenth-century England and her American colonies. The

people to develop a sense of national connection and define some of the elements of that nationalism, albeit in ways that continued to be contested. See, for example, David Waldstreicher, *In the Midst of Perpetual Fetes: The Making of American Nationalism, 1776–1820* (Chapel Hill: University of North Carolina Press, 1997); Simon P. Newman, *Parades and the Politics of the Street: Festive Culture in the Early American Republic* (Philadelphia: University of Pennsylvania Press, 1997); Len Travers, *Celebrating the Fourth: Independence Day and the Rites of Nationalism in the Early Republic* (Amherst: University of Massachusetts Press, 1997); François Furstenberg, *In the Name of the Father: Washington's Legacy, Slavery, and the Making of a Nation* (New York: Penguin, 2006).

birthdays of royals, Coronation Day, Pope's Day (remembering the foiled gunpowder plot to blow up Parliament in 1605), and several other annual holidays brought people into public spaces across the empire, to toast, dance, parade, and perhaps to listen to speeches, the peal of bells, or the boom of cannons.[3] In 1766, for example, the *Virginia Gazette* reported that on the King's birthday, "the [royal] Governour, with some of the principal Gentlemen of this city, met at Mr. Pullett's tavern, and spent the evening in honour of his Majesty; and several houses were illuminated, as also the flag displayed on the Capitol." The paper noted that there was no ball or "public rejoicing," however, since the town was half-deserted for the summer. Instead, "the 25th of October, the anniversary of the accession of our Most Gracious Sovereign to the throne, will for the future be observed in the same manner as his Majesty's birthday used to be, a great deal of company generally being in town at that season of the year."[4] In a later edition, *Gazette* readers learned about the celebration of the King's birthday in Philadelphia, which had been marked by a fine dinner for the members of the legislative assembly hosted by the royal governor, while "a great number of respectable citizens assembled on the banks of the river Schuylkill, to celebrate the same, where an elegant entertainment was provided." The evening included "many loyal and constitutional toasts," and "bells were rung, the ships in the harbour displayed their colours, and other demonstrations of loyalty and joy were shown on the happy occasion."[5]

North Americans similarly participated in state-led rituals to mark the deaths of kings and other prominent members of the royal family. Reports of public mourning of this sort began to appear in the colonies in the early eighteenth century, but perhaps the clearest example of transatlantic grief in the first British Empire came in the final days of 1760, when inhabitants of North American port towns learned of the October 25 death of King George II. In Britain, the news had sparked unprecedented public clamoring to display symbols of mourning, ranging from crape bands and

[3] For the emergence of a formal system of imperial holidays, see Brendan McConville, *The King's Three Faces: The Rise and Fall of Royal America, 1688–1776* (Chapel Hill: University of North Carolina Press, 2006), 56–70, 73–80; Waldstreicher, *Midst of Perpetual Fetes*, 21–24; Peter Benes, "Night Processions: Celebrating the Gunpowder Plot in England and New England," *Dublin Seminar for New England Folklife Annual Proceedings* 25 (2000): 9–28.

[4] *Virginia Gazette*, June 6, 1766. The King's birthday coincided in 1766 with the arrival of news of the repeal of the Stamp Act, which did not alter the *forms* of the celebrations so much as the enthusiasm expressed during them.

[5] *Virginia Gazette*, June 20, 1766.

ribbons to black drapery for coaches, windows, mirrors, and the like – a spontaneous prelude to the far more elaborate and scripted official court mourning that would go on for the entire following year. In the words of one Londoner, "'Twas astonishing to see the amazing consternation, bustle, and confusion an event like this, quite unexpected, made in the metropolis . . . [the news] was published about twelve, when instantly the streets were in a buzz, the black cloth carrying about, and in half an hour every shop was hung with the appendages of mourning."[6] The London papers reported on merchants' desperate rush to secure supplies of crape to resell, so that "not less than 12 Post Chaises, we can assure our Readers, had set out by Noon on Saturday for Norwich," and the prices of crape and other mourning accouterments immediately began to soar.[7]

The provincials may have been far from the imperial center, but they, too, seemed to "bustle" with mourning upon hearing the news. In Boston, all the bells in the city began to toll when the first ship arrived bearing late-October London newspapers on December 27. City leaders organized a seventy-seven-gun salute that afternoon (the number corresponding to the fallen King's age) at Fort William in the harbor. Government officials immediately donned mourning attire. Shops closed. Likewise, in New York, "the Gentlemen, and most of the Inhabitants of this City, entered into Mourning for the Death of our late most gracious Sovereign GEORGE the SECOND; when it was observed with great Reverence and Decency. The several Churches in Town were hung in Mourning, and Sermons preached in each of them suitable to the Occasion."[8] In Philadelphia, just a few days after the royal governor received word of the King's passing, "the Gentlemen in public Office, and other principal Inhabitants, having assembled at the GOVERNOR's House, agreeable to Notice, proceeded to the Court House" in a carefully ordered procession where they were received by "all the Officers of the Army now in Town, together with a

[6] Paul S. Fritz, "The Trade in Death: The Royal Funerals in England, 1685–1830," *Eighteenth-Century Studies* 15 (spring 1982): 308. For the history of English royal mourning, see Peter Metcalf and Richard Huntington, *Celebrations of Death: The Anthropology of Mortuary Ritual*, 2nd ed. (New York: Cambridge University Press, 1991), 162–81; John Wolffe, *Great Deaths, Grieving, Religion, and Nationhood in Victorian and Edwardian Britain* (New York: Oxford University Press, 2000), 11–27; Olivia Bland, *The Royal Way of Death* (London: Constable, 1986); Paul S. Fritz, "From 'Public' to 'Private': The Royal Funerals in England, 1500–1830," in *Mirrors of Mortality: Studies in the Social History of Death*, ed. Joachim Whaley (1981; Routledge, 2012), 61–79.

[7] A reprint of this story appeared in the *Virginia Gazette* on January 16, 1761.

[8] *Boston Gazette and Country Journal*, December 29, 1760; *Pennsylvania Gazette*, January 22, 1761.

Party of the Royal Welsh Volunteers, under Arms." There they listened to a declaration that both bemoaned the nation's loss and proclaimed George III as the new sovereign.[9] Within a few days, funeral sermons emanated from churches all over the colonies, shot through with the language of *national* loss. The sermon of Presbyterian minister and Princeton College president Samuel Davies was emblematic in the way he weaved together the language of national unity and collective sorrow:

> George is no more! George, the mighty, the just, the gentle, and the wise; George, the father of Britain and her Colonies, the guardian of laws and liberty, the protector of the oppressed, the arbiter of Europe, the terror of tyrants and France; ... Britain expresses her sorrow in national groans .... The melancholy sound circulates far and wide. This remote American continent shares in the loyal sympathy. The wide intermediate Atlantic rolls the tide of grief to these distant shores; and even the recluse sons of Nassau-Hall feel the immense bereavement, with all the sensibility of a filial heart; and must mourn with their country, with Britain.[10]

Similarly, William Cooper of Brattle Street Church in Boston, in a sermon delivered to the Massachusetts legislature and then printed as a tract, proclaimed that George II "falls lamented, as the Friend of human Kind, the Patron of Justice, the common Father of his Subjects; and his Worth is attested by the Sighs and Tears of a whole Nation."[11]

Although in 1760 colonial newspapers still had fairly small numbers of subscribers, their contents traveled the colonies both by seagoing connections, which facilitated the common practice of clipping and reprinting, and through more informal means such as reading aloud and distributing news through letters and conversations.[12] Mourning sermons also quickly

[9] *Pennsylvania Gazette*, January 22, 1761.

[10] Samuel Davies, "Sermon LX: On the Death of His Late Majesty, King George II," in *Sermons on Important Subjects by the Late Reverend and Pious Samuel Davies*..., 5th ed., 3 vols. (New York: T. Allen, 1792), 3: 344.

[11] Samuel Cooper, *A Sermon upon Occasion of the Death of Our Late Sovereign George the Second* (Boston: John Draper, 1761), 26, 27.

[12] For a discussion of the rise of newspapers in eighteenth-century North America and the circulation of news, see Richard D. Brown, *Knowledge Is Power: The Diffusion of Information in Early America, 1700–1865* (New York: Oxford University Press, 1989); Michael Warner, *The Letters of the Republic: Publication and the Public Sphere in Eighteenth-Century America* (Cambridge: Harvard University Press, 1992); Charles E. Clark, *The Public Prints: The Newspaper in Anglo-American Culture, 1665–1740* (New York: Oxford University Press, 1994); David A. Copeland, *Colonial American Newspapers: Character and Content* (Newark: University of Delaware, 1996). The most influential work on the relationship between the press and the rise of nationalism is still Benedict Anderson, *Imagined Communities: Reflections on the Origin and Spread of Nationalism* (New York: Verso, 1983).

appeared as tracts and became accessible far beyond the initial audiences. Through all these channels, King George's death and the accompanying rhetoric of national loss became widely known and so, too, did news of public mourning rituals. North Americans could inform themselves of the exact nature of the King's funeral procession in London, including the positioning of his pallbearers and the placement of the hundreds of yards of black cloth along the route.[13] They could read and hear about local performances in remembrance of the King and also those in other colonial cities and towns, making it possible to imagine a "national" grief that tied the colonies to the metropole.[14]

Such public commemoration, when focused on the royals, took on the language of nation, but collective grief could also be a profoundly local phenomenon. Colonial newspapers are rife with descriptions of the passing of well-respected ministers, local officeholders, prominent merchants, model household heads, and devoted and devout wives who became the objects of community mourning that reached well beyond the immediate circle of family and friends. There was a rich elegiac publishing tradition that also speaks to this social phenomenon. These local rituals, always concluding with what was described as a "decent" interment, referenced close bonds within communities. Take as just one example the 1769 obituary of Mrs. Elizabeth Willis, of Gloucester County, Virginia. While she was mourned as "the best of wives, the tenderest of parents, and the most kind of mistresses," she was also described as "well known to the poor and indigent by that charitable assistance which she was ever ready to afford them; and is universally lamented, particularly by the poor in her neighbourhood."[15] In texts such as these, the social networks that bound people together in neighborhoods are repeatedly made visible and even celebrated.

[13] See, for example, *Boston Gazette*, January 5, 1761; *Pennsylvania Journal*, January 22, 1761; *New Hampshire Gazette*, January 9, 1761; *Virginia Gazette*, January 16, 1761. See also Max Cavitch, *American Elegy*, 309 n 23; Fritz, "The Trade in Death," 291–316.

[14] The January 29 issue of the *Pennsylvania Gazette* reprinted reports from London of King George III's first speech before Parliament (including laments at the loss of his grandfather), reports from Boston of the spread of the news of George II's death and the concomitant tolling of bells and the delivering of funeral sermons, reports from New York of the arrival of sad news from both London and Boston, and an elegiac poem likely written by a Philadelphian. The poem particularly made explicit the colonial connections to nation on this occasion: "Ev'n on *Sylvania's* Shore the humble Maid/Far from th' Influences of her Prince's Eye/ Tho' not in public Pomp of Woe array'd/Drops the soft Tear, and joins *Britannia's* Sigh."

[15] *Virginia Gazette*, May 11, 1769, supplement. A search of the colonial obituaries indexed in genealogybank.com brings up hundreds of examples of this sort. For public death rituals in the eighteenth-century British North American colonies, see Robert V. Wells, *Facing the*

Alongside the deaths of "national" figures and local notables, newspapers reported many other losses of the kinds that would one day bring Americans together – catastrophic storms, fires, accidents, and murders most foul. Yet before the imperial crisis, such events, although attracting interest, mostly appear to have been curiosities, unless they happened very close to home. Responses to the massive fire that razed Charlestown, South Carolina, in November 1740 illustrate the point. This "great" fire reduced a considerable portion of the city to ash, destroyed the warehouses that held much of that year's rice crop and deer skins, and made as many as a third of the city's inhabitants homeless. News of the blaze was reprinted in other papers, and South Carolina's governor wrote to the executives of several other colonies requesting aid. Responses beyond the colony's borders, however, were limited and decidedly calm in tone. The Massachusetts governor, for example, dutifully put out a public notice asking that "charitable well-disposed Persons" in the Bay Colony "put on Bowels of mercy, and cheerfully deny our selves to contribute freely for their Relief; which we trust will be a Sacrifice highly acceptable to God, and will doubtless be remembered by our Neighbours to our own Advantage, if it should please God to bring the like Calamity upon us." Some material aid did come from this campaign, but absent were reports of deep sympathy or descriptions of public acts of mourning.[16] North Americans were similarly unperturbed by news of a devastating hurricane that struck that same city in September 1752, reportedly causing a hundred deaths as well as enormous loss of property. Many colonial newspapers reprinted news of the damage to the city, ships, and cargo, as well as the human costs. But the reports offered no discussion of shared grief or even sympathy. A single elegiac poem appeared in some newspapers. It focused on the hurricane as an object lesson on the suddenness with which life's circumstances can change and the necessity to be prepared for the afterlife – not quite the tone one expects from mourning literature.[17] In sum, although the language and gestures of public grief were common among colonials, they seem to have been

"King of Terrors": Death and Society in an American Community, 1750–1990 (New York: Cambridge University Press, 2000), 13–34; David E. Stannard, *The Puritan Way of Death: A Study of Religion, Culture, and Social Change* (New York: Oxford University Press, 1977).

16 *New England Weekly Journal*, May 5, 1741; Matthew Mulcahy, "The 'Great Fire' of 1740 and the Politics of Disaster Relief in Colonial Charleston," *South Carolina Historical Magazine* 99 (April 1998): 139, 147–48, 149.

17 This paragraph was based on a search for "hurricane" (1752–1753) in the newspapers collection of genealogybank.com, which provides access to several Boston, Philadelphia, and New York papers for that year, as well as for the *Virginia Gazette*. For the poem, see (Philadelphia) *Pennsylvania Journal*, December 19, 1752.

reserved primarily for important local losses or deaths among the British leadership, whereas a sense of "national" feeling extended *between* colonies only in far more limited ways.[18]

All this changed rapidly with the escalation of conflict between colonial leaders and the metropole after 1763. Many historians have noted the appropriation of public mourning rituals in popular protest of the Stamp Act, the Boston Massacre, and numerous other moments in the imperial crisis, and they chart the rapidly rising awareness of and sensitivity to the experiences of fellow colonials in distress. When North Americans took to the streets to demonstrate their dissatisfaction, they borrowed liberally from British public celebration and mourning rituals, often in combination, to make their point. Parading with an effigy of the tax man or royal governor and processioning to symbolically bury the liberty that such men had murdered by upholding Parliamentary policies bore more than a passing resemblance to mourning rituals for the absent King, as well as to celebrations such as Pope's Day. When the King himself became the object of these symbolic rituals in the mid-1770s, the echoes of the mourning for King George were at times front and center.[19]

The War for Independence then redirected the acts and words of mourning toward the formation and celebration of a new, albeit nebulous, nation aborning. The war inevitably reshaped the context in which North Americans thought about leaders, heroes, and "national" tragedies, simultaneously marking a sharp departure from the past as well as maintaining some key continuities. Very early in the war, the deaths of a select few individuals became rallying points. The "martyr" of Bunker Hill, Dr. Joseph Warren, and Major General Richard Montgomery, killed while leading the December 1775 Quebec City attack, have been particularly highlighted by historians. Warren fought as a common soldier in June 1775, but his role as a prominent local politician, an active Son of Liberty, and a two-time orator at the Boston Massacre annual commemoration were enough to propel him to the ranks of the patriot leadership in the public mind and set the stage for his transformation into a hero after his death. Public eulogies, an elaborate second burial ceremony after the British evacuation of Boston, and a cascade of published accounts of his sacrifice,

[18] This point is beautifully illustrated in Matthew Mulcahy, *Hurricanes and Society in the British Greater Caribbean, 1642–1783* (Baltimore: Johns Hopkins University Press, 2006), 141–64.

[19] Waldstreicher, *Midst of Perpetual Fetes*, 25–26; McConville, *King's Three Faces*, 301–11; Eran Shalev, "Dr. Warren's Ciceronian Toga," *Common-Place* 7 (2007), www.common-place.org.

borrowed from past British mourning traditions, turned him from a local notable to a national symbol.[20] Along these same lines, Montgomery's death occasioned a requisition by the Continental Congress for a monument and a commission for a funeral sermon delivered in the largest house of worship in Philadelphia after local and national elites led a procession through the city, witnessed by thousands along the streets. General Montgomery was the subject of numerous elegiac plays, poems, sermons and tracts, countless wartime toasts and tributes, and a blanket of newspaper coverage that fixed a sense of "national" mourning around his death, even as the nation itself was all but undefined.[21] Through the use of traditional rituals and words of grief, the general public was invited to conceive of an American elite of socially and militarily prominent men – a new republican "royalty" around whom the nation could rally in remembrance as a single people.

After independence, Americans persisted in traditions of public mourning that in many ways echoed those of the colonial and revolutionary past. George Washington's death in December 1799 is perhaps the best-known example of early American public mourning.[22] When news of Washington's death first broke, church bells rang and shops closed in a widening circle from its Virginia origin point. The U.S. Congress immediately sought to take control of the public mourning process, donning arm bands, draping the Speaker's chair in black cloth, and visiting the sitting president, John Adams, to express their condolences, almost as if to say "the King is dead – long live the King," before a congressional subcommittee planned and executed a "state" funeral, with a carefully ordered procession through Philadelphia (then serving as the capital), the playing of muffled

[20] Samuel Forman, *Dr. Joseph Warren: The Boston Tea Party, Bunker Hill, and the Birth of American Liberty* (Gretna: Pelican, 2012), 307–24; Purcell, *Sealed with Blood*, 11–23; Charles Royster, *A Revolutionary People at War: The Continental Army and American Character, 1775–1783* (Chapel Hill: University of North Carolina Press, 1979), 44–45.

[21] Purcell, *Sealed with Blood*, 24–38. See also Michael P. Gabriel, *Major General Richard Montgomery: The Making of an American Hero* (Cranbury: Fairleigh Dickinson University Press, 2002), 173–90; Royster, *Revolutionary People*, 122–26.

[22] The mourning and apotheosis of George Washington has been the focus of a number of fine studies. For example, see Furstenberg, *In the Name of the Father*; Gerald E. Kahler, *The Long Farewell: Americans Mourn the Death of George Washington* (Charlottesville: University of Virginia Press, 2008); Max Cavitch, "The Man That Was Used Up: Poetry, Particularity, and the Politics of Remembering George Washington," *American Literature* 7 (June 2003): 247–74; James H. Smylie, "The President as Republican Prophet and King: Clerical Reflections on the Death of Washington," *Journal of Church and State* 18 (spring 1976): 233–52; Wells, *Facing The King of Terrors*, 28–29.

"death marches," the tolling of bells, the firing of sixteen guns (one for each state), a sermon and eulogy, thousands of onlookers, and the promise of a monument (with the body of the great American hero entombed beneath) in the future national capital. From the federal government down to the smallest town meeting, civic leaders orchestrated public displays of loss. Military leaders required officers to wear mourning crape, drew down flags to half-staff, and held various ersatz funeral services. Many state legislatures put on arm bands and adjourned. Local governments went into mourning as well, enforced regulations on business closures, and oversaw a multiplicity of smaller ceremonies of mourning for the fallen hero. Congress resolved that Washington's birthday, February 22, would be a time to gather to express grief and hear speeches, sermons, and eulogies, stretching out the grieving process for two months.[23]

Echoes of the response to George II's death are impossible to overlook in all this: the bells, guns, crape, processions, and sermons, directed by those in official power, drew their inspiration from the well of British tradition. These grief performances and the widespread coverage of them in America's newspapers allowed Americans to imagine themselves as united in sadness. Although Washington's Virginia roots were certainly mentioned occasionally, and Virginians were delighted to claim him as their native son, the language of nation far outstripped regional distinctions in this context. The one area of debate concerned the dispensation of Washington's body. Congress wished his remains to be interred in the nation's capital, but the hero himself had expressed in his will his desire to be buried in the family plot at Mount Vernon. Washington rests at his Virginia home, but this was not a case of local, or perhaps southern, claims asserted over those of the nation in 1800. Rather, relocation of the remains was delayed for more than thirty years by a failure to raise funds for his national monument, and only then did a Washington descendant refuse the request for relocation, in a pointedly different historical context.

Washington's memorialization may have strongly resembled that of a King, but it was also distinctive from royal mourning in important ways. This was the death of a republican father, and those who called on his memory made reference to the man who had consistently refused the trappings of monarchy in establishing presidential tradition throughout his two terms. John Adams's official letter notifying Congress of Washington's passing set the tone for the rest. He labeled Washington "our excellent fellow-citizen." John Marshall called Washington "our departed friend"

[23] Kahler, *Long Farewell*, 12–13, 27–37.

and advanced a resolution to form a committee to plan a state funeral to honor "the memory of the man, first in war, first in peace, and first in the hearts of his country."[24] The emphasis on Washington's status as the best of citizens and the best of men, but not more than that, appeared everywhere in subsequent months. The ceremonies constructed by governments at every level then called on Americans to respond as citizens, not subjects. Most particularly, as historian François Furstenberg has argued, the "civic texts" produced around Washington's death collectively constructed him as a distinctly republican leader and called on readers to emulate his civic virtues as the most fitting way to honor the man (and to advance the causes of the nation).[25]

In the first dozen years of the nineteenth century, two subsequent incidents of public mourning with origin points in Virginia reinforced this theme of "republican" national grief, and, in both instances, a potential regionalism was completely overshadowed by nationalist rhetoric. In the early summer of 1807, Norfolk, Virginia, was the site of a public funeral for a sailor killed aboard the USS *Chesapeake* shortly after it left that port. The *Chesapeake-Leopard* Affair is probably best known as an episode in the breakdown of British–American relations, leading toward open war in 1812. When the HMS *Leopard* fired on the *Chesapeake* and British sailors boarded her in search of deserters, it provoked fury throughout the United States and demands for a political response. The first recounting of the news, published in the Norfolk papers where the *Chesapeake* returned to port for repairs and offloaded its injured and the bodies of three "tars" or sailors who died was perfectly clear on this point: "We are now to present our readers with the details of a most unexampled outrage, in the perpetration of which the blood of our countrymen has been shed by the hand of violence and the honor and independence of our nation insulted beyond the possibility of further forbearance."[26] Norfolk residents immediately called a meeting of citizens and ratified a series of resolves outlining how they would respond to the outrage. They pledged to refuse all communication with British ships and to withhold the

[24] Kahler, *Long Farewell*, 27, 28.

[25] Furstenberg, *In the Name of the Father*, esp. 25–70. Max Cavitch's study of the hundreds of elegies produced after Washington's death notes the subtle ways in which this long-used form of public mourning was adapted to republican principles as elegists downplayed Washington as a "singular" person and commended the edification available to all by modeling their lives after him; see Max Cavitch, *American Elegy: The Poetry of Mourning from the Puritans to Whitman* (Minneapolis: University of Minnesota Press, 2007).

[26] *Norfolk Gazette and Publick Ledger*, June 24, 1807.

services of local pilots needed to guide them into port, essentially closing their harbor to English shipping until "satisfaction" could be obtained. They subsequently lobbied leaders in other port cities to do the same. The tactics echoed those of the revolutionary era: town meetings, boycotts, correspondence campaigns to promote solidarity. But these deaths, unlike prerevolutionary ones, were understood as an affront to the *sovereignty* of the United States as a separate nation. Responses to the attack called on good citizens of the republic to feel the loss of their countrymen *and* the threat to their rights as Americans.[27]

That the language of nation was used on such an occasion is hardly surprising; more interesting are the complex acts of public mourning that followed. The death of injured *Chesapeake* tar Robert MacDonald became the occasion for a massive performance of public grief as political theater. According to the *Norfolk Gazette and Publick Ledger*, at least four thousand people processed through Norfolk and participated in a funeral service for MacDonald.[28] The sailor's body first made its way from Hospital Point to the city by barge with a large waterborne escort. The paper reported that "Minute Guns from the artillery fired during the time, all the American shipping with colors at half mast." Once MacDonald's coffin was taken ashore, a large and carefully planned funeral procession "marched up Market Square, through Catharine Street, to Freemason-Street, and from thence to Christ Church where an appropriate, impressive, and patriotic discourse was delivered to a most numerous congregation." The Norfolk paper printed the order of the procession, which involved naval officers and crew, the city's mayor and other office holders, the surgeons of the hospital, a band playing muffled music, and, of course, common citizens. Included was a sketch of MacDonald's coffin and notations informing readers that three "masters of vessels" served as pall bearers on each side.[29] One can hardly escape the similarities to the reporting on George II's funeral procession, with its careful list of participants and pall bearers. The only striking difference, in fact, was that one performance honored the sovereign of a global empire while the other paid tribute to a common sailor.

That distinction, however, is important. MacDonald, unlike the kings, presidents, and generals who were mourned before him, was in no way a

[27] For an excellent treatment of public mourning and remembrance of this event, see Robert Cray Jr., "Remembering the USS *Chesapeake*: The Politics of Maritime Death and Impressment," *Journal of the Early Republic* 25 (fall 2005): 445–74.

[28] *Norfolk Gazette and Publick Ledger*, June 29, 1807.

[29] *Virginia Argus*, July 4, 1807.

public figure. He did not lead, or die first, or die heroically by the usual definitions. He was in the wrong place at the wrong time, part of a routine mission to transport lumber to the Mediterranean. If he seemed an unlikely hero, he also does not appear to have been a local favorite in Norfolk. He apparently did not have family or deep personal ties in town, beyond the casual ones that most sailors developed over time if they plied the waters of the Chesapeake Bay.[30] In other words, he might have been known in the ale and boarding houses but would have been a complete stranger to almost everyone who planned, paid for, and attended his funeral. That he would be the focus of such a massive act of mourning suggests that he represented something important to those crowds, something that transcended his personal history.[31]

MacDonald's funeral could have been a local event, or a Virginian one, but descriptions of it were rapidly republished in newspapers across the United States, allowing Americans – Federalist and Republican, North and South, East and West – to vicariously participate and turning Norfolk itself into a patriotic symbol. Soon, some other cities began to stage their own forms of public mourning for those killed on the *Chesapeake*. For example, when New York City's General Committee of Arrangements published the details of their plans to celebrate the Fourth of July a few days after the incident, they instructed New Yorkers to "wear a crape on the left arm on that day, in testimony of their indignant regret at the death of the American Seamen recently killed on board of the American frigate the Chesapeake."[32] As was typical of Independence Day celebrations, the centerpiece of the day was a procession through the city and then a sermon at church. But this time, New Yorkers saw citizens parading with black armbands affixed, symbolically transforming a patriotic celebration into a public funeral procession. A few days later, readers of the *Richmond Enquirer* learned that Fourth of July celebrations in Virginia's capital included toasts to "Joseph Arnold, John Lawrence, John Sharkely, and Robert MacDonald, their infamous murder shall be avenged by their country," and to "The People of Norfolk, Portsmouth, and Hampton, sympathy for their sufferings, honor for their patriotism, and revenge for their wrongs."[33] In Philadelphia, they toasted to "John Bull, the curse of nations and cursed

[30] John C. Emmerson, Jr., *The Chesapeake Affair of 1807* (Portsmouth: by the author, 1954), 33.

[31] Cray, "Remembering the USS *Chesapeake*."

[32] (New York) *American Citizen*, July 3, 1807.

[33] *Richmond Enquirer*, July 7, 1807. See also the toasts at the New Haven, Connecticut, July 4 celebration; *Connecticut Herald*, July 7, 1807.

by them – one heart and one arm to avenge our wrongs and to punish piracy and murder."[34]

As with previous expressions of public mourning, the deaths of MacDonald and the others became rallying points that unified Americans around a common sense of loss and a common affront to their nation. What stands out in such reporting is the underscoring of the citizenship status of those who suffered and died. It was the simple "Americanness" of MacDonald and the others that made their "murders" into a national tragedy. Similarly, it was the patriotism of the common citizens of ports that voluntarily closed to British shipping, to their own economic detriment, that deserved to be honored and remembered as well. In the mourning for the Chesapeake tars, in sum, is witnessed the appropriation of old rituals of mourning in service to a relatively new nation, but also the borrowing of those rituals to apply to a new kind of symbol, the common citizen, to be praised and remembered merely for acting dutifully, although not necessarily bravely or with leadership. In this process, Norfolk was transformed into national ground, and its regional associations were suppressed or forgotten.

Four and a half years later, a horrified public yet again learned of deaths in Virginia that were unexpected and undeserved. Processions, arm bands, heartbroken citizens, and funeral sermons dominated the press. But this time, the victims – a cross-section of citizens – died while participating in a far more ordinary event, and they were not in any way overt symbols of nationhood. On the day after Christmas, 1811, a fire tore through a crowded theater in Richmond, Virginia, during a performance. A simple accident brought a lit chandelier stage prop up into the rafters among the highly flammable scenery. Flames jumped up the sides of the painted canvases and began to lick at the dry, rosin-dappled pine boards of the unplastered theater roof. In moments, a blaze raged overhead as panicked theater-goers, alerted far too late to the danger, bolted from their seats in search of the exits. By some miracle, more than five hundred ticket holders managed to escape, but at least seventy others lost their lives. Their passing represented anything but "good deaths" – some were crushed and trampled by the panicked crowd, others were killed leaping from the windows, suffocated by smoke, or, to everyone's particular horror, burned alive. Within ten minutes, according to various eyewitness reports, the roof caved in and the building itself started to come down. The dead included a

[34] *Aurora General Advertiser*, July 7, 1807. See also *Poulson's American Daily Advertiser*, July 6, 1807.

few prominent men: Virginia's governor, George William Smith; one of its retired Congressmen and Senators, Abraham B. Venable (also the president of the Bank of Virginia); prominent lawyer Benjamin Botts; and naval officer James Gibbon. But most of the dead were lesser known members of Virginia's middling and planter families. The majority were women and children.[35]

To say that Richmonders were traumatized by the event is a wild understatement. People described the scene out in the street that night as utter, horrifying chaos. Once the fire bells began to ring, the whole city seemed to rush to the theater, where people formed a panicked, unhelpful mob. People ran madly around the site, searching for their loved ones, and those seriously injured by the blaze were strewn everywhere as nearby homes quickly became makeshift hospitals. Editors of two of Richmond's newspapers were present that night, but even these wordsmiths were so unhinged by the event that they could hardly narrate for their readers what they had witnessed. The *American Standard*'s editor explained that "The fire flashed into every part of the house with a rapidity, horrible and astonishing, and alas!! ... No tongue can tell, no pen ... can describe, the woeful catastrophe .... There was but one door for the greatest part of the audience to pass. Men women and children were pressing upon each other, while the flames were seizing upon those behind ...." On the top floor, "Those nearest the windows ... were afraid to leap down, whilst those behind them, were seen catching on fire, and writhing in the greatest agonies ... At length, those behind, urged by the pressing flames pushed those out who were nearest to the windows, and people of every description began to fall, one upon another; some with their clothes on fire; some half roasted; Oh wretched me! Oh afflicted people! ... Who that saw his friends and dearest connections devoured by fire, and laying in heaps at the door, will not regret that he ever lived to see such a sight! ... A sad gloom pervades this place, and every countenance is cast down to the earth."[36]

[35] The overview of the fire and its aftermath is drawn primarily from accounts in the *Richmond Enquirer* and *Virginia Argus* for December 1811 and January 1812, as well as *Full Account of the Burning of the Richmond Theatre* (Richmond: J. E. Goode, 1858); Harl LaPlace Jeffers, "Richmond Theatre's Tragic Fire: Out of the Ashes to Monumental Church," *Olde Times* 2 (winter 1987/8): 2–11; William H. Gaines, Jr., "The Fatal Lamp, or Panic at the Play," *Virginia Cavalcade* 2 (summer 1952): 4–8; Harry Kollatz Jr., "A Monumental Recovery," *Richmond Magazine*, October 2005, 200–10; Raymond P. Rhinehart, "Fire!" *Richmond Magazine*, February 1975, 14–19; Meredith Henne Baker's excellent monograph on this subject, *The Richmond Theatre Fire: Early America's First Great Disaster* (Baton Rouge: Louisiana State University Press, 2012).

[36] "Most Dreadful Calamity," *American Standard*, December 27, 1811.

The editor of the *Richmond Enquirer*, Thomas Ritchie, wrote similarly emotional and repetitive descriptions, closing with "The whole town is shrouded in woe. Heads of families extinguished forever – many and many is the house in which a chasm has been made that can never be filled up. We cannot dwell on this picture. We must drop the pen . . .. Oh miserable night of unutterable woe!"[37]

From the first, accounts of the fire included stories of lost family members, of paternal and maternal grief, of the chasms created in individual hearts. But within hours, the dead also began a rhetorical transformation into "citizens" and the mourners into "fellow citizens" in everything from private correspondence to news coverage to government resolutions. An ostensibly private catastrophe became public business, and performances of community grief were orchestrated by the city government, with the city's inhabitants playing key roles as well. Although the deaths of the Governor and a few others were particular public losses, the emphasis remained squarely on the seventy-odd theater-goers as a whole.

Even as the wreckage of the theater smoldered the next morning, the city government met to consider how it could best respond. Its first act was to form a committee to collect remains and move them "to the public burying ground, with all proper respect and solemnity." The ordinance also required that the city's inhabitants receive notice of when and where the removal of remains would take place, that "necessary refreshments" be provided, and that the graves be marked with "such tomb or tombs as they [the committee] may approve, with such inscriptions as to them may appear calculated to record the melancholy and afflicting event." The point, the ordinance stipulated, was both to manage remains and to "sooth and allay . . . the grief of the friends and relations of the deceased."[38] Although the city fathers were not, as of yet, planning a full-blown public funeral, they did not treat the occasion as entirely a private undertaking either. The councilmen urged that citizens cease all business for two days. The meaning and intention here is ambiguous: they may have intended simply to calm the city with this pause in activity, or they may have been edging toward recommending a public performance of mourning. Clearer was their final ordinance of the day – prohibiting for four months "any public show or spectacle" and forbidding anyone to "open any public dancing Assembly"

[37] *A Concise Statement of the Awful Conflagration of the Theatre, in the City of Richmond* . . . (Philadelphia: n.p., 1812), 7.

[38] *Narrative and Report of the Causes and Circumstances of the Deplorable Conflagration at Richmond* (Richmond: Shaw & Shoemaker, 1812), 15.

in Richmond – restrictions that clearly echoed of the sort of public grieving that had been expected on the death of kings and other major figures of state in earlier times.[39]

If the city government waffled on reading the disaster as an occasion for public mourning, the citizenry itself did not. That same afternoon, Richmonders held a public meeting and drafted a series of resolutions that clearly transformed the ambiguous city ordinances into a full-blown plan for public grieving. They resolved to request "the citizens of Richmond to observe Wednesday next, as a day of humiliation and prayer, in consequence of the late melancholy event, and to suspend on that day their usual occupations." They passed a resolution to essentially turn the collection of unclaimed remains into a ceremonial public funeral by calling on the city's committee to "regulate the time and order of the funeral procession" and by asking that the "legislature, the executive and the judiciary branches be respectfully requested to attend."[40] They added a formal funeral sermon to the event, to be given by one of the two most prominent ministers in Richmond, and they expanded the proposed tombstone into a more grandiose monument to which all were invited to financially contribute. Finally, they resolved to ask that Richmonders perform a collective act of mourning by wearing "crape for one month" for the "worthy and meritorious citizens who fell a sacrifice to the flames."[41] Not only did the community itself serve as the engine for public mourning (while drawing, of course, on age-old rituals), but they did so by invoking the language of citizenship at every turn. Both the fallen and those who mourned them were held together by the bonds of citizenship, and their collective grief was rooted in that commonality.

The city government, guided by public opinion, then completed the process of turning the fire into an occasion for public mourning. Collection of the victims' corpses proved more difficult than anyone at first imagined because the fire had burned so hot that human remains could not be easily distinguished or moved. City officials decided to purchase the theater lot, inter the victims there, and place a monument on the site as a public reminder of the tragedy. Before consecrating the cemetery, a funeral procession would wind through the city: the order was to be the "Corpse[s], Clergy, Mourners

[39] Ibid., 15–16. It is possible that a governor might merit such a response, but Smith was not singled out. As with the mourning of the *Chesapeake* dead, grief rituals normally reserved for the elite were applied to common citizens in this case.

[40] Ibid., 17.

[41] Ibid., 18, 40–41.

and Ladies" followed by the city's Executive Council and the directors of the Bank, reflecting the loss for the governor and the bank president. Then would come the "Judiciary. Members of the Legislature. Court of hustings. Common Hall. Citizens on foot. Citizens on horseback."[42] It was the making of a full-blown public funeral, akin to the processions for George II in 1760 and George Washington in 1799.

The fire and Richmond's responses to it were reported in full detail in newspapers across the United States, setting the tone for countless acts and words of sympathetic mourning that took personal losses occasioned by the fire and transformed them into collective ones. In Petersburg, twenty-some-odd miles south of Richmond, the deaths were felt most acutely, and local mourning clearly mimicked that taking place in Richmond. On New Year's Day, the "whole town exhibited, in silence and dejection, a melancholy participation in the sorrow and affliction" by attending public religious services and suspending all business, and even the "vessels in the harbor displayed their colors in sign of woe."[43] The city government also passed resolutions to "recommend to the citizens to wear crape" and to suspend "all public exhibitions for one month, as an expression of their deep sorrow and condolence."[44] In Norfolk, a hundred mile away, citizens set aside a day "to express their sympathy and condolence for ... the city of Richmond."[45] A large crowd of "different orders of citizens" assembled in Market Square and processed to the Presbyterian Church, where they listened to a funeral sermon. The editor of the Norfolk paper explained that this was a solemn occasion of "real" mourning, not "the empty pageant of a volatile crowd, fond of novelty and parade." "Never did we behold so great a concourse of people assembled at once on any former occasion in this Borough," he continued, "and since the funeral rights in honor of WASHINGTON, the nation's savior and benefactor, never and so mournful a one." The city purchased an urn which, "supported by eight citizens, was taken into the procession" and delivered to the church to the strains of a "solemn dirge." Afterward, the mourners, bowing under the weight of the urn, processed to Christ Church where the vessel and its symbolic contents were "deposited, and the mournful ceremonies concluded." Participants wore black, guns were fired, bells rung, and ships at their moorings drew their colors down to half-mast. Norfolk, in sum,

[42] Ibid., 21.
[43] *Richmond Enquirer*, January 4, 1812.
[44] *Charleston City Gazette*, January 6, 1812; *Columbian Centinnel*, January 11, 1812.
[45] *Charleston City Gazette*, January 16, 1812.

reenacted for the citizens of Richmond many elements of a royal or presidential funeral, although the rituals, in this case, were for "departed friends and brethren."[46] The dead and those who mourned were depicted as fellow "citizens," and Richmond as a whole was sympathized for, as part of a larger, unnamed collectivity, be it state or nation.[47]

In Washington DC, Congress came close to declaring the catastrophe a focus of national grief, resolving to don mourning in recognition of Richmond's losses. The language of national unity is impossible to miss in these resolutions. On December 30, Virginia congressman John Dawson called for thirty days of crape on the left arm from the floor of the House of Representatives. "It is to us a great national calamity," Dawson proclaimed. His resolution was unanimously adopted to "testify the respect and sorrow which this nation feels for the deceased, and to prove that we sympathize with the afflicted." In the Senate, a similar resolution was submitted "in testimony of the national respect and sorrow for the unfortunate persons, who perished." Senators wore arm bands in honor of their former colleague, but their resolution more broadly defined the subjects of their mourning. As representatives of the nation, they modeled the nation's sorrow over the loss of so many fellow Americans.[48] Interestingly, a New York newspaper editor complained in print that Congress's actions did not go far enough. In his view, the fire was one of several recent events, including the Battle of Tippecanoe, the New Madrid earthquakes, and a series of diplomatic conflicts pushing the nation toward war, which necessitated a national day of "FASTING, HUMILIATION *and* PRAYER." In his view, "If it ever was the peculiar duty of the Nation, in a time of general and wide felt calamity, to bow with humiliation and reverence, before THE RIGHTEOUS SOVEREIGN OF THE UNIVERSE, surely it becomes ours, in the present eventful day."[49]

In major seaboard cities, expressions and performances of "national" grief were also in evidence. About one hundred Virginia sons attending medical school in Philadelphia met on New Year's Day, resolved to wear crape for a month, and planned to process to church to hear a funeral

[46] *Richmond Enquirer*, January 9, 1812.

[47] Several other Virginia communities organized their own public mourning events, although none with quite the thoroughness of Norfolk. The *Richmond Enquirer* reported such activity in Falmouth, Smithfield, Alexandria, and Winchester; *Richmond Enquirer*, January 4, 1812; January 9, 1812; January 14, 1812; January 25, 1812.

[48] (Washington City) *National Intelligencer*, December 31, 1811.

[49] *New York Spectator*, January 4, 1812.

sermon in order to express their "piercing and deep sorrow for the loss of their connexions, friends and countrymen."[50] In sympathy, "young men of Philadelphia" convened a public meeting in which they decided to join the Virginians in wearing crape and processing to a memorial ritual. They also wrote a condolence letter to the mayor of Richmond, which was published in the Philadelphia papers. The language of the letter reveals how a terrible, personal tragedy for many Richmond families became for others an occasion to express a sense of national connectedness. The transition from the local and personal to the national and empathetic is hard to miss: "The conflagration that has recently involved the domestic scene of Richmond in terror, anguish and despair, becomes a national calamity not by the political operation of the government, but by the social virtues of the people, and all who have the soul to feel, possess the privilege to deplore."[51] Similar expressions of national sympathy and the symbolic connections of citizenship came out of Boston, New York, and Charleston as well.[52] In the last city, the council resolved that its citizens wear crape for a month in sympathy with the citizens of Richmond, a feeling that they believed would "be universal." The *City Gazette* was itself garbed in the black border ink of mourning on January 4, "as a mark of respect for the memory of the dead, and condolence with the living, citizens of Richmond."[53]

The circulation of print reinforced the message of national unity among citizens in mourning for unfortunate theater-goers in Richmond. The *Richmond Enquirer* was the main source of news about the fire. Papers across the country reprinted excerpts, informing fellow Americans about the horrors of the fire itself, the magnitude of the losses, and the crippling grief that seized the city. They described performances of public mourning and the sharing of that grief by inhabitants of other cities. Nearly every newspaper reprinted Congressman Dawson's resolution that the House of Representatives wear crape, including his words of citizenship, nation, and sorrow. If Congress mourned, did not the whole nation? In early 1812, more than a dozen stand-alone tracts related to the fire also appeared. Several of these simply compiled newspaper accounts, making narratives of public grief readily available to the reading public long after newspapers

50 *Richmond Enquirer*, January 9, 1812.

51 *Poulson's American Daily Advertiser*, January 9, 1812.

52 *Richmond Enquirer*, January 18, 1812; January 25, 1812; January 30, 1812; February 6, 1812, February 25, 1812.

53 *Charleston City Gazette*, January 9, 1812.

ceased to address the topic.[54] The majority of the tracts, however, were reprints of sermons that, not surprisingly, emphasized the sudden and horrible deaths in Richmond as a warning to all Christians to recognize how fleeting life is and to repent their sins and live according to God's laws daily. Some went considerably further, however, to advance a "nationalist" message by reading the fire as a warning to all Americans to repent not only for their own good, but also for the good of the United States itself. For example, Episcopalian minister George Dashiell, speaking to his Baltimore parish, put it this way: "I consider these unhappy brethren as suffering not for themselves particularly, but especially for us. They are victims immolated for their country's good. I believe that God yet looks with an eye of mercy upon this country." But, he explained, so long as moral degeneracy such as is tolerated in the theater continues, how can the vision be realized? "May our country hear, and obey the warning voice!"[55] See Figure 5.

Black armbands, crape drapery, carefully ordered processions, funeral sermons, elegiac writing, bans on public amusements, lowered flags, tolling bells, and published laments – all comprised a common language for Americans that allowed them to imagine themselves as unified in grief. These performances and texts of public mourning in the early nineteenth century consistently employed the language of nation and articulated a

[54] See, for example, *Calamity at Richmond, Being a Narrative of... the awful Conflagration of the Theatre in the city of Richmond ...* (New York: Largin and Thompson, 1812); *Distressing Calamity. A Brief Account of the Late Fire at Richmond...* (Boston: Repertory Office, 1812); *Particular Account of the Dreadful Fire...* (Baltimore: J. Kingston, 1812); *A Concise Statement of the Awful Conflagration of the Theatre; Narrative and Report of the Causes and Circumstances.*

[55] George Dashiell, *A sermon occasioned by the burning of the theatre in the city of Richmond, Virginia on the Twenty-sixth of December, 1811 by which disastrous event more than one hundred lives were lost ...* (Baltimore: J. Kingston, 1812), 8, 9. See also William Hill, *A sermon delivered in the Presbyterian meeting-house in Winchester, on Thursday the 23d January 1812: Being a day of fasting and humiliation, appointed by ... late calamitous fire at the Richmond Theatre* (Winchester: *Wincester Gazette*, 1812), 5, 7, 10; Samuel Miller, *A Sermon, Delivered January 19, 1812, at the Request of a Number of Young Gentlemen of the City of New-York, Who had Assembled to Express their Condolence With the Inhabitants of Richmond on the Late Mournful Dispensation of Providence in that City* (New York: Whiting and Watson, 1812); James Muir, "Sign of the Times," in *Ten Sermons* (Alexandria: Cotton and Stewart, 1812). Perhaps the most detailed and full discussion of the sins of the United States as a nation and the need for Americans to correct them is found in George Richards, *Repent! Repent! Or Likewise Perish!: The Spirit of an Evening Lecture, February 16, 1812, On the Late Calamity at Richmond, Virginia, Most Respectfully Inscribed to the Universalist Church, Philadelphia, at Whose Request it is Published* (Philadelphia: Lydia R. Bailey, 1812).

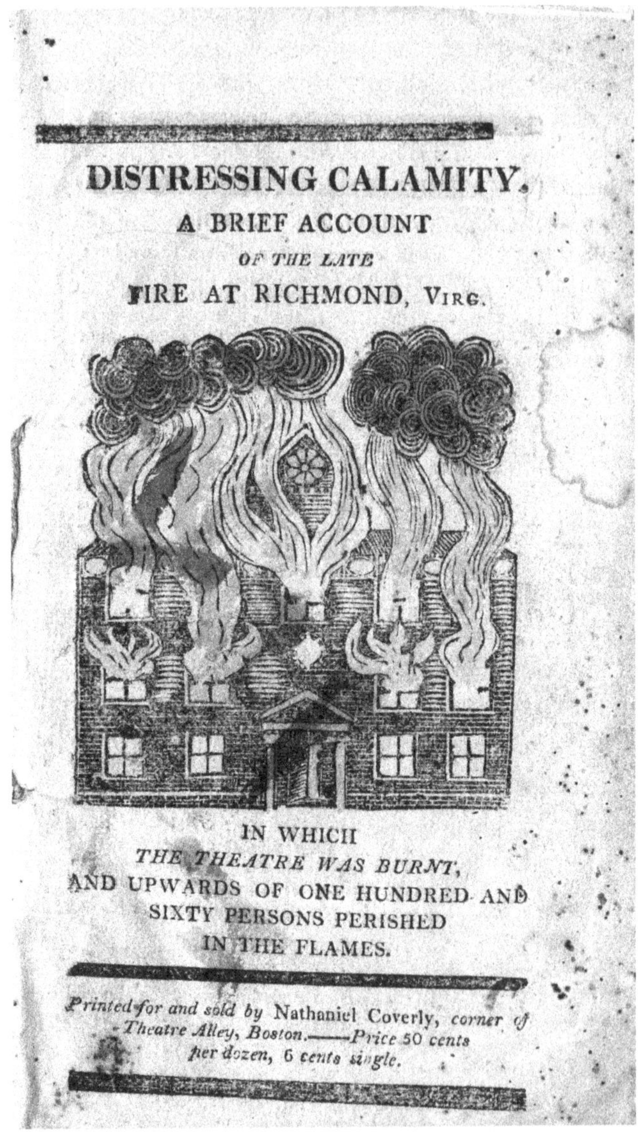

DISTRESSING CALAMITY.

A BRIEF ACCOUNT

OF THE LATE

FIRE AT RICHMOND, VIRG.

IN WHICH

THE THEATRE WAS BURNT,

AND UPWARDS OF ONE HUNDRED AND SIXTY PERSONS PERISHED IN THE FLAMES.

Printed for and sold by Nathaniel Coverly, *corner of Theatre Alley, Boston.——Price 50 cents per dozen, 6 cents single.*

FIGURE 5. The Richmond theater fire became a widely publicized tragedy and played a role in the coalescence of a "national" form of mourning.
Source: *A Distressing Calamity: A brief account of the late fire at Richmond, Virg. in which the theatre was burnt, and upwards of one hundred and sixty persons perished in the flames* (Boston: Nathaniel Coverly, 1812), cover image. Courtesy of the Library of Virginia, Richmond.

sense of common American identity. Notably absent from the narratives of tragedy and mourning examined here is any semblance of regionalism. Bostonians, New Yorkers, and Philadelphians all treated Norfolk and Richmond as fully integrated with the "nation" and its inhabitants as "fellow citizens." Those who grieved with and for Virginia in 1807 and 1812 very rarely referenced these events as regional or local. Norfolk modeled the mourning ritual as patriotic performance for the United States in 1807, and in 1812, the dead and bereaved in Virginia's capital were consistently framed as fellow citizens and mourned and sympathized with on that basis.

Revealing a moment when tragedy readily overcame regionalism in forging a sense of national connectedness, these incidents also show us the work that Americans continued to do after Washington's death to define a distinctive form of national mourning. Washington was grieved as a military hero, a president, and as symbol of the nation, even as he was held up as a fellow-citizen. Americans mourned for *Chesapeake* tars a few years later with similar acts and language, attached to an international and politically charged incident, bursting with potential political meanings and "national" consequence. Yet their focus on undistinguished seamen and the ubiquitous use of the language of "citizenship" suggest a continued evolution in thinking about what it was to be American. Response to the Richmond theater fire even further evinced a shift toward a more inclusive notion of public mourning and American belonging. The deaths of Virginia's governor, a former Senator and bank president, and a naval officer occasionally drew particular notice, but what stands out is the thoroughly apolitical nature of this moment of national grief. The Richmond victims were not (and could not have been) turned into martyrs for a national cause – there *was* no cause, except perhaps to improve safety standards in public buildings. Instead, what arose was the idea that any American victims, even ordinary heads of household or ladies who "ornamented" the social scene, were a loss to the nation and worthy of a collective show of sadness.

5

To Claim One's Own: Death and the Body in the Daily Politics of Antebellum Slavery

Jamie Warren

In 1856, a young southern physician submitted an article to a medical journal regarding a troubling, and ultimately fatal, case of peritonitis in an enslaved woman. Detailing the woman's illness and the doctor's many failed attempts of remedy, the article is heavy with the vexed practitioner's uncertainty. After eleven days of medicines, teas, oils, poultices, and tinctures, the patient died "calmly and easily" with a "clear mind," leaving the doctor perplexed and in search of an explanation. Believing the answers lay in the enslaved woman's corpse, he sought permission to perform an autopsy, directing his request, unsurprisingly, to the master who claimed ownership over the woman during her life. Yet the answer to the doctor's request came not from the slaveowner, but from the deceased woman's enslaved husband. This man, likely stricken with grief and tormented by the idea of his wife's body mutilated under the dissector's blade, emphatically defended the body of his kin – and won. The physician's request for a postmortem examination was denied. The disappointed practitioner penned his frustration, "As this was rather a doubtful case and a very interesting one, it is very much to be regretted that a postmortem examination could not be obtained. I requested the privilege of making an examination but the husband of the woman was so much opposed to it that the master was unwilling to do violence to his prejudices and feelings."[1]

The enslaved man's successful claim to his wife's body raises important questions for historians of the slave South. Why did the slaveholder in question acquiesce to his bondsman's demands? Perhaps the doctor's

[1] A Young Practitioner, "Report of a Case of Disease Supposed to be Peritonitis," *The Monthly Stethoscope and Medical Reporter* 1 (June 1856): 364.

account was correct – the white slaveowner simply did not want to deal with the turbulence of upsetting his slave's "prejudices." Perhaps the slaveholder shared similar beliefs about the sacred boundaries of the corpse's flesh. Or, possibly, the slaveholder questioned the legitimacy of his own claim over the body of the dead woman. Certainly, he could lay claim to her body during her life, but did his dominion extend beyond the reach of death as well? To whom, exactly, did this corpse belong? Although we cannot know why the slaveholder refused the doctor's request for a postmortem autopsy, we can know that, in this instance, a white master recognized a slave's claim to the corpse of his kin. By the nineteenth century, moments like this were quite common – although they did not always work out this way – and are thus revealing of the daily politics of slavery and ownership in the antebellum South.[2]

This essay explores the vast range of treatments that black corpses received in the antebellum South, arguing that death and the dead bodies of the enslaved were important sites for expressing and challenging social claims in others. The treatment of the dead in the slave South reflected, in magnified terms, how planters and bondspeople thought of themselves and each other. A close examination of how antebellum Southerners handled the dead – whether it involved washing and shrouding, dissecting and mutilating, or simply leaving a body to exposure and rot – reveals how blacks and whites used the corpse to express social identity, stake claims of family, and navigate the boundaries of slave ownership.[3]

Black and white Southerners, like their northern counterparts, revered the dead and held the corpses of their kin in deep regard. Indeed, nineteenth-century America, regardless of region, was marked by an obsession with death and a ritualistic care of corpses.[4] However, the pervasive presence of a slave labor system based in part on concepts of commodified, racialized bodies produced a distinctly southern understanding of the value and potency of corpses. In a social and economic system in which one's physical

[2] Sharla Fett, *Working Cures: Healing, Health, and Power on Southern Slave Plantations* (Chapel Hill: University of North Carolina Press, 2002), 156; Marie Jenkins Schwartz, *Birthing a Slave: Motherhood and Medicine in the Antebellum South* (Cambridge: Harvard University Press, 2006), 219–23.

[3] In his work on nineteenth-century autopsies, Michael Sappol has argued that during the tumultuous changes of the early to mid-century, Americans increasingly turned to the body and consequently the corpse to express a fixed social identity; see *A Traffic of Dead Bodies: Anatomy and Embodied Social Identity in Nineteenth-Century America* (Princeton: Princeton University Press, 2002).

[4] Ibid., 15.

body largely determined whether he or she was enslaved, the corpse – passive, yet deeply imbued with meaning – became a site for expressing, challenging, and strengthening the ideologies of mastery and slavery. Examining the various treatments of corpses in the Old South reveals a complex value system wherein slaves and masters turned to the dead to mark out their claims in each other and articulate what a life meant under the system of slavery.

The literature on enslaved peoples' experiences of death and dying in the American South has tended to emphasize either the resistance of African Americans against whites' attempts to dehumanize slaves in death or the oppressive totality of a slaveholder's power. Scholarship that emphasizes resistance, for example, may focus on evidence of African cultural retention in burial practices, pointing to the ways enslaved people maintained traditional cosmologies and rituals. In contrast, historians who focus on the role of death in the maintenance of planter dominance tend to emphasize masters' mortal and postmortem violence and their complete disregard for enslaved peoples' deathways.[5] Death, it seems, was either a moment for slaves to transcend the oppression of a life of enslavement, or it was the final stage for the master to act out his dominion over his bondspeople. However, this essay begins from the premise that to understand the daily politics of slaves' experiences of death, we must move beyond the dichotomy of oppression and resistance. More than a site of rebellion or oppression, death in the context of slavery is better understood as an important transformation where something new might be created – a time when the daily politics of slavery cracked open, allowing space to carve out new meaning. In short, to die a slave was not always the same as having lived as one.

In a similar vein, focusing only on one kind of planter behavior – violence – obscures the ways in which antebellum slaveholders employed

[5] Howard Thurman, *A Strange Freedom: The Best of Howard Thurman on Religious Experience and Public Life*, ed. Walter Earl Fluker and Catherine Tumber (Boston: Beacon Press, 1998), 57. See Philip Morgan, *Slave Counterpoint: Black Culture in the Eighteenth-Century Chesapeake and Low-Country* (Chapel Hill: University of North Carolina Press, 1998), 640–57 for a discussion of slave burial practices as sites of cultural retention and resistance. For examples of scholarship that emphasizes planters' oppressive violence toward slave deathways, see Douglas Egerton, "A Peculiar Mark of Infamy: Dismemberment, Burial, and Rebelliousness in Slave Societies," in *Mortal Remains: Death in Early America*, ed. Nancy Isenberg and Andrew Burstein (Philadelphia: University of Pennsylvania Press, 2003), 149–60; Franny Nudelman, *John Brown's Body: Slavery, Violence, and the Culture of War* (Chapel Hill: University of North Carolina Press, 2004), 40–69. For an analysis of the limits of viewing slave death experiences through the lens of oppression and resistance, see Vincent Brown, "Social Death and Political Life in the Study of Slavery," *American Historical Review* 114 (December 2009): 1231–49.

more paternalistic responses to their slaves' deaths. The ideology of paternalism during the early nineteenth century increasingly encouraged masters to symbolically honor the corpses of their slaves. During the late seventeenth and eighteenth centuries, slaveholders understood that violating a slave's corpse, by beheading an executed man for example, worked as an effective tool for terrorizing and thus compelling compliance from their bondspeople. Although postmortem violence and disregard for black bodies never disappeared, by the antebellum period, such behavior took its place alongside more "benevolent" responses. For example, Charles Colcock Jones, a Georgia planter, clergyman, and strong advocate of slaveholders' paternalist obligations to the enslaved, reminded his white readers that their bondsmen and women "weep over us when we die, prepare us for burial, and carry us to the house appointed for all the living." It was only right, Jones argued, that slaveholders should acknowledge such intimate labor by attending slaves' funerals and by helping the enslaved honor their dead. "It is cold, heartless, senseless heathenism that neglects death," he admonished.[6] Obviously, such advice cannot be taken as evidence of all planters' behavior, yet the documents of slaveholders and the testimony of former slaves indicate that some antebellum masters paid heed to such instructions and found postmortem violation of slaves' bodies disagreeable. Cruel postmortem violence sadly persisted through the antebellum period, even as it was increasingly targeted by admonishing voices. As the beliefs surrounding the duties of masters changed, southern death customs shifted to accommodate this vision of the extended plantation "family."[7]

[6] Charles Colcock Jones, *The Religious Instruction of Negroes in the United States* (Savannah: Thomas Purse, 1842), 166, 232.

[7] Historians have long debated how to best interpret nineteenth-century slaveholders' use of the term "family" to describe their bondspeople. Eugene Genovese argued that the oft presence of the notion "Our family, white and black" in planters letters and journals cannot be dismissed as propaganda or ideological rationalization and claimed that the extended "family" of the plantation household provided masters with a "sense of who they were as individuals and as a people, their sense of moral worth, their sense of honor"; "'Our Family White and Black': Family and Household in the Southern Slaveholders' Worldview," in *In Joy and Sorrow: Women, Family, and Marriage in the Victorian South, 1830–1900*, ed. Carol Bleser (New York: Oxford University Press, 1991), 71; Craig Thompson Friend, "Little Eva's Last Breath: Childhood Death and Parental Mourning in 'Our Family, White and Black,'" in *Family Values in the Old South*, ed. Craig Thompson Friend and Anya Jabour (Gainesville: University Press of Florida, 2010), 62–85. Others have asserted that such language should be interpreted as no more than a guise meant to mask the more prominent justification for slavery – property in persons. I am less interested in measuring the sincerity of slaveholders' claims and instead focus on understanding how this ideology of family affected plantation life and customs.

Death and the dead body are important sites for historians' analyses, precisely because Southerners used them to stake claims of kinship and respectability. To understand antebellum southern beliefs about who belonged to whom, we need to look closely at their intimate proximity with the dead and examine the value this intimacy held for the living. Disputes over dead bodies reflected the sometimes uncertain nature of kinship. When North Carolinian John Wilfong's daughter, Caroline, died only one month after marrying, he and his wife demanded that her new husband return her body to be buried in South Carolina near them. Perhaps the brevity of her marriage caused Wilfong and his wife to question their son-in-law's claim to Caroline's body. Given that Caroline died rather suddenly from "fits," Wilfong's grief was no doubt confounded by being absent during his daughter's passing. It is not difficult to imagine their sadness, and perhaps anger, when they received a letter saying that Caroline had already been buried, an enclosed lock of her hair their only consolation.[8] By caring for and burying their dead, white Southerners laid claim to the people they believed belonged to them. Such claims were more difficult, and in that sense, all the more salient for black Southerners.

Although most antebellum Americans were wary of postmortem disturbance to the corpses of their families, African-American slaves in particular were deeply protective of the corpses of their kin. Slaveholders may have dismissed such vigilant custody as superstition, but in the context of chattel slavery, the enslaved response to the bodies of their kin makes sense. Beginning in early childhood, African Americans held in bondage lived daily with the struggle to feel a sense of possession over their own bodies and thus their own identity. At its base, the chattel slavery system claimed black bodies and placed these bodies under the purview of whites. From the buying and selling of their persons to the taking of black women's breast milk for the feeding of white mistresses' babies to sexual exploitation and physical violence, enslaved Southerners were often reminded that their bodies legally belonged to someone else. The fact that their living bodies by law belonged to their master made claiming the corpses of their kin all the more important.

Consider the story told by James Carter, an escaped Virginia slave, about the struggle over his brother's corpse. James's brother, Henry, fled from his owner in the early nineteenth century after he had learned that he

[8] Mary Bobo to John Wilfong, February 24, 1845; Charles Bobo to John Wilfong, February 24, 1845, both in John Wilfong Papers, David M. Rubenstein Rare Book and Manuscript Library, Duke University, Durham, NC.

was to be sold to a planter known for his cruelty. The slave patrollers found Henry in neighboring woods and, when he attempted to escape by swimming through a river, the white men stoned him, leaving his body in the water. James and his family heard the news of Henry's death and the abandonment of his body five days after the fact. James recalled that he implored his master to let him go with his father to search for his brother's corpse, wherein his master refused, sending James on an errand instead. At his mother's insistence, James managed to make it back to the plantation before nightfall, and he and his parents searched the river for Henry's body. With the help of slaves from neighboring plantations, they eventually found his corpse several miles down river. They then floated the body back to their wagon and secreted the corpse in a barn overnight. James recalled staying with his brother's five-day-old remains in the barn that night, waiting until morning when his father returned with help to transport Henry's body to the plantation burial ground where his open grave was waiting.[9]

To wrestle with the significance of this event, we must try to imagine what was at stake in the quest to claim Henry Carter's body. If his family had not been able to recover his remains, there would be no burial and perhaps no funeral gathering. They would be faced with the dreadful sadness and horror that their kin's body laid rotting and decomposing in the river. And his death, perhaps, would take on the same meaning as his life – an existence and end characterized primarily by bondage. He died attempting to escape and was stoned for it. Leaving his body to endure the continued postmortem violence perpetuated by the slaveholding class meant allowing the meaning of his death to fall under the ownership of these men as well. James's status and that of his parents as enslaved people did not change as a result of Henry's burial. Yet, by finding and recovering his body at considerable risk to themselves, Henry's family cared for him in death and claimed his passing – and in some sense his life – as belonging to them. The circumstances surrounding Henry's death were particularly acute, and therefore his burial by kin all the more poignant. However, commonplace deaths are just as revealing of the troubling daily politics of enslavement and mastery and the saliency of the dead body in the making of these politics.

To appreciate the role of the corpse in the making of kinship claims among slaves and slaveholders, we must look closely at the labor of

[9] Linda Stanley, comp., "James Carter's Account of his Suffering in Slavery," *Pennsylvania Magazine of History and Biography* 105 (July 1981): 335–40.

tending to the dead, for in such labor family ties were both confirmed and challenged. Tending to corpses provided antebellum Southerners a crucial means for confirming kinship claims, imagined or real, between the living and the dead. In a social world where kinship ties existed in painful flux – where masters called their bondspeople family, and enslaved folks' kin lines could be severed by that same master's whim – the labor of laying the dead to rest was rich with meaning. Antebellum Southerners understood that the work of tending to the dead should be performed by close relatives; by performing such labor, the living could claim the dead as their own.[10] This labor involved stripping and washing the body, shrouding or dressing the corpse in winding cloth or funerals clothes, building and adorning coffins, sitting up with and watching over the body, and finally digging a grave and burying the corpse. Indeed, the work of death produced a particularly intimate arena of labor for slaves and, at times, their masters as well. Like much of the labor performed in the slave South, this work was largely organized by gender.

Enslaved women performed a great deal of the corpse care on slave plantations for both white and black bodies. Black women's roles as plantation healers, domestic servants, wet nurses, and "mammies" often pulled them into troublingly close proximity and unwelcome intimacy with the planter family, and the work surrounding death was no exception.[11] Consider, for instance, the task of washing the dead. This was typically done with vinegar, lavender, or homemade soap. A former slave recalled that bondswomen washed the plantation's dead with "hot water and homemade soap" made by enslaved women.[12] Washing the dead body made practical sense, particularly if the deceased had suffered a long and gruesome illness before passing. But this practice also held metaphysical importance, as bathing the body of the dead symbolically washed away the soil of life and sickness and prepared the individual to be reborn in death. Thus, caring for the dead was a sacred duty, and it was work that was often performed by enslaved women. Former slave Sarah Augustus recalled the domestic nature of death and dying in her years as a slave in the Old South. "The colored

[10] See Gary Laderman, *The Sacred Remains: American Attitudes toward Death* (New Haven: Yale University Press, 1999), 27–29 for a discussion of antebellum Americans' understanding of the familial nature of death labor.

[11] Thavolia Glymph, *Out of the House of Bondage: The Transformation of the Plantation Household* (New York: Cambridge University Press, 2008).

[12] Interview with former slave, in *The American Slave: A Composite Autobiography*, ed. George P. Rawick, 19 vols. (Westport: Greenwood Press, 1972), 13: 20.

people washed and shrouded the dead bodies," she remembered. "My grandmother was one of the ones who did this."[13]

Black women's death labor was not confined to the slave quarters or the preparation of black corpses. A former bondman from Texas, Leo Moulton, remembered watching his mother and another enslaved woman tend to the dead body of their white owners. "When my mistress die," Moulton recalled, "my mother and another old colored woman lay her out. I had to hold her feet when they put her dress on. That dress shine so it hurt my eyes. That night I remember sitting by the fire and thinking about how she used to rub my head when I was standing by her knee."[14] Being a child when his mistress died, Moulton's memory of laying out her corpse conjures the mix of sadness, fear, and strangeness the event must have held for him. The woman once positioned near the head of the plantation hierarchy now lay lifeless and nude and under the ply and care of two enslaved women. Although we cannot know how Moulton's mother or her fellow bondswoman felt that night, it is not a stretch to assume that such moments must have been incredibly fraught with conflicting emotions.

Tending to the deceased was a sacred affair that African Americans approached with deep respect and care. In performing such duties, enslaved women assumed the sacred and intimate role of caring for the vulnerable dead. Yet, at the same time, being forced to perform such intimate labor for members of the slaveholding family also reflected the most profound exploitation of women's labor. The dual implications of intimacy and exploitation must not have been lost on slave women as they performed such work, taking on the role of sacred postmortem caretakers of their own enslavers. Although direct evidence of black women's role in tending to the dead on plantations is limited in quantity, it is substantiated by what we know about the type of nursing and body care enslaved women performed for white and black families in the South.[15] Black women spent much of their lives caring

[13] Interview with Sarah Augusts, in ibid., 14: 53–55.

[14] Interview with Leo Moulton, in ibid., supplement series 2, 7: 2814.

[15] The roles of domestic servant and plantation nurse as performed by enslaved women required such intimacies as breastfeeding and bathing members of the white family. Additionally, black women often fulfilled the role of midwife on plantations, assisting both white and black women with childbirth. For a discussion of black women breastfeeding white infants, see Morgan, *Slave Counterpoint*, 325–26. For a discussion of black women's roles as midwives in the Old South, see Sharla Fett, "Consciousness and Calling: African American Midwives at Work in the Antebellum South," in *New Studies in the History of American Slavery*, ed. Edward Baptist and Stephanie Camp (Athens: University of Georgia Press, 2006), 65–86.

for the white bodies of plantation households. There was little reason for that to change when whites died.

Enslaved women's labor of plantation health work and tending to the dead also provided moments of authority and important opportunities to shape the stories surrounding plantation deaths. The mysteries that surrounded death in the Old South yielded speculation as to what caused one's demise and who or what was to blame. Death also brought a chance to recount – and reshape in memory – the deceased's character. Access to the dead gave enslaved women the chance to influence these postmortem narratives and thus shape the social dialogue about those living and dying in their midst. When John Walker's slave, Eliza, died on his Virginia plantation, he wasted no time blaming her for her own death, calling her imprudent and lambasting her character. Walker believed that Eliza had suffered from consumption and prescribed her medicine accordingly. Her death, he believed, resulted from her own unwillingness to submit to his treatments and take the medicines he ordered her to take. "I have great faith in the medicine," he wrote in his plantation journal in 1834, "and I believe Eliza would have been cured if she had of used proper means." Yet, two days after this entry, Walker made an interesting correction: he was informed by his slave women who had shrouded Eliza that she had not died from consumption after all, but rather from venereal complaints.[16] Clearly then, the slave women who tended to their fellow bondswoman's corpse held the authority of diagnosing cause of death. Indeed, as Walker played the part of plantation doctor and condemned the character of his slave, the death labor performed by the enslaved women challenged his interpretations enough to make him acknowledge in his journal that he had been wrong.

Tending to the needs of corpses, like other nursing labor, was work that enslaved women sometimes performed alongside white women of the plantation household. Slaveholding mistresses often assumed the role of directing bodily care and then took credit in their letters and journals for the labor performed by enslaved women.[17] For example, Martha Brown Callendar Forman turned to her journal in 1824 to describe her experience in tending to the death of her overseer. After staying by his bedside through

[16] Plantation Journal, July 5, 1834, John Walker Papers, Southern Historical Collection, University of North Carolina, Chapel Hill.

[17] In her work on healing and health on slave plantations, Sharla Fett writes, "the crux of the matter was that when mistresses saw to healing work or had the sick tended to, enslaved women did the actual labor"; *Working Cures*, 117.

his painful and troubling passing, Callendar "took the sheets to lay him out," making do without her husband's help, as he was away.[18] One has to wonder, though, about the possible help she may have received, although not recorded in her journal. It is difficult to imagine that Forman did this work on her own. More likely, she relied on the help of her bondspeople to tend to the dead body of their overseer.

Following the cleaning of the body, the living shrouded the corpse in either funeral cloths, winding sheets, or regular clothes in preparation for laying out. Shrouding the body reflected an older worldview in which the dead body existed in close proximity with the living but was regarded as a vulnerable thing apart – a precarious entity that required protective partitioning from the living. By the mid-nineteenth century, however, concepts of death had begun to shift so that dead bodies were no longer wrapped to mark them as separate from the living. Instead, they were dressed in clothes and made to look as alive as possible. Most slaves continued to be shrouded rather than dressed, however, because few enslaved folks had the luxury of owning clothes suitable for funerals or to bury perfectly good clothes that the living could use.[19]

The sewing of funeral clothes and winding sheets provided white and black women an opportunity to work together and socialize.[20] Sewing was an activity intrinsically bound to white women's identities. They taught their daughters and some of their female slaves, but, during most sewing bees, slave women assisted the white seamstresses. For example, Maria Davies described an afternoon in 1852 that she spent sewing a burial cloth with a group of women while reading aloud from *Uncle Tom's Cabin*.[21] Given the literature, it is unlikely that there were very many slave women in the room. Still, the demographics highlight plantation owners' investments in burying their slaves properly. By providing funeral clothes for

[18] Diary of Martha Brown Callendar Forman, February 20, 1824, MS 1779, Manuscripts Division, Maryland Historical Society Library, Baltimore. Also published in *Our Common Affairs: Texts from Women in the Old South*, ed. Joan Cashin (Baltimore: Johns Hopkins University Press, 1996).

[19] James J. Farrell, *Inventing the American Way of Death: 1830–1920* (Philadelphia: Temple University Press, 1980); Sappol, *A Traffic of Dead Bodies*; interview with Emma Hurley, in Rawick, ed., *The American Slave*, 12: 274.

[20] Interview with former slave, in Rawick, ed., *The American Slave*, 18: 12. For a study of white and black women's household production of cloth and clothes, see Lynn Kennedy, "Out of Whole Cloth? Sewing and Family in the Old South," in Friend and Jabour, eds., *Family Values in the Old South*, 111–33.

[21] Kennedy, "Out of Whole Cloth?" 119, 123; Maria Dyer Davies Diaries, November 18, 1852, David M. Rubenstein Rare Book and Manuscript Library.

corpses of the enslaved, thereby demonstrating grief and respect for a slave's passing, slaveholders used the window of death to thread sentimental attachment to ownership of people and bind them to "our family, white and black."

White antebellum Southerners used the passing of their slaves to demonstrate their *benevolent* mastery. In a letter to her husband, for instance, Mary Colcock Jones described the acute emotion of helping her enslaved woman die and the aftermath of her death. As she sat by the side of the woman's corpse, Jones wrote, she felt more intensely than any other moment "the responsibility of being an owner."[22] Consider, as well, the corpse care provided by Virginia Shelton and her family when their slave, Lythe, passed. The enslaved woman's body was "neatly laid out" and dressed in "a beautiful night gown." Her body was then shrouded by a cloth cut by a neighboring white woman and her head adorned with a funeral cap. The cap had been made and sent by Shelton's mother "for just this purpose" and had been carefully stored until needed.[23] Given that her body was primarily visited and viewed by her fellow bondspeople, it follows that this elaborate care for the dead was less about demonstrating status to fellow planters and more about presenting themselves as certain kinds of masters to their slaves.

Another possibility is that Shelton and her white kin felt deep bereavement at Lythe's passing and sought to comfort themselves by honoring her corpse. Shelton wrote to her mother that she felt overcome with loneliness and grief, writing that her "head was but a fountain of tears," as she gave way to weeping. She added that Lythe's coffin was made of fine cherry, "as neat as any white person's."[24] Treating Lythe's dead body as if it were white, in Virginia's estimate, was the highest honor her family could bestow on their servant. In death, Lythe's enslaved body could be transformed through sorrow and ritual into a white body. Relying on sentimental language and ritual, Shelton's letter and the scene she described point to the ways in which white Southerners used nineteenth-century traditions of sentimentality to deny difference and bodily particularities during moments of death. In claiming that Lythe's body was handled just as if she were white, Shelton at once tried to evoke a goodness and worthiness in her

22 Mary Jones to Charles Colcock Jones, May 17, 1837, Charles Colcock Jones Papers, Louisiana Research Collection, Tulane University, New Orleans.

23 Virginia Tabitha Jane Shelton to her mother, July 22, 1843, Campbell Family Papers, David M. Rubenstein Rare Book and Manuscript Library.

24 Ibid.

slave by denying in death that Lythe's body had, in fact, been enslaved throughout her life.[25] By evoking whiteness to elevate the status of Lythe's corpse, Shelton and her family did not transgress racial difference in death but rather affirmed it through a sentimental affection exposed by death and the dead body.[26]

Blacks, too, sensed the erasure of racial differences in death. Although enslaved men and women were often denied proper baptisms and weddings, the handling and burial of black and white bodies were, at times, the same.[27] Millie Forward recounted a story surrounding the death of a fellow slave who drowned. Her mistress was quite ill and nearing death but was "that good," Millie recalled, "that she sat up in bed and made the shroud" for the deceased slave. Soon after they buried the drowned man, the plantation mistress passed away as well. Millie claimed that "the day she died, I cried all day."[28] Millie pointed to her mistress's care for a slave's corpse as the evidence of her good character and dedication to the slave community. Moreover, Millie's recollections are not unique. The quality and appearance of coffins was also emphasized when ex-slaves remembered death practices during slavery. Jasper Battle recalled, "The coffins was just the same for the white folks as it was for their slaves."[29] Another former bondsman told his interviewer that when a slave died, "their measure was taken and a coffin was made and blackened up until looked right nice .... They fixed up the

25 Scholars of rhetoric and cultural studies have pointed to the ways antebellum white women, in particular, used sentimental language to emphasize an emotional bond at the expense of the body or, as Arthur Riss described it, evoking the sentimental through "blindness to the body"; *Race, Slavery, and Liberalism in Nineteenth-Century Literature* (New York: Cambridge University Press, 2006), 93. Regarding the significance of Shelton's use of the term "white" to describe her slave, I am drawing from Karen Sánchez-Eppler who described such emotional conventions as the "obliteration of blackness." White women writing during the nineteenth century, Sanchez-Eppler argued, attempted to highlight the goodness of enslaved African Americans by washing blackness white; *Touching Liberty: Abolitionism, Feminism, and the Politics of the Body* (Berkeley: University of California Press, 1991), 31.

26 Riss argued that American traditions of liberalism and sentimentalism, which relied on abstract notions of the person and emotional bonds of sameness, were actually invoked to mark racial difference during the antebellum period. He writes, "During the antebellum period, however, the sentimental crucially extended liberal rights not because it generated abstract identities but because it cherished difference. The problem with attributing a universalizing imperative to either liberalism or the sentimental is that such an account removes the object of sentimentality and the subject of liberal thought from the very debate in which both are inevitably embedded: the debate over who counts as a 'person'"; *Race, Slavery, and Liberalism*, 96.

27 Interview with Ila Prine, in Rawick, ed., *The American Slave*, 6: 69.

28 Interview with Millie Forward, in ibid., 4: 48.

29 Interview with Jasper Battle, in ibid., 12: 66.

corpses nice . . . they made new clothes for them and buried them in a decent graveyard."[30]

Still, death was a leveler only where whites were amenable to the possibility. In contrast to Jasper Battle's experience was the work of other enslaved men who measured bodies, built coffins to size, and, in some cases, decorated or stained the wood, confronting in the process the social hierarchies of the plantation. Testimony of former slaves reveals a deep resentment toward masters who allowed for nothing more than crude boxes for slave burials. Rachel Adams recalled that on the plantation where she lived, black corpses were buried in "just a square pine box. Now warn't that terrible?"[31] As black men built the strikingly different coffins, they participated in unequal and differentiated care for black bodies.

In some instances, particularly in more urban settings, masters often purchased coffins for the corpses of their slaves from a local furniture maker or funeral home. Although purchased coffins were typically modest in construction and cost – ranging from fifty cents to five dollars – the fact that antebellum slaveholders purchased coffins for their bondspeople at all indicates shifting beliefs about what masters owed their slaves.[32] During the seventeenth and eighteenth centuries, it was rather uncommon for slaves to be buried in coffins. Not until the nineteenth century did coffins for the enslaved become at all prevalent.[33] The testimony of former slaves indicates that African Americans, as well, valued this cultural practice and were deeply offended when the bodies of their kin were denied such demonstrations of respect.

After the deceased had been ritually prepared for the grave, family and friends sat vigil for one to three days. The importance of seeing the dead, of gazing at the body in the company of kin, was an important part of processing loss and creating a narrative of death. For enslaved people, the claiming of this social rite was fraught with struggle and sadness because they were subjected to a master's prerogative on the matter. It is not difficult to imagine the grief enslaved people experienced when the

30 Interview with former slave, in ibid., 12: 262.

31 Interview with Bill Heard, in ibid., 12: 141; interview with Robert Sheppard, in ibid., 13: 251–52; interview with Rachel Adams, in ibid., 12: 5.

32 Gus Sellers Graveyard Account Book, Mss. 404, Robert Stewart Papers, Hill Memorial Library, Louisiana State University, Baton Rouge; Receipts, 1826, William Family Papers, Virginia Historical Society, Richmond.

33 Vincent Brown analyzed the use of coffins for the enslaved, arguing that slaves' demands for coffins point not only to the transformation of African burial practices, but also to the ways in which enslaved people used symbols of social hierarchy to claim status in a slave society; *The Reaper's Garden*, 245, 246.

news of their loved one's passing reached them too late to commune with the body. Enslaved men and women who did manage to attend the "sitting up" for a deceased friend or family member used such opportunities to showcase their strong connection to the deceased and the social worthiness of the body of their dead. Former slaves recalled "all the neighbors far and nigh gathered around to sit up with the family," singing and praying through the night. The loved one's corpse would likely be laid out on a cooling board, and the living kin would take turns watching over the body, day and night. A special meal might be prepared and served in the late hours, as folks sat in solemn and sometimes joyful reverence with the dead. Indeed, one ex-slave referred to these nights as "a big sitting up party."[34] Sitting vigil with the dead body of a loved one was so important that even when masters explicitly prohibited such visits, some slaves risked punishment by "slipping in after dark" to attend the gathering and "slip back before day."[35]

Nighttime vigils between the living and the dead point to the social value of the corpse and the role of death in the making of social ties for enslaved African Americans. Although such reverence for the dead was shared by white and black Southerners alike, the experience of living in bondage gave such postmortem care and ritual unique salience for blacks. When white men and women of the slaveholding home gathered around the body of a deceased family member, they communed with and bid farewell to a social tie that was honored and sanctioned by southern custom and law. When enslaved Southerners gathered around the corpse of their kin, sometimes in secret and perhaps after traveling some length, they were closing circle around one of their own and claiming in death what was often denied during life.

Caring for the dead provided a valued space for claiming kin among the enslaved, and some slaveholders used "benevolent" corpse care to express a paternalistic sense of ownership. Indeed, slaves could not necessarily expect that their corpses would be honored postmortem or that their families would be able to respectfully lay them to rest. Although some antebellum planters increasingly made attempts at proper corpse care, or at least allowed their slaves to do so, the dead bodies of the enslaved remained volatile sites of conflict. Precisely because slaveholders understood the importance of caring for the dead among the enslaved, some masters turned to the dead bodies of

[34] See interview with Arrie Binns, in Rawick, *The American Slave*, 12: 77; interview with Bill Heard, in ibid., 12: 141; interview with Paul Smith, in ibid., 13: 329; interview with Abraham Chambers, in ibid., supplemental series 1, 1: 87.

[35] Interview with Ann Mathews, in ibid., 16: 45.

their bondspeople to intentionally circumscribe blacks' claims of kinship and embodied social ties.

Former slave and abolitionist Henry Bibb invoked the mistreatment of slaves' corpses in his autobiography, complaining that "As to the burial of slaves, very little more care is taken of their dead bodies than if they were dumb beasts."[36] Frederick Douglass, too, referenced the horrible neglect that slave bodies faced after death, as he imagined his isolated grandmother's corpse laying exposed and untended on the ground.[37] Similarly, an author writing for the abolitionist newspaper *The Provincial Freeman* described a slave baby's corpse denied nearly everything essential for a proper burial. He recalled an enslaved woman digging a grave for her infant, "which lay by her side, shroudless and coffinless! The mistress of that mother had sent her thus to bury her child, refusing to buy grave-clothes and a coffin!"[38] This deliberate, callous neglect of black corpses enflamed abolitionists' messages. Side by side with descriptions of bodily pain and familial disruption, images of desecrated bodies reflected the most profane abuses suffered by bondspeople.[39]

Indeed, by the mid-nineteenth century, Africans and African Americans held in bondage had experienced a long history of fighting to claim the dead bodies of their kin. In addition to their struggle to procure proper burials and resting grounds for their dead, enslaved men and women were forced to contend with their masters' use of postmortem violence against black bodies to exact submission. British colonial planters became familiar with West African cosmological beliefs that a person's soul could not join her ancestors in the afterlife if her corpse had been desecrated. Thus, planters resorted to beheading the corpses of executed slaves and placing mutilated bodies on display.[40] This postmortem violence prohibited enslaved people not only from claiming the bodies of their own, but also from exercising the role of

36 Henry Bibb, *Narrative of the Life and Adventures of Henry Bibb: An American Slave* (New York: privately printed, 1849), 118.

37 Frederick Douglass, *Narrative of the Life of Frederick Douglass* (1845; reprint, New York: Doubleday, 1963), 41.

38 H. Jessup Names, "The Slave Mother," *The Provincial Freeman*, November 10, 1855.

39 In his work on death and slavery in colonial Jamaica, Vincent Brown had a similar finding. He argued that, by 1780, British antislavery advocates "made the dead central players in the politics of antislavery"; *The Reaper's Garden*, 157. Although the reformers under Brown's analysis focused more on mortality rates than on the direct mistreatment of dead bodies, the point remains pertinent: death was an important trope for the abolitionist message.

40 Vincent Brown, "Spiritual Terror and Sacred Authority in Jamaican Slave Society," *Slavery & Abolition* 24 (2003): 24–53.

spiritual caretaker for the deceased's soul. American colonial courts also used black corpses to deny claims of kinship by refusing to allow bondswomen to bury their husbands after executions.[41]

By the nineteenth century, such practices became less common. One North Carolina planter, for example, received a letter from his overseer in 1816 that expressed concern over the extreme violence a fellow slave manager used against the dead body of a slave. After hanging an enslaved man in the presence of his fellow bondspeople, the slave manager then cut the heart out of the dead man's chest and fed it to a dog.[42] Another overseer, William Capers, also used the body of a dead slave who had committed suicide to threaten the men and women under his rule. The deceased, a young man named London, had chosen to drown himself. Seeking to undermine such acts of self-possession, Capers prohibited London's fellow bondspeople from caring for the body, ordering that the corpse remain in the river where he had drowned. "This I have done," Capers wrote, "to let the negroes see when a negro takes his own life they will be treated in this manner."[43] Capers's cruelty was a deliberate and explicit attempt to strip slaves of their death rites and thus undermine the legitimate claims of kin to provide physical and spiritual custody for their own. London's dead body floated in plain sight of his family and friends, uncared for and left for the oblivion of the water. This was not simply an act of disregard or social control on the part of the slave manager. London's decomposing corpse served as a horrible reminder of the possible reach of slavery's claim on the enslaved.

Although such overt postmortem violence no doubt haunted enslaved people's psyches, the most commonly feared corpse desecration was the autopsy. From the late eighteenth through the early nineteenth century, anatomical research and dissection became increasingly important for the professional training of medical students. Yet most Americans, regardless of race or region, abhorred the notion of having their own body or the body of a loved one mutilated by the anatomist's scalpel under the gaze of eager medical students, and many went to great lengths to protect corpses.[44] Faced with a shortage of dead bodies available for dissection, medical students

[41] Egerton, "A Peculiar Mark of Infamy," 149.

[42] Overseer to Iverson L. Brooks, April 17, 1850, Iverson L. Brooks Papers, Southern Historical Collection.

[43] William Capers to Charles Manigault, June 13, 1860, in *Life and Labor on Argyle Island: Letters and Documents of a Savannah River Rice Plantation, 1833–1867*, ed. James Clifton (Charlottesville: University of Virginia Press, 1978), 300.

[44] Sappol, *A Traffic of Dead Bodies*.

often resorted to grave robbing to procure needed cadavers. Although all graves were in some danger of violation, the graves of the poor, of immigrants, and of African Americans were disproportionately robbed.[45] Grave robbing was so much a concern for African Americans that one antebellum black newspaper even advised its readers how to guard against potential body snatchers: "As soon as the corpse is deposited in the grave, let a truss of long wheaten straw be opened and distributed in layers, as equally as may be with every layer of earth, until the whole is filled up. By this method the corpse will be very effectually secured."[46]

In the Old South, medical colleges worried about the same lack of bodies, yet their students did not always have to resort to digging up their specimens in graveyards. Slaveholders willingly consigned the corpses of their bondspeople to medical researchers, keeping southern medical colleges in regular supply.[47] Slaves did all they could to protect their own from such desecration, but it could be difficult to escape the reach of the dissector's blade. The body of an enslaved Georgia woman almost made it to the grave intact after suffering from intestinal worms. On the evening after her death, however, physician Edward Eve, who had tended to the woman during her illness, intercepted her corpse just before burial at her graveside, cut open the corpse's belly, and removed her stomach for investigation.[48]

Such practices are revealing of the confounding racial ideology at work in the American slave system. On the one hand, the fact that anatomists went searching for clues about the workings of the human body by dissecting black corpses suggests an implicit notion of sameness between races underlying the scientific/medical concepts of the body. Yet, on the other hand, the disproportionate use of black bodies in such research reflects a deep understanding of the perceived social insignificance of black corpses. In cutting and dissecting black corpses, the anatomist denied the cultural practices that made corpses meaningful to slaves.

White men of the slaveholding class did not necessarily view the dissections of slaves' corpses as violence against the dead or as being in conflict with their self-perception of benevolence. Everard Green Baker, a

[45] Ibid.; Todd Savitt, *Race and Medicine in Nineteenth and Early Twentieth-Century America* (Kent, OH: Kent State University Press, 2006); Nudelman, *John Brown's Body.*

[46] *Freedom's Journal*, March 30, 1827.

[47] Savitt, *Race and Medicine*; Steven Stowe, *Doctoring the South: Southern Physicians and Everyday Medicine in the Mid-Nineteenth Century* (Chapel Hill: University of North Carolina Press, 2003), 60.

[48] Paul F. Eve, "An Essay Read before the Medical Society of Augusta, January 10th, 1839," *Southern Medical and Surgical Journal*, March 1839, 329, cited in Fett, *Working Cures*, 241.

small cotton planter in Mississippi, wrote briefly in his farm journal about the death of a young slave girl under his ownership. He did not mention her name, nor did he describe her deathbed scene in any detail. Yet he did make a note of the fact that he was at her side and holding her hand as her "last gasp was taken." He then described the dead girl's skin after death, "moist and warm," and wrote that the young corpse "was opened" revealing a wad of worms in her intestine.[49] Baker apparently experienced no conflict as he shifted his description from an intimate deathbed moment to a discussion of the girl's dissection.

Even when their masters allowed for proper burials, the corpses of the enslaved were still vulnerable in their graves. Although grave robbing was illegal, young doctors hardly worried about prosecution for stealing black bodies from the ground. Yet, in rare cases, the historical record demonstrates that southern courts punished the theft of black bodies, recognizing white ownership over slaves' corpses but, in the process, also enabling slaves' social claims to the bodies of their own brethren. The language from an 1856 court indictment of two grave robbers in Upson County, Georgia, is particularly revealing of white Southerners' complex regard for black corpses. Two men of their mid-twenties – one a doctor, the other a carriage maker – were found guilty and sentenced to pay a fine for digging up the body of an enslaved man named William who had lived under the ownership of Hillard Marby. Marby had pressed charges upon discovering the violation of his slave's grave, and the court fined each accused man twenty dollars plus court costs.[50]

Marby's reasons for pressing charges are unknown to us. Perhaps he was offended by what he perceived as trespassing against his property – the body of his bondsman. William was buried in a public burial ground for African Americans, so Marby's offense could not have been rooted in the trespassing of his land. The court edict supported Marby's claim of ownership in his slave's body, even after death, noting that the accused had taken the body without Marby's consent. Yet the indictment continues to condemn the two men by pointing out that they had "removed the dead body of a human being" but had not obtained consent to take William who "had been the property of Marby while living." "The property of another while living": does such language indicate that the legal status of William's

[49] Diary of Everard Green Baker, August 22, 1850, Southern Historical Collection.

[50] *The State v. Clark W. Upson and Simeon S. Oslin* (May 26, 1856), Criminal Record Book A, 85, Upson County Superior Court, GA, www.files.usgwarchives.net/ga/upson/court/mabry.txt.

body after death was in question? Moreover, the indictment continues by pointing out that the two grave robbers had failed to gain the consent "of the friends of the negro man." Assuming William's friends were fellow slaves, does such language indicate that the bodies of the enslaved, although belonging to another while living, became the domain of black kin upon death?

This question reveals a profound and important ambiguity at the heart of southern law and the culture of slavery. On the one hand, the fact that Marby – a white slaveowner – acted as the plaintiff in this case and was duly rewarded by the court, exemplified the ideological underpinnings of chattel slavery. Yet, on the other hand, the court's reference to the enslaved man's "friends" indicated the possibility that the court may have recognized enslaved people's claims in one another. This recognition of postmortem claiming reflects much more than legal practicalities or accepted death customs. The court's mentioning of the man's "friends" indicated, at the very least, an uncertainty of the reaches of southern slave law. As one historian has argued, the protection of corpses from grave robbers and the dissector's blade in the nineteenth century was marked by profound stratification because the marginalized poor could be designated as "unclaimed" and thus more vulnerable to desecration. Indeed, in instances such as the passage of the British Anatomy Act of 1832, the state went one step further and actually laid claim to the indigent, "unclaimed" poor who died under public care, donating these bodies to medical schools for the purpose of anatomical study.[51] Although nineteenth-century law varied by state in the American setting, by 1860, five states had passed similar statutes in hopes of simultaneously solving the scarcity of bodies for burgeoning medical schools and curtailing the illegal black market in corpses.[52] Thus, when Marby sued over the violation of his slave's grave, he did so in a social and legal context in which only the "unclaimed" were deemed beyond the purview of postmortem protection. The court indicated that, in this instance, the dead body was in fact claimed, albeit by a member of the slaveholding class. Yet, at the same time, the finding suggests that the slave's "friends" might have been accorded that same social power.

At first glance, southern slaveholders' power and authority over the bodies and lives of the enslaved appear nearly all-encompassing in the historical record. Yet by the antebellum period at least some Southerners, including proslavery advocates, were beginning to rethink masters' claims

[51] Ruth Richardson, *Death, Dissection and the Destitute* (London: Penguin Books, 1988).
[52] Sappol, *A Traffic of Dead Bodies*, 4–5.

to their slaves' bodies. Indeed, southern laws and the courts that enforced them struggled not only to determine the scope of slaves' legal personhood, they struggled at least as much to define their bodies as property.[53] What did it mean to claim that one person owned another?

Wary of the political and theological implications of total ownership of human beings, some proslavery advocates began espousing the claim that the body and soul of any person could never be truly owned by another. Responding to the increasingly passionate condemnations of slavery by antebellum abolitionists, southern slaveholders defended their system by claiming to possess a less overt ownership in their slaves.[54] E. N. Elliot, for example, argued in 1860, "The person of the slave is not property ... but the right to his labor is property." Another proslavery writer argued, "We lay no claim to the soul of the slave ... only a right to the labor and lawful obedience of the slave." If the master owned only the labor of a slave, his claim to the slave's body ceased when that body could no longer produce, and the slave's soul was never his to release.

Interestingly, as proslavery advocates attempted to minimize slaveholders' claim to the people they held in bondage, abolitionists emphasized the opposite. The master's property claim in his slaves was complete, body and soul, as William Goodell maintained: "It remains to be observed that this claim of property in slaves ... as carried out into everyday practice ... is manifestly and notoriously a claim, not only to the bodies and physical energies of the slave, but also to his immortal soul." For, without the soul, Goodell pointed out, the body "would be a dead carcass of no value."[55] Although Goodell may have been correct that slaveholders laid claim to much more than the living bodies of their bondspeople, he was wrong that the "dead carcass" of the enslaved held no worth in the eyes of masters.

The bodies of enslaved people were valuable to slaveholders in two distinct ways: as sources of labor and as sources of ideological power. Clearly, the corpse was no longer useful in physical service. However, the dead bodies of the enslaved did continue to serve the ideology of southern patriarchy. Masters who prided themselves on their benevolence offered token gestures of respect or simply acknowledged the living kin's needs to

[53] Thomas D. Morris, *Southern Slavery and the Law, 1619–1860* (Chapel Hill: University of North Carolina Press, 1996), 61–71.

[54] Ibid., 62; E. N. Elliot, *Cotton is King and Proslavery Arguments* (Augusta: Pritchard, Abbott, and Loomis, 1860), vii; Albert Taylor Bledsoe, *An Essay on Liberty and Slavery* (Philadelphia: J. B. Lippincott & Co., 1856), 89.

[55] William Goodell, *The American Slave Code in Theory and Practice* (New York: American and Foreign Anti-Slavery Society, 1853), 41.

care for their own. In this way, the dead slave served the slaveholder's need to fashion his or her own self-image and shape the contours of the daily politics of the master–slave relationship. Conversely, for masters seeking to control their slaves through violence and terror, the black corpse was disposable. The dead body of a slave could no longer produce material wealth, but the ideological profit was still there for the stealing.

6

Nativists and Strangers: Yellow Fever and Immigrant Mortality in Antebellum Charleston, South Carolina

Jeff Strickland

In the wake of the 1858 yellow fever epidemic, Dr. William Hume criticized Charleston's establishment for prioritizing commerce over the lives of immigrants: "It seems to be conceded by one party that the importation of one thousand hogsheads of sugar and molasses, advances the prosperity of the city more than the immigration of one thousand Irish and German candidates for permanent citizenship." Between 1849 and 1858, five epidemics struck the city, and each took a greater toll on immigrant populations than on any other group. For many Charlestonians, that was an acceptable solution to the problems posed by mid-century immigration. "Opinion is divided between the receipt of an annual income from commerce, and a permanent capital from population," Hume continued, "for, in the state of our knowledge, derived from the experience of the past, an increase of population is incompatible with the occasional prevalence of a mortal pestilence." Since yellow fever "destroys those who settle, and deters others from settling," the doctor urged the city to develop public health policies to protect its human resources. Failure to protect *all* Charlestonians, Hume concluded, emanated from Anglo-American Charlestonians' resentment of "petty German traders and Irish laborers [who] supply their places." "Our pride and prejudices are excited against them," he continued, "and it is not uncommon for a native to rejoice at the advent of fever, because he knows that the evil is to be diminished by the funerals of many."[1]

[1] William Hume, "On the introduction, propagation and decline of Yellow Fever in Charleston, during the summer of 1854," *Charleston Medical Journal and Review* 10 (July 1855): 1–2.

Yellow fever was a regular visitor to the Old South, and Charleston had the displeasure of bearing the brunt of yellow fever mortalities, rivaled only by New Orleans and Savannah in death rates. Yellow fever first appeared in Charleston in 1699 or 1700, and its virulence varied over the next century and a half. It returned in 1703 and again in 1728, when the fever killed "an immense number" of whites and some blacks. Fearing the disease, colonial planters refrained from contact with the city, reducing the import of foodstuffs and adding to Charlestonians' misery. Physicians could not successfully treat the disease. Dr. Thomas Simons explained,

> The calamity was so general, that few could grant assistance to their neighbors. So many funerals happening every day, while so many lay sick, white persons sufficient for burying the dead were scarcely to be found. Though they were often interred on the same day that they died, so quick was the putrefaction, so offensive and infectious were the corpses, that even the nearest relations seemed averse from performing the necessary duties.

The fever appeared again in 1732 and 1739, killing ten to twelve people per day at the height of the epidemics, and it reappeared in milder form in 1745 and 1748. There were a few cases in 1753 and 1755, but then a lull for the next four decades. In 1792, the "new era of yellow fever" began, according to Dr. David Ramsay. The disease ravaged Charleston for ten of the next dozen years, particularly striking younger children and immigrant groups. African Americans were not immune, but they often experienced lighter symptoms, as did black and white migrants from the West Indies. The fever appeared again in 1817 and 1819, three more times in the 1820s, and three times again in the 1830s. In 1838, 353 people died, including 281 adult males, 31 adult females, and 28 children.[2]

But the true "new era of yellow fever" occurred between 1849 and 1858, when epidemics brought large-scale mortality to the city. Nearly two thousand people died in the five epidemics, and the two deadliest in 1854 and 1858 accounted for two-thirds of those deaths. European immigrants who settled in Charleston died at higher rates than native white Southerners for a variety of reasons, mostly related to lack of resistance to the disease but also indicative of social class and gender. Irish immigrants accounted for 37.1 percent of the casualties and Germans for 24.1 percent. Of course, the two immigrant groups represented distinct minorities of the total population. In 1850, Irish and Germans comprised 10.5 and

[2] Thomas Y. Simons, "An Essay on the Yellow Fever as it has occurred in Charleston, including its origin and progress up to the present time," *Charleston Medical Journal and Review* 6 (November 1851): 7–9.

6.9 percent of the free population, respectively. Within a decade, the Irish population rose to 12.5 percent, despite the intermittent yellow fever epidemics, and the German population similarly increased to 7.3 percent. In addition to the 1,100 deaths among those two groups, an additional 224 foreign-born persons died of the disease between 1849 and 1858.[3]

Historians have long argued that yellow fever shaped public policy in southern cities, but they tend to focus on the last quarter of the nineteenth century, especially the 1878 epidemic that killed twenty thousand people in the lower Mississippi Valley. Their conclusions center on public health: physicians researched the disease, developed theories about its origins, and served on health boards and committees that made recommendations to city councils regarding quarantine and sanitation policies.[4]

Earlier in the nineteenth century, when authorities lacked understanding about the nature of yellow fever, especially the role of mosquitoes in its transmission, they still sought to enact public health policy – although we would hardly qualify it as such today. Authorities aimed to prevent the disease with a port quarantine that proved ineffective. Their efforts targeted poor, "unclean" immigrants – Irish and German – whom they believed carried the disease, leading to an invidious provincialism and surge in nativism. Not surprisingly, many white Southerners thought yellow fever useful for thinning out immigrant populations, and the Know Nothing Party became particularly active during the deadly epidemics of the 1850s.

By 1849, Charleston was a densely populated southern city, and European immigration was taxing the city's sanitary capacity. Other antebellum cities similarly experienced phenomenal physical and demographic growth that degraded sanitary conditions and increased mortality.

[3] Tim Lockley, "'Like a clap of thunder in a clear sky': differential mortality during Savannah's yellow fever epidemic of 1854," *Social History* 37 (May 2012): 166–86; City of Charleston, Return of Deaths within the City of Charleston, 1819–1926, The Charleston Archive, Charleston County Public Library, Charleston, SC.

[4] Peter McCandless, *Slavery, Disease, and Suffering in the Southern Lowcountry* (New York: Cambridge University Press, 2011); Margaret Humphreys, *Yellow Fever and the South* (New Brunswick: Rutgers University Press, 1992); John H. Ellis, *Yellow Fever & Public Health in the New South* (Lexington: University Press of Kentucky, 1992); Khaled J. Bloom, *The Mississippi Valley's Great Yellow Fever Epidemic of 1878* (Baton Rouge: Louisiana State University Press, 1993); Deanne Nuwer, *Plague among the Magnolias: The 1878 Yellow Fever Epidemic in Mississippi* (Tuscaloosa: University of Alabama Press, 2009); Mariola Espinosa, *Epidemic Invasions: Yellow Fever and the Limits of Cuban Independence, 1878–1930* (Chicago: University of Chicago Press, 2009); Jeanette Keith, *Fever Season: The Story of a Terrifying Epidemic and the People Who Saved a City* (New York: Bloomsbury Press, 2012); M. Foster Farley, *An Account of the History of Stranger's Fever in Charleston, 1699–1876* (Washington: University Press of America, 1978).

Immigration so swelled Boston's inner city, for example, that mortality rates skyrocketed.[5] Charleston, too, experienced a demographic boom so that building construction, including housing, never met demand.

All the while, urban land development and sanitation challenges created new breeding grounds for mosquitoes. Charleston's relatively small peninsula and heavy population density provided a perfect opportunity for mosquitoes to spread yellow fever. The acute viral disease is transmitted by the bite of a female mosquito (*Aedes aegypti*). The victim soon develops symptoms: headaches and fever for about three days and pains in the stomach and upper abdomen, often accompanied by black vomit resembling coffee grounds. With the vomiting comes bleeding from the nose, gums, ears, and even the fingernails. Damage to the gastrointestinal system is so severe that the victim soon begins to vomit venous blood as well. Blood circulation becomes languid, the skin yellows, except along the spinal column where the skin appears blue and mottled. The victim's breathing slows and becomes laborious, interrupted by heavy and deep sighs, and sometimes hiccoughs.[6]

Breeding in the estuaries that lined Charleston harbor and in the rainwater that pooled in streets, backyards, and buckets, mosquitoes began feeding on humans as temperatures reached sixty degrees Fahrenheit. Inevitably, they would find an infected host – a newly arrived sailor or ship passenger, often from Havana. The incubation period lasted four days to two weeks, after which the newly contaminated mosquito began to infect humans who then transmitted the disease back into neighborhoods, sharing their infected blood with previously uninfected mosquitoes that, in turn, infected more humans. During a typical epidemic, mosquitoes initially spread yellow fever along the docks and wharves on the Cooper River. Within a couple of weeks, Charleston residents living along the river fell ill. Everyone who visited the docks became a potential victim, and they returned to their own neighborhoods, infecting mosquitoes there. At this stage, yellow fever infections reached epidemic levels.[7]

5 Richard A. Meckel, "Immigration, Mortality, and Population Growth in Boston, 1840–1880," *Journal of Interdisciplinary History* 15 (winter 1985): 395, 397, 413.

6 Simons, "Essay on the Yellow Fever," 796; Henry R. Frost, "Review of the Weather and Diseases of the two preceding years. Reported to the Medical Society of South Carolina at the anniversary of the same," *Charleston Medical Journal and Review* 10 (January 1855): 53–54.

7 K. David Patterson, "Yellow Fever Epidemics and Mortality in the United States, 1693–1905," *Social Science & Medicine* 34 (August 1992): 855–65; J. J. Chisolm, "A brief Sketch of the Epidemic Yellow Fever of 1854, in Charleston," *Charleston Medical Journal and Review* 10 (November 1855): 434.

Because mosquitoes were present every summer and the yellow fever was not, however, nobody realized that the insects carried the disease. Resident Charlestonians instead related yellow fever epidemics to heavy summer rains, and those who could afford to do so fled the city immediately following torrential downpours. Physician Henry R. Frost wrote in his notebook on June 25, 1854, that the number of mosquitoes was greater than he had ever seen. But it was another six weeks before cases of yellow fever began to be reported. In his documentation of heavy immigrant mortality that year, Dr. D. J. Cain dismissed the mosquitoes as a contributing factor: "Prominent among the exciting causes of the disease were a wetting by rain and sleeping in the open air, either under an awning, or without any covering overhead. Almost all who were seized on shipboard stated, that on account of the heat and the mosquitoes in the cabin, they slept on the decks of their respective vessels, some under an awning, others without covering." At the height of the 1858 epidemic, George A. Gordon noted how "Mosquitoes are very troublesome, just now," but he did not make the connection.[8]

Complicating matters, physicians found it difficult to diagnose yellow fever because the symptoms resembled those of scarlet and other fevers and of hepatitis. Some believed that other types of fever presented themselves alongside yellow fever, including typhus and typhoid, and bilious remittent and bilious intermittent fevers. They relied on a standard treatment program for yellow fever: blistering the epigastrium, calomel (mercury chloride), and saline cathartics. Unaware of its toxicity, they prescribed mercury chloride to stimulate salivation and bowel movements. They also tried lead acetate and opium, castor oil, brandy toddies, and chicken or beef stock. In some cases, they applied mustard plasters if the extremities were cold, used leeches to bleed the head and spine, and employed cold affusion and warm baths. Dr. Simons supplemented his treatments with Seneca snakeroot, which was believed to help with the flow of blood. Dr. Cain prescribed calomel, sometimes combining it with rhubarb, followed by Epsom salts or castor oil. He also plied his patients with opium to induce sleep, ice pellets and ice water, beef tea, chicken and veal broths, milk, and sometimes one or two tablespoons of brandy. If the patient survived the

[8] Frost, "Review of the Weather and Diseases," 50; D. J. Cain, *History of the Epidemic Yellow Fever in Charleston, South Carolina in 1854* (Charleston: T. K. & P. G. Collins, 1856), 14; George A. Gordon to Krilla, October 11, 1858, Gordon Papers, David M. Rubenstein Rare Book & Manuscript Library, Duke University, Durham, NC.

most virulent form of yellow fever, a full recovery took as long as six months.[9]

Yellow fever was a terrible way to die, and nearly everyone feared it. Native-born white Charlestonians were less likely to die from the disease than were immigrants from the North and Europe, and they were well aware of that fact. Between 1849 and 1858, 1,954 people died from the disease, only 363 of whom were native-born white Southerners. Yet, a correspondent for the *Christian Inquirer* described the anxiety natives and immigrants felt about yellow fever: "In the fall, it is death to sleep without the city of Charleston .... The stranger's fever is a dreadful disease; after a few days of violent fever, the patient will suddenly feel himself entirely relieved, feel strong, wish to be dressed, to go out, to eat; and, in half a day – be a dead man! Nothing is so much dreaded as this sudden appearance of convalescence."[10]

The very wealthiest abandoned Charleston altogether in July and August, choosing to summer in New York City or Europe. They returned to their plantations for the December holidays and went to Charleston for the theater season in February. In March, they again returned to their plantations until April, spent a month in Charleston, and then left. A few planters, however, dared the disease, spending summers in Charleston because it was "perfectly safe, oftentimes, to dwell in the city, when Death is knocking with dreadful riot at all its gates." In 1854, Edward Barnwell wrote how "I am not apprehensive of taking it, although I take some few precautions." H. Barton wrote from Augusta, Georgia: "Our city has been in a dreadful state of excitement for some days in consequence of a few cases of fever, the nature of which is a matter of dispute with the medical men. There is no cause for alarm."[11] See Figure 6.

For most, however, the yellow fever was the "king of terrors." In late September 1854, A. S. Gibbes wrote his son James, "The City has been most sickly, you hear of one theme alone – yellow fever and Broke bone which often terminates in yellow fever. The prevailing epidemic but as

[9] Lockley, "'Like a clap of thunder in a clear sky,'" 167–68; Cain, *Yellow Fever*, 16, 17, 19; Benjamin Rush, *An Account of the Bilious Remitting and Intermitting Yellow Fever, as it appeared in Philadelphia, in the Year 1794* (Philadelphia: Thomas Dobson Benjamin Rush, 1796); Hayne, "Notes on Yellow Fever of 1849," 342, 347, 349, 356; Simons, "Essay on Yellow Fever," 29.

[10] *Christian Inquirer*, January 9, 1847.

[11] Ibid.; Edward Barnwell to William H. W. Barnwell, September 1, 1854, Lowcountry Digital Library, lowcountrydigital.library.cofc.edu; H. Barton to Ziba B. Oakes, September 18, 1854, Ziba B. Oakes Papers, MS Am. 322, Rare Books and Manuscripts Department, Boston Public Library.

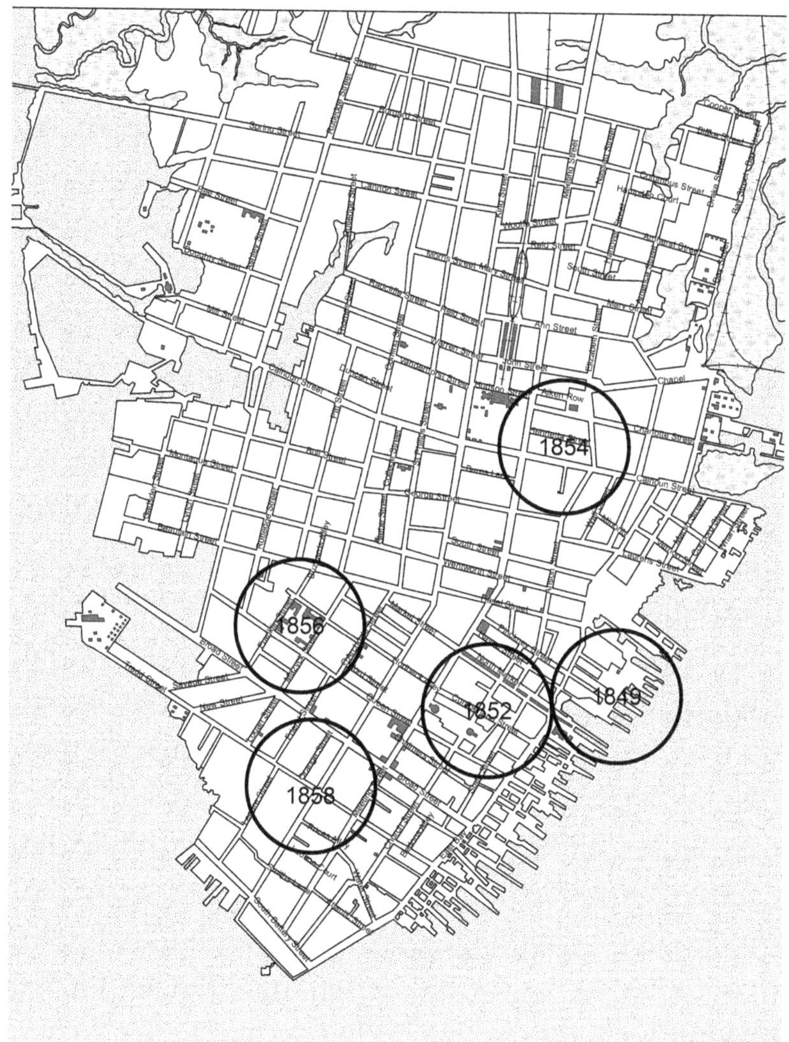

FIGURE 6. Between 1849 and 1858, 1,954 Charlestonians died from yellow fever, with each epidemic centered in a different neighborhood.
Source: Map prepared by and in possession of the author.

melancholy as it is here, what an awful state has Savannah been in from the commencement of the disease until now." Two weeks later, in October 1854, Gibbes informed his son that a number of their family friends had died: Sam Prioleau, Jefferson Bennett's wife and son, George Beese's child, Rutledge Parker's three-day-old son, and Arthur Holmes's daughter (despite that she lived adjacent to the Battery, which was considered a haven from yellow fever cases). "Alas! How many hearts have mourned," Gibbes lamented, "how many houses have become desolate by this terrible fever. Hundreds have hurried into eternity – unprepared for their changed living in open rebellion against their maker and regardless of that doom which the bible tells us awaits every unrepentant sinner." He recommended that his son remain in New York a couple more weeks until the epidemic ebbed.[12]

On November 6, 1854, John F. Blacklock wrote his nephew that he had been preoccupied with "business and looking after sick friends." "We have had a sad time of it here this summer as scarcely a family has escaped without the loss of some member of it and nearly all that have been fortunate enough to escape loss have been visited with great sickness." He speculated that it was not yellow fever but a violent bilious fever that had subsided with the onset of cold weather. His children had gone to New York for the summer and were waiting out the epidemic before returning. His wife and niece had spent the summer in Summerville, just outside Charleston, without incident. Four years later, Blacklock again wrote on yellow fever, this time from Aiken where his children dealt with other diseases: all three daughters suffered from whooping cough, and one also contracted a chill and fever. He wanted to take them to visit a doctor in Summerville but heard of two cases of yellow fever there. Blacklock determined, "the Fever seems to have been more malignant than usual. I am glad that William has escaped it and think the slight attack which he had early in the summer must have prevented a more serious one."[13]

Local physicians debated the origins of the disease, primarily whether it was imported from other ports or endemic to the city, and the majority of them concluded it was "liable to occur from a peculiar state of the atmosphere" and "not introduced by contagion or infection." Still, municipal authorities enacted quarantine regulations that functioned "efficiently without injuring commerce." Because many yellow fever victims became ill after they arrived at port, however, quarantines were not very effective.[14] Yellow fever's appearance in Charleston typically coincided with its arrival at other ports, like Savannah, leading to suspicions that the disease was related to the environment. Few physicians believed the disease was

[12] A. S. Gibbes to James Gibbes, September 25 and October 9, 1854, Gibbes Papers, David M. Rubenstein Rare Book & Manuscript Library.

[13] John F. Blacklock to Elizabeth Boyle, November 6, 1854 and October 19, 1858, Gadsden Family Papers, 1703–ca. 1955, South Carolina Historical Society, Charleston.

[14] Thomas Y. Simons, *A Report on the History and Causes of the Strangers or Yellow Fever of Charleston: Read Before the Board of Health* (Charleston: W. Riley, 1839), 16, 17.

contagious because most people who came in contact with yellow fever patients did not contract it. The few who did become ill – nurses, family members, and friends – were categorized by physicians as victims of sanitary, constitutional, and atmospheric conditions.

Still, physicians sought ways to minimize yellow fever's impact. Dr. Thomas Y. Simons of Charleston and a member of its city council promoted a "wise system of medical police" that included washing of docks, cleaning of drains in winter, and removing scavengers' offal. He also encouraged keeping streets and yards clean, draining and filling low lots, ensuring cellars were dry and properly ventilated, the prohibition of future cellars, burying dead outside of the city, and providing a plentiful supply of fresh water. The city council created a drainage system, filled up low-lying lots, required cellars be watertight or closed up, and prohibited future cellars, thus reducing the accumulation of water lying in low spots or cellars. Simons assumed the chairmanship of the Board of Health, which was empowered to enforce the new laws. Less formally, Simons tried to protect populations particularly susceptible to yellow fever: "the greater proportion of those who sickened and died were Irish laborers, and I regard it as an important system of medical police to avoid employing such as are unacclimated in the summer, exposing them to all the exciting causes of disease, and some effort should be made to prevent emigrants being brought to the city in the summer months."[15]

Yellow fever also threatened people legally defined as property. Charleston was an urban slave society, and when slaves died of yellow fever, the monetary losses inspired slaveholding elite to support public health measures. Still, in comparison to other populations, African Americans died in fewer numbers as a result of yellow fever. One possible factor in low African American mortality was that slaveowners hired private physicians to protect their slave property. Typically, patients with physician care recovered much more often than did patients who ended up in hospitals.[16]

Instead, it was disruption to the slave trade that frustrated planters most. In September 1854, slave broker A. J. McElvine notified slave trader Ziba B. Oakes that he had purchased a fourteen-year-old male slave but refused to send him on to Charleston because of the yellow fever. William Wright complained to Oakes from Savannah in August 1854 that "on

[15] Ibid., 22; Chisolm, "A brief Sketch of the Epidemic Yellow Fever of 1854," 172; Simons, "Essay on the Yellow Fever," 186.

[16] Simons, "Essay on the Yellow Fever," 10; idem, *Yellow Fever*, 14; Kenneth F. Kiple and Virginia H. Kiple, "Black Yellow Fever Immunities, Innate and Acquired, as Revealed in the American South," *Social Science History* 1 (summer 1977): 419–36.

account of the prevalence of yellow fever in this city business of all kinds has become entirely stagnant and in consequence of which I have been unable to close sale of woman Nelly [and] now am at a loss to say when business will again become what it usually was not until cold weather I presume." In October 1856, J. A. Bitting wrote Oakes, "I would like to buy a few negroes in your market. We hear bad account of Yellow Fever. You will please inform me what the chance is at present to buy boys and girls and also whither much danger from fever." In early August 1856, John Cox notified Oakes that his friend General G. N. Pillow wanted to purchase a few slave girls and that Cox had recommended he purchase them through Oakes. One month later, Pillow wrote Oakes, "I have purchased a lot of girls here of a trader who purchased them in the Richmond market. After the receipt of your former letter announcing the appearance of Yellow Fever in your City, I abandoned all idea of being able to do anything in your market the present season, and consequently do not now wish to make any further investments."[17]

In contrast to African Americans' higher rate of survival against yellow fever, what became very apparent to physicians and other observers was immigrants' greater susceptibility to the disease. In 1838, a fire had burned one-third of Charleston, and by summer, municipal authorities had not yet removed the debris. Some observers called for the debris to be burned, hoping a more sanitary environment would decrease the intensity of the fever (unaware that the smoke would reduce the influence of mosquitoes). Hundreds of immigrant workers arrived in Charleston to remove the debris. At night, they either slept outside or crammed into small living quarters. When yellow fever struck that summer, 281 male immigrants and 30 female immigrants died.[18] In 1838, as in all the yellow fever epidemics of the mid-nineteenth century, immigrants bore the brunt of mortality, and as immigration increased so did the mortality figures.

Unlike wealthy white Southerners who had the luxury of avoiding Charleston in order to protect their slave investments (and the African Americans who benefitted from such decisions), European immigrants had far fewer choices, often arriving on Charleston's docks while the fever raged. The mid-nineteenth-century United States drew thousands of European immigrants, with most settling in the Northeast and Midwest. For those

[17] A. J. McElvain to Ziba B. Oakes, September 18, 1854; William Wright to Ziba B. Oakes, August 30, 1854; J. A. Bitting to Ziba B. Oakes, October 25, 1856; John Cox to Ziba B. Oakes, August 7, 1856; Ged J. Pillow to Ziba B. Oakes, September 10, 1856, all in Ziba B. Oakes Papers.

[18] Simons, *Yellow Fever*, 8.

who elected to reside in the South, the immigrant experience differed in two significant ways: large-scale interaction with slaves and death from yellow fever.[19]

German and Irish immigrants began settling in large numbers in Charleston during the late 1840s, and the pace accelerated during the 1850s, ceasing only when the Civil War erupted. German immigrants worked in skilled occupations, operated wholesale grocery firms, owned retail grocers, and sometimes served as petty traders. Many operated retail groceries called "Dutch corner shops" that kept small stocks and made modest revenue from illegal liquor sales to slaves and free blacks. Although a few Irish immigrants owned successful businesses, the Irish mainly served as laborers and semi-skilled workers, often competing directly with free and enslaved African Americans for work.[20] Relations between Irish and African Americans were generally more hostile than those between Germans and black Southerners.

Many immigrants had not been socialized to racism, and they were slow to react to the norms of southern society, especially as racial lines hardened in the late antebellum era. Social and economic interaction between German and Irish immigrants and African Americans clouded racial lines, as petty traders dealt with slaves and free blacks and as Irish laborers worked alongside slaves. And neither Germans nor Irish had the means to purchases many slaves.[21]

Native-born white Southerners had long blamed yellow fever on immigrants. The editor of the *Southern Quarterly Review* argued, "It is the introduction of these strangers among us, that brings Yellow Fever. If we had no strangers, there would be no such disease." Many white Southerners opposed immigration, especially the influx of impoverished laborers

[19] John Duffy, "Yellow Fever in the Continental United States during the Nineteenth Century," *Bulletin of the New York Academy of Medicine* 44 (June 1968): 687–701.

[20] Ira Berlin and Herbert G. Gutman, "Natives and Immigrants, Free Men and Slaves: Urban Workingmen in the Antebellum American South," *American Historical Review* 88 (December 1983): 1175–1200; Dennis C. Rousey, "Aliens in the WASP Nest: Ethnocultural Diversity in the Antebellum Urban South," *Journal of American History* 79 (June 1992): 152–64.

[21] Ira Berlin, *Slaves Without Masters: The Free Negro in the Antebellum South* (New York: New Press, 2007); Richard C. Wade, *Slavery in the Cities: The South, 1820–1860* (New York: Oxford University Press, 1964); Jeff Strickland. "How the Germans Became White Southerners: German Immigrants and African Americans in Charleston, South Carolina, 1860–1880," *Journal of American Ethnic History* 28 (fall 2008): 52–69; James Oliver Horton, *Free People of Color: Inside the African American Community* (Washington: Smithsonian Institution Press. 1993); Edna Bonacich, "A Theory of Middleman Minorities," *American Sociological Review* 38 (October 1973): 583–94.

who supplanted black workers: "We are losing a valuable, manageable, and healthy population, for one, in every sense, the reverse. We see the submissive, acclimated, non-voting negro pushed aside by the turbulent, feverish, naturalized foreigner. These men come among us with habits adapted to far different climates, and constitutions prone to every febrile disease." Immigrant funerals that took place during the epidemics drew the ire of white Southerners who condemned the "constant scenes of revelry and drunkenness" that accompanied wakes and internments. Intoxicated, grief-stricken men and women lined the road to Magnolia Cemetery, and the excessive drinking continued into the night, filling the streets with drunks. Adopting nativist rhetoric and scapegoating immigrants, many whites blamed them for the renewed presence of yellow fever. The American Party or Know Nothings enjoyed considerable political success in the city during the decade.[22]

Yellow fever mortality rates for German and Irish immigrants were notably high. Between 1849 and 1871, 2,343 people in Charleston died from yellow fever, 24 percent of whom were German and 33 percent of whom were Irish. So, half of all deaths were immigrants. More importantly, the high death rates eroded the stability of immigrant communities. Immigrants tended to settle in Charleston's lower wards, especially the first and third wards, closest to the wharves. Crowding into the first and third wards, immigrants lived in densely populated neighborhoods with degraded sanitary conditions. Additionally, immigrants' immune systems were ill-prepared for the disease because they had not been "seasoned." When yellow fever struck, then, conditions were ripe for catastrophe. Between 1849 and 1858, yellow fever's toll was heavy, reducing German immigrant populations by 23 percent and Irish immigrant populations by 24 percent.[23]

22 "Yellow Fever in Charleston," 142–43, 144, 152; Tyler Anbinder, *Nativism and Slavery: The Northern Know Nothings and the Politics of the 1850's* (New York: Oxford University Press, 1992); W. Darrell Overdyke, *The Know-Nothing Party in the South* (Baton Rouge: Louisiana State University Press, 1950). On earlier Southerners' attitudes toward yellow fever, see McCandless, *Slavery, Disease, and Suffering in the Southern Lowcountry*, 105–11.

23 McCandless, *Slavery, Disease, and Suffering in the Southern Lowcounty*, 113–18; Meckel, "Immigration, Mortality, and Population Growth in Boston," 395, 397, 413; Gerald N. Grob, *The Deadly Truth: A History of Disease in America* (Cambridge: Harvard University Press, 2002); Philip D. Curtin, *Death by Migration: Europe's Encounter with the Tropical World in the Nineteenth Century* (New York: Cambridge University Press, 1989); City of Charleston, Return of Deaths within the City of Charleston, 1819–1926, the Charleston Archive.

Ironically, some public health initiatives put immigrants' lives in even greater jeopardy. Upon arrival, Irish immigrants sought whatever jobs they could find, and white Charlestonians often preferred to hire Irish laborers during yellow fever season rather than risk slaves. So, in 1849, when the city council embarked on a variety of public works projects of "extensive and deep excavations" aimed at draining marshland and improving the sewage system, they turned to Irish laborers to dig sewage drains on Hasel and Market Streets between Church Street and the wharf. This put the immigrants at the epicenter of a yellow fever epidemic that took 208 lives, including ninety-five Irish and forty-four Germans. Only thirty-three native white South Carolinians died, including a mere two from Charleston. Because the excavation of raw sewage coincided with the appearance of yellow fever, health officials speculated that the disease had come out of the ground. Dr. John Porter explained how "Every street in the vicinity or near Union wharves was in a shocking state of sanitary police .... All of these streets were very unhealthy ... Linguard Street was ravaged by the fever, and the physicians who had a large amount of practice in this street during the epidemic, regard the extensive excavations as being the main cause of its malignity." "For a stranger to have slept in any of these streets, during the summer of 1849, would have been at the peril of his life," Porter concluded.[24]

Dr. A. P. Hayne, the almshouse physician, treated yellow fever victims and conducted autopsies on the dead during the summer of 1849. His first case arrived on August 25. He treated fifty-three patients, twenty-three of whom died. Hayne attributed the high mortality rate to ill patients usually of low socioeconomic status who waited until the third or fourth day of infection to seek medical attention because they could not afford a doctor and hoped the illness would pass. Poverty, vice, and intemperance, Hayne concluded, "offered but a sad and discouraging field to the labors of the physician."[25] It was not just male laborers who became victims. Three female prostitutes died of yellow fever in the almshouse; each lived among the bars and sailors' boarding homes adjacent to the wharves where the epidemic originated.

[24] John B. Porter, "On the Climate and Salubrity of Port Moultrie and Sullivan's Island," *American Journal of the Medical Sciences* 60 (January 1855): 60; idem, "On the Climate of Salubrity of Fort Moultrie and Sullivan's Island," *American Journal of the Medical Science* 27 (January 1855): 29, 57; Simons, "Essay on the Yellow Fever," 10, 782.

[25] A. P. Hayne, "Notes on Yellow Fever, as it prevailed in Charleston during the summer of 1849," *Charleston Medical Journal and Review* 5 (March 1850): 340, 341.

Dr. Hayne's treatment of Alice Leroy, a twenty-four-year old Irish woman and the second person to die of the disease at the almshouse, evidences the typical yellow fever case. Leroy complained of pains in the upper abdomen, back, and extremities, especially her calves. She also suffered from an intense headache and irritated stomach. Other symptoms included red eyes and face, flushed cheeks, a dejected countenance, and a rapid pulse (ninety beats per minute). Her tongue had redness along the edges and the center was covered with a light brown film. She had not vomited, but her bowels were costive and irregular. She continued to drink alcohol as her own medicinal response, but Hayne prescribed blistering the abdomen, saline cathartics, and calomel (mercury chloride) to stimulate salivation and bowel movements. Hayne believed his treatment had improved Leroy's condition until evening, when her extremities became cold, and her face and neck turned yellow, dark, and blotted. Then her gums began to bleed. Hayne used stimulants, a warm bath, and injections but nothing worked, and she died on September 14, only one week into the infection and just two and a half days after her admission to the hospital. Her stomach contained black vomit – the tell-tale "dark coffee grounds" fluid.[26]

Hayne similarly treated other patients. Ellen Weims, a prostitute from New York, had been living in the city for ten months. Hayne ordered a shower bath, a blister to her abdomen to be dressed with mercurial ointment, and small doses of calomel, opium, and acetate of lead every two hours. On the seventh day of infection, she died in a delirious state with yellow skin, cold extremities, and unable to urinate. Peter Mayorick was a thirty-year-old Italian who had lived in the city for ten months. Mayorick sold plaster figures for a living. His symptoms included intense pain and tenderness over the epigastric region; pain in the back, loins, and extremities; headaches; and an uneasy feeling in the pit of his stomach. He had a distressed countenance, and his face was flushed and his eyes red and watery. He had been sick three days before arriving at the almshouse, and he vomited just before Hayne examined him. Hayne prescribed one powder of acetate of lead and opium every two hours, a blister to the epigastric region, and weak brandy toddy at intervals. The next day, Mayorick had a weak pulse and cold extremities. His skin was yellow, and he could not speak. Mayorick died on September 23, a week after he first became ill. Hayne also treated John Dugan, a forty-three-year old Irish immigrant and member of the City Guard who had been living in Charleston for seven years. Hayne prescribed calomel and castor oil, and Dugan seemed to

[26] Hayne, "Notes on Yellow Fever," 342.

improve for a couple of days before declining rapidly and dying with the usual symptoms of yellow skin and cold extremities.[27]

In 1852, yellow fever again visited Charleston, striking an area bordered by Market Street on the north, the wharves on the east, Queen Street on the south, and Meeting Street on the west, with a few cases along King Street. The Irish population had grown since 1849, and a large number had only lived in Charleston for less than two months, having not spent a single summer in the city. Even during the 1852 epidemic, four to five hundred additional immigrants arrived in Charleston, unchecked by unsympathetic public health officials. The city, once again, had embarked on a variety of public works projects aimed at improving the sewers and draining inundated land, priming the environment for a yellow fever epidemic. Irish immigrants were employed on those projects, with devastating consequences. "Destitute of means," Dr. John Porter recalled, the Irish "were compelled to do laborious work, such as excavating the earth, paving the streets, &c., and having miserable accommodations. At the new custom house, a great number of Irishmen were employed in excavating the earth and piling, of whom a great many were taken sick and died." Irish laborers were exposed to infected mosquitoes day and night, and they had not built up any antibodies to fight the disease. Porter identified a variety of factors that spread yellow fever in immigrant populations: intemperance among immigrants, fatigue and exposure among laborers, bad ventilation in places where immigrants lived, high temperature, humidity, defective drainage, poor sanitary conditions, bad water, and heavy rains. The results were catastrophic, claiming 267 lives, half of whom were Irish.[28]

In 1854, two sailors died of yellow fever on the ship *Aquatic* en route to Charleston from Havana. When the ship docked at Union Wharf on July 21 with hogsheads of molasses, the stevedore employed African Americans to work in the cargo hold and Irish immigrants to work above deck, believing that the fever was contained below decks. When the Irish laborers asked the Customs House officer why he had not boarded the ship as usual, he replied that yellow fever was aboard and he preferred to remain on the wharf. The stevedore replied, "And, by jabbers, is it Yellow Fever that's aboard this vessel, and divil a turn more will we give the windlass." The

[27] Ibid., 344, 347, 482.

[28] Porter, "On the Climate and Salubrity of Port Moultrie and Sullivan's Island," 60: 391–99; idem, "On the Climate and Salubrity of Port Moultrie and Sullivan's Island," *American Journal of the Medical Sciences* 38 (July 1854): 341–66; "Yellow Fever in Charleston," *Southern Quarterly Review* 7 (January 1853): 151; City of Charleston, Return of Deaths within the City of Charleston, 1819–1926.

Irish laborers demanded higher wages in lieu of the greater risk. After the ship's hold had been emptied, the stevedore descended into the cargo hold, accompanied by M. Garvey and McLean, and they washed it out with a fire hose. On August 12, Garvey died of yellow fever at a house in Pinckney Street. Yellow fever quickly spread through the neighborhood bounded by Tradd Street to the south, Wentworth to the north, King to the west, and the harbor to the east. It extended as well to Calhoun and Franklin Street, a low and damp street that had recently been reclaimed and was crowded with laboring foreign populations. Within a month, the fever extended beyond the old confines, however, spreading along the freshets of the Cooper and Ashley Rivers where fresh water collided with salt water. A number of fatalities on Franklin Street followed, including an Irish woman and her infant daughter. The Marine Hospital and city jail became hotbeds of the fever, as well as the streets surrounding Citadel Square.[29]

Yellow fever epidemics could be particularly tragic for women, many of whom did not have the means to escape the disease. Margaret Sage, an Irish immigrant, died in Tradd Street on August 16, 1854. She had worked as a nurse for a family that lived on East Bay Street, opposite Commercial Wharf. Mrs. Gorman, an Irish woman on Calhoun Street, fell ill on August 15. That afternoon, her friend Ann Corran from Mill Street, found Gorman without assistance and remained to nurse her. Three days later, Gorman died, and Corran prepared her for the wake. After attending her friend's funeral, Corran returned to Mill Street and died of yellow fever on September 3. Corran's two-year-old daughter fell ill on September 17 and died throwing up black vomit three days later. On September 8, a violent storm that lasted three days left low parts of Charleston submerged, a perfect breeding environment for mosquitoes. Within one week, another 129 people died.[30]

One physician estimated that during the 1854 epidemic 20,000–25,000 people had caught the fever – one out of every two residents – and 627 people had died, including 256 Irish, 131 Germans, and 78 other European and West Indian immigrants. As a testament to the advantages of being "seasoned," only forty-three native white Charlestonians and only five native black Charlestonians died. Dr. D. J. Cain determined that many

[29] Chisolm, "A brief Sketch of the Epidemic Yellow Fever of 1854," 436; Cain, *Yellow Fever*, 8, 22–23; William Hume, "On the introduction, propagation and decline of Yellow Fever in Charleston, during the summer of 1854," *Charleston Medical Journal and Review* 10 (January 1855): 6–8, 22.

[30] Lockley, "'Like a clap of thunder in a clear sky,'" 170–71; Hume, "On the introduction, propagation and decline of Yellow Fever," 6, 8, 24; Cain, *Yellow Fever*, 3–7, 32.

Charlestonians had remained in the city that summer and risked exposure. The community was not panic stricken: the banks continued operations, shops remained open, and people walked the streets. Those Charlestonians who did flee went to Columbia where fires burned to keep the disease away. Dr. Frost wrote, "Thus passed two months of the most trying scenes ever witnessed in this city. The physicians have been kept busiest, some of them to sickness – nurses have been in the utmost requisition – the city in the greatest agitation. Parents, in many instances, lamenting the loss of some favourite child, husbands or wives – friendship's ties abruptly severed."[31]

Although Americans lacked scientific knowledge of bacteriology, municipal governments like that of Charleston claimed the authority to deal with epidemics. Certainly, most victims who could afford to hire a physician early in their illnesses certainly did so. The best option for poor Charlestonians was Roper Hospital, funded through the city council and private philanthropy. In 1854, physician William T. Wragg treated 254 yellow fever patients at Roper Hospital, including 131 Irish and 51 Germans, most of whom had been living in Charleston for less than a year.[32]

Following the epidemic of 1854, public health experts, primarily the physicians who served on the local boards of health and treated victims of the terrible disease, debated whether yellow fever emanated from local sanitary conditions or foreign ports. There was considerable deliberation over whether yellow fever was a contagious disease or not and whether it was brought to Charleston from the West Indies or endemic. Contagionists favored a port quarantine that would keep the disease from arriving seasonally. Noncontagionists believed that yellow fever originated locally and from a particular circumstance of soil and climate. They were primarily concerned with improving sanitary conditions and eliminating pools of standing water in cellars and low-lying areas.[33]

31 Cain, *Yellow Fever*, 8–10; Chisolm, "A brief Sketch of the Epidemic Yellow Fever of 1854," 43; Frost, "Review of the Weather and Diseases," 53–54, 56; *Baltimore Sun*, September 26, 1854; William T. Wragg, "Report on closing the Roper Hospital after the Yellow Fever Epidemic of 1854," *Charleston Medical Journal and Review* 10 (January 1855): 67–68.

32 Meckel, "Immigration, Mortality, and Population Growth in Boston," 404; William J. Novak, *The People's Welfare: Law and Regulation in Nineteenth-Century America* (Chapel Hill: University of North Carolina Press, 1996), 191–234; Wragg, "Report on closing the Roper Hospital," 67–68; Chisolm, "A brief Sketch of the Epidemic Yellow Fever of 1854," 438.

33 Hume, "On the introduction, propagation and decline of Yellow Fever," 33; Porter, "On the Climate and Salubrity of Port Moultrie and Sullivan's Island," 29–30; Chisolm, "A brief Sketch of the Epidemic Yellow Fever of 1854," 28.

In response to concerns that wetlands produced yellow fever, officials began the "modern process" of filling up marsh lots with carrion and garbage. But J. J. Chisolm, a noncontagionist, believed that the process of filling such areas and inhibiting drainage actually contributed to yellow fever outbreaks. For example, several yellow fever cases had occurred in a square on Calhoun Street, bounded by Meeting, Elizabeth, and Henrietta Streets. Irish families occupied this particular unsanitary area of the city. The lots were "very low and boggy," and water stagnated on them because the streets were higher than the lots, hindering drainage. Chisolm identified a second area bounded by East Bay, Laurens, and Calhoun Streets and the river. In this section, there were numerous low unoccupied lots, covered with water at spring tides, and partially filled up with decomposing vegetable matter and other garbage. A third section was the city's western portion, a mud flat recently reclaimed from the river, which was being filled up with the city's garbage and offal from the streets.[34] By 1856, Charleston had both a quarantine policy and had begun instituting sanitation measures for low-lying areas.

The epidemic of 1856 was less intense but most ironic because it began on the quarantine docks. John Abbott arrived from Havana on the *St. Andrew* on July 8. By July 27, he was ill and sent to Sullivan Island in Charleston harbor, which served as a lazaretto. Within two weeks, he was joined by Michael Denning, a laborer who had helped to unload the bark *Industria* at the quarantine docks. The bark had arrived from Cuba on July 13 with several ill sailors. Between May 2 and September 6, only 41 of 105 arriving ships were allowed to come to port after inspection by the port physician. Another twenty-nine came into the city after the cargos and vessels were disinfected. But the efforts were insufficient: twenty-three sailors and passengers were quarantined for yellow fever at the lazaretto.[35]

The 1858 epidemic killed more people than any other outbreak in Charleston's history, and native-born whites expressed little sympathy for the immigrants who died. The disease took 715 people, including 202 Germans and 188 Irish. Public health officials boldly acted on their nativist impulses, relocating Irish immigrants from their homes to a quarantine ship anchored offshore. George A. Gordon, editor for the *Courier*, wrote his fiancée that when several Irish immigrants died in a house

34 Wragg, "Report on closing the Roper Hospital," 68; Chisolm, "A brief Sketch of the Epidemic Yellow Fever of 1854," 28.

35 William T. Wragg, William Hume, and James M. Eason, *Report of the Committee on Health and Drainage on the Origin and Diffusion of Yellow Fever in Charleston in the Autumn of 1856: To the City Council of Charleston* (Charleston: A. E. Miller, 1856), 3, 4, 6.

on Tradd Street, "the authorities bundled off the whole family to the Quarantine, whitewashed and thoroughly renovated the establishment. Since which no case has occurred within the city limits. It made a stampede of the Irish population and crowded the steerage of the *Columbia*. No general alarm was felt." The quarantine seemed to slow yellow fever's progress through the city, at least until it "broke out among the German population, and has thus far, except one or two Irish policemen, kept entirely among the Germans." Gordon continued, "I account for this from their frequent visitings and familiar intercourse with each other. Not a Dutchman could be sick, but he would have crowds of his countrymen to see him, and the consequence has been that cases are scattered all over the city."[36]

After a series of heavy rains in early July 1858, authorities prepared for the possibility of a greater outbreak. The mayor required all building owners to drain their cellars. Summer heat also accelerated decomposition of garbage and offal, and the rotten odor seemed to confirm everyone's fears. The mayor required all city residents to leave their garbage at the curb every morning, except on Sundays. Moreover, residents were to keep the streets and gutters in front of their buildings clean. The penalty for neglecting either requirement was a two-dollar fine and five dollars each time thereafter. In early August, a local minister having just returned from the country requested the mayor to lift the quarantine because it reflected poorly upon the city, but the mayor refused, arguing that it might lead to more deaths. It did not matter: the fever soon became an epidemic.[37]

In mid-August, editors at the *Courier* did not believe there was reason for concern, asserting that only one death had been reported the previous week. Although there had been ten or twelve deaths from yellow fever since July 18, the *Mercury* pronounced the victims "entirely among the poor of recent migration." There was no yellow fever at the Marine Hospital or at the docks. Strangely, however, the *Augusta Dispatch* reported sixteen cases of yellow fever in Charleston and the deaths of five of seven patients who had been admitted to Roper Hospital, even as the *Courier* continued to deny yellow fever's presence. Instead, the *Courier* dismissed the few deaths: "To any one acquainted with the habits and circumstances of the class of population furnishes the cases admitted to the Roper Hospital, it need not

[36] Hume, "On the introduction, propagation and decline of Yellow Fever," 11–12; *Charleston Mercury*, July 31, 1858; George A. Gordon to Krilla, July 27, 1858; George A. Gordon to Krilla, August 18, 1858, both in Gordon Papers.

[37] (Charleston) *Courier*, July 10, 1858; Hume, "On the introduction, propagation and decline of Yellow Fever," 11–12.

be stated that the relative mortality in such cases is no criterion whatever of the character of the disease under other conditions, or of the condition of the city, as regards the health and safety of any persons of southern acclimation." When the *Norfolk Herald* claimed yellow fever in Charleston, the *Mercury* denied it. A few days later, the *Courier* reiterated that no official declaration had been reported and that it was merely a rumor.[38]

Yellow fever spread slowly but relentlessly through Charleston during the summer of 1858. On July 15, Mr. Garcia, a Spaniard and twelve-year resident of the city, succumbed to the disease. John Abbott, an Irish police officer, fell ill and died on July 19. On August 4, Thomas Nevins, an Irishman who had lived in Charleston for seven years, also succumbed. A day later, Larry, the twenty-two-year old black slave of C. B. Northrup, died. Four casualties in three weeks: the first three living on Tradd Street. Yellow fever seemed to gain little traction in Charleston until early August, when the city experienced its first torrential rains of the summer. The rainstorm and subsequent high temperatures stimulated the mosquito population. The disease intensified soon thereafter, claiming six victims the following week: three Germans living on Tradd, an Irishman on Stoll's Alley, and an English woman and French Canadian man in Roper Hospital. The following week, the disease reached epidemic status, claiming twenty-eight people, including Michael O'Brien, an Irishman who lived at 67 Tradd Street where John Mehrtens, a German, died three days earlier. Yellow fever spread northward across Broad Street along Linguard and Queen Streets, while continuing to affect Tradd and East Bay Streets and Bedon's Alley. As late as the first week of September, the disease remained south of Calhoun, but a few cases had been discovered in the northern portion of Charleston. By mid-October, the disease had spread throughout the city. Among the German immigrant population alone, 222 died from yellow fever between mid-August and mid-November.[39]

In the aftermath of the 1858 epidemic, Mayor F. D. Hutchinson targeted the prevention of yellow fever as Charleston's most pressing concern because "during the last ten years, its visits have been biennial, and materially retarded our prosperity, and lessened that confidence in our progress .... The fact that Yellow Fever can be imported can no longer be doubted by us." Most physicians and engineers continued to argue,

[38] McCandless, *Slavery, Disease, and Suffering in the Southern Lowcounty*, 121; *Courier*, August 14, 18, 20, and 26, 1858; *Mercury*, August 20 and 23, 1858.

[39] Robert Lebby, *Report of the Committee of the City Council of Charleston upon the Epidemic Yellow Fever of 1858* (Charleston: Walker, Evans & Co., 1859), 11–18; *Deutsche Zeitung*, December 2, 7, and 9, 1858.

however, that poor sanitation, including stagnant water, assisted in the spread of yellow fever, and the city council continually worked to improve the city's streets and drains. Dr. William Hume disagreed that sanitation had anything to do with the disease, pointing out that filth had always existed in the city but yellow fever did not. He advocated for a more rigorous quarantine: vessels arriving from the West Indies between May 31 and October 1 would drop anchor across from Fort Johnson for thirty days after their arrival and twenty days after the cargo had been discharged; the port physician would board the vessel to examine the crew; nobody would be allowed to leave the vessel for twelve days from the date of arrival, and they could not leave for fifteen days after the last reported illness.[40]

In early August 1858, the editor of the *Mercury* summarized the crux of the quarantine debate: "The subject of quarantine, in its municipal and legislative as well as its medical relations, has very properly engaged, in large measure, the attention of our city government and of intelligent citizens for several years, and is still prominently before the public mind in all cities that enjoy a maritime commerce. The great problem of the day is to adjust and enforce a system with the maximum of prevention and security against all communicable diseases, with the minimum of restraint against commerce and the right of personal locomotion, which is cherished as one of the prominent characteristics and distinctions of *Anglo-American liberty*." The problem, apparently, was immigration, whether from the West Indies, Ireland, or Germany.[41]

Hume recommended total cessation of commerce during the four months when yellow fever most often appeared. Not surprisingly, business leaders opposed shutting down the port. Urban elites were concerned with public health, but they were unwilling to pay for it in the form of restricted commerce. Hume chastised the economic elite for opposing the quarantine, likening them to criminals for promoting foreign commerce that brought yellow fever and death to the city. If a strict quarantine were enacted, "Charleston will be exempt from the great cause that prostrates her energies," Hume argued, "and may yet realize the golden dreams which have stimulated her to compete with more favored cities in attaining both population and wealth. Sad experience has taught us that Yellow Fever is fatal

40 *Courier*, July 10 and August 25, 1858; October 31, 1859; Porter, "On the Climate and Salubrity of Port Moultrie and Sullivan's Island," 56; Hume, "On the introduction, propagation and decline of Yellow Fever," 10–11, 14–15, 31; Thomas Y. Simons, "Observations in reply to William Hume, M.D.," *Charleston Medical Journal and Review* 10 (January 1855): 170, 186.

41 *Courier*, August 12, 1858; *Mercury*, August 12, 1858 (emphasis added).

to all trade in our city." As long as native-born white Charlestonians and their native-born black slaves did not bear the heaviest burden of yellow fever mortality, the city council remained lukewarm to quarantines that would damage commerce.[42]

Yellow fever never visited Charleston again with the same vengeance. Immigration also declined in the post-Civil War era as immigrants chose to settle in the North's industrializing cities. In his report on the epidemic, Charleston's city registrar J. L. Dawson wrote, "The fatality of the past year, 1858, will long be remembered in the history of this city, not only on account of the fearful mortality which it records, but the unprecedented panic amongst the foreign and native population." Determined to protect their own interests, native-born white Charlestonians failed to find ways to help immigrants survive yellow fever, instead using epidemics as social control. But such prejudices inhibited public health policy not just for immigrants, but for all Charlestonians. The epidemic of 1858 demonstrated this total failure: "Yet the solemnity which pervaded every class of the community," Dawson continued, "plainly evinced the destroying angel had, day after day, added some loved object to the 'city of the dead.'"[43]

[42] William Hume, "The Yellow Fever of Charleston, considered in its relations to the West India commerce," *Charleston Medical Journal and Review* 15 (January 1860): 1, 3–4, 28, 31; *Courier*, August 12, 1858.

[43] Lebby, *Yellow Fever of 1858*, 6.

7

"Cumberer of the Earth": Suffering and Suicide among the Faithful in the Civil War South

Diane Miller Sommerville

The most famous suicide of the American Civil War was undoubtedly that of Edmund Ruffin, fire-eating secessionist from Virginia whose actions bookended the Civil War. Ruffin fired the first shot of the war – he was given the honor of detonating the first volley at Fort Sumter – as well as the last, when on June 17, 1865, he blew his brains out with a silver-plated rifle.[1] Most historical treatments, and virtually all popular ones, have fixated on the Confederacy's loss as the impetus for Ruffin's suicide. Ruffin was a high-profile public figure, well known outside the South as well as within as an ardent supporter of secession and independence. A political explanation for his suicide thus corresponds with the man

The author wishes to acknowledge the excellent feedback she received from Richard Bell and David Silkenat. Mitchell Snay graciously read the manuscript and offered insightful comments. Many thanks also to Andrew Menfi who provided critical research assistance. The research and writing for this project was generously supported by grants from the National Endowment for the Humanities, the Dean of Harpur College at Binghamton University, Southern Baptist Historical Library and Archives, North Caroliniana Society, and the Virginia Historical Society.

[1] Ruffin's biographers disagree over the date of his suicide: see David F. Allmendinger, Jr. and William K. Scarborough, "The Day Ruffin Died," *Virginia Magazine of History and Biography* 97 (January 1989): 75–96; David F. Allmendinger, Jr., *Ruffin: Family and Reform in the Old South* (New York: Oxford University Press, 1990), 152–85; Betty L. Mitchell, *Edmund Ruffin: A Biography* (Bloomington: Indiana University Press, 1981); idem, "'Superfluous Lags the Veteran on the Stage': The Death of Confederate Edmund Ruffin," *Virginia Cavalcade* 32 (winter 1983): 126–33; Kenneth S. Greenberg, *Honor and Slavery: Lies, Duels, Noses, Masks, Dressing as a Woman, Gifts, Strangers, Humanitarianism, Death, Slave Rebellions, The Proslavery Argument, Baseball, Hunting and Gambling in the Old South* (Princeton: Princeton University Press, 1996), 88–98; Bertram Wyatt-Brown, *The Shaping of Southern Culture: Honor, Grace, and War, 1760s–1880s* (Chapel Hill: University of North Carolina Press, 2001), 189–90.

and all he stood for. But most accounts focus only on a brief portion of his lengthy twelve-page suicide note in which he indeed excoriated "the Yankee race" and adamantly declared his refusal to live under "Yankee domination and despotism." Even Ruffin's son and namesake Edmund Ruffin Jr. assured his own sons – Ruffin's grandsons – that "the subjugation of our country has weighed heavily on his mind and determined him to take the final step."[2]

Although the prospect of living in a defeated South surely contributed to Ruffin's decision to end his life, a fuller, closer examination of his rather lengthy, researched, and contemplative explanation of that decision, including an interrogation of religious texts to justify the deed, illuminates important notions about suicide at the mid-nineteenth century. Ruffin's suicide serves as both a starting and ending point for a discussion of how religious white Southerners viewed suicide in the wake of war and loss.

Before the war, the vast majority of Americans walked in lock step with Christian theological doctrine that condemned suicide as a mortal sin, although a few isolated voices, Ruffin's among them, dissented. By the Civil War, and certainly after, many Southerners had begun to challenge the institutional churches' harsh treatment of suicide victims, ushering in a sea change in attitudes toward suicide.[3] The war proved an important catalyst in reorienting the way white Southerners viewed suicide and those who ended their own lives. For generations, ministers had admonished the faithful to countenance suffering and not give in to suicidal impulses, but the onslaught of misery, death, and destruction bared the limits of what Christian Confederates were able to endure physically and psychologically. Many southern believers were simply no longer able to reconcile the theological call for stoic forbearance in the face of prolonged agony and grief, and they came to realize that stress and depression, once interpreted as spiritual failings, were understandable consequences of the sacrifices and hardships of war, worthy of empathy rather than condemnation and

[2] "Death of Edmund Ruffin," *Tyler's Quarterly Historical and Genealogical Magazine* 5 (January 1924): 193–95.

[3] Southern Christians in the Civil War era associated with one of three denominations: Baptist, Methodist, and Presbyterian, encompassing 94 percent of all churches located in the Confederate states; see Daniel W. Stowell, *Rebuilding Zion: The Religious Reconstruction of the South, 1863–1877* (New York: Oxford University Press, 1998), 12. The classic survey of religion in the South before the Civil War is Donald G. Mathews, *Religion in the Old South* (Chicago: University of Chicago Press, 1977). See also Randy J. Sparks, "Religion in the Pre-Civil War South," in *A Companion to the American South*, ed. John B. Boles (Malden: Blackwell Publishing, 2002), 156–75; Mitchell Snay, *Gospel of Disunion: Religion and Separation in the Antebellum South* (Chapel Hill: University of North Carolina Press, 1997).

judgment. Suicide came to be viewed less as a sin or a sign of moral weakness and more as the result of tragic circumstances, a sad but natural result of war-generated suffering.

Edmund Ruffin readily conceded in his suicide note that popular opinion was "almost universal" in believing suicide to be a sin against God, forbidden by the Bible, a belief he condemned as "mistaken." A thorough, methodical analysis of relevant texts in both Old and New Testaments revealed, to his mind, no such proscriptions. Ruffin emphatically rejected the Christian definition of suicide as a form of murder, the most common explanation offered by religious authorities in denouncing suicide as sinful. Because the act is voluntary and directed toward one's self, Ruffin asserted, it fails to rise to the level of either sinful or criminal. Ruffin employed an analogy of fasting, which if done voluntarily to one's self is not criminal, yet when forced on another constitutes a crime. Finding no explicit Biblical prohibition of suicide, Ruffin then surveyed ancient Jewish history, a time when Jews were "fanatically devoted to every requirement of God's law." Yet Jews often committed suicide. In fact, Jewish law required suicide under some conditions, such as after defeat or rather than surrender, as in the case of the siege of Masada and the mass suicide of nearly a thousand Jewish warriors. "Suicide is not simply, of itself, a crime, or even a sin," Ruffin concluded.[4]

Despite asserting as he did that killing one's self did not constitute an affront to God, Ruffin did not embrace a fully libertarian view of suicide. He differentiated between good suicides and bad suicides. One had to consider circumstances and motives. Suicide was bad when intended to duck duties and obligations to family, like providing financial and material support, and to the state, such as offering defense. In these cases, "suicide would be cowardly and base as well as criminal in high degree." In contrast – and here he described what he saw as his own circumstances – when death would not deprive family or country of service or duty or would not contribute to losses or the physical suffering of anyone, then suicide was neither criminal nor an act of disobedience to God. Suicide might actually "remove incumbrances [sic], lessen evils, or ward off dangers to others," in which case the act of self-destruction might even be "commendable." Ruffin then laid out a case for his own "commendable" suicide. He bulleted the significant things he had done for family

[4] William Kauffman Scarborough, ed., *The Diary of Edmund Ruffin, vol. III: A Dream Shattered, June 1863–June 1865* (Baton Rouge: Louisiana State University Press, 1989), 935–46. Ruffin's suicide note was written on June 16, 1865, while at his Redmoor residence.

(generously provided for his children, including the dispersal of property) and nation (promoted agricultural improvements in the region and sustained the southern secession and independence cause); and he laid bare his dependent, helpless condition, having lost everything as a consequence of the war. Having satisfactorily fulfilled his duties as father and countryman, and no longer able to contribute to his own or anyone else's support, Ruffin had become "merely a cumberer of the earth, and a useless consumer of its fruits."[5] His, he concluded, was a good suicide.

A rehearsal of sorts for Ruffin's suicide and its justification occurred a quarter-century before when his close friend and aging mentor, Thomas Cocke, killed himself in February 1840. In the days before his death, Cooke discussed with Ruffin in veiled terms the topic of suicide. News of Cocke's death by his own hand deeply shook Ruffin and was made worse by the gruesome sight. Ruffin assisted with the cleanup, which required gathering the remains of Cocke's skull and brain matter near the large oak where Cocke had fired a gun into his mouth. Yet, Ruffin refused to rebuke Cocke for taking his life. Although he would not go so far as to justify or excuse Cocke's suicide – what Ruffin termed the "greatest offence" of Cocke's life – he resisted joining the "universal cry of condemnation."[6] Ruffin's tentative and inchoate reflections on Cocke's 1840 suicide expose an inner conflict about the act that, by the end of the Civil War, had congealed into a reasoned and fully researched justification for taking one's life.

Ruffin's tolerant views on suicide stood in stark contrast to official denominational Christian doctrine, which entertained no extenuating circumstances. (The Universalists proved the notable and significant exception.) Church teachings ordained that suicide fell under the auspices of the proscription against murder located in the Sixth Commandment. To take but one example, the Presbyterian Church's catechism, printed in the 1850s but written by two theologians from the eighteenth century, forbade suicide – "self-murder" – under any circumstances. The tract condemns suicide as an unnatural act, "opposed to the natural principle of self-preservation implanted in us." Citing the Old Testament account of Job, the catechism denounces self-murder as an act of the "highest impatience," a reflection of "rooted discontent with our lot in the present world."

[5] Ibid.

[6] Edmund Ruffin, "Statement of the Closing Scenes of the Life of Thomas Cocke," in *Incidents of My Life: Edmund Ruffin's Autobiographical Essays*, ed. David F. Allmendinger, Jr. (Charlottesville: Virginia Historical Society, 1990), 179–88.

Furthermore and perhaps paramount, suicide represented an encroachment on God's authority, for only God determines when a life ends: "it is an impious invasion of the prerogative of God, as the sole author and disposer of life." What made suicide a unique and especially heinous act was that, unlike all other sins, a suicide victim ended his or her time on earth, thus denying the sinner an opportunity for redemption. Consequently, those who died at their own hands suffered "an awful eternity" for they were unable to ask for and receive forgiveness.[7] Presbyterians, like most other mainstream Protestants, unequivocally denounced suicide as a form of murder and hence a sin, and a mortal one at that.

Clerical consensus on the anathema of suicide carried the day in antebellum America. In the years of the early republic, theologians regularly delivered harsh, unequivocal denunciations of suicide. The ministers' tenor on the topic of suicide was often strident, their positions rigid and intransigent. One of the most expansive and thorough theological ruminations on the topic of suicide was delivered in 1805 by a Presbyterian minister in New York City. Samuel Miller's widely disseminated treatises on suicide left no doubt where organized religion stood: "suicide is really a crime" – a crime against God, a crime against human nature, and a sin against society. Miller considered but rejected the common motives for suicide: feelings of uselessness, depression and melancholy, embarrassment, physical suffering. In truth, he countered, "pride, vanity, impatience, cowardice, a criminal love of the world, a false estimate of happiness, the most unworthy and degrading selfishness" stood as the real causes of suicide.[8]

[7] James Fisher and Ebenezer Erskine, *An Essay Towards an Easy, Plain, Practical and Extensive Explication of the Assembly's Shorter Catechism* (Pittsburgh: United Presbyterian Board of Publication, 185–); Ashbel Green, *Lectures on the Shorter Catechism of the Presbyterian Church in the U.S.A.: Addressed to Youth* (Philadelphia: Presbyterian Board of Publications, 1841); William S. Plumer, *The Law of God as Contained in the Ten Commandments, Explained and Enforced* (Philadelphia: Presbyterian Board of Publication, c. 1864), 251, 408–12, 566, 589, 642; John Brown, *An Essay Towards an Easy, Plain, Practical and Extensive Explication of the Assembly's Shorter Catechism* (New York: Robert Carter, 1845), 248–49. Colonial statutes against suicide can be traced deep into English history; Keith Burgess-Jackson, "The Legal Status of Suicide in Early America: A Comparison with the English Experience," *Wayne Law Review* 29 (fall 1982): 61–65.

[8] Samuel Miller, *The Guilt, Folly, and Sources of Suicide. Two Discourses, Preached in the City of New York, February 1805* (New York: T. and J. Swords, 1805). On Miller, see Howard I. Kushner, *American Suicide* (New Brunswick: Rutgers University Press, 1991), 31–32; Richard Bell, *We Shall Be No More: Suicide and Self-Government in the Newly United States* (Cambridge: Harvard University Press, 2012), 1, 22–23, 30, 33, 37. For other early nineteenth-century clerical denunciations of suicide, see Joseph Lathrop, *Two Sermons on the Atrocity of Suicide and on the causes which lead to it …* (Springfield: Henry Brewer, Printer, 1805); *Gracious Interpositions; or, "Do Thyself No Harm"*

Ministers like Miller who expressed draconian views on suicide built on a theological and cultural foundation of orthodoxy when it came to suicide.[9] But three overlapping developments in the early republic contributed to further entrenchment by clergy on the subject of suicide. The first was a postrevolutionary move in some states to decriminalize suicide, as well as a growing reluctance by coroners to issue verdicts for suicide. Virginia's suicide statutes, to take one example, required confiscation of the victims' property. None other than Thomas Jefferson decried the severity of the laws and called for their repeal. Ministers pushed back against the sentiments that undergirded the secular relaxation of harsh suicide law. Second, clergy also launched strident missives against suicide in response to a perceived wave of postrevolutionary suicides. Miller and other theologians urged extreme measures to stave the rising number of victims in an ostensible suicide epidemic.[10]

Third, the first half of the nineteenth century witnessed an entrenchment by mainstream Protestant sects on suicide doctrine in the face of a growing Universalist challenge, much of which refracted over the issue of self-murder. Universalists proved irksome to Protestant denominations, not only because they competed for souls, but also because Universalism embraced radical doctrines anathema to mainstream churches, like universal salvation and antislavery, and rejected mainstay beliefs of Protestantism like the trinity and original sin. Universalism adopted a loving, inclusive philosophy and a belief

(London: Baptist Tract Depository, 18–), microfilm, Southern Baptist Historical Library and Archives, Nashville, TN; Richard Watson, *Theological Institutes: Or, a View of the Evidences, Doctrines, Morals and Institutions of Christianity*, 2 vols. (New York: Nelson & Phillips, 1829).

9 Literary and popular condemnations of suicide abounded and reinforced religious denunciations in the eighteenth century; see "Arguments Against Suicide, From the Rev. Herries' Sermons," *The Massachusetts Magazine; or, Monthly Museum* (December 1793): 726; T. Warton, "The Suicide," *New York Magazine, or Literary Repository* 3 (March 1792): 3; "The Columbian Parnassiad," *The Columbian Magazine* (February 1790): 121; "On Suicide," *The Gentleman and Ladies' Town and Country Magazine* (July 1789): 312; D. S., "Suicide," *The Gentleman and Ladies' Town and Country Magazine* (July 1789): 328; "Summary of Late Intelligence," *Worcester Magazine* 3 (June 1787): 164; "An Antidote Against Suicide," *Weekly Museum* 5 (July 7, 1792): 2; "A Letter to a Friend on Suicide and Madness," *The Gentleman and Ladies' Town and Country Magazine* 8 (December 1784): 329; "On Suicide," *Worcester Magazine* 5 (May 1786): 61; Marquis Beccaria, "An Essay on Crimes and Punishments, Chapter XXXII, Of Suicide," *The New-Haven Gazette and the Connecticut Magazine* 1 (May 4, 1786): 90; John Herris, "An Address to the Public on the Frequent and Enormous Crime of Suicide," *The Pennsylvania Magazine, or, American Monthly Museum* 1 (January 1775): 38.

10 Bell, *We Shall Be No More*, 18–23; Burgess-Jackson, "The Legal Status of Suicide in Early America," 66–67.

that all people, sinners of all sorts, would be reconciled with God. Universalists did not denounce suicide like most of their brethren. They denied that suicide victims would suffer eternal damnation, instead embracing a more compassionate view of God who, they believed, would save all, including those who died at their own hands.

A veritable print war between Universalists and virtually everyone else broke out in the first half of the nineteenth century, much of it debating the sinfulness of suicide. Mainstream theologians attacked dissenting Universalist views on suicide, reinforcing long-standing, intractable positions on the sinful nature of self-destruction.[11] Thus, when a northern Methodist minister in 1861 delivered a sermon equating the start of the Civil War with suicide and noted as an aside, "Suicide has always been considered, by Christian moralists, the most culpable form of murder," he was affirming a long-standing religious tradition of antisuicide thought that permeated the sensibilities of most laypeople, including antebellum Southerners.[12]

Religious proselytization on the subject of suicide proved effective and greatly influenced popular ideas about the sinfulness and immorality of self-murder. The admonition that those who took their own lives faced eternal damnation certainly deterred many antebellum Southerners from such a path, as it was intended to do. Newly apprenticed lawyer Enoch Faw of North Carolina wrote despairingly over his future prospects for employment in 1858, even contemplating suicide, which he admitted "would be eternal death."[13] Like Faw, a suicidal H. T. Brown well understood the stigma attached to suicide in the antebellum period. The planter/land speculator from Wilkesboro, North Carolina, confessed that he often felt "weary of the long monotonous road before me and I have often felt an inclination to voluntarily abandon it but then everyone who reflects on such a subject must know that it is base and cowardly to do so and then if there is any truth in the Bible what comes after death is a weighty

11 For an illustration of an anti-Universalist tract in the late antebellum period, see Rev. E. B. Tenny, *Suicide Profitable, or A Good Bargain Soon Made: A Sermon* (Binghamton: Cooke & David, 1840). On the rift between Universalists and mainstream Protestant denominations over suicide in the early republic, see Bell, *We Shall Be No More*, 160–200.

12 Daniel Steele, *The Cause, the Crime, and the Cure of our National Suicide. A National Fast Day Sermon Delivered in the Baptist Church, Springfield, September 26, 1861* (Springfield: Samuel Bowles & Co., 1861).

13 October 25, 1858 entry, Diary and typescript, 1851–1861, 78, Enoch Faw Papers, David M. Rubenstein Rare Book and Manuscript Library, Duke University, Durham, NC. The powerful influence of evangelical Protestantism shaped ideas of even non-churchgoers; Frances M. Clarke, *War Stories: Suffering and Sacrifice in the Civil War North* (Chicago: University of Chicago Press, 2011), 18.

consideration." John Wesley Halliburton recounted in a letter in February 1861 that a classmate of his at Chapel Hill had died by his own hand, overdosing on laudanum. Halliburton, too, believed that the consequence of suicide was suffering in the hereafter: "A self-murder as this has received the awful doom which sentences him to eternal death."[14]

Church doctrine and clerical scorn over suicide, notably the threat of eternal damnation, contributed significantly to the considerable stigma that pervaded antebellum southern society and shaped popular attitudes toward self-murder. Occasionally, religious and popular derision of suicide resulted in the community's revocation of burial rites for suicides, which most religious Southerners held as sacred.[15] Mississippi planter Thomas Dabney received word while away from home that his children's tutor had killed himself following a failed attempt to live a life of sobriety. Although Dabney had regarded the young man as a son, he grew outraged upon learning that the teacher had been buried alongside Dabney's two deceased sons. Dabney ordered the disinterment of the tutor's body, insisting that no suicide should rest by the side of his "pure children."[16]

So-called "profane" burials for suicide victims, though, usually fell under the purview of clergymen. William H. Taylor, for many years the

[14] January 11, 1858 entry, H. T. Brown Diary, vol. 23: 1855–1859, Hamilton Brown Papers; "Cousie" to "My Silent Darling," February 14, 1861, John Wesley Halliburton Papers, both in Southern Historical Collection, University of North Carolina, Chapel Hill.

[15] Early modern European punishments for suicide, which included postmortem desecration and confiscation of the victim's property, had largely disappeared in the United States by the nineteenth century. On early punishments for suicide, see Terri L. Snyder, "What Historians Talk About When They Talk About Suicide," *History Compass* 5 (March 2007): 658–64; Burgess-Jackson, "The Legal Status of Suicide in Early America," 76–80; Kushner, *American Suicide*, 19–23; R. S. Guernsey, *Suicide: History of the Penal Laws Relating to it in Their Legal, Social, Moral and Religious Aspects in Ancient and Modern Times* (New York: L. K. Strouse & Co., 1883), 17–31.

By contrast, suicide victims could still be prosecuted posthumously for felony until 1870 in England. If convicted, they were declared civilly dead and their property forfeited to the Crown; Olive Anderson, *Suicide in Victorian and Edwardian England* (Oxford: Clarendon Press, 1987), 220. Until 1882, a suicide's body had to be buried by police in unconsecrated ground late at night and without benefit of religious rites; Victor Bailey, *"This Rash Act": Suicide across the Life Cycle in the Victorian City* (Stanford: Stanford University Press, 1998), 67. As late as 1792 in Amsterdam, the body of a suicide victim was ordered to be hanged by the legs in the gallows field "to be consumed by the air and the birds"; Machiel Bosman, "The Judicial Treatment of Suicide in Amsterdam," in Watt, ed., *From Sin to Insanity*, 9. On punishments for suicide in the medieval period, see Gwen Seabourne and Alice Seabourne, "The Law on Suicide in Medieval England," *Journal of Legal History* 21 (April 2000): 21–48.

[16] Susan Dabney Smedes, *Memorials of a Southern Planter* (Baltimore: Cushings & Bailey, 1888), 120–21.

coroner of Richmond, relayed a childhood memory of a suicide victim who was denied a Christian burial by local ministers.[17] Suffering from delirium tremens, the "poor creature" had jumped from a window of a Richmond building. The victim's friends, Taylor relayed, appealed to a number of ministers to perform a Christian interment. All refused. Out of desperation, the friends turned to an ostracized clergyman recently arrived in the city and propagating "the heterodox tenets of so-called Universalism." The Universalist minister mortified the more orthodox ministers in town when he performed what "he believed to be Christian rites" and had the "effrontery" to speak of the pathetic drunk as "our brother."[18]

Despite considerable animus expressed by many clergy and some followers toward the act of suicide, lay attitudes showed signs of relaxing by the late antebellum period. In William Taylor's account of ministers who refused to perform Christian burial rites for the suicidal drunk, the response of clerical leaders stood in contrast to that of community leaders who "applauded" the unconventional funeral performed by the Universalist preacher not so much because they approved of the Universalist doctrine on suicide, but because they saw that in treating the suicide victim with compassion, the itinerant minister showed himself to be "more Christ-like than were others who had arrogated to themselves the Christian name." Although official church teachings on the sinfulness of suicide remained unchanged throughout the long nineteenth century and persisted well after the war, laypeople and even some ministers began to show greater compassion toward suicide victims, as well as displeasure with draconian and condemnatory church canon on self-murder, exposing a fissure between theological doctrine and churchgoers.[19]

Writing in 1847, a man self-identifying as "a Southern physician" penned a thoughtful essay on suicide, drawing on historical, religious, legal, medical,

[17] On English clerical practice on burial rites for suicide victims, see Anderson, *Suicide in Victorian and Edwardian England*, 269–81; MacDonald and Murphy, *Sleepless Souls*, 44–50. On the burial restrictions for suicide victims in England and thirty-one other countries, see Guernsey, *Suicide*, 18, 20–31.

[18] Because Taylor was born in 1834, I'm estimating that this incident occurred some time in the 1840s; William H. Taylor, "The Burial of Ophelia," *Old Dominion Journal of Medicine and Surgery* 1 (January 1903): 156–64. On the conflict between Protestant denominational leaders and Universalists over the question of suicide in the nineteenth century, see Bell, *We Shall be No More*, 160–200. On Russian burial practices of suicide victims, see Paperno, *Suicide as a Cultural Institution in Dostoevsky's Russia*, 52, 54, 58, 64–65, 227 n 87, 228 n 94.

[19] Taylor, "The Burial of Ophelia," 163. Even by the turn of the twentieth century, some theologians continued to defend their harsh view of suicide as a sin; see for example, "Suicide," *The Methodist Review* 10 (July–August 1894): 620.

and philosophical treatments of suicide. He observed a "sentiment of profound pity for the unhappy suicide" and expressed confidence that God, "most merciful, and most just Judge," will "abundantly pardon" those who die at their own hands. Mirroring Ruffin's refusal to condemn the suicide victim, the anonymous essayist implored others to act compassionately and "say to our most unhappy brother, 'Neither do I condemn thee!'" A Georgia man identified only as a "young lawyer formerly of Columbia County" who died in 1856 likewise challenged prevailing harsh attitudes toward suicide, expressing profound sympathy and compassion for the suicide victim. He admonished others to "think not harshly of the suicide – we seldom if ever understand, or appreciate the feeling, that impel him to the commission of so sad and rash an act." Those who voluntarily end their own lives, he penned, "should be met with all fortitude and patience."[20]

By the outbreak of Civil War, a small but growing divide between official church doctrine and lay beliefs on the sinfulness of suicide existed in southern sources. Clergy in the early nineteenth century had launched a vigorous counterattack against the tide of Enlightenment thought, Universalist dissent, and the decriminalization of suicide. They failed, however, to stem that tide entirely and, as evidenced by the anecdotes just presented, harsh popular attitudes about suicide showed some signs of relaxing by mid-century.

The widespread physical and material suffering, loss of life, anxiety about the war's outcome, and ultimate loss of the war prompted many Southerners – those on the battle front and on the home front – to change their minds about suicide. Confederate veterans returned home, many thousands of them afflicted with emotional and psychological damage, including post-traumatic stress disorder, brain damage, and other manifestations of war trauma. Quite a few contemplated suicide as a last means to stop their suffering.[21] Those who considered ending their own lives

[20] A Southern Physician, "Suicide," *The American Review: A Whig Journal of Politics, Literature, Art and Science* 6 (August 1847): 137; quote from republished version in *U.S. Democratic Review* 34 (November 1854): 417; *Thomasville* (Georgia) *Times*, August 5, 1876, 1.

[21] On veterans who returned home from the war with physical and/or emotional wounds, consult James Marten, *Sing Not War: The Lives of Union and Confederate Veterans in Gilded Age America* (Chapel Hill: University of North Carolina Press, 2011); Jeffrey W. McClurken, *Take Care of the Living: Reconstructing Confederate Veteran Families in Virginia* (Charlottesville: University of Virginia Press, 2009); Eric T. Dean, Jr., *Shook Over Hell: Post-Traumatic Stress, Vietnam, and the Civil War* (Cambridge: Harvard University Press, 1997); Brian Craig Miller, "Confederate Amputees and the Women Who Loved Them," in *Weirding the War: Stories from the Civil War's Ragged Edges*, ed. Stephen Berry

through self-murder no doubt weighed the religious proscriptions and social taboos attendant with suicide. When men did take their own lives, family members, friends, admirers, and neighbors were left to make sense of the deaths; sometimes they rejected the long-standing religious denunciations of suicide. The gap between the church's position on suicide and the attitudes of laypersons, shaped by personal experience, grew considerably. Although the war did not change the doctrinal proscription against suicide or its definition as a form of murder, it did affect the attitudes of ordinary Southerners who, in the midst of unprecedented human suffering, began to reconsider its depiction as sinful.[22]

Southerners' evolving views about suicide cannot be understood without first considering the emotional and psychological toll exacted by war and loss, as well as the failure of religion, so integral to the lives of nineteenth-century Southerners, to address the mental anguish experienced by many soldiers and civilians. White Southerners' religious convictions were put to the test on multiple fronts as a result of the Civil War. As historian George Rable noted in his important work on religion and the Civil War, *God's Almost Chosen Peoples*, the "scale of the suffering and sacrifice in turn raised large and difficult questions about the providential meaning of slaughter on such a massive scale."[23]

Theological tenets about suffering – the pervasiveness and inevitability of human suffering and the religious assurance that with sufficient faith one would survive life's most challenging trials – implicitly reinforced doctrinal taboos against suicide. Southern Christian churches taught that, because of the fateful decision of Adam and Eve to eat of the

(Athens: University of Georgia Press, 2011), 301–20; Diane Miller Sommerville, "'Will They Ever Be Able to Forget?' Confederate Soldiers and Mental Illness in the Defeated South," in Berry, ed., *Weirding the War*, 321–39. On suicidal behavior of southern soldiers during the Civil War, see Diane Miller Sommerville, "'A Burden Too Heavy to Bear': War Trauma, Suicide, and Confederate Soldiers," *Civil War History* 59 (December 2013): 453–91.

22 David Silkenat makes this argument in *Moments of Despair: Suicide, Divorce and Debt in Civil War Era North Carolina* (Chapel Hill: University of North Carolina Press, 2011), 53–74.

23 George Rable, *God's Almost Chosen Peoples: A Religious History of the American Civil War* (Chapel Hill: University of North Carolina Press, 2010), 178–79; Drew Gilpin Faust suggests that the Civil War created a religious crisis that caused many Americans to redefine or reject their faith. Others, however, relied heavily on their faith as a survival mechanism that enabled them to resist succumbing to psychological collapse; see *This Republic of Suffering: Death and the American Civil War* (New York: Knopf, 2008), 171–210; idem, "'Without Pilot or Compass': Elite Women and Religion in the Civil War South," in *Religion and the American Civil War*, ed. Randall M. Miller et al. (New York: Oxford University Press, 1998), 250–59.

forbidden fruit and thereby invoke God's wrath, man was destined to a path of suffering and misery. Because of original sin, all must suffer. To escape earthly misery and affliction through self-murder subverted God's will. Moreover, the coming of Christ brought a new contract with God's people, one that required a painful and tortuous end to his life in order to provide Christian followers with salvation. In the New Testament, Christ figures as a model of suffering, a source of inspiration for those who, like him, faced considerable tribulations in life. Jesus, like any other man, dreaded his trial and sought to avoid it, even praying to God to allow him to escape the suffering that he prophetically knew awaited him: "My father, if it be possible, let this cup pass from me." But, as the son of God, he recognized that his path of intense sorrow and anguish was required to save God's people and so resigned himself to the misery that would follow.[24] As one Georgia minister expressed, God "laid upon him the iniquity of us all – that by his stripes we may be healed."[25]

By exalting Christ's fortitude and resignation in the face of suffering, theologians and ministers provided the anguished and tormented a model for Christian comportment in the face of adversity while reminding them that they were the direct beneficiaries of his suffering. Christ bore his challenges bravely and stoically; so should they. The example of Christ's forbearance provided solace to those afflicted with sorrow and served as an important source of consolation in nineteenth-century America. For example, a North Carolinian offered condolences to "Aunt Sade," a relative of William Lenoir who committed suicide in the spring of 1861. The author shared how she took, and by implication how Sade should have taken, solace in Christ's example: "it was the greatest comfort to me to feel that Jesus had suffered grief." A book of religious reflections published in 1860 assured readers that "[Jesus] knows my sorrows, for he has *felt* them!" In a sermon prepared for Confederate soldiers, Rev. C. T. Quintard implored his audience to remember that "Whatever be the intensity of sorrow that bows and presses the heart of man, remember that, for every grief you suffer, the meek and Holy One suffered a thousand." The preacher urged the soldiers to garner strength from Christ's example: "wherever we turn, whatever be

[24] Robert Foster Bradley, "The Cause and Cure of Suicide," in *Divine Decrees and Other Pamphlets* (n.p.: Index Publishing Company, 1913), 3–4; Winslow, *The Anatomy of Suicide*, 41. Frances Clarke describes the centrality of the notion of suffering in Victorian America and its links to evangelical religion in *War Stories*, 8–27.

[25] Rev. Adolphus W. Mangum, *Myrtle Leaves, or Tokens at the Tomb* (Raleigh: Branson & Farrar, 1864); Sermon, August 30, 1855, William McKay Papers, 1865–1906, Columbia Theological Seminary, Decatur, GA.

our shade of grief, we are but feeble copyists of the great sufferer, who, in His own person, exhausted every variety of human sorrow."[26]

Nineteenth-century Protestant ministers regularly counseled parishioners on suffering and its requisite place in the Christian schema, reminding them that faith would provide no insulation from pain. Echoing the convictions of many, one Southern Baptist clergyman cautioned that faith alone was no inoculation to affliction: "Immunity from trial is not guaranteed or promised. Rather the reverse." God's followers needed to understand that the inevitable and ubiquitous trials they faced served a godly purpose. "It is a good schooling of the heart to visit the couch of suffering and pain, to come into contact with sorrow," countenanced the Reverend William McKay, a Presbyterian minister who served Georgia churches in the late nineteenth century. "Sorrow is one of the world's greatest teachers." Adversity instilled in Christians the virtue of piety. Earthly trials only sweetened the fruits of paradise in the afterlife, a time that would usher in "praise and love and joyous gladness for the very things which had brought weeping and sorrow upon earth."[27]

Simply put, Christians had a responsibility to bear their trials with the same strength as Christ their savior had done because they were part of God's plan for salvation. Ministers counseled congregants to not to give in to despair, "a cowardly sort of refuge from misfortunate – a sort of moral suicide, which disgraces manhood." Christians should model themselves after Jesus Christ who persevered in the face of torment and sorrow. Such was the sentiment behind the rebuke delivered by the eminent Presbyterian minister from South Carolina James Henley Thornwell to his brother-in-law, A. J. "Jack" Witherspoon, also a minister, who felt so despondent about his feeble health that he considered taking his own life. Henley sternly warned him, "You have no right to commit suicide."[28]

26 Rable, *God's Almost Chosen People*, 172; Sermon, August 30, 1855; R. N. L. to Aunt Sade, April 12, 1861, Personal Correspondence, 1861–1865, Lenoir Family Papers, Southern Historical Collection; J. R. MacDuff, *Soldiers' Text-Book, or Confidence in Time of War* (Raleigh: General Tract Society, 1862), 14; C. T. Quintard, *Balm for the Weary and the Wounded* (Columbia: Evans & Cogswell, 1864).

27 Sermon #2 notes, "Funeral Discourses," Lansing Burrows Papers, Southern Baptist Historical Library and Archives, Nashville, TN; Sermon, August 30, 1855; *The Christian Index and Southwest Baptist*, February 24, 1866, 35; Sermon #10, "Funeral Discourses," Lansing Burrows Papers.

28 Rable, *God's Almost Chosen People*, 171; Sermon, December 29, 1847, William Anderson Crawford Papers, Columbia Theological Seminary; *The Daily Phoenix* (Columbia, SC), August 22, 1865; James Henly Thornwell to A. J. Witherspoon, June 17, 1851, in *The Life and Letters of James Henley Thornwell*, ed. B. M. Palmer (Richmond: Whittet & Shepperson, 1875), 349–50.

The antebellum Christian worldview of the role of suffering, including the charge that a good Christian soldier should suffer in silence because suffering was a gift from God, proved inhospitable to those enveloped by melancholy, the nineteenth-century term used to describe depressive behavior.[29] To the contrary, Christians should find bliss in life. "We must be joyful," preached a South Carolina Presbyterian minister before the war. "We have no business to go mourning all our days.... It dishonours him when we are downcast and sad." A Southern Baptist newspaper reminded Southerners after the war that "manliness and Christianity forbid the indulgence of a despondent, gloomy spirit."[30] Melancholy was thought to represent spiritual weakness. Those who succumbed to gloomy thoughts were giving in to temptation; they needed to pray for greater inner strength to face life's struggles. In fact, colloquial phrases used to describe melancholy, "the blue devils" or "devils in the heart," signify the vestiges of the historical association of depression with temptation and the influence of Satan. Moreover, suffering served an important purpose: it built character by teaching important lessons about failure, disappointment, patience, and, importantly, trusting God.[31]

Among early nineteenth-century Christians, then, melancholy or nervousness was often perceived as spiritual failing.[32] Christians under

[29] A melancholic was defined by the medical field as someone who possessed "no present enjoyment, no hope, no confidence; everything wears a gloomy aspect, every contemplation is sad and nature, with all its loveliness, is somber darkened and cheerless"; Samuel B. Woodward, "Observations on the Medical Treatment of Insanity," *American Journal of Insanity* 7 (July 1850): 19.

[30] Rev. A. F. Dickson, *Plantation Sermons, or Plain and Familiar Discourses for the Instruction of the Unlearned* (Philadelphia: Presbyterian Board of Publication, 1856), 136–37; *Christian Index and Southwestern Baptist*, March 28, 1867, 54.

[31] Nancy Tomes, "Devils in the Heart: A Nineteenth-Century Perspective on Women and Depression," *Transactions and Studies of the College of Physicians of Philadelphia* 13 (December 1991): 364; James J. Walsh, *Religion and Health* (Boston: Little, Brown, and Co., 1920), 254–64. Few ministers and laypeople in the nineteenth century continued to believe that demonic possession was the cause of insanity; Norman Dain, *Concepts of Insanity in the United States, 1789–1865* (New Brunswick: Rutgers University Press, 1964): 187.

[32] On colonial views of melancholy (depression) as resulting from temptations by the devil, see Kushner, *American Suicide*, 16–17. For an antebellum northern case study of a religious woman's battle with depression and suicidal thoughts, see Tomes, "Devils in the Heart," 363–86. On the medieval roots of conceiving of depression (melancholia) as sinfulness, see Stanley W. Jackson, *Melancholia and Depression from Hippocratic Times to Modern Times* (New Haven: Yale University Press, 1986), 325–27; Roy Porter, *Madness: A Brief History* (New York: Oxford University Press, 2002), 17–28; Clark Lawlor, *From Melancholia to Prozac: A History of Depression* (New York: Oxford University Press, 2012). For a recent treatment of the history of depression, consult

emotional strain simply needed to turn to God. "When your heart is heavy you must return to the Lord," advised an antebellum southern minister. "Pray to him to comfort you, to take away your sin, and to make you rejoice." God alone was the source of "strength" and "peace," the virtues that would see Christians through their troubled times. A handbook for soldiers counseled, "The two things I most need – strength to bear and to suffer; peace in the midst of much to cause uneasiness and pain."[33]

When men and women in despair took their own lives before the Civil War, then, the acts were often viewed as symptoms of spiritual failing and the victims as unable or unwilling to bear life's trials as Christ had modeled. A Louisiana newspaper in 1841, for example, reprinted a Baltimore account of a young woman who hanged herself because her beau refused to marry her. "Had she feared God as much as she appears to have loved man," the newspaper proclaimed, "she would have wiped her lover's last kiss from her lips, and been resigned to the loss of a heartless wretch."[34] The love-struck woman was ridiculed for her fateful act and denied compassion in this instance because she had failed an earthly test. Instead of trusting God to see her through her tribulations, she succumbed to one of many life difficulties and became a cautionary tale of what happens when God's followers fail to heed pastoral calls to forbearance in the face of adversity.

The Civil War, and the extensive and widespread suffering it unleashed, exposed the limits of these Christian tenets on suffering and Christianity's ability to comfort and sustain the distraught and afflicted. Husbands, sons, and brothers were dying; families faced deprivations of staples like food; destruction of dwellings left many homeless; fears of an invading army pervaded pockets of the South. To be certain, Christian teachings on suffering and the admonition to remain stalwart in the face of earthly troubles sustained some Southerners during the war. A New Orleans woman wrote to her husband during the war that "If it were not for ... religion that keep[s] me up, I would kill myself."[35] But growing numbers of Southerners lost faith in assurances that suffering served a purpose or that God was merely testing them.

Edward Shorter, *How Everyone Became Depressed: The Rise and Fall of the Nervous Breakdown* (New York: Oxford University Press, 2013).

[33] Dickson, *Plantation Sermons*, 137; MacDuff, *Soldiers' Text-Book*, 12.

[34] *Concordia* (Louisiana) *Intelligencer*, June 16, 1841.

[35] Anais to My Dear Husband, April 29, 1863, quoted in Drew Gilpin Faust, *Mothers of Invention: Women of the Slaveholding South in the American Civil War* (Chapel Hill: University of North Carolina Press, 1996), 182. For illustrations of women whose faith sustained them, see 180–84.

Religious Southerners whose psychological and emotional stamina were taxed by the war viewed the resulting depression and anxiety as weakened faith rather than mental illness. The very religious Mary Jeffreys Bethell of North Carolina, for example, confessed on the eve of the war that she was "miserable" and "surrounded by darkness, doubts and gloomy fears." The prospect of sacrificing two grown sons to the cause no doubt accounts for much of her personal despair, but she also had been beset by a bevy of woes: two children had died, two others were sick, a daughter had scalded her ankle, a son had been kicked by a horse and left close to death, and her husband had been gone for six weeks. Bethell viewed her slip into depression not as a natural response to crises and stress in a war zone, but rather through a religious lens. These feelings represented spiritual shortcomings, and she sought comfort in the Lord, whom she confessed seemed as if he had forsaken her. "I wept and prayed to Jesus Christ to remove my burden of fears, and gloom." A year later, the war and the sacrifices it demanded from Bethell tried her faith. "The Lord's face is hid from me. Darkness and gloom surrounds mc," she wrote. Two years into the war, she confessed that "severe and fiery trials and temptations" left her "low-spirited" and feeling like a "poor, helpless sinner." Georgia mother Julia Cumming, a month into the war that eventually took all four of her sons, similarly lamented that she felt wracked with anxiety despite efforts to keep it in check. She blamed her weak faith: "A true Christian faith should give me more confidence and serenity than I now feel."[36] Anguished diary entries that would strike modern readers as manifestations of a compromised mental state instead to Bethell, Cumming, and their contemporaries represented sinfulness and faltering faith.

As the war progressed, suicide thus became a real possibility for some anguished Southerners, many of whom had previously been very religious and took seriously the church's condemnation of suicide. Not all who contemplated suicide did so, of course. But the war left a number of Southerners feeling abandoned by God and therefore willing to rethink suicide as a viable alternative to end the suffering.

Take, for instance, the wartime experience of twenty-four-year-old Grace Elmore of Columbia, South Carolina, whose diary entries over

[36] Entries for April 2, 1861; April 29, 1862; September 26, 1862; October 1, 1862; May 15, 1863; June 4, 1863, all in Mary Jeffreys Bethel Diary, 1853–1873, typescript copy, Southern Historical Collection; Cumming quoted in LeeAnn Whites, *The Civil War as a Crisis in Gender, Augusta, Georgia, 1860–1890* (Athens: University of Georgia Press, 1995), 36.

time reveal a transformation of her ideas about suicide. In the last six months of the war, she grew increasingly concerned about advancing Federal troops. Despair over Confederate military setbacks, apprehension over Yankee raids, the deaths of two cousins in the war, and the prospect of living under "the Yankee nation" prompted her to consider suicide. "I have *almost* determined suicide in such circumstances would be justifyable [sic]." But she could not quite get herself there. The best she could do was to pray for God to bring about her death, taking the choice away from her: "God grant me death sooner than a life amongst the abomination of abominations, the Yankee nation." Two months later, still awaiting the arrival of Sherman's army and clearly worried about the prospects of rape, she again broached the topic of suicide, but this time openly as she considered that God might permit the act of self-murder in the face of such trying conditions: "Would to God I felt sure that life could be destroyed without sin, under such circumstances. That God would justify the self destroying hand, when life had become a burden and a shame through the wickedness of man." If robbed of what she "values more than all things" – her virginity – death by her own hand was preferable to living with the dishonor. "God forgive me, if I had to choose between death and dishonor, I could not live .... That which was taken could never be restored. God will, God must justify the deed."[37] Elmore was a deeply religious woman brought up in the Episcopal church and well understood that suicide constituted an affront to God, and she struggled with what she knew were the teachings of her church. Yet, the war-related trials she faced were unprecedented and overwhelming. In a leap of faith, quite literally, she came to believe that God would forgive her for choosing to take her own life rather than live with the taint of Yankee rape. Her reasoning was less intellectual than Edmund Ruffin's but nonetheless ended up at the same place: under some circumstances, suicide was a reasonable response. Elmore did not commit suicide; she merely contemplated it. But the war and its consequences had brought her face to face with the taboo of self-destruction as a way to end suffering.

The psychological crisis that grew in the wake of war enveloped thousands of Southerners, many of whom manifested symptoms of mental illness, including suicidal behavior, during and after the war. Asylums

[37] Marli F. Weiner, *A Heritage of Woe: The Civil War Diary of Grace Brown Elmore, 1861–1868* (Athens: University of Georgia Press, 1997), entries for September 25, 1864, 73 (emphasis added) and November 26, 1864, 81–82. On Elmore during the war, see also Faust, *This Republic of Suffering*, 192; idem, *Mothers of Invention*, 194–95.

quickly filled to capacity with men and women, many of whom had attempted self-injury.[38] A clergyman ministering to Confederate troops in Wilmington, North Carolina, in May 1861 and concerned about the increase in soldier suicides in the first weeks of hostilities, preached: "And, already, men heretofore of firm and well-ordered character, have committed suicide from the pressure of this one distracting thought, the troubles of the country." Another southern minister delivered a sermon to soldiers entitled, "It is a Fearful Thing to Live," a rebuke, it would seem, to those who might be considering taking their own lives rather than face battle: "He who lives in this world must live forever. Live we must."[39] Southerners during and after the war faced the juxtaposition of a religious culture that denounced suicide as sinful against the stark new reality of war trauma, which had increased the specter of suicide.

During the war, Confederates acted on their suicidal impulses in unprecedented numbers.[40] A Raleigh newspaper acknowledged in 1864 that

[38] The Georgia insane asylum, which first opened its doors in 1842, was severely taxed by the increase in patients after the war, although most of its patients were civilians. Thomas Green, superintendent and resident physician of the asylum, reported in 1867 that the facility was "greatly overcrowded" and filled "almost to capacity." In the final year of the war, it housed a total of 275 patients; Thomas F. Green, "Report of Superintendent and Resident Physician to Board of Trustees, October 2, 1867," in *Report of the Trustees, Superintendent Resident Physician and Treasurer of the Lunatic Asylum of the State of Georgia for the Year 1866–7* (Milledgeville: Federal Union Book and Job Office, 1868); idem, "Report of the Superintendent and Resident Physician to Board of Trustees," in *Report of the Trustees, Superintendent, Resident Physician and Treasurer of the Lunatic Asylum of the State of Georgia, for the Years 1868–69* (Atlanta: Samuel Bard, Public Printer, 1870). The large number of Union soldiers deemed "insane" were centrally hospitalized at the Government Hospital for the Insane in Washington. The superintendent of the Washington asylum consequently noted an increase in the number of military patients in the facility. During the fiscal year 1864–1865, for example, 83 percent of the inmates were military patients; Albert Deutsch, "Military Psychiatry: The Civil War," in *One Hundred Years of American Psychiatry*, ed. J. K. Hall et al. (New York: Columbia University Press for the American Psychiatric Association), 379–83. To date there is only one study of a southern insane asylum, Peter McCandless's book *Moonlight, Magnolias and Madness: Insanity in South Carolina from the Colonial Period to the Progressive Era* (Chapel Hill: University of North Carolina Press, 1996).

[39] Thomas Atkinson, "Christian Duty in the present Time of trouble. A Sermon Preached at St. James' Church, Wilmington, N.C., on the Fifth Sunday after Easter, 1861" (Wilmington: Fulton and Price, 1861); Rev. Andrew Broaddus, "It is a Fearful Thing to Live" (Raleigh: s.n., ca. 1861 and 1865), both in Southern Historical Collection.

[40] Because of poorly kept or nonexistent Confederate military records and vital statistics throughout much of the South, there is no way to conduct a quantitative study of suicidal behavior in the South over time. We are left with ample anecdotal and impressionistic evidence, however, that is strongly suggestive of an increase of suicidal behavior during and after the war.

"anguish of the mind has driven thousands to suicide." More than a few Confederate soldiers died at their own hands, even before seeing the front lines. The postwar years saw even more acts of self-destruction as broken men returned home from the front to find their fortunes gone, families emotionally and financially devastated, dwellings destroyed, and slaves vanished. Josiah Gorgas, the chief ordinance officer for the Confederacy and later president of the University of Alabama, noted the high number of suicides in the South in 1867: "I can now understand how those poor, doomed, wretches whose self destruction we daily see chronicled are forced to their doom. To many, annihilation must be the only thing left. Nothing is so terrible as despair." Southern newspapers were peppered with observations about the increase in suicides. The Atlanta *Weekly Sun* in 1871 asked the rhetorical question, "is suicide epidemical?" in response to "an epidemic of suicide [that] is prevalent in the country."[41] Two years later, the Atlanta *Daily Sun* remarked on the nonchalance with which people responded to news of suicides, as well as their putative causes: "Suicides have become so frequent that people take the most frivolous excuse for 'shuffling off this mortal coil,' with the coolest sort of indifference." The *Richmond Whig* in 1866 referred to a national "suicide epidemic" and listed a number of self-murders from throughout the country.[42] "The crime of suicide," wrote the *Tri-Weekly Sumter* (Georgia) *Republican* in 1870, "is becoming frightfully common."[43] In fact, one writer levied a charge of sensationalism against newspapers that, to his mind, had gone so far as to characterize "self-destruction in the light of heroism."[44]

Faced with the suicides of friends or family members in the maelstrom of suffering and despair, Southerners began to reconsider the harsh attitudes

41 Raleigh *Weekly Standard*, October 26, 1864; Sommerville, "'Too Heavy a Burden to Bear'"; Josiah Gorgas Journal, entry for January 7, 1867, typescript copy, 76, Southern Historical Collection; (Atlanta) *Weekly Sun*, August 16, 1871.

42 (Atlanta) *Daily Sun*, March 27, 1873, 2; *Richmond Whig*, March 9, 1866.

43 *Tri-Weekly Sumter* (Georgia) *Republican*, May 12, 1870. For additional postwar newspaper accounts commenting on the increase of suicides and describing them as epidemics or mania, see the *Thomasville* (Georgia) *Times*, August 5, 1876 and May 3, 1879; *Weekly Sumter* (Georgia) *Republican*, October 1, 1875; *Albany* (Georgia) *News*, February 28, 1873; *Daily Phoenix* (Columbia, SC), April 17, 1868; *Savannah* (Georgia)*Daily News and Herald*, February 11, 1868; Charleston *News & Courier*, July 10, 1883; *National Police Gazette*, October 26, 1867, 23; Macon (Georgia) *Telegraph*, August 2, 1865; New Orleans *Times*, July 12, 1866. Additional sources that comment on the rise of suicides in the country include William Mathews, "Civilization and Suicide," *North American Review*, April 1, 1891, 470, 477; Horace Mellard DuBose, "Suicide – Its Causes and Cures," *Quarterly Review of the Methodist Episcopal Church, South* 21 (1884): 36.

44 (Atlanta) *Daily Intelligencer*, January 12, 1870.

toward suicide preached from the pulpits of their churches and taught in catechism classes. The war amplified Southerners' emphasis on the afterlife, which inadvertently contributed to assuaging popular abhorrence of suicide. Protestant orthodoxy denouncing suicide as sinful rested precariously alongside the theological glorification of death as a peaceful destination where suffering and sorrow no longer existed. Death was not to be feared but rather welcomed, for "to die will be thy eternal gain .... death hath no terror for thee ... come, welcome death." The Christian view of an afterlife devoid of suffering was intended to persuade the faithful that death was a portal to eternal life and, thus, not to be feared. The depiction of Heaven as a place "where suffering and sin shall never more be either felt or feared" was intended to pacify Christians' concerns about the fate of loved ones after death, notably dead soldiers. Whereas conceptions of "Heaven" certainly predated the war, the image of Heaven transformed from a vague, distant place to a comforting, blissful home away from home, a conceptual construction intended to comfort those who lost or stood to lose loved ones in war. Representations of a peaceful paradise soothed worries about the departed's state in the hereafter: "No sickness there – No weary wasting of the frame away.... No hidden grief, no wild and cheerless vision of despair.... No tearful eyes, no broken hearts are there! ... The storm's black wing is never spread athwart celestial skies!"[45]

Depicting death as a beautiful, serene retreat from the misery of an earthly life – notably, the carnage and torment of war – risked making suicide a tempting alternative to human suffering. Soldiers heading into battle were counseled not to fear it. One typical soldiers' guidebook advised, "In an unsinning and unsorrowing Heaven, war, tumult, pain, sickness, battle, bloodshed, shall be words unknown." Ministers consoled those who had lost loved ones in the war by describing the afterlife as an ethereal haven devoid of pain and anguish. Southern believers could take solace in the promise that in death all "our sorrows are coming to an end." Although institutional religion roundly condemned suicide, insisting that only God determined the timing of one's death, ministers preached that death should be welcomed because it brought escape from suffering. Messages intended to bolster those reeling from loss perhaps offered

45 *The Working Christian* (SC), July 15, 1869; MacDuff, *Soldiers' Text-Book*, 19. On war-era representations of the hereafter, see Mark S. Schantz, *Awaiting the Heavenly Country: The Civil War and America's Culture of Death* (Ithaca: Cornell University Press, 2008), 38–69; Philip Shaw Paludan, "Religion and the American Civil War," in Miller et al., eds., *Religion and the American Civil War*, 30–31; *Christian Index and Southwest Baptist*, March 15, 1866.

severely depressed Confederates an avenue to peace, inadvertently enticing weary Confederates to end their earthly torment and become one of "the blessed dead! ... [one of] those who no longer suffer and are tried."[46]

Suicide during and after the Civil War, and in the wake of vast and unprecedented suffering, became a more understandable, reasonable option for those afflicted with emotional distress. It was no longer merely the act of the insane or impious. Condemning fellow Southerners for ending their own lives or castigating the tormented as spiritually weak no longer resonated so strongly among a war-ravaged people. A more compassionate response was required. The few voices like Edmund Ruffin's before the war increasingly constituted a chorus of calls for a nonjudgmental, sympathetic reaction to instances of suicide. A poem – "At the Grave of a Suicide" – published in 1886 by Sarah Morgan Bryan Piatt, a Kentucky woman, reflects the softening attitude toward those who died by their own hands.

> You sat in judgment on him, – you, whose feet
> Were set in pleasant places; you, who found
> The Bitter Cup he dared to break still sweet,
> And shut him from you consecrated ground
> Come, if you think the dead man sleeps a whit
> Less soundly in his grave, – come, look, I pray:
> A violet has consecrated it.
> henceforth you need not fear to walk this way.[47]

The poetess reprimands those who dare judge suicide victims. In particular, she chastises those who denied suicides burial rites in church cemeteries. Piatt emphatically rejected the church's long-standing belief that self-murder destined one to eternal suffering. Here, death brought peace – an end to earthly suffering – to the troubled soul, symbolized by the sprouting of a solitary humble flower, the violet, which serves to "consecrate" the grave when heartless mortals would not.

Newspaper obituaries of suicidal deaths after the war similarly reflect a softening of harsh attitudes on suicide. At the beginning of the nineteenth century, newspaper accounts of suicide often condemned the deceased. After the war, deaths by suicide – whether war participants or not – more often elicited sympathetic commentaries; condemnation all but disappeared. When an unidentified ferry passenger threw himself overboard in

[46] MacDuff, *Soldiers' Text-Book*, 35; Dickson, *Plantation Sermon*, 137; *The Working Christian* (SC), September 23, 1869.

[47] Sarah Morgan Bryan Piatt, "At the Grave of a Suicide," *Atlantic Monthly* 58 (July 1886): 76.

April 1865, the *Daily Picayune* acknowledged that while the action defied "canon against self-slaughter" and is "generally regarded as a cowardly act," it nonetheless had been sanctioned by such historical luminaries as Saul, Hannibal, Brutus, and Mark Anthony. After the wife of an abusive, alcoholic veteran took her own life in 1871, the Atlanta *Weekly New Era* printed a letter recounting the details of her death that included thoughts on suicide that she had shared with friends after a failed attempt. She defended "its moral right, saying that there were some wrongs, some miseries, which only a self-inflicted death could end." The piece then ended with a line from the victim's own suicide note: "Judge not, that ye be not judged."[48]

Postwar obituaries of suicides regularly reported on displays of sympathy for the victims and their families, such as in the case of twenty-nine-year-old John M. Parkman, a former president of the First National Bank of Selma who drowned himself in 1867. Parkman left a wife and two children "overwhelmed with the sad calamities of a few weeks, and exciting the tenderest sympathies of the entire community." An eighteen-year-old Georgia woman's suicide by drowning in 1879 prompted the local paper to remark that her parents had the sympathy of the entire community. Postbellum obituaries reflected a significant change in the way society perceived suicide by voicing greater empathy for the men and women who killed themselves, acknowledging that extenuating circumstances could (understandably) lead one down the path of self-destruction. Encapsulating this new attitude was a short editorial that ran in the Atlanta *Weekly Sun* in 1871 advocating a more tolerant view of suicide: "There come to every one of us times ... when we find no happiness either in the crowded assembly or in the quiet parlor, when companionship is rather an annoyance than a pleasure. ... Life is burdensome, existence is tasteless. Not knowing whither to turn, is it any wonder he dreams of suicide, and is it any matter if his dream 'comes true'?"[49]

Changing attitudes toward suicide victims can also be seen in coroners' reports. In the early nineteenth century, inquests on dead bodies that

[48] Silkenat, *Moments of Despair*, 11; *Weekly New Era* (Atlanta), May 24, 1871. David Silkenat observes this change in suicide obituaries in North Carolina newspapers as well; *Moments of Despair*, 25–32.

[49] (Atlanta) *Daily Intelligencer*, May 29, 1867; *Weekly Sumter* (Georgia) *Republican*, December 12, 1879; (Atlanta) *Weekly Sun*, July 26, 1871. For other obituaries noting sympathies for the suicide victims' families, see *Weekly Sumter* (Georgia) *Republican*, May 24, 1878. Parkman may have been J. M. Parkman from Selma who served in a local defense militia during the war and who after the war received a presidential pardon that allowed him to engage in banking in Selma.

resulted in a finding of suicide typically ended with a turn of phrase pointing out the deceased's lack of religiosity. For example, an 1808 coroner's investigation into the drowning of Simon Taylor of Frederick County, Virginia, led to a finding of suicide resulting from Taylor "not having God before his eyes." Similarly, after inmate Robert Wimm of the Frederick County poorhouse cut his throat with a razor in 1839, the coroner attributed the suicide to Wimm's "not having the fear of God before his eyes but being ... seduced by the instigation of the Devil."[50]

After the war, religious references all but disappeared from coroners' reports. A shift from the sacred to the secular is in evidence in postbellum coroners' reports that depicted the act of suicide as an affront to the state, not God. When Fred Dollfender, a storeowner from Charleston, shot himself to death in 1883, he did so "against the peace and dignity of the state."[51] There was as well a striking absence of religious condemnations in verdicts in the postwar years. For example, John Black, the magistrate of

[50] Inquest on body of Simon Taylor, March 14, 1808, and Inquest on body of Robert Wimm, December 7, 1839, both in Inquests on Dead Bodies, Frederick County Miscellaneous Records, Library of Virginia, Richmond. See also the suicides of Macknep B. Goode, September 8, 1827, and Inquest on body of James, a negro, July 15, 1828, both in Coroners' Inquests; Official Appointments, 1770–1870, Charlotte County Miscellaneous Records/Bonds/Commissions/Oaths/Estrays (1774–1785); Inquest on body of William Blackaby, June 24, 1831, Coroner's Inquests (1833–80), City of Lynchburg Miscellaneous Records/court records: various courts, Library of Virginia. Attributing suicide to the work of the devil was common in colonial tracts; Bell, *We Shall Be No More*, 16–18.

[51] Inquest on body of Fred Dollfender, July 9, 1883, Charleston County Coroner's Books (L 10173), Vol. 2 (1883–1893), sec. 1, South Carolina Department of Archives and History, Columbia.

Despite language that situated suicide as an affront to the state, suicide for the most part was no longer a felony in the South. The American Revolution and Enlightenment thought had shepherded in a wave of decriminalization, but the language of coroners suggests that officials continued to view self-murder as a slight against the state. A perusal of nineteenth-century statute compilations of slaveholding states failed to identify a single statute addressing suicide and its punishment in the antebellum period, suggesting that suicide was no longer regarded a crime by the Civil War. Mississippi, Virginia, Tennessee, Alabama, and Missouri all passed laws well before the Civil War ensuring that the estates of suicide victims would not be treated differently from those who died of natural causes; *Revised Code of the Laws of Mississippi* (Natchez: Francis Baker, 1824, sec. 21), 541; *The Revised Code of the Laws of Virginia* (Richmond: Thomas Ritchie, 1819), sec. 58, 613; R. L. Carruthers and A. O. P. Nicholson, comps., *A Compilation of the Statutes of Tennessee* (Nashville: Steam Press of James Smith, 1836), art. I, sec. 12, 689; Harry Toulmin, *A Digest of the Laws of the State of Alabama* (Cahawba: Ginn & Curtis, 1828), art. I., sec. 21, 916; *The General Statutes of the State of Missouri* (Jefferson: Emory S. Foster, 1866), ch. 207, sec. 24, 826. In fact, most states likely decriminalized suicide in the wake of Revolutionary-era Enlightenment thought, as did Virginia and North Carolina; Bell, *We Shall Be No More*, 20; Henry Potter, John Louis Taylor, Bartlett Yancey, George C. Mendenhall, comps., *Laws of the State of North-Carolina ... Volume 1* (Raleigh: J. Galem, 1821), Law of 1787, ch. 280,

Anderson County, South Carolina, presented the jury's findings on the hanging death of Hutson B. Sullivan in August 1866 and concluded that he had come to his death by "self murder" and did "voluntarily and feloniously himself did kill against the peace and dignity of the state."[52]

All of the evidence that Southerners after the Civil War exhibited greater tolerance of suicide than before the war coincided with a growing chorus of voices critical of church authorities who continued to toe the harsh line on suicide; some even challenged church leaders to take positions more "Christ-like." William Taylor, the Richmond coroner, criticized the church's harsh attitude toward suicide by invoking the Shakespearean tragedy of Ophelia's suicide and her brother's rebuke of the priest for conducting "maimed" funeral rites, that is, withholding a full burial ceremony for those who died at their own hands. Taylor acknowledged that it had only been "within a period quite recent that society has sympathized" with Ophelia's brother, an indication that "society" was moving toward a sympathetic view of suicide victims that rejected the "barbarities inflicted under the sanction of the Christian religion upon the bodies" of suicide victims. As Taylor saw it, one of the chief duties of the church was to console "the wretched," to serve as their "rock of refuge in a sea of troubles." By denying Christian suicide victims full burial rites, the church had "perverted its office" and was "painfully at variance with the attribute of tender compassion we intuitively ascribe to it." As Edmund Ruffin had done in 1865, Taylor scoured the Bible for an explicit proscription against suicide and found none. Taylor concluded that there now existed a "large number who do not sympathize with the authorities of the Church in their harsh treatment of suicides." In fact, he noted that "in recent times, some Christian denominations have, in their attitudes toward suicide, become liberal."[53]

One Presbyterian minister seems to have proven Taylor right. In 1870, George Howe, a minister and professor at Columbia Theological Seminary in Decatur, Georgia, from 1831 to 1883, published a two-volume history

581. In the absence of statutes pertaining to suicide one must consider that common law may have provided opportunities for prosecution, as suggested by a Louisiana jurist, although he offered that punishment lay outside of law in custom: "The punishment of murder could not be applied to the person committing suicide, but in his reputation and fortune he was made to atone for his crime"; Albert Voorhees, *A Treatise on the Criminal Jurisprudence of Louisiana* ... (New Orleans: Bloomfield & Steel, 1860), 122.

52 Inquest on the body of H. B. Sullivan, August 13, 1866, Coroner's Inquests, 1830–1883, Anderson County Court of General Sessions, South Carolina Department of Archives and History.

53 Rocellus Sheridan Guernsey, *Ecclesiastical Law in Hamlet: The Burial of Ophelia* (New York: Bretano Bros., 1885); Taylor, "The Burial of Ophelia."

of the church in South Carolina in which appeared a brief biographical sketch of William Richardson, a late-colonial minister in the Waxhaw settlement. Richardson died under a cloud of suspicion – some thought he committed suicide, others that he was murdered by his wife – but Howe concurred with the former, believing Richardson had in fact taken his own life in 1771. Richardson had struggled with melancholy his whole life. More compelling, he had been found dead in his study with a bridle around his neck, which persuaded many at the time that Richardson had committed suicide. His friends apparently suppressed the circumstances of the death in order to conceal the apparent suicide. Richardson had, the official story went, "died an untimely death, by what instrumental cause we cannot determine, and the delicacy of the case forbids a conjecture." Howe used the biographical exercise as an opportunity to express a softened attitude toward suicide victims, one far different from that of those who shrouded the good reverend's apparent suicide in the late eighteenth century. "These doubts" about Richardson taking his own life, he proclaimed, were "all founded on the popular belief among Christians, that God would never so forsake his children as to leave them to the awful death of a suicide." In marrying theological and medical reasoning in a way that anticipated later developments in mainstream thought about the psychological (as opposed to physiological) causes of mental illness, Howe explained that, since youth, Richardson had suffered from a disease of the mind every bit as real as those of the body. "A heavy, melancholic disposition" and "vapory disorders" plagued him much of his life and had grown worse in his last months. Howe concluded that Richardson "died the victim of a mental malady which had been gaining strength ... for some time."[54] Howe's sensitivity to what we today would recognize as Richardson's

[54] George Howe, *History of the Presbyterian Church in South Carolina* (Columbia: Duffie & Chapman, 1870): 416–19. My thanks to Peter N. Moore for sharing this citation. On Richardson's death, see Moore, "The Mysterious Death of William Richardson: Kinship, Female Vulnerability, and the Myth of Supernaturalism in the Southern Backcountry," *North Carolina Historical Review* 80 (July 2003): 279–96. Nineteenth-century understanding of "insanity" and its causes was very much in flux and often confused symptoms with causes. Most American psychiatrists in the antebellum period, though, saw insanity as a physical disorder but disagreed over whether the cause was somatic or psychological (environmental or moral). Disagreement also characterized the designation of proximate (immediate) and predisposing (underlying) causes of insanity, although most asylum caretakers seemed to privilege physical over psychological factors as proximate. On early American psychiatry and the supposed causes of insanity, consult Edward Jarvis, "Causes of Insanity," *Boston Medical and Surgical Journal* 45 (November 12, 1851): 289–305; Gerald Grob, *The Mad Among Us: A History of the Care of America's Mentally Ill* (Cambridge: Harvard University Press, 1994), 5–128; idem, *The State and*

history of mental illness and the role it played in his possible suicide is significant. Importantly, as a Presbyterian minister and as an instructor at a theological seminary, Howe would have been painfully aware that his empathetic stance on death by suicide contradicted official Presbyterian doctrine. Nonetheless, his dissenting remarks appear in an official church publication after the Civil War.

William Taylor, a coroner who saw first-hand the tragic consequences of suicide; George Howe, who recognized the symptoms of mental illness of a suicide victim; Edmund Ruffin, a religious man who could find no Scriptural basis for the stigmatization of suicide: they all numbered among the many postwar Southerners who expressed more open-minded views about suicide and challenged church orthodoxy on the issue. They, like thousands of others, had witnessed or experienced the consequences of four years of brutal warfare, the mounting cost in human casualties and material wealth, and the despair and suffering that hung over the postwar South like a dark cloud. Historians only recently have begun to zero in on a more accurate accounting of the massive scale of destruction and cost of the war in both lives and treasure. Collectively, these many stories suggest a much more horrific experience than has previously been imagined, one that had far-reaching influence and effected profound transformations well into the twentieth century.[55] Americans, but Southerners particularly, tried to make sense of the pervasive suffering and death that defined the Civil War. As the foremost scholar on death and the Civil War, Drew Gilpin Faust asserted that "Death transformed the American nation as well as the hundreds of thousands of individuals directly affected by loss."

the Mentally Ill: A History of Worcester State Hospital in Massachusetts, 1830–1920 (Chapel Hill: University of North Carolina Press, 1966), 51–61, 229–32; Dain, *Concepts of Insanity*, 1–113; Richard W. Fox, *So Far Disordered in Mind: Insanity in California, 1870–1930* (Berkeley: University of California Press, 1978), 7–15; Nancy Tomes, *The Art of Asylum-Keeping: Thomas Story Kirkbride and the Origins of American Psychiatry* (Philadelphia: University of Pennsylvania Press, 1984), 77–87.

[55] On the demographic impact of the deaths of vast numbers of soldier dead, see J. David Hacker, "A Census-Based Count of the Civil War Dead," *Civil War History* 57 (December 2011): 306–47. Some historians have referred to this recent burst of scholarship that takes aim at the massive costs of the war in bodies and material treasures as the "War is Hell" school. A sample of such works includes Jim Downs, *Sick from Freedom: African-American Illness and Suffering during the Civil War and Reconstruction* (New York: Oxford University Press, 2012); Megan Kate Nelson, *Ruin Nation: Destruction and the American Civil War* (Athens: University of Georgia Press, 2010); Clarke, *War Stories*; Kathryn Shively Meier, *Nature's Civil War: Common Soldiers and the Environment in 1862 Virginia* (Chapel Hill: University of North Carolina, 2013); Marten, *Sing Not War;* McClurken, *Take Care of the Living;* Faust, *This Republic of Suffering*; Schantz, *Awaiting the Heavenly Country.*

The emergence of "this republic of suffering," as Faust aptly refers to the wartime nation, forced Americans to make sense of the meaning of death and dying.[56] Southerners, who experienced greater losses than Northerners, thus had every reason to reconstitute their worldview of suicide. Because suicide had become a regular visitor to Southerners, they developed a greater capacity and willingness to sympathize with those who ended their lives at their own hands.

Indeed, the Civil War did not merely contribute to the mitigation of harsh attitudes on suicide; it eventually opened the door to the valorization of suicide. In 1877, Lost Cause propagandist George Bagby published a poem lamenting the disappearance of "The Old Virginia Gentleman." He includes a stanza on Edmund Ruffin:

> He was the first to fire the gun
> When Sumter was assailed,
> He it was who life disdained
> When our Great Cause had failed,
> And ever in the van of fight
> The foremost still he trod
> Until on Appomattox' height
> He gave his soul to God,
> Like a good Virginia gentleman,
> All of the olden time.[57]

Ruffin's suicide, far from being condemned in this elegiac prose, was hailed as martyrdom: his death was nostalgically transformed into a symbol of holy sacrifice, a harkening of some imagined lost world when suicide constituted a noble death. (Later versions of his suicide had Ruffin wrapping himself in a Confederate flag before taking his life.) This cultural reformulation would not have been possible without the catalyst of the Civil War, which played a significant role in destigmatizing suicide, in creating a space where news of a suicide provoked compassion, not ridicule. Edmund Ruffin, in the minds of many, became a patriot who chose death, a final act of rebellion, rather than life under Yankee rule. Who would judge him for his act of self-destruction? Who would cruelly denounce the self-inflicted fatal wounds of the many Confederate soldiers who returned home broken at war's end? Who would condemn to eternal damnation the stalwart women of the home front who collapsed under the

[56] Faust, *This Republic of Suffering*, xiii.

[57] George W. Bagby, *Selections from the Miscellaneous Writings of Dr. George W. Bagby*, 2 vols. (Richmond: Whittet & Shepperson, 1884), 1: 45.

weight of unprecedented responsibility and fear of an advancing enemy? In the wake of war and the pervasive despair that it ushered in, more postbellum Southerners had embraced the sentiment expressed by Ruffin twenty-five years earlier on the death of his good friend, Thomas Cocke: "It is not for man to judge of, but for God – and may the merciful God judge of it in mercy!"[58]

[58] Ruffin, "Statement of the Closing Scenes of the Life of Thomas Cocke," 188.

8

The "Translation" of Lundy Harris: Interpreting Death out of the Confusion of Sexuality, Violence, and Religion in the New South

Donald G. Mathews

In the cemetery at Oxford, Georgia, about a mile from where Emory College was founded in the 1830s, stands the headstone of a young Methodist. On it are engraved the youth's name followed by this inscription: "*Born May 9, 1867; Born again, June 12, 1878; Translated June 15, 1885.*" The word "translated" was defiantly optimistic. The family of the deceased wanted the world to know in Whom and unto what he had hoped: Christ Jesus and the Church Triumphant. Death was the logical outcome of the first date, but not of the second. Having been "born again," the young man had presumably been living a life in which physical death would have been merely the means through which he would realize the life of a pure Christian. Being "translated" was a fitting if archaic usage resurrected by the revivals of the eighteenth century. The concept had once meant entrance into Heaven without having died. By the late Middle Ages, however, it had come to refer to the death of the righteous, and, to the parents of this young man, "translated" carried not only this meaning but also a triumphant Hope. Sad as his death was, the young man's rebirth in Christ and His Resurrection promised "translation," a change beyond human understanding and knowledge. The young man's family had translated his life, rebirth, and dying, as they understood them, within the context of Faith and Hope. That testimony is far different from that

Research for this and other essays was made possible by the Louisville Institute through a generous grant and the University of North Carolina at Chapel Hill through a leave of absence. Sylvia Hoffert, Leslie Banner, and Kathryn Lofton were generous with their time and invaluable comments. I hope they are not too disappointed at the result. Elizabeth Farrior Buford offered valuable suggestions, observations, and insights and was encouraging when it helped the most.

attached to the death of another Methodist whose remains lie thirty yards away. The Reverend Lundy Howard Harris was interred there after committing suicide in September 1910.

Harris's translation was dramatically different from that imagined by the younger Methodist's family; his death triggered a flurry of translations. They began when one of Atlanta, Georgia's major newspapers, *The Constitution*, reported that the "widely Known Churchman and Educator" had sought relief from ill health and despondency through an overdose of morphine. Bishop Warren Akin Candler of the Methodist Episcopal Church, South (MECS), who was a much more "widely known Churchman and Educator" than Harris, paid tribute to him as a "most brilliant man and an accomplished professor."[1]

If that is all that Harris had been, his self-destruction would probably not be worth noting by anyone interested in culture, death, suicide, religion, and the South. But Harris was so much more than an "accomplished professor" – and unfortunately, less. When he killed himself, he was famous enough to have the *New York Times* and *The* (Philadelphia) *Public Ledger* each devote an entire page to his suicide, primarily because of who and what his wife was. Corra Harris was a popular writer and a former literary critic for *The Independent*, a New York magazine.[2] Lundy's suicide was transformed into a martyr's death because of his wife's stories in the *Saturday Evening Post*, published between hard covers in early 1910 as *A Circuit Rider's Wife*. In the translation of Yankee reporters, the "Circuit Rider" had killed himself: Why? The answers lie in the following "translation," which flows from a life wracked by a confluence of trends both southern and national: changing gender roles, professional standards, religious discourse, interracial sexual relations, and lynching.

Lundy Harris had once been a "golden Boy" of sorts. Bishop Atticus Greene Haygood had mentored him and Warren Candler to be future "players" in renewing the MECS. Lundy was "adopted" by Haygood while the future bishop was president of Emory College in Oxford, Georgia, as well as editor of the church's *Wesleyan Christian Advocate*. Haygood made the young man his assistant editor and, in 1881, took him to an international Methodist meeting where Lundy must have been affected by his mentor's positive and emotional interaction with African-American ministers. Lundy's importance to Haygood was reaffirmed when the president

[1] *The* (Atlanta) *Constitution*, September 20, 1910.

[2] *The* (Philadelphia) *Public Ledger*, September 25, 1910, Corra Mae White Harris Papers, University of Georgia Library, Athens. See also *The New York Times*, September 25, 1910.

then appointed him to take charge of students preparing to enter Emory College. Lundy was on the path to success, and then he stumbled – badly. At a Sunday morning worship service in Oxford, in the spring of 1882, Harris rose to confess to an embarrassed congregation that he had just resigned his position with the College because he had engaged in a drunken "debauch." It seemed to have happened at a brothel in nearby Covington.[3]

He fled the world of "cap and gown" to one of his mother's farms, hoping to purge himself through physical labor. If he succeeded in doing something he hated, he confessed, it would be a positive sign for the future. He still attended church, he told his grandmother, but found the sermons to be irrelevant and the worshippers to be "scandal mongers." By 1885, Lundy had given up farming to teach in an academy and, in early 1887, he married one of his youngest and brightest colleagues, Corra Mae White, daughter of a Confederate veteran and planter. Lundy had already insisted to his friend Warren Candler that he now relied on Christ and was ready to meet "God's demands on the soul." He then became a preacher serving country churches in north Georgia. In 1888, to the great relief of the Harrises, Candler, as the newly elected leader of Emory College, invited Lundy to rejoin the faculty. The president and Atticus Haygood knew that he would be "absolutely loyal" to them both.[4] The path was clear once again.

To the community and college, Lundy Harris seemed to thrive. He was a popular if not scholarly professor; he invited students into his home for conversation that could inspire them to value ideas in a new way; he encouraged them to have confidence in themselves and to live responsible public lives. The problems of the late nineteenth century, he once told the student body, demanded "the energies of all the most holy, the most stainless and the most devoted spirits of our time." He hoped that his audience included at least a few such "spirits." But he himself could not summon the confidence he encouraged in others to believe that he could be steadfastly "holy," "stainless," or "devoted." In the privacy of their home,

[3] Atticus Greene Haygood to Young John Allen, September 25, 1881, Young John Allen Papers, Robert W. Woodruff Library Special Collections, Emory University, Atlanta; R. F. Burden to Warren Akin Candler, April 21, 1882, Warren Akin Candler Papers, Robert W. Woodruff Library Special Collections.

[4] Lundy Howard Harris to "My Dear Grandma," September 8, 1882, Burge Family Papers, Robert W. Woodruff Library Special Collections; *The Emory Phoenix*, June 1888, 3; Atticus Greene Haygood to Warren Akin Candler, December 31, 1888, Warren Akin Candler Papers; John Talmadge, *Corra Harris: Lady of Purpose* (Athens: University of Georgia Press, 1968); Catherine Oglesby, *Corra Harris and the Divided Mind of the New South* (Gainesville: University Press of Florida, 2008).

almost from the very beginning of their marriage, Lundy afflicted his wife with a mercurial depressiveness and sense of guilt that at times left her convinced that she was living with a "madman." She often feared he would take his own life. She carried this dread secret in silence, perhaps too willing as the "birthright of married life" to "suffer" alone until forced to reach out to Warren Candler in the spring of 1898. Then she appealed to the newly elected bishop because she could no longer in solitude "carry my burden of fear, that has sapped my life all these years." She desperately needed Candler's help.[5]

So did Lundy. He had once again done something to justify his being cast out of the Methodist Garden of Eden. He had sinned; and perhaps worse, he had been discovered to be something less than what he pretended to be. The second fall from grace began in early 1898, when President Candler hired Andrew Sledd to be professor of Latin. Sledd had a master's degree from Harvard where he majored in Greek literature. Upon his arrival, he asked Lundy (who had earlier been appointed Seney Professor of Greek literature) to join him in studying selected classical Greek texts. Lundy demurred. Sledd then discovered that his new colleague had little knowledge of the classics and that he relied on English translations to study the few that he did claim to understand. Lundy was a fraud. When another professor was discovered, with the aid of Lundy's wife, to have plagiarized one of Lundy's articles, the man was forced to resign. Fraud once exposed might have been revealed again. Lundy's propensity for shame and guilt must have sent him into a depression, which he was able to hide until after he and his wife hosted a grand party for students and faculty to celebrate the end of term. Shortly thereafter, Lundy disappeared, leaving his family so that he could find "the Spirit" in Texas – but he looked in the wrong places. He suffered a complete breakdown, apparently in an Austin sporting house. Finding haven in his brother Henry's home, he then took on a self-inflicted penance that included far too many embarrassing public confessions to drunkenness and sexual intercourse with black women. A brother thought him temporarily insane, his wife thought him dangerously depressed, his colleagues thought him unnecessarily talkative, and he thought himself shamefully

[5] Henry Stiles Bradley to Mrs. L. H. (Corra) Harris, October 3, 1910, Corra Mae White Harris Papers; Elam Dempsey to his parents, November 28, 1897, Elam Dempsey Papers, Robert W. Woodruff Library Special Collections; Lundy H. Harris, "Speech of Professor Lundy H. Harris," *The Emory Phoenix*, March 1892, 11, 13; Corrie Harris to Warren Akin Candler, June 17 and 24, 1898, Warren Akin Candler Papers.

disgraced.[6] He was right. The community seized on his sexual escapades; only Sledd knew of his flaws as a scholar. Corra took him back; Emory College did not.

After a brief separation, Corra gradually took over Lundy's life. She fumed at his betrayal of her and his recklessness with black women – maybe even a family maid or cook. The evidence lies in the way she became de facto head of household, a famed literary critic, and a short story writer. Corra's transformation began with her response to a spectacular lynching. Almost a year after what she called Lundy's "Austin debauch," she published her first essays in *The Independent*. The first one "explained" the burning of Sam Hose in April 1899 near Newnan, Georgia. The next three condemned black women for creating the domestic conditions within which black men embraced a licentiousness that endangered every white woman in the South. Hose, Corra implied, had been one of those "brutes."[7]

Her fury with black women intensified with each essay; she seemed to be responding not to what had happened in Newnan, but to what had happened between Lundy and unnamed black women. Those vixens, she believed, had perfected a loathsome sexuality that dominated their relations with all males; it had shaped their religious expressiveness and entrapped white men in a "cesspool of vice." She ignored critics who pointed out that it was the white men who had (at best) seduced or (at worst) raped the African-American women she condemned. Her anger with Lundy – his "madness," his weakness, and his betrayal – was dangerous to her. It was obvious in her first letters to Candler in the spring of 1898, but it receded until it was transformed into a displaced fury with women whom Lundy himself believed he had wronged. Much later, she confessed that she had had to speak out because she was in so much "trouble and pain." The "spirit" from that pain encouraged editors of *The Independent* to believe they had discovered a feisty southern woman who could – despite her atrocious views – add a new dimension to the magazine.[8]

6 William P. Lovejoy to Bishop Warren Akin Candler, June 30, 1898, Warren Akin Candler Papers; Luke G. Johnson to Candler, June 16, 1898, Warren Akin Candler Papers; Corra Harris to Candler, "One Sunday" in June 1898, Warren Akin Candler Papers; Corrie Harris to Candler, June 12 and 18, 1898, Warren Akin Candler Papers; "Dr. Moore's Successor," *The Emory Phoenix*, December 1897, 97; *The Emory Phoenix*, February 1898, 187; Terry Lee Matthews, "The Emergence of a Prophet: Andrew Sledd and the 'Sledd Affair of 1902'" (Ph.D. diss., Duke University, 1989), 76–89.

7 Mrs. L. H. Harris, "A Southern Woman's View," *The Independent*, May 18, 1899, 1354–55.

8 Hamilton Holt to Mrs. L. H. Harris, June 29, 1899, Corra White Harris Papers; Corrie Harris to Warren Akin Candler, June 27, 1899, Warren Akin Candler Papers; Lundy Howard Harris to Candler, October 31, 1899, Warren Akin Candler Papers; Mrs. L. H. Harris, editorial, *The*

Soon, Paul Elmer More, famed literary editor for *The Independent*, taught Corra how to improve as a writer and critic; they eventually wrote an epistolary novel together. Letters from Corra to More suggest an emotional attachment on her part that was liberating as she learned how to analyze and evaluate texts, a process that revealed a new world of ideas and judgments that made her both uncomfortable and happy. More became her inspiration, her mentor, and, probably to his regret, her confidante. She treasured any sign of approval from him: "Your last letter was generous," she once told him, "and I was so pleased that you think my work is improving. I always think that a word of praise wrung from a man with the 'Greek' accent of mind and spirit is a great concession to a barbarian like me." She wrote to him freely, trying out phrases, words, and ideas that seemed to help her find what she called "a strange world of a new life." The world in Oxford had gone out "in one lightening [sic] fizzle," but then, she recalled, she had ascended far above that "ground." She thought her chattering to him would make her "grow wise," but she was not passive or hesitant to challenge him. She complained of More's aloof and sometimes cold demeanor – almost to the edge of teasing. She chided him for his lack of "feeling." But she absorbed the duality of emotion and reason, female and male, private and public, and empathy and indifference that grounded his innate conservatism as well as hers. By the end of their association, Corra had developed a "different voice," biographer Catherine Oglesby pointed out, and "crafted a new identity for herself." More's obvious intellectual rigor and broad knowledge of world religions helped Corra continue her flight from Lundy's religious miasma of shame and guilt. As she struggled with the limits of her knowledge, she recruited her husband to be her research assistant as the life of the household gradually became her intellectual domain. She sent him to the library to read articles, mine books, check references, and dig up details for reviews and essays. She then used her connection with Warren Candler to wrangle a position for him as assistant secretary of the Board of Education for the bureaucracy of the MECS, in Nashville. She had taken charge of their lives.[9]

Independent, June 22, 1899, 1703–704; idem, "Negro Womanhood," *The Independent*, June 22, 1899, 1687–89; idem, "The Negro Child," *The Independent*, October 26, 1899, 2884–86; idem, "A Southern Woman's View," *The Independent*, May 18, 1899, 1354–55; idem, *My Book and Heart* (Boston: Houghton Mifflin Co., 1924), 181–82.

9 Mrs. Lundy H. Harris to Paul Elmer More, May 4 and July 2, 1901; March 3, 1902; April 9, 1903, Paul Elmer More Papers, Princeton University, microfilm at the University of Georgia; Oglesby, *Corra Harris*, 17–70, 96–113, esp. 61, 62, 66, 70. Corra did not mention Candler by name, but she did claim that she had the connections to get Lundy appointed to this relatively lucrative position. Her best connection was Candler now that Haygood was deceased.

In the Tennessee capital, Lundy seemed to thrive once again: he even began serving a nearby church without taking a salary. Publicly, he seemed to be doing very well, but privately he returned to nurturing his deadly depression with alcohol. He felt compelled to escape once again, this time not to Texas but into the void Corra had always feared he would leap. In March 1908, he bade her "Goodbye" in a brief note. "You have been infinitely good & loving to me, and it is hard to part, but it is better so," he told her. He mentioned his love for her, their daughter, and their deceased son and closed with a true assessment of her relationship to him: "You have been the noblest of all wives – the most faithful, the most loving – the most forbearing." He could not "overcome the drink habit" and decided to "take this way of ending the struggle." Then he thrust scissors into his throat.[10]

As with most of his ways of coping with depression and failure, Lundy could not get this one right either. He survived and began to heal emotionally as well as physically throughout the spring and summer. By autumn, Corra thought that he had "found peace in God," that he felt more "at home" with his surroundings "than I have ever known him to be. . . . Now he is like a man that has been delivered from a great darkness." His deliverance was surprising, she confessed, because he had continued to suffer the "ferocious enmity" of a bishop for "treason" against the MECS. Corra had also felt the bishop's temper for essays she had written about the church, and she had been "vengeful," but her husband achieved a strange new calm that gave her peace. The "terrible place" into which Lundy's attempted suicide had thrown her was gone: "Nothing else can be that hard for me."[11]

To her daughter Faith, however, Corra was less optimistic and confessed her apprehensions. When he returned to work after his recuperation, Lundy was thrown back into the maelstrom that had been afflicting the MECS since 1905. Bishop E. E. Hoss and many of his colleagues began to fight for ecclesiastical control of Vanderbilt University, despite the fact that the church had never invested any funds in it. The issue was whether Vanderbilt's Board of Trust could appoint its own members. The university charter empowered the Board of Trust, but Hoss wanted the MECS

[10] See suicide note on stationery of the Board of Education of the MECS and several bills for the Nashville sanitarium where he convalesced thereafter, June 1908, Corra Mae White Harris Papers; Talmadge, *Corra Harris*, 38; David Silkenat, *Moments of Despair: Suicide, Divorce, & Debt in Civil War Era North Carolina* (Chapel Hill: University of North Carolina Press, 2011), 33.

[11] Corra Harris to Warren Akin Candler, April 3, 1909, Warren Akin Candler Papers; Corra Harris to Faith Harris, April 14, 1909, Corra Mae White Harris Papers.

Board of Education to do it. After five years of sometimes intense and mean-spirited controversy, all but three bishops submitted a bill against the Vanderbilt University Board of Trust asking the Court in effect to affirm the right of the General Conference of the MECS to rule the university. A sometimes-hysterical Hoss became outraged when the Methodist General Board of Education and its secretary, John D. Hammond, refused to take sides in the controversy.[12]

Lundy and Corra were friends with Vanderbilt's Chancellor, James H. Kirkland, believing that he was fighting for the integrity of higher education against ecclesiastical "bigotry." Corra wrote articles supporting the university's position against Hoss, provoking Hoss's wrath. When Secretary Hammond resigned in June 1910, Hoss succeeded in having an ally appointed to replace Hammond, and he immediately targeted Lundy who was given instructions that he refused to follow on principle. Lundy was forced to resign.[13]

Once again, Lundy lost an important position and his self-respect, even though it could be argued that his latest resignation was in fact quite honorable. He felt contaminated, and he began to bathe himself obsessively. He needed rest. Corra asked an influential friend to find haven for Lundy away from Nashville: a farm near Pine Log in north Georgia seemed to be just right and when, in early September, he arrived at Clarence Anthony's home, Lundy plunged enthusiastically into the farm's daily chores. He devoted evenings to writing Corra long letters that rambled on about everything from Greece and Cromwell to the flora of rural Georgia. He needed to tell her repeatedly how much he loved her, how much he longed to hold her: "I love you with all my heart – more and more every day." It became his mantra. "I think of you," he seemed to whisper, "with infinite tenderness."[14] He seemed to relax.

[12] Bishop E. E. Hoss to James H. Kirkland, December 21, 1909, James H. Kirkland Papers, Heard Library, Vanderbilt University; Bishop Eugene B. Hendrix to Chancellor James H. Kirkland, November 2, 1905, James H. Kirkland Papers. After an appeal four years later, the Supreme Court ruled against the bishops and on behalf of the Board of Trust; Paul K. Conkin et al., *Gone with the Ivy: A Biography of Vanderbilt University* (Knoxville: University of Tennessee Press, 1985), 149–84.

[13] Corrie Harris to Mrs. James H. Kirkland, May 8, 1904; Corra Harris to "My Dear Friends," March 22, 1914; Lundy Howard Harris to James H. Kirkland, May 27, 1908; James H. Kirkland to Mary Kirkland, January 26, 1904, all in James H. Kirkland Papers; Corra Harris to Dr [Stonewall] Anderson, September 24, 1910; Lundy Harris to Kirkland, August 10, 1904, both in Corra Mae White Harris Papers; *Nashville Christian Advocate*, June 3, 1910; July 22, 1910.

[14] Lundy Harris to Corra Harris, September 7, 8, 10, 13, 15, 16, and 17, 1910, Corra Mae White Harris Papers.

Somehow, he had escaped his alcoholic addiction and began to imagine a future.[15] He quit taking two baths a day and planned on bathing only once a week after sweating profusely enough somehow to expel the deadly poisons in his mind. He anticipated that "I'll understand what the clod [earth] is saying" after he became "saturated with the rains." He looked forward to sleep, which soothed the soul as it came gently from "the healing silence of the country" and its "soft medicinal winds." Sleep promised salvation and strengthened him to do what he had come to Pine Log to do. Finally, like the good bureaucrat he had been throughout his life, he wrote instructions, listed his assets, told his executor to buy the cheapest coffin available, and bade Corra once again "Goodbye." "Nobody knows that this act is contemplated and nobody is to blame but me," he wrote, "My family relations are unusually happy and my trouble is not due to any business wrong. I'm simply tired of living." He had been hoarding morphine for this moment and now ingested it. His last message to Corra was the shortest of the previous eleven days: "The end has at last come. Goodbye, my darling. My last thoughts are of you and Faith. I shall love you both eternally – if love is hereafter permitted. You have been unutterably good to me all our days together."[16]

Nashville, from which Lundy had escaped only two weeks before his funeral, must have been abuzz with rumors and knowing expressions of "the real truth" about his death – "bless his heart." Many remembered his previous attempt at suicide and his terrible drinking problem. Church bureaucrats knew that he had just lost his job. Maybe the truth could be that he was a casualty of Vanderbilt University's fight for independence. Corra certainly considered this interpretation as part of her own truth, and she did hint at it in obituaries and feature stories, albeit without great specificity. He had been a scholar of the "deepest piety" who had been in poor health for some time and had gone to Georgia for a much-needed rest. His piety had been exemplified in a disregard for worldly wealth. When he died, he had $2.16 in his pocket, $116.00 in the bank, 400 books in his

[15] Corra Harris to Faith Harris, April 14, 1909, Corra Mae White Harris Papers, in which Corra reassured her daughter that "Your father is all right. He says that he does not even crave liquor any longer. Anyhow, I do not have to hide it from him if I have it in the house. He never notices it. He is never morbid or blue anymore, but he is high strung as ever and as easy to fly off the handle with his temper. Only you do not mind because he never broods [with you]."

[16] Lundy Harris to Coroner, to Austen, to others, September 17, 1910; Lundy Harris to Corra Harris, September 9, 10, 13, 15, and 17, 1910, all in Corra Mae White Harris Papers.

library, and a coffin worth $85.00 in the ground (definitely not the "cheapest" one available). His character could be inferred from the fact, Corra claimed, that he had given $1,200 a year to charities – nearly his entire annual salary. He had pensioned an "outcast" woman and an old soldier; he had sent two "Negro" boys to school and supported "a family of 5." His wife added that he had been persecuted for three years prior to his death and that he had been the person upon whom she had modeled William Thompson, the hero of her "circuit rider stories."[17]

It was as the "Circuit Rider" that Lundy was remembered in the Philadelphia and New York newspapers on September 25, 1910. The stories would surely have saddened him or at least evoked a sardonic and self-deprecating grimace, for they did not capture Lundy so much as the fictional circuit rider whom Corra had imagined. As with almost everything else in his later life, it was as Corra's husband – and therefore as her creation – that he was remembered. Corra's likeness accompanied the articles, not Lundy's image. Engravings from her book illustrated the stories that became, in her mind and on the page, a condemnation of the ways in which the Church treated its minor clergy. Additionally, there was the leit-motif of theological failure attributable to The New Theology and manifested in a muddled report of Lundy's own theological reflections, followed by the last story in *A Circuit Rider's Wife*. The effect of this translation was to make one pause in respect for the poverty-stricken and extraordinarily pious preacher who had taken his own life because the church, contaminated by heartlessness and ecclesiastical politics, did not appreciate his selfless ministry.[18] The sentimentality may have cautioned a few readers, but Corra's fictionalized husband, William Thompson, was about to be confirmed in popular culture by Lundy's very real suicide. He had not only lost his life but also his identity.

We are left to wonder how Lundy Harris came to the most fateful decision of his life. In one sense – and the one that Lundy himself must have felt as he gathered his morphine – he was a failure as a professor, a Christian, a husband, a man, a minister, and a bureaucrat. Not all "failures" kill themselves, however, and in many ways he was definitely not a failure: he inspired his students, befriended the friendless, fed and educated the poor, tendered anonymous kindnesses to his enemies, and preached an

[17] Unidentified newspaper clippings, Corra Mae White Harris Papers.

[18] William R. Hutchison, *The Modernist Impulse in American Protestantism* (Cambridge: Harvard University Press, 1976); *The Public Ledger*, September 25, 1910, Corra Mae White Harris Papers; see also *The New York Times*, September 25, 1910.

evocative gospel in which he could frequently believe. Neither did faithlessness nor his chronic depression necessarily lead him to overdose on morphine. Depressives who mourn the loss of faith have toughed it out, acquiring new centers of trust and value, losing themselves in diversions, and even finding creative outlets that elicited praise from others for their intensity, insight, and profundity. Lundy struggled to do some of these things – giving away his salary to educate and support both blacks and whites and refusing to act in a way he considered irresponsible and dishonorable.

His last confession was that he was "tired of living." To be sure, the loss of a position in the church that he had tried to serve in an honorable way may have helped to nudge him over the edge, but he had been hoarding his cache of morphine for a long time before his resignation. There was something else tormenting him – something which, in his own mind, labeled him a failure as a husband and a man. Years later, Corra remembered Lundy's state of mind after *A Circuit Rider's Wife* had been published in early 1910. People had visited him that summer expecting to discover that he was in fact the deeply religious and profoundly committed William Thompson about whom his wife had written, but he had insisted in a "crestfallen" way that he was nothing like the sainted William. As husband and wife talked about the widespread acclaim for the book, Corra came the closest to being really happy, she recalled, as at any time in her entire life; but Lundy was not. As she shared with him her joy and plans for them both to be happy, he responded with a look of "terrible apprehension" that she never forgot.[19] Much earlier, he had watched her be "born again" under More's tutelage and now he watched her change once more through the joy of widespread popular approval. She had surpassed his own public persona; she had been doing so for a long time, even as she continued to be "unutterably good" to him. Maybe he was tired of it.

Taking one's own life is a special kind of death, and embracing death as a Christian bereft of the opportunity for martyrdom also sets one apart because it suggests a repudiation of divine grace bestowed both in the gift of life and the offer of salvation. Although Lundy Harris would be buried in what was in effect hallowed ground, there was a general sadness (by all accounts) at the failure of faith in this flawed but good man. His wife was shocked, stunned, and enraged. She had labored so hard to prevent this, and he had betrayed her yet again. For the next several months, she

[19] Oglesby, *Corra Harris*, 37; Harris, *Book and Heart*, 268–70.

relived the years of "agony and suspense" and thought about him in terms of scandal, shame, and defeat. She contemplated the haven of an asylum or of going "the way that Lundy went." Lundy Harris's suicide was not merely his failure, she believed, but her own as well. She had been his sanctuary; she had been his keeper, his patron, his Providence – or at least she had tried to be – but "in the end," his daughter Faith was convinced, "he did what he had pre-ordained in himself." It was, she wrote Corra, "impossible to save him."[20]

Lundy himself had often felt he was irredeemable: when visiting his brother Henry in Florida, he had been especially arrested by the terrible depression that afflicted them both and wondered if they should not have been "strangled as they were born."[21] Perhaps chemical deprivation of serotonin had thrown the Harris brothers into various episodes of despair, but Lundy's suicide was nonetheless his own within a complex and broad web of human relationships, and it had implications for those who knew him.

He had traveled too far out to the margin of life and self-esteem to withstand the suicidal logic that seemed to promise haven. As Corra confessed almost hysterically to Warren Candler in 1898, she feared he would kill himself many times during their marriage, especially when he was depressed by "the memory of that first sin" that was like a "crawling serpent [leaving] its trail across [his] youth." She feared the "Austin debauch" had condemned him once again to a "madness" with which she could not cope, but he seemed to come to his senses when he realized how seriously he had damaged his family. He returned to a semblance of normality and seemed to be in no danger of killing himself. He seemed at times still to be afflicted by that "crawling serpent" of guilt and the inability to receive a "witness of the Spirit," which was the Wesleyan phrase for a subjective confirmation of ones becoming a "child" of God. Much later, Corra "remembered" how Lundy's torment lay in an unrealistic search for religious assurance and perfection when a simple faith should have sufficed. She wanted him to embrace the gospel of forgiveness that he preached to others and get on with life, if not for Heaven's sake then at least for *her* sake.[22]

[20] Susan Leech to Harry Leech, February 28, 1911; Faith Harris to Corra Harris, February 7, 1911, both in Corra Mae White Harris Papers.

[21] Lundy Harris to Corra Harris, January 18 and February 3, 1908, Corra Mae White Harris Papers.

[22] Ronald W. Maris with Bernard Lazerwitz, *Pathways to Suicide: A Survey of Self-Destructive Behaviors* (Baltimore: Johns Hopkins University Press, 1981), 1, 169, 206, 234; Corra Harris to Warren Akin Candler, June 24 and 28, and July 1, 1898, June 6,

Lundy's quandary was similar to that of a fictional minister whom Harold Frederic imagined in a novel published in 1896: *The Damnation of Theron Ware*. Both Harris and Ware came out of a rural background into the Methodist ministry; both were sexually tempted outside their marriages; both yearned to slough off their ministerial "calling," at least momentarily; both were humiliated in confrontations that revealed their hollowness; both found solace in drink. Ware did not commit suicide but, in discovering philosophical atheism and a sophisticated aestheticism, the Methodist church became dead to him.[23] Both the damnation of the fictional preacher and the suicide of the real man revealed the tensions, losses, and failures of professional men overwhelmed by the challenges brought on by an accelerating modernity.[24]

Like Ware, Lundy may not have heard the voice of forgiveness because he was not sure anyone was there to forgive. Both of Corra's biographers agree that he was afflicted by religious doubt and confusion, which may have approached a pious but emotionally draining agnosticism.[25] He recognized that Southern Methodism had been torn by religious dissension, suspicion, and frustration as believers tried to sustain an authentic faith against discoveries and values that seemed to belie it. Evangelicals of all Protestant denominations shared the conviction that a Creator God, the Bible, the Cross, an experience of God's grace, and a disciplined Christian

1899, Warren Akin Candler Papers; Corra Harris, *As A Woman Thinks* (New York: Houghton Mifflin Co., 1925), 83, 100–103, 152.

[23] Harold Frederic, *The Damnation of Theron Ware* (1896; imprint, Mineola: Dover Publications, 2012). Ware becomes infatuated with a beautiful red-haired woman, Celia, who finally damns him in effect for his naiveté, presumption, arrogance, and failure to understand what their interaction with a Roman Catholic priest actually means. Lundy, of course, did not bed white women or carry on affairs with black women. His sexual enticement was more impersonal, demoralizing, demeaning, exploitative, and physical.

[24] In *This Republic of Suffering: Death and the American Civil War* (New York: Alfred A. Knopf, 2008), 171–210, Drew Gilpin Faust analyzes the writings of Emily Dickinson, Ambrose Bierce, and Herman Melville, and points out that critics have found in each "characteristics associated with 'modernity.'" The challenge to certainty is an important dimension of this designation; each of these writers grapples with religious doubt, and all adopt an irony that reflects anxiety about deception and delusion. All three seek, to borrow Melville's word, to "undeceive" (207).

[25] Talmadge, *Corra Harris*, 24–27, 53–55; Oglesby, *Corra Harris*, 31, 36–37. Oglesby argues that Bishop Haygood's agnosticism in his declining years may have affected Lundy, citing Harold Mann's fine biography, *Atticus Greene Haygood, Methodist Bishop, Editor, and Educator* (Athens: University of Georgia Press, 1965), 183. Mann is correct in believing that Haygood's theology changed over time, and he may have sloughed off or at least declined to believe in the divinity of Christ. But latter-day Socinianism does not mean he doubted the existence of God or the truth of the Beatitudes. Doubt and adjustment are functions of faith as much as they are of faithlessness.

life were the bases of Christian faith. Beyond the simplicity of this foundation, however, lay the complexities and anguish of definition. New, rigorous, disinterested studies in geology, biology, archaeology, sociology, ethnology, history, textual criticism, comparative religions, and the philosophy and psychology of religion combined to undermine certainty. The languages of these different disciplines demanded "new translations." Even conservatives believed that "Christ" had to be explained in the language of the new century rather than that of the old ones. As historian Drew Faust points out, the problem was greater than one of translation: the "crisis of language and epistemology as much as one of eschatology ... about not just whether there is a God and whether we can know him but whether we can know or communicate anything at all."[26]

Consequently, there was a wide range of attempts to communicate – and excommunicate. Conservatives worried that unthinking naïfs might come to believe that the Creator God had acted and continued to act through "evolution." They suspected that secret "heretics" were interpreting Christ's crucifixion in ways that diminished or even denied his divinity, that such people accepted the "higher criticism" of the Bible that made it less authoritative and that they were substituting "Christian education" for a radical experience of being "born again." Some "Christians" had even accepted secularism by dancing, drinking, playing cards, reading scandalous novels, and attending the theater. To counter such activities, some Wesleyans insisted that true Christians experience not only a first "blessing" of conversion but a "second blessing," or subjective confirmation of Christian discipleship. The Methodists' *Christian Advocate* announced in 1909 that heresy should not be condoned, but no one should be labeled "heretic" just because he or she sometimes went "wrong" in his or her thinking or actions. "True heresy," the editor insisted, "is more a frame of mind than a specific form of error. ... [T]he worst heresy – the only absolutely unpardonable one – is a bad life."[27]

[26] Faust, *Republic of Suffering*, 208; Claude Welch, *Protestant Thought in the Nineteenth Century, Volume 2: 1870–1914* (New Haven: Yale University Press, 1985); Charles D. Cashdollar, *The Transformation of Theology, 1830–1890* (Princeton: Princeton University Press, 1989); William P. Lovejoy, "The Christ of the Twentieth Century," *Methodist Quarterly Review* 50 (1901): 61–73.

[27] *The* (Nashville) *Christian Advocate*, September 10, 1909; Hunter Dickinson Farish, *The Circuit Rider Dismounts: A Social History of Southern Methodism 1865–1900* (1938; reprint, New York: De Capo Press, 1969); Christopher H. Owen, *The Sacred Flame of Love: Methodism and Society in Nineteenth Century Georgia* (Athens: University of Georgia Press, 1998): M. B. Chapman, "Evolution as a Method of Creation," *Methodist*

Lundy Harris wondered as much: in 1907, "bad" was his alcoholism. To escape its clutches, Corra had urged him to take temporary leave of his job and visit his brother; doing so would be restorative. In Florida, he talked with Henry about poetry, religion, science, sociology, socialism, New Thought, and health fads. They probably talked about Ernst Renan's *Life of Jesus*, too, because Henry had just written an article for *The Methodist Quarterly Review* in which he discussed what a later generation would call the androgyny of Jesus. Henry relied on Renan for his understanding of the Nazarene, whom the French author claimed was not divine although he did cause "his fellowmen to make the greatest step towards the divine."[28] This heresy Lundy did not mention: it was merely part of "intelligent conversation" during his visit. But he could not avoid confessing that he did not "understand the ways of God" even as he wondered if he and Henry "ought to have been strangled as they were born."

Even as he expressed these theological questions in his correspondence to Corra, he transitioned quickly to a question that became an obsession: "You will love me, will you not – even if I am a Harris?" He needed to know: "Do you love me? Your letters have mighty little to say on that line." He required her "love & fidelity." "Do pray try to love me," he pleaded, "I crave & need your love." He was "hungry for one or two love words." If she would tell him that she loved him, he hoped Corra would "say it with the accent of conviction." He wanted reassurance, but he feared that he did not deserve it: "I only wish I were worthy of you." Perhaps to stoke the fire a little, he assured her that he was "coming back into the peace I had last year," but he lied and soon thereafter made his first suicide attempt by slashing his throat.[29]

His mood swings had continued. To his daughter's classmates and friends, he appeared charming. Sometimes he was as "sweetly at home among men" as Corra had ever known him to be. Other times, Lundy was "high strung" and easily enraged. The "blue" moods turned to anger as the religious propriety of Nashville suffocated him: he exploded about the

Quarterly Review 17 (1894): 224–31; E. D. McCreary, "Three Decades of Evolution," *Methodist Quarterly Review* 9 (1890): 79–100; Wilbur Fisk Tillett, "A Wesleyan Arminian Confession of Faith," *Methodist Quarterly Review* 10 (1891): 282–99; idem, "The Higher Criticism," *Methodist Quarterly Review* 17 (1895): 321–32.

[28] Ernst Renan, *The Life of Jesus* (1863; reprint, New York: Prometheus Books, 1991), 226; Henry F. Harris, "The Absence of Humor in Jesus," *Methodist Quarterly Review* 34 (1908): 460–67.

[29] Lundy Harris to Corra Harris, January 13, 14, 16, 25, 26, and 30, 1908; February 3, 1908; suicide note on stationery of the Board of Education, all in Corra Mae White Harris Papers.

"shams & conventions & artificialities" that surrounded him. Once again in need of rest, he fled to his brother William Albinus "Al" Harris who had recently survived a crisis of faith and found renewed confidence in a "living God" instead of the god of "obsolete creeds." The visit did not help. Lundy railed at the stifling intellectual atmosphere of the Methodist bureaucracy that choked him into silence "because I do not know how to talk to the dead" or "to breathe through formulas." He announced to Corra his intent to return to a simple, country-defined faith where Nature could cleanse him. If she and Faith would not go with him, he would go alone "though it means breaking asunder of the very cells of life and reason." This was not what either woman wanted to read. Faith was planning her wedding, and Corra was writing a book. Only upon returning home to nurse Corra through convalescence after two serious operations did he begin to calm down. And then he was forced to resign from Vanderbilt.[30] He badly needed "rest" once again; he headed for north Georgia with the cache of morphine from Corra's convalescence in his bag. His hope for peace lay with neither Nature nor God, but with death.

Lundy's letters to Corra hide as much as they reveal, but he also kept a small notebook – part of the debris from the wreck of his life as a professor – filled with Greek words and, in English, some of his inner musings. He revealed *moral judgment* of friends, of authority figures, and of self; *anger* with Corra and himself; *dismay* with marriage and religion; *frustration* at ignorance and the conventional; and *questions* about divinity, innocence, and sex.

During the trip in which he began to jot down his thoughts, Lundy had sought a "living God" beyond creeds. Within Lundy's Wesleyan tradition, the dialectic of dead creed and living God was axiomatic: John Wesley believed that the Apostle's Creed was ineffectual as a statement of truth if the believer had not been received by the Spirit of God. Every Methodist minister of Lundy's generation knew that the witness of the spirit came only to those certain in issues of faith.[31] Lundy tried to use rituals of charity

[30] Corra Harris to Faith Harris, April 14, 1909; Faith Harris to Lundy Harris, May 2, 1909; Lundy Harris to Corra Harris, January 23, 1910, all in Corra Mae White Harris Papers; Corra Harris to Warren Akin Candler, April 1 and 3, 1909; Lundy Harris to Warren Candler, May 25, 1910, all in Warren Akin Candler Papers.

[31] Lundy Harris to Corra Harris, January 23, 1910, Corra Mae White Harris Papers. Methodist ministers would have schooled in the witness of the spirit by John Wesley and Thomas N. Ralston, *Elements of Divinity* (Nashville: Cokesbury Press, 1924), 435–72. Also see Robert W. Burtner and Robert E. Chiles, eds., *A Compend of Wesley's Theology* (New York: Abingdon Press, 1954), 95–105; and Edward H. Sugden, ed., *Wesley's Standard Sermons*, 2 vols. (London: Epworth Press, 1955), 1: 199–236, 2: 341–59.

and service to compensate for his lack of certainty. He seemed almost desperately to need that witness of the spirit; it was the one religious theme that Corra recalled as having condemned Lundy to despair.[32]

The first of his jottings was about faith – "Is God is? . . . What does a wife mean?" – under which he listed questions and comments that defy order but contain themes that come and go throughout the notebook. Lundy seemed to be "screaming for a God who cares," as he had in a poem he scribbled in a letter to Corra. He rejected the sentimentality that found God in human emotions: did God "exist" in a grin or tear? He knew facile ministers who seemed to believe it, but he did not. He wondered if the chaos of his own internal life and his dismay at the dead formulae of theology and the equally dead formula of marriage were not all the same. He played with the idea of *innocence*, represented by children and Eden but not – to this publicly and domestically uxorious married man and father – with *women*. If innocence were a condition in which one lived heedless of law in prelapsarian righteousness, then *women* were strangely "against the laws" for they were connected, in his free association, with an "unlawful" sexuality. "People [wives] don't like pencils," he wrote among a group of phrases. "Why? Is it because we have something unlawful between our [legs]? The point of comity between a man and a woman is – a point."[33] One wonders how clever Lundy thought he was for imagining the pencil with which he wrote as a phallus in search of a meaningful connection between men and women.

More than cleverness, however, the analogy was the natural expression of a man for whom the association of sex with humanity and divinity was compelling. Sexual intercourse was problematic between him and Corra. She was reticent even to talk about sex and thought that writers such as Jack London who did so were desecrating literature and defiling American culture.[34] Corra had become pregnant three times, but she and Lundy had not slept together for years after she discovered his infidelity. Still, those sexual encounters with black women had been essential to his pilgrimage

32 Harris, *Book and Heart*, 25, 65, 98–101, 126–27; idem, *A Circuit Rider's Wife* (1910; reprint, New York: Houghton Mifflin Co, 1933), 31, 88–94; Lundy Harris to Corra Harris, January 23, 1910; William Albinus Harris to Corra Harris, February 4, 1910; Lundy Harris Notebook, all in Corra Mae White Harris Papers.

33 Lundy Harris to Corra Harris, January 23, 1910, Corra Mae White Harris Papers; Lundy Harris Notebook.

34 At a banquet celebrating American authors, London teased Corra Harris about her reticence to think of sex in a free and open way; she was horrified and tried to get away from him, eventually fleeing the banquet hall in a panic; Corra Harris to Dear Miss Adelaide W. Neall, February 14, 1914, Corra Mae White Harris Papers.

of faith for they had led him long ago to confess his sins. It is not surprising, therefore, that sexual imagery should come so naturally to him in his private confessional: it reflected neither shame nor guilt so much as vexation with conventional marital assumptions and a sense of irony at the incongruity of the sacred within the profane – and the profane within the sacred. He imagined "God in a sporting house" – a sanctuary in which God would have to rely on the more experienced Lundy for protection! His initiation of God into the mysteries of a brothel was ironic, contradictory, offensive, humorous – all at once. He had little doubt in the power of sex, but he was less sure of the power of God and unconvinced that any deity would or could "care" for men such as he, or indeed for anyone.

From phallus and sporting house, Lundy intellectually journeyed to the futility of the Methodist Episcopal Church's missionary activity in Cuba, a special project of Bishop Candler. "Cuba is a pretty small island to put a Bishop to so much trouble," he scrawled. He could not avoid the sexual metaphor: "Why can't God save Cuba by sticking Florida through it 'a la hat on peg'"? In his previous contemplations of God's sexual prowess, Lundy had labeled Cuba a "nigger republic." Conflating salvation with the white rape of black Cuba not only reflected current domestic and international politics, but Lundy's own personal experiences: his sexual encounters with black women had been a form of salvation.[35]

Memory, inquiry, pride, and awe flooded Lundy's passages on innocence and divine sexuality, evoking dismay: "God don't you understand?" It is difficult to judge whether he was addressing God or himself or Candler, whether he was cursing or praying, whether thinking of his failure with Corra or her failure with him, whether ashamed or proud of his sexual knowledge: probably all of these possibilities.[36] In his doodling about God, sex and chaos, Lundy contemplated the meaning of "wife" and wondered about societal dictates that people live together as couples. He chafed at expectations of respectability and jotted a few words suggesting "insult" associated with New York, *The Independent*, and More, its one time literary editor. Lundy seemed to be angry that Corra had turned to More as her indispensable mentor: "Am I worth more than they all? If so, why?" The context suggested despair over any protestations of care from Corra. Did he really think of her as Socrates' bothersome wife, Xantipe, as

[35] R. R. Burden to Warren Akin Candler, April 21, 1882; Lundy Harris to Warren Akin Candler, October 31, 1899, both in Warren Akin Candler Papers.

[36] Lundy Harris Notebook.

he wrote? His anger with her, scrawled in his notes, starkly contrasted with protestations of eternal love during the week he spent preparing his death. It was probably safer for the anger to remain hidden in Greek analogies and probably truer to both of them.

Lundy's greatest anger was at God whom he could not grasp, understand, or concede. His mind wavered between scriptural authority ("Can a man by searching, find out God. No man hath seen God") and his own quest. "Why are men afraid to search for God," he asked, but he was actually tortured by the fact that they were *not* afraid to do so. The God-question had tormented him for years as he awaited divine Grace. Lundy's questions were conventional and troubling and existential. Perhaps his unrealized intention to read William James was a feeble concession to concerns that were leading him on a lonely voyage to "the undiscovered land where God comes & goes like flickering lights on the wall." Lundy seemed to be enmeshed in a game of cosmic hide and seek that he thought he could not win. The void left Lundy alone, small, confused, and "tired." He had hoped the Universe was a "cradle," but he feared it was a "grave."[37]

Lundy was playing at the edge of propriety and faith, frustrated at his lack of understanding that would have helped him establish his place in a plausible reality. He was unable to solve his God-sex-wife problem. The question was not far from his consciousness when Harris unexpectedly met Warren Candler – the most significant authority figure of his life save perhaps his wife. One way to solve his problem was to accuse the bishop of having failed to help men such as Lundy. It was a relatively easy indictment that placed responsibility on those in authority but solved nothing. Candler's formula for salvation lay in the manifestation of God's love for the world through Christ. Lundy had tried to embrace it: in his lectures and sermons at Emory College, he labored to "instill in our youth a noble Christian manhood"; he had celebrated Christmas as the promise of "hope and holy joy in human hearts"; and he seemed at times to have been a cheerleader for Christian commitment. In a poem he wrote on the back of a letter to his wife, he intoned a canticle of affliction in which a forgotten, benighted, and "naked soul" screams in anguish: "Is there a God Who cares?" Lundy tried to incarnate his flickering and shadowy God in a "cross-stained" Christ who dragged "bleeding hearts from hell." It was a sentimental solution that employed the sermonic form of asking on behalf of the wretched if there is a God who cares and answering with the familiar

[37] Ibid.

formula that by observing Christ in agony upon the cross we can know that He does.[38]

Rather than reason, emotion and intuition commend poetry, even bad poetry, and Lundy's poem was sufficiently resonant with conventional Protestant piety to convince editors of *The Independent* to publish it.[39] But there is no evidence that Lundy found the poem's message any more compelling than the most skeptical of the magazine's readers did: it expressed his anguish, not his salvation. In his dreadful solitude, he knew that he could not affirm what he had been taught to believe. He decided to escape into eternal sleep; it seemed to meet his need, which is to say, his own understanding of salvation. But it would be a mistake to conclude that religious angst brought Lundy to his final decision, if religion is conceived as one way of understanding, among others, independent of human relationships, personal identity, social solidarity, and sexual expression. If these things, however, are understood as interwoven webs of meaning associated with love, transcendence, and commitment, then Lundy's protracted crisis was indeed religious. He could not mesh the meanings of wife, phallus, love, and God in a positive way: "tired" as he was, he resolved futility with oblivion.

Lundy told us why he thought he was leaving. But the letters and notebook do not reveal how he thought things out; we do not have access to his four hundred books. He did not write essays on any of the issues that concerned him. He hid from us the ways in which he wrestled. So our sources are incomplete as we try to understand the act, which involves the individual's entire life experience, as people who have studied suicide point out. Lundy's letters and notebook were not only about him, but also about his culture. His culture was not merely southern: he was an avid reader of English novels, essays, and poems (especially Tennyson), and he read his wife's reviews for *The Independent*. Victorians on both sides of the Atlantic had moved beyond driving stakes into the bodies of suicides and submerging them in lime at a crossroads. If they had not yet arrived at a consensus on how to think about suicide, they did believe it to be caused by some sort of mental breakdown. Lundy's note had denied any wrong doing; he simply professed existential exhaustion, and this explanation could be easily folded into Victorian views that suicides were "the lonely,

[38] "Editorial," *The Emory Phoenix*, November 1889, 1; Lundy Howard Harris, "Christ and Christmas," *The Emory Phoenix*, December 1895, 3; Lundy Howard Harris to Corra Harris, January 23, 1910, Corra Mae White Harris Papers.

[39] Oglesby, *Corra Harris*, 36.

the lovelorn, the mad, [or] the ruined" – lost souls at the end of their "emotional tether."[40] Late nineteenth-century Americans who learned of Lundy's death would have been primed to believe much the same thing. Thus, when newspapers reported his suicide, the articles attributed the cause to "ill health and despondency."[41]

The publisher of *The Independent* tried to reassure Corra that, simply because a "maladjustment of the nervous system" had made Lundy unable to "judge wisely," his suicide had stained neither him nor her. Letters to Corra suggest that those who knew her best wanted her to believe that Lundy was simply too good. He was emotionally unable to contend with "selfish, striving, warring men" such as, one writer implied, the ecclesiastical bullies intent on controlling Vanderbilt University. He was a "tender spirit," one "too delicately pursed" for this world, one too thoroughly "misunderstood" but nonetheless set apart by his "consciousness of God."[42] A minister captured Lundy in the idiom of sentimental evangelicalism: "His beautiful soul recoiled from hard and uncouth ways and lived in a kind of sorrowful and wondering isolation. It is not strange that the whole grim spectacle at length became unbearable to him. But God must have a place for those rare ones who know only love and pity – to whom strife and selfishness are forever detestable. Into the holy peace of the great brightness your husband has gone." The theme continued in a stark, unsentimental, and unforgiving way when the official and decidedly unfriendly *Christian Advocate* of Nashville reported Lundy's suicide: "Morphine poisoning self-administered was the cause of his death, and for this reason there is added sorrow." The reporter continued: spells of despondency had unbalanced Lundy's mind, and his friends had feared something like this would happen – conclusions that would have infuriated Lundy.[43] It was a conclusion for which Victorian Americans were well prepared.

[40] Maris, *Pathways to Suicide*, 1–5, 8–11; Barbara T. Gates, *Victorian Suicide: Mad Crimes and Sad Histories* (Princeton: Princeton University Press, 1988), 1–7, 40; Olive Anderson, *Suicide in Victorian and Edwardian England* (Oxford, UK: Clarendon Press, 1987). See an article on the readings habits of Emory faculty in *The Emory Phoenix*, November 1894, 9.

[41] *The* (Atlanta) *Constitution*, May 11 and 18, 1910; July 16, 1910; September 7, 20, and 30, 1910; November 23 and 29, 1910; December 31, 1910.

[42] William Hayes Ward to Corra Harris, September 20, 1910; E. B. Chappell to Corra Harris, September 26, 1910; Mary Sperry to Corra Harris, September 20, 1910; G. B. Winto to Corra Harris, September 22, 1910; W. Woods White to Corra Harris, September 26, 1910; Mary Helm to Corra Harris, June 29, 1911; William Hayes Ward, September 1910, all in Corra Mae White Harris Papers.

[43] E. B. Chappell to Corra Harris, September 26, 1910, Corra Mae White Harris Papers; *The* (Nashville) *Christian Advocate*, September 23 and 30, 1910; Lundy Harris to Warren

If students of the twenty-first century are not Victorians, they are nonetheless influenced by Victorian scholar Emile Durkheim who, after studying the sociology of suicide, believed that it was one of the markers of an industrialization that eroded traditional values and created new rules for how people worked, thought, disciplined themselves (or not), and related to each other, including leaving them rudderless and feeling "isolated." Of course, factories and capitalists did not do Lundy in. Still, a sense of normlessness, lack of certainty, failure of self-confidence, and loss of identity permeated the writings that he left behind. Support for the Frenchman's views appeared in the "popular press and in fictionalized portrayals of suicide rather than in medical literature." American psychiatrists were reluctant, medical historian Howard Kushner points out, "to integrate Durkheim's sociological theory into explanations for the etiology of suicide," concluding instead that suicide was a "symptom of individuals rather than social dysfunction."[44] But the two points of view were not mutually exclusive: Lundy's troubles were indeed personal and imbedded in his inner life, but his was a life affected by changes in higher education, religion, and gender roles.

The New South was changing as America was changing, if at a few furlongs behind: a region growing cities and cotton mills as well as cotton, changing the way people worked and lived. Some of its universities strove for professional faculties freed from ecclesiastical control. Lundy's pilgrimage from country to city paralleled the move of Emory College from rural Oxford to Decatur (next door to Atlanta) and its transformation into a university where his nemesis, Andrew Sledd, became a noted New Testament scholar and professor. Perhaps most important for Lundy, there was what historian Jane Censer has called a "reconstruction of white southern womanhood." Marriage, sexuality, religion, and domestic life were changing in ways that encouraged women to become publicly active in lobbying legislators to adopt policies favorable to and protective of women. Even though feminists of the time may have been angered at Corra Harris's antifeminist invective, she was nonetheless part of this

Akin Candler, August 8 and 13, 1899; October 31, 1899; Corra Harris to Warren Akin Candler, June 29 and July 1, 1899, Warren Akin Candler Papers.

44 Emile Durkheim, *Suicide: A Study in Sociology*, ed. George Simpson (1951; reprint, New York: Free Press, 1979); George Howe Colt, *The Enigma of Suicide* (New York: Summit Books, 1991), 187–98; Howard I. Kushner, *Self-Destruction in the Promised Land: A Psychocultural Biology of American Suicide* (New Brunswick, NJ: Rutgers University Press, 1989), 59–60, 61.

"reconstruction," both as a literary critic and an author.[45] In public she created an idealized Lundy that seemed finally to have shamed him; in the family, she presided as Lundy's caretaker and "mother," negotiating his career after being forced from Emory. In his writings, she almost disappeared as a "woman ... against the laws." She had told him she loved him, but he felt worthless compared with New York, *The Independent*, and More.

Lundy's intrapersonal conflicts were obviously most about gender and faith, but behind all his "failures," secrets, and compulsions were the ways in which white Southerners related to black Southerners. Like many thousands of white men before him, Lundy found solace, release, and mastery in sexual relations with dependent black women. Corra's fury at black women who "contaminated" her life through her husband's infidelities and his funding for the education of two "Negro" boys suggests the reach of white people's criminal lack of empathy and casual use of African Americans who, at best, became objects of charity and, at worst, were lynched. Just how much that lack of empathy toward blacks had been "normalized" throughout the nation was evidenced through Corra's rise into middle-brow literary culture through the "spirit" she exhibited in justifying a spectacular lynching and blaming black women for it. That Corra so adamantly ignored and suppressed her knowledge of her husband's use of black women – and that Lundy in his secret musings and anguish also refused to reflect on that use – suggests a pathology of avoidance that had become common among middle-class white Southerners.[46]

Lundy knew he was not the sainted Circuit Rider, but he also knew he could not reveal who he really was – if he, in fact, knew. He served a church and encouraged others to trust in the "blood-stained" Christ, but he himself could not do it. He paid for the education of two "Negro" boys and seduced married black women. He sometimes possessed a unique "consciousness of God," leading Corra to complain of his exaggerated piety, but

[45] Jane Turner Censer, *The Reconstruction of White Southern Womanhood 1865–1895* (Baton Rouge: Louisiana State University Press, 2003); Regina D. Sullivan, *Lottie Moon: A Southern Baptist Missionary to China in History and Legend* (Baton Rouge: Louisiana University Press, 2011); Oglesby, *Corra Harris*, 73.

[46] In contrast to Corra Harris stood Lilly Hardy Hammond, the wife of Lundy Harris's boss in Nashville. Lily Hardy Hammond eventually became a well-known racial liberal for her day. She was a pioneer among southern women who insisted that whites realize the evil inherent in their racial prejudice; see, for example, L. H. Hammond, *In Black and White: An Interpretation of Southern Life* (New York: Fleming H. Revell Co., 1914): 40–44; idem, *In the Vanguard of a Race* (New York: Council of Women for Home Missions and Missionary Education Movement of the United States and Canada, 1922).

he confessed terrible loneliness in the "voyage to the undiscovered land where God comes & goes like flickering lights in the wall." He wondered if God existed (which was not strange even for a saint), but he had difficulty even positing an answer (which laid bare his qualifications as a cleric and a teacher). He professed undying love to his wife, but he coupled with black prostitutes. He pleaded with her to love him, but he could not provide the loving support of an uxorious husband.[47]

Not all of these seeming polarities are mutually exclusive, of course, but they all suggest a duality that afflicted Lundy and his brother, Henry. Lundy would have known through their conversations that the younger man's ministry was a "torture" to Henry because he thought religion could not answer the "deepest questions of the heart." Henry had been fascinated by discovering the "horror" of humanity's two natures as revealed in Robert Louis Stephenson's *Dr. Jekyll and Mr. Hyde*, and he should have been more horrified at Oscar Wilde's *Picture of Dorian Gray*.[48] Stephenson wrote about a scientist whose experiments created a macabre dance between the good (Jekyll) and the evil (Hyde) in humanity; Wilde wrote about a man whose hidden picture revealed the monstrous reality behind his charming public persona. Such "two-ness" dramatically befits fiction, but the condition itself is not unusual in reality, and most people manage it well enough. Lundy was neither Henry Hyde nor Dorian Gray, but his duality still afflicted him: he was unable to find an integrated self with whom he could live; he was tired of trying.

Harris's suicide dramatizes a personal dimension of change in the early twentieth-century South, especially for religious and professional men. He experienced change as loss. For more than fifteen years, his suffering eventually wore him down. On a cold Sunday morning in January 1896, his friend and mentor Bishop Haygood died; Haywood had guided Lundy's life since the latter was eighteen years of age. In 1898, Lundy lost the guidance and protection of President Candler who was elected Bishop. That same spring, Lundy lost much of his self-respect when Andrew Sledd exposed him – privately to be sure, but the experience was nonetheless devastating. Lundy lost his Eden, and he retreated into the haven of whiskey, extramarital sex, and religious penitence. He briefly lost his wife when they separated

[47] Harris, *As a Woman Thinks*, 81, 90–93, 177, 194, 206; idem, *A Circuit Rider's Widow* (Garden City: Doubleday, Page & Co, 1916), 133, 135, 136, 190–91; idem, *The Happy Pilgrimage* (Boston: Houghton Mifflin Co., 1927), 111; idem, *Justice* (New York: Heart's International Library, 1915), 53; idem, *Book and Heart*, 213; Oglesby, *Corra Harris*.

[48] Henry Harris, "Comment," *The Emory Phoenix*, December 1893, 7.

physically, and he lost her once again as she flourished under the tutelage of Paul Elmer More. He lost something of himself when Corra's popular stories about a circuit rider and his wife dramatized just how far he was, he believed, from being the model minister. He slipped into alcoholic despair to be reclaimed once again but was then fired from his position in Nashville when he refused to obey episcopal directives. Loss upon loss upon loss. He seemed to have lost his religion, too, although one wonders if he could have lost what he felt he had never really found. He told Candler in 1886 that he had found "Christ," but his wife remembered his despair at not receiving the subjective certification of "religion" that he had so desperately wanted and which evangelical Protestantism – and especially traditional Methodism – demanded. Baptized into a culture that spoke the language of experiential faith, Lundy learned to speak it so well that he attained respectable positions in the Church, but in the interior consciousness of his musings the approved language was trumped by sexuality, skepticism, and the abyss. He could not resolve the merciless contradictions of his private, interior, and public selves.[49]

If Lundy's "failures," losses, secrets, and compulsions were primarily about gender, sex, and faith, they existed under a canopy of race. Like generations of southern white men, he certified his manhood through sexual relations with black women, experiences that seemed to allow him to feel they were a more certain pathway to knowledge than any association with "God." His charitable support of education for those unnamed black boys, which his wife mentioned in his obituary, may have been prompted by guilt or a sense of personal responsibility, but the act was on the edge of his consciousness as he ended his life. He seems to have avoided any association with Paine Institute, the school supported by both white and black Methodist denominations. He did not blame black women for his adulteries as Corra did; it was his own moral failing, he insisted, and not theirs. But there is no indication that he could share the relatively liberal views of race expressed by his supervisor, who became president of Paine, and the man's wife whom he knew while serving the MECS bureaucracy. Of course, race was absent from his mind as he confessed the exhaustion that devastated him. He fled to a rural haven, into a child-like utopia, befriending and playing with children as if they could teach him things far more important than the lessons of academy and church. As he gathered strength to take the morphine, he seemed at times

[49] Lundy Howard Harris to Warren A. Candler, March 8, 1886, Warren Akin Candler Papers.

to be obsessed by the triviality of everyday existence until he exploded in a short note at the stupidity of people who thought that breaking a lantern's glass chimney was an occasion for lament. Such people did not know what was really important! They had not peered into the abyss as had he. The last thing he could feel, or knew he should have felt, was his love for Corra. He told her, "My last thoughts are of you and Faith. I shall love you both eternally – if love is hereafter permitted. You have been unutterably good to me all our days together."[50] He ended his life with a real truth if not the whole truth. If his suicide attracted scholarly attention because it appeared to be an anomaly, it was not that to Lundy. He was tired; explaining why should not be lost in translation.

[50] Lundy Harris to Corra Harris, September 9 [incorrectly dated in archives, actually 7 and 8], 10, 13, 15, 16, and 17, 1910, Corra Mae White Harris Papers.

9

"He's Only Away": Condolence Literature and the Emergence of a Modern South

Kristine M. McCusker

When Nashvillian Eugene Crutcher died in January 1921, family, friends, and colleagues rushed to comfort his widow, Annie, the president of the Tennessee State Parent/Teacher Association. Friends and colleagues wrote her sympathy letters, bemoaning her loss and vowing to mourn with her. Eugene's loss was one that should be grieved, but writers promised Annie she was not alone, that Jesus was her constant companion as she waited to be reunited with Eugene upon her own death. Showcasing the etiquette common to a condolence note, Ella M. Hussey wrote,

> It is hard to find words in which to try to comfort those who have lost their nearest and dearest, not lost, no, we never really lose them, the loving Father has only called them to a higher better life, and we shall go to them in His own good time. But human hearts are lonely and life can never again be just the same. Grieve not, dear friend, as one who sorrows without hope, for Jesus, our dear elder Brother walks with you, as he walked with your loved one when he was called to pass through the deep waters.[1]

Two decades later, changes in technology and etiquette, as well as the overwhelming losses from World War II's distant battlefields, provided a new context for condolence notes. When Tuskegee Airman William J. Faulkner Jr. died over Austria in November 1944, friends, family, and even strangers wrote his parents, the Reverend William J. Faulkner Sr. (chaplain and Dean of Students at Fisk University) and his wife, Bess,

This project was partially funded by NIH/NLM Grant #1 G13 LM010074–01.

[1] Ella M. Hussey to Mrs. Crutcher and family, ca. January 1921, Crutcher Family Papers, Tennessee State Library and Archives, Nashville; "Prominent Citizen Called by Death," *Nashville Banner*, January 18, 1921.

using new tropes and ideas about death. For one so young to die on a distant battlefield, his death – rather than the life he lived – became noteworthy and meaningful as a sacrifice to the nation and its noble ideals. Reverend William Cash wrote, "He paid with honor the supreme sacrifice that all peoples everywhere might have freedom." But preprinted cards, now easily available, embossed in multiple colors, and cheap to buy, were quite prevalent in the Faulkner papers, too, many reading only "With Sympathy" or "He's only away."[2]

In the early twentieth century, condolence notes – brief letters restricted solely to consolation – were a relatively new death ritual and a new genre of writing in its own right that became a central feature of "modern" southern death care: the burial of the dead, the mourning of the loss, and the comfort extended to the grieving. Typically, scholars have argued that death care is a mirror of society; in this case, condolence notes were reflective of the South's transformation during and after World War I into a more industrial, urbanized region. However, condolence notes and other death rituals were also catalysts in making that modern South, as a common etiquette and language of death gave Southerners the means to assess not only the deceased but the whirlwind of economic, political, and social transformations reimagining political and social systems of race, power, and economics.

It was through the language of grief and sympathy and the substantive industrial changes that made this language possible that evangelical Christians and others imagined a modern South. Writing about death with a Victorian flourish, but firmly rooted in Christian theology, writers of the 1910s and 1920s acknowledged that death had occurred and that the recipient felt real sorrow. "The Father has called them to a higher, better life," evangelical Christians wrote, and the note of condolence assumed that each life had lived out its purpose in achieving God's mission on earth. Those assumptions became the foundation on which southern letter writers constructed the condolence note as a new genre of literature. By the 1930s, however, new purposes and solaces became apparent as a civic language of death and other secular succor like time and memories provided a comfort that God no longer monopolized. Preprinted cards, with messages such as "he's only away" – as if the deceased were on

[2] Reverend William L. Cash to Reverend and Mrs. Faulkner, January 20, 1945; and Reverend Edward K. and Laura D. Nichols to Rev. and Mrs. William J. Faulkner, Sr., ca. January 1945, both in William J. Faulkner Sr. Papers, Moorland-Spingarn Research Center, Howard University, Washington DC.

vacation – further undermined the seriousness of death as portrayed by evangelical Christianity. Still, the familiar language of evangelical Christianity remained an anchor that helped Southerners endure the Great Depression and World War II.

Historians of death have argued that over the course of the late nineteenth and early twentieth centuries, there occurred a "dying" of death: namely, that the topic became taboo in American discourse. Twentieth-century southern condolence writers, however, complicate this narrative. Death did not become a taboo topic of conversation because the dead continued to exist in a romanticized afterlife that religious Southerners acknowledged in their everyday lives and imagined joining upon their own deaths. Evangelical Christian language embraced a belief that the dead lit a path to Heaven where they awaited the faithful and repentant. Certainly, the idea was not exclusive to southern evangelicals, but it was quite forceful in the South even as secular influences recast the language and rituals associated with death. Condolence notes were therefore part of the evolving death rituals and identities of a transforming South in which letter writers came to terms with not only the dead but with the consequences of being a modern evangelical Christian.[3]

New death care rituals were the outcome of a substantive industrialization process in the early 1900s in which many moved into the middle class and secured a new "place" in the transition from a New South to a Modern South. What had been initially imagined by *Atlanta Constitution* editor Henry Grady in 1874 as a New South rooted in an industrial order came to fruition by the 1920s with an industrial and urban economic base, a consumer ethic (Southerners no longer made coffins, for example; they purchased them), and a Progressive reform movement that attempted to lower the region's high mortality rates.

The condolence note, as one of the outcomes of these changes, evinced a shift in both the ways a death was announced and the expected response. In rural southern areas, locals often learned of deaths from tolling church bells that rang for each year of a person's life. Sometimes, in smaller communities, a child – typically black – ran from house to house with

[3] Philippe Ariès, *The Hour of Our Death* (New York: Knopf, 1981); Ray Stannard, *The Puritan Way of Death: A Study in Religion, Culture and Social Change* (New York: Oxford University Press, 1979); James J. Farrell, *Inventing the American Way of Death, 1830–1920* (Philadelphia: Temple University Press, 1980); Gary Laderman, *The Sacred Remains: American Attitudes Toward Death, 1779–1883* (New Haven: Yale University Press, 1996); Drew Gilpin Faust, *This Republic of Suffering: Death and the American Civil War* (New York: Knopf, 2008).

the news. The deceased's family expected the news to prompt friends and family into action, namely in preparing the body and grave for burial. They were then to sit up with the dead and, finally, attend the funeral within a day or two. Thus, death care was, in the rural South, a collective response to a death.

The condolence note assumed a relationship, originally intimate but increasingly more formal, between people who may not have been able to see each other daily. In fact, some notes acknowledged their responsibilities to attend to the dead, but then offered up reasons to renege on those responsibilities because of physical distance. As morticians increasingly took control of preparing the body, the community as a whole no longer provided death care as a communal act. As communities no longer laid hands on the body, they shifted their focus from the deceased to the grieving, privatizing and rooting the new focus in a relationship between letter writer and letter recipient. The condolence note also evidenced the region's expanding industrial base and communication and transportation (especially railroad) networks, making the news of death over greater distances necessary for those who could not hear a church bell or receive a message from a neighborhood boy.

Changes to announcements of and receptions to news of death reflected larger transformations to the region's racial and power structures, particularly in terms of "place." White Southerners rigidly assigned themselves and others to their "places" – the gendered, racial, and class positions within society that reinforced whites' authority. Etiquette – the idealized behaviors required at various social situations like births, weddings, and funerals – claimed and reinforced "place" in the southern social hierarchy. Appropriate etiquette, as determined by upper-class Southern whites, marked one as at least middle class and white and reinforced an illusion of exclusiveness. In condolence and letter writing, even when writing an intimate friend, women of status inscribed "Mrs." in a parenthetical next to the sender's name – for example, Lillian Palmer Gregson (Mrs. William S.) – to demonstrate they were "ladies." White Southerners did not accord black women the right to be "Mrs." Continuing a practice established in the slave era, upper-class Southerners well into the twentieth century continued to call lower-class women and men by their first names and specifically referred to lower-class blacks as "uncle" or "aunt," reminding blacks as well as white working-class Southerners of their lowly status. Death care reinforced social and racial status, depriving blacks and working-class white Southerners of the opportunity to write notes of condolence. To cross the racial border between white and black by sending a condolence note, then, was available to only the most elite black Southerner and only in very rare, very specific circumstances (elite black men wrote to the sons of deceased white men, for example, but never to a mother or wife).[4]

The New South ushered in a new southern middle class of men and women eager to secure their status within the larger American middle class that emerged in the early twentieth century. They required education on the best practices for writing condolence notes and other status-promoting activities, and a flood of etiquette books attempted to teach them appropriate manners. Between 1918 and 1929, sixty-eight books on etiquette were published. Over the next fifteen years, five more etiquette books on average came out each year. The best known and longest lasting of these etiquette gurus was a Marylander, Emily Post. In her 1922 book, appropriately entitled *Etiquette in Society, in Business, in Politics, and at Home*, Post acknowledged the importance of controlling death's abruptness when she wrote, "the last place in the world where we would look for comfort at such a time is in the seeming artificiality of etiquette; yet it is in the moment of deepest sorrow that etiquette performs its most vital and real service."[5] Etiquette was an anchor in chaos, but it was also an opportune moment to use prescribed rituals to firm up social boundaries that might be ignored. Moreover, when a family suffered economically and potentially in social status at the death of a breadwinner, good manners reassured that family of its place.

Beginning in the 1910s, those who received and collected condolence notes tended to be elite, whether black or white, and the condolence letters in their family archival collections often number in the hundreds. But what changed was who sent a letter: elite *and* middle-class Southerners fully accepted the responsibilities of sending condolences. The note of condolence, according to Post, approximated the handclasp and displayed a sincere sympathy for a family's loss. That sincerity implied an intimacy between sender and recipient, creating an emotional alliance between upper- and middle-class Southerners.

[4] Lillian Palmer Gregson to Mary Daniel Moore, ca. May 1929, John Trotwood Moore Papers, Tennessee State Library and Archives; James Watkins, quoted in John C. Inscoe, *Writing the South through the Self: Explorations in Southern Autobiography* (Athens: University of Georgia Press, 2011), 2.

[5] Emily Post, *Etiquette in Society, in Business, in Politics and at Home* (New York: Funk & Wangnalls, 1922); Arthur M. Schlesinger, *Learning How to Behave: A Historical Study of American Etiquette Books* (New York: Cooper Square Publishers, Inc., 1968), 51; Ted Ownby, ed., *Manners and Southern History* (Oxford: University Press of Mississippi, 2011).

Social etiquette relegated grief to a private concern, not one to be openly shared in public except at the funeral. Since the community no longer shared in death duties, family and friends no longer shared in mourning in the same ways they had in the nineteenth century. Distance was now required to allow the bereaved to privatize grief, away from others' eyes. A condolence note implied, then, the recipient's choice when she or he might open it and read its contents. A telephone call, although appropriate to spreading the initial word that someone had died, did not allow the same choice and challenged the privatization of grief. Thus, a phone call was taboo, as Elsie M. Slopes realized when she called Nashvillian Mary Daniel Moore after her husband, John Trotwood Moore, died in May 1929. Slopes apologized to Moore for "telling you over the phone that I'd been in constant sympathy with you lately. It was not a subject for telephone conversation but my impulse to let you know how deeply I felt for you got the best of my judgment." Her transgression, in fine southern form, required a note of apology. The prescriptions against a phone call continued well into the 1940s. Martha Harris wrote Reverend Faulkner when his son was reported missing in action during World War II (his death was later confirmed), "I won't disturb you by calling but I wanted you to know that I'm thinking of you and hoping and praying with you that he will be all right."[6]

Letters tended to follow prescribed guidelines that would have been heartily approved by Post. In general, appropriate paper had to be used, something more formal than school tablet paper, and letters had to be written in ink. Advances in printing press technology allowed Southerners to buy stationery embossed in black that announced their sympathies as well as their own grief. The new style, made famous in old folk music by the song "Letter Edged in Black," allowed writers to announce their own mourning status. Dark clothing that indicated one as grief-stricken could not be seen at a distance; stationery had to make the announcement of grief. Mrs. Reuben Reynolds Banks and Mrs. John F. Campbell sent small, preprinted cards edged in black to Mary Daniel Moore. The message was simply "Sympathy."[7] The black edging let Moore know that they, too, mourned.

[6] Elsie M. Slopes to Mrs. Moore, May 30, 1929, Moore Papers; Martha Harris (Dr. and Mrs. S. P. Harris) to Reverend and Mrs. William J. Faulkner, Sr., Faulkner Papers.

[7] Mrs. Reuben Reynolds Banks to Mary Daniel Moore, ca. May 1929; Mrs. John F. Campbell to May Daniel Moore, ca. May 1929, both in Moore Papers.

Still, most individuals continued to personalize condolence notes with their own words rather than those of a printer. Many notes evinced a fine and careful hand that wrote with appropriate grammar and spelling, suggesting an educated person. Handwritten notes were plentiful, although by the end of the 1920s, typed notes – typically produced by men – were almost as common. A typed note announced the sender as a professional who knew it was in good taste (and good business) to send his sympathies. Most letters, whether typed or handwritten, opened with "My dear" as in "My dear Mrs. Gregory" and ended with a formal signature. Finally, there was an expectation that one wrote as soon as possible, and an apology was offered if the letter was tardy. "I hope you will pardon my delay in writing but I have been out of town," Jean Carroll Bradford wrote Annie Crutcher upon the death of Crutcher's mother in 1918.[8]

Once letters were received, the recipient, revealing his or her own good taste, thanked the sender for the letter. Handwritten notations on received letters, detailing the sender's full name and address, as well as lists with senders' names and addresses with check marks next to names suggest that thank-you notes were a formal undertaking. Men as well as women had their lists of thank-you cards to write. Dr. Merrill Moore kept his own list of thank-you notes to send, an act that indicated his own good taste and status. If a thank-you note was not received, the original sender might offer a gentle reminder. Writing to the secretary of Alabama congressman and Speaker of the United States House of Representatives William Bankhead upon his death in September 1940, Ray Knight hinted, "This is the second letter I've written to you since Speaker Bankhead's death. The other one must have been lost since you no doubt have had hundreds and hundreds of letters about the Speaker."[9]

Even the content of condolence notes was scripted. Letters typically documented how the sender heard of the news and his or her immediate reaction. By the 1910s, few children or churches announced the news in urban areas. Rather, information came from local or national newspapers, telegrams and telephone calls, and, later, radio. "Last night only, I received the, to us, sad information that once again the inevitable Messenger had invaded our fast narrowing circle," wrote John Lord to his cousin Manny Howell when her mother died in 1913, "and that not again in this particular phase of our existence would we be able to get an audible response to

[8] Jean Carroll Bradford to Annie Crutcher, May 20, 1918, Crutcher Family Papers.

[9] Ray Knight to Carter Monasco, October 13, 1940, William Bankhead Papers, Alabama Department of Archives and History, Tuscaloosa.

our hearts call for our dear '*Auntie!*'"[10] Lord, who lived in Mississippi, wrote his cousin in Tennessee relatively soon after his aunt's death, suggesting that he heard the news in a telegram. Regardless of how Lord heard the news, acknowledging its receipt was a formal part of condolence writing.

Next, writers eulogized the deceased, ascribing meaning to a well-lived Christian life and, by implication, a "useful" life worthy of a trip to Heaven. "After our transactions with him both in selling and buying, we said he was certainly our real estate man for any other business we might have for we found him so accommodating honest, upright and such a perfect Christian gentleman," Mr. and Mrs. Gregory Molder wrote Crutcher upon the death of her businessman husband. "Professor Gregory has been a beacon light among the educational forces of his day and generation and light will Continue to shine in the lives of those whom he has taught and influenced," I. J. Gregory wrote of a former Howard University professor. "His was a full rounded life of usefulness," James Daughtery wrote Nashvillian Manny Howell when her husband died in June 1929. In many cases, the attainment of certain material and professional standards made deceased men especially exalted in writers' eyes.[11]

Writers also found ways to refer to death in a genteel language that implied a continuing Victorian melodramatic flourish. Euphemisms suggested the deceased "went home," had experienced his "homegoing," or had "gone away" (subtle references to the family reunion that awaited the repentant). Others labeled death as "your sad misfortune" or as "the sorrow that has come to you and your family." News of death was a "sad message." Bereavement and grief were "your great trouble," a "dark hour," a "black cloud," "the shadowy days of sorrow," or "the supreme anguish with which it has pleased God to visit you." Mary Tarbell Gordon wrote Manny Howell, noting she was "holding out my hand to you in love while you're walking in this shadowy place on the road."[12]

[10] John Lord to Mannie, April 22, 1913, Joseph Toy Howell Family Papers, Tennessee State Library and Archives.

[11] Mr. and Mrs. George B. Molder to My Dear Mrs. Crutcher, January 24, 1921, Crutcher Papers; L. J. Gregory to Mrs. Fannie Gregory, December 19, 1915, Thomas Montgomery Gregory Papers, Moorland-Spingarn Research Center; James A. Daughtery, June 17, 1929 to Mrs. J. T. Howell and Son, Howell Papers.

[12] Minnie and George to Annie Crutcher, April 22, 1918; and Nelle B. Lowe to Annie Crutcher, ca. January 1921; Mrs. R. L. Kennedy to Annie Crutcher, January 26, 1921; and Mr. and Mrs. Clarence M. Baker to Mrs. Crutcher, February 1, 1921, all in Crutcher Family Papers; Ada Hayes to Cousin Mamie, May 18, 1929; Mary St. John Jones, Washington D.C., to Cousin Mary, May 23, 1929, both in Moore Papers; Eileen

As the South modernized, shifts in death ritual instilled a palpable sense of helplessness as many struggled to use words to comfort friends from a distance. No longer was their physical presence necessary in the burial of the dead, and letter writers understood the potential superficiality of a note in place of that comfort. "I know that no words of mine can assuage your poignant grief, but I simply want you to know that I weep with you," the Commanding General of the local United Confederate Veterans organizations wrote Annie Crutcher. Dr. E. C. Denton noted in a letter of condolence to Floyd Jenkins upon his wife's death in 1937, that "Any words which we might utter on such an occasion seem futile and was but empty statements."[13]

Evangelical Christian language promised some succor to the writer, supplying biblical references and imagery as words of comfort and providing an explanatory power not found in secular language, words that evoked God's mystery (as in "we cannot know why the beloved was taken"), God's comfort, and the hope of reunion. Frequent references to John 14:2 "In my Father's house are many mansions" and John 14:21 "He that hath my commandments, and keepeth them, he it is that loveth me" outlined the standard evangelical southern belief that death reunited the deceased with family members who had already died, and writers used them to remind the grieving that their loss was a temporary "human" one. Lizzie Bloomsteen, writing her "dear sweet Friend" Annie Crutcher, attempted to assuage Annie's grief: "But dear friend, there *is* 'balm in Gilead.' 'In my Father's house are many mansions, if it were not so, I would have told you.' He has become a golden link between you and Heaven and will thus fulfill the promises given through the psalmist, 'There is a blessed candle of Faith burning for you near your beloved while he sleeps.'"[14]

Letter writers assured the bereaved that the world was a poorer place without the deceased. Harry Byrd wrote Bishop Carter Wormley's wife how the Bishop's death in 1938 meant that "Richmond [Virginia] will never be the same without him. My whole family is very deeply distressed." The

R. Cunningham to Sadie Warner Frazier, July 15, 1927, Sadie Warner Frazier Papers, Tennessee State Library and Archives; Mary Tarbell Gordon to Mannie Howell, June 1929; Kate Eastman to Manie Howell, June 22, 1929; and Mary Tarbell Gordon to Manny Howell, ca. June 1929, all in Howell Papers.

[13] Jno. P. Hickman to Mrs. Eugene Crutcher, January 18, 1921, Crutcher Family Papers; Dr. E. C. Denton to Floyd Jenkins, September 1, 1937, Floyd Franklin Jenkins Papers, Virginia Historical Society, Richmond.

[14] Lizzie J. Bloomsteen to My dear, Sweet Friend, January 22, 1921, Crutcher Family Papers. The biblical references are (in order of appearance) Jeremiah 8:22 and John 14:2. It is unclear to which psalm the writer was referring. All biblical citations are from the King James Version.

Ladies Aid Society of Franklin, Virginia, wrote Varina Jenkins's husband that the group had "suffered the irreparable loss of one of its most active, devoted and lovable members. A loss felt and shared also by the church at large." In many cases, those at a distance held memorial services when they could not attend actual funerals, reporting those services in condolence notes. Kate A. Monahan from the State Teachers College (she does not indicate which state) wrote that "This school devoted the chapel period today to the memory of Mr. Moore whom we have always considered our friend." Amy Rose Ellis wrote actress Tallulah Bankhead when her father, Speaker Bankhead died, "I know you aren't a Catholic, but I am and if you don't mind I'm going to have a mass said for your father. This doesn't appear to be very much but to a Catholic it is the greatest thing that can be done for anyone, living or dead."[15]

Condolence letters, however, were meant to remind the receiver of his or her social status and obligation as much as evidence that of the sender. Letters written in the Progressive-era South reminded the grief-stricken that, despite their losses, their work on earth had not ended and they had to remember their responsibility to the living. Civic duties could not be shirked; neither could irrational emotions be allowed to overwhelm survivors. Mrs. E. H. Leathy reminded Annie Crutcher, using Old Testament language from Moses that "With your faith and depth of reasoning, I am quite sure you will be led to see through the heavy veil that hangs over you and have a bigger, better vision of the great beyond." The Child-Welfare Circle of Athens was more blunt in reminding Crutcher that her work as a progressive activist was not finished:

> We realize the splendid work you have been doing in the training of mothers and the future citizenship of the state of Tennessee and we deeply regret that any sorrow should have come to you. We wish to assure you of our continued love and our prayers that the merciful Heavenly Father will send you comfort and sustain you that you may do further work for the many women and children who need just such a soul and mind as yours.

Handle this grief rationally, writers to Crutcher emphasized, your labor is needed. The tendency to note a recipient's "usefulness" was another reminder to not let grief overwhelm one's labors. Thus, letter writers

[15] Harry F. Byrd to Mrs. Carter W. Wormeley, September 14, 1938, Wormeley Family Papers, Virginia Historical Society; The Ladies Aid Society, Congregational-Christian Church, Franklin, VA., to F. F. Jenkins, ca. August 1937, Jenkins Papers; Kate A. Manahan to Mary Daniel Moore, May 20, 1929, Moore Papers; Amy Rose Ellis to Miss Bankhead, September 15, 1940, Tallulah Bankhead Papers, Alabama Department of Archives and History.

wanted their words to both comfort and motivate those who grieved. Upon the 1925 death of famed Baptist minister A. C. Dixon (brother to Thomas Dixon, author of *The Clansman*), Mars Hill College correspondents noted to his wife how familiar they were with her "wonderful work and hope that it will even have great growth yet.... We are praying for you and your work." Manny Howell's sister reminded her after her husband's death that "there is still a great chapter in your life to be lived."[16]

The evolving etiquette of letter writing reinforced the South's racial and class barriers, drawing sharp distinctions between public announcements of death, like a newspaper obituary, and private conversations about grief. Knowing someone was crucial: crossing that intimate boundary could elicit rancor. Someone who was black, working class, or both had to find other means to express grief and sympathy since only those with the good taste of a middle-class or elite Southerner were supposed to know letter-writing etiquette. If a letter writer was not sure the recipient knew her or him, reminders had to be included to assure the bereaved that the sender acted appropriately. Margaret Bybee Anderson added a postscript to her letter to Mary Daniel Moore, "If I've slipped from your memory, will refer you to the Adair book."[17]

Only very elite African Americans wrote condolence notes to whites. At John Trotwood Moore's death, Fisk University administrators Dean Ambrose Caliver and A. F. Shaw wrote Moore's son (but not the widow, suggesting a sensitivity to white concerns about the threat of black men to white women). Drawing upon evangelical imagery and their own good taste, they consoled that "We feel that there is no death, only a transition to higher service." In the process of condolence, however, Shaw claimed his own elite status by referencing his own wife as Mrs. Shaw, a title white Southerners did not accord black southern women.[18]

Beginning in the late 1920s and well into the 1940s, more secular language began to appear in condolence letters, evidencing the evolution of the South and the incorporation of a modern aesthetic with traditionalism. In some cases, a language of citizenship replaced or merged with the language of evangelical Christianity. The death of Tennessee State Librarian John Trotwood Moore in May 1929 affords an especially

[16] Mrs. E. H. Leathy to Annie Crutcher, January 24, 1921; The Child-Welfare Circle, Athens, TN, February 18, 1921, both in Crutcher Papers; unnamed correspondents to Mrs. A.C. Dixon, June 21, 1925, A. C. Dixon Papers, Southern Baptist Historical Library and Archive, Nashville, TN; Jennie, Sheffield to Mannie, June 23, 1929, Howell Papers.

[17] Miss Margaret Bybee Anderson to Mary Daniel Moore, May 14, 1929, Moore Papers.

[18] A. F. Shaw to Merrill Moore, May 13, 1929, Moore Papers.

revealing example. Both a southern historian and an apologist for a romanticized Old South, Moore was the author of books such as *The Bishop of Cottontown: A Story of the Southern Cotton Mills* (1906). His work fostered a romanticized resurgence of the noble plantation class that simultaneously depicted demeaning images of black Southerners, a mythology eventually given later visual force by *Gone with the Wind*. In doing so, he created the foundation for a modern white southern citizenship that validated a Confederate past and a reimposition of racial structures appropriate to that plantation mythology. Those racial structures were never more apparent than at Moore's own funeral: former Tennessee governors serving as "honorary" pallbearers looked on benevolently as black porters from the Tennessee Statehouse actually bore the burden of his casket. In symbolic form, the governors were the southern patriarchs, managing once again black labor for their own benefit.[19]

The condolence letters sent to Mary Daniel Moore numbered in the hundreds and eulogized Moore's ability to resurrect and romanticize the Old South. What is astonishing about Moore's letters, however, is the near absence of evangelical Christian language. In many cases, white writers appealed to a new religion in their letters – that of the mythological Old South, an appropriate language for a man who, in their eyes, had redeemed the region and its past. Dozens of letters lauded Moore's ability to resurrect the plantation South. One writer said, "But your sorrow is shared by Tennessee – the loss is hers as well as yours." Others proclaimed him "Dixie's poet laureate and brilliant novelist" and his "defense of the South" as his life's noble work.[20] Few notes declared his Christian life had made him fit for Heaven.

Civic losses were common to black Southerners as well and appeared in condolence notes upon the death of a noble citizen who had fought for his community. In December 1939, Howard University poet and noted sociologist and mathematician Kelly Miller died. Miller was especially well-known for his work in introducing sociology into the university's curriculum. His death was a devastating loss, as one writer noted, since his "greatly fruitful life" of seventy-six years had spanned the era of African-Americans freedom. He had "rendered a major service to his people and to his country," Mordecai Johnson wrote. T. L. Hungate,

[19] Fred Arthur Bailey, "John Trotwood Moore and the Partician [sic] Cult of the New South," *Tennessee Historical Quarterly* 58 (1999): 16–33.

[20] Jeannette Tillotson Acklen to Mary Daniel Moore, ca. May 1929; and Murfreesboro United Daughters of the Confederacy to Mary Daniel Moore, May 30, 1929, both in Moore Papers.

chair of Howard University's Board of Trustees, addressed Mrs. Miller, assuring her that "Dr. Miller will continue to live in the minds of the community both for what he did and for what he was. The university family with which he associated so long will feel the loss keenly." That civic life served as an example for his survivors. "I trust the memory and the influence of his life will be a help to you the rest of your life," an official of the National Association for the Advancement of Colored People (NAACP) wrote Miller's son.[21]

Other civic losses were literal. Passing away in September 1940, Speaker of the United States House of Representatives William Bankhead's twenty-three-year tenure as an Alabama Congressman and his four-year tenure as Speaker of the House (begun in 1936) had guided the nation through the Great Depression and New Deal and had helped Franklin Delano Roosevelt sustain America during a trying time. His death was a loss not simply for Alabamans or his family, but to the nation. "In the death of your honored husband," Birmingham native John Shelby Chadwick wrote Florence Bankhead, "the nation sustains a great loss." Family friends consoled Florence that "It must be a comfort to you to remember that a whole nation mourns with you in the loss of so fine a man and so great a statesman." Bryce Harris noted that Bankhead's death in the midst of the Great Depression was devastating because, "We are sorely in need of more statesmen like your late husband to handle the affairs of our government in these trying times."[22] The grieving nation joined the family in mourning, these writers insisted.

When the deceased was a person of note, condolence letters often acted as fan letters, demonstrating little etiquette. The deaths of Moore, Miller, Bankhead, and the latter's famous daughter actress Tallulah Bankhead provided opportunities for perfect strangers to send letters, cloaking their fan mail in the language of condolence. Tennessean Newman Barndon admitted in his handwritten letter that he had never known Moore, but had "admired him very much." "Altho I am a stranger to you, I feel as

[21] Telegram, Mordecai W. Johnson to Earl Brown, Editor, *Amsterdam News*, ca. December 1939; T. L. Hungate to Mrs. Annie May Butler Miller, January 4, 1930; and William Pickens, Director of Branches, NAACP, to Dr. Kelly Miller, Jr., January 2, 1940, all in Kelly Miller Papers, Manuscripts, Archives, and Rare Book Library, Emory University, Atlanta.

[22] Anna I. L. Mahler to Miss Bankhead, September 15, 1940, T. Bankhead Papers; John Shelby Chadwick to Florence Bankhead, September 15, 1940; J. V. and Mrs. Dickinson to Florence, September 16, 1940; and Bryce W. Harris to Mrs. Bankhead, September 17, 1940, all in Bankhead Papers.

if I know you well," wrote Mrs. J. O. Cheairs to Mary Daniel Moore. Although hardly harbingers of the celebrity culture of the mid- to late-twentieth century, such letters did relate a familiarity with strangers that had been unacceptable in southern etiquette but was becoming more common and, if not welcomed, was at least condoned.[23]

Secular language also manifested in condolence notes in another way: God no longer provided an exclusive succor to grief caused by death. Time, memories, and work were set forward as ways to heal those same wounds. Industrialization heightened Southerners' preoccupation with time, for industrial success depended on the efficient use of time. Not surprisingly, then, references to time became part of condolence language. Mrs. Moore's niece wrote that "time is the only thing that really eases this intense longing for our loved ones." Joseph Toy Howell's death in 1929 placed him in the "hands of the Creator who 'doeth all things well,'" but James Daughtery noted to Howell's widow, "as time passes it will be consoling to remember that the loss of your husband and Father was not alone yours." Appeals to memories became as common in condolence notes as reassurances of reunion with dead kin. Jennie Blackburn wrote Mary Daniel Moore, promising her memories would soothe her grief, "For you to have had such a husband has been a great good fortune. Then, remembering this, let us be happy in the thought that such a sacred memory is ours to cherish." And the ethic of work became an outlet for grief, especially in the Progressive and Depression-era Souths. Louise Meriweather noted to Moore that "I can understand fully your sorrow and shock for your experience was almost identical with my own," but urged her to keep busy: "After all, work is the greatest panacea for sorrow and loneliness."[24] Certainly, Christian theology was included in some of these assessments, but it was not an exclusive language anymore.

These shifts in language – the references to time and memories, the notation of a civic death – accompanied another remarkable shift in sympathy letters. By the mid-1930s, the condolence note was no longer new but a traditional ritual of death care. The expectation of receiving letters

[23] C. K. Decherd, Meriden to Mary Daniel Moore, May 14, 1929; Congressman E. E. Eslick, Seventh Congressional District, Tennessee to Mary Daniel Moore; Newman Barndon to Mary Daniel Moore, May 14, 1929; and Mrs. J. O. Cheairs to Mary Daniel Moore, n.d., all in Moore Papers. "Dropped Stitches" was a column that Mrs. Moore wrote.

[24] James A. Daughtery, June 17, 1929 to Mrs. J. T. Howell and Son, Howell Papers; Jennie G. Blackburn to Mary Daniel Moore, May 18, 1929; Louise H. Meriweather to Mary Daniel Moore, June 6, 1929; Pearl to Mary Daniel Moore, May 27, 1929; Mal to Mary Daniel Moore, May 14, 1929, all in Moore Papers.

provided its own level of comfort, a noteworthy change for Southerners who had earlier in the century expected face-to-face condolence for the grieving. Walter Newman wrote Floyd Jenkins when his wife, Varina, died in 1937, "I know that there is very little that your friends can do in such a situation, but I shall never forget what it meant to me to have letters expressing friendship and sympathy coming to me when I experienced loss in my immediate family."[25]

Unexpected trauma like the Great Depression inspired a return to evangelical Christian language in condolence notes, but such language did not supplant more secular themes that had begun to appear or the importance of the condolence note in comforting the grief-stricken. If the Depression left Americans anxious and fragile, deaths of family members or friends simply amplified the trauma. These new circumstances required more common use of new scriptural language, particularly the Twenty-Third Psalm ("The Lord Is My Shepherd"). The psalmist promised that "Yea, though I walk through the valley of the shadow of death, I will fear no evil: for thou art with me; thy rod and thy staff they comfort me." Emphasis on the Twenty-Third Psalm metaphorically connected individual death to the trials of the Depression, assuring recipients that God would serve as a guide for the trials and tribulations for the living. The Fidelis Sunday School wrote Viola Wood Goodwin when her husband died in May 1930, using the Twenty-Third Psalm, "[I]n our Sunday School class, we spoke of your journey through the Valley of the Shadow and we knew you were guided and comforted by the Good Shepherd. Your high faith, the beautiful Christian life your husband led, the absolute certainty of being with him again, soon, the gentle and strong Master who walks by your side – all these will comfort and sustain you."[26]

In the death of "Heck" Heckman in May 1931, the intersections between individual death and the Depression, biblical language, and secular references to time are most apparent. A well-known public official in Richmond, Virginia, Heckman died a young man, leaving behind a grieving fiancé, Mollie McLaughlin. McLaughlin's friend, Ethel, reminded her that "we have to go on just the same relying on our Heavenly Father for strength to bear these sorrows that come to us. May the God of all comfort be with you." Mollie's helplessness at the loss was palpable, but so, too, was the futility of those attempting to comfort her. "Mollie," her family

[25] Walter S. Newman to Floyd Jenkins, September 2, 1937, Jenkins Papers.

[26] Fidelis Class, via Principal, Dunbar School, Richmond Public Schools, to Viola Wood Goodwin, May 2, 1930, James Dennis Goodwin Papers, Virginia Historical Society.

wrote, "How sorry we are words cannot express ... do try to brace up for we are so worried about you and only wish some of us could be with you." Some letter writers blamed the Great Depression for his death. In mid-1931, McLaughlin's friend Robert wrote, "The past year or so has been a great strain on so many people, we have heard of so many young men being taken off suddenly that we have commenced to about dread opening the mail at least five of our acquaintances have had sudden deaths, none over fifty years of age. One day they were playing golf and the next day gone." Her aunt reminded her, "God knows best," even as she reported on the closings of family-owned mills due to the lack of orders – another loss to be accepted stoically. Another friend, Emmett Taylor, consoled that "In time the light will come to you, just try to think that the man that loved you would not have you grieve your life away." Like death interrupting the life of a young man, the Depression disrupted the modernization of the South, eliciting responses in both traditional and new languages.[27]

Even as the Depression made life difficult for many Southerners, the benefits of modernization were beginning to emerge, particularly in health care. One might expect privation and malnutrition to have lowered life expectancy in the Depression-era South, but mortality rates, particularly among infants, actually improved over the 1930s, most likely due to the intrusive influences of the New Deal and its health policies. "Death Rate Declines," announced the Memphis *Press-Scimitar* in 1940, noting how the city's infant mortality rate had declined from 14.8 percent in 1930 to 10.8 percent in 1939. Improvement to life expectancy elicited new ways of considering death among Southerners. When death did come, its presence was considered an abrupt, destructive force, something that "broke" families apart rather than a temporary rupture that would be healed once the family reunited in heaven. In that destruction, writers counseled their friends and intimates to be "brave," "gallant," or "courageous," to not give in to the emotional despair unleashed by the devastation of death. In their rush to assuage Florence Bankhead's grief at her husband's death, her close friends bemoaned her now "broken" household. Meta Crawford wrote of a poem sent to her by "one who knew our home that was broken by death." Another friend expressed thanks for her own as yet "unbroken

[27] *Richmond Times Dispatch*, May 22, 1931; Cora J. Moore to Mollie McLaughlin, May 22, 1931; Nelia to Mollie, ca. May 1931; Robert to Molly, June 16, 1931; Old Aunt Lola to Mollie, May 13, 1931; Emmett Taylor to Mollie, June 1, 1931; Flora to Mollie, June 2, 1931, all in Mollie Belle McLaughlin Papers, Virginia Historical Society.

household." That brokenness caused some to fear that those in mourning might dissolve into an emotional frenzy; that the grief might so overwhelm them that they ceased to be useful people. Ruby O'Neale, in her note to Florence Bankhead, hoped that God would "give you strength to bear this and to live on courageously."[28]

Changes in printing press technology in the 1930s and 1940s also contributed to shifting attitudes toward death. Preprinted cards were cheap, became more attractive with a greater availability of colors (purple, the color of Christian royalty, and silver were most common), and included images (like Easter lilies that symbolized the resurrection of Jesus Christ). The written text not only expressed sympathy but also provided different ways to console. Preprinted sympathy cards also inspired preprinted thank-you notes. No longer would friends and family have to imagine what to write in a condolence note, and no longer would families have to handwrite thank-you notes for the cards that they received. The Bankheads simply sent out a card that read, "The Bankhead families acknowledge with grateful appreciation your kind expression of sympathy." One consequence of this diminution of handwritten notes was the incorporation of broader American ways of grieving into southern condolence literature. But the new practices also expanded the number of people who could share sympathies because the cards allowed a more distant formality. There was nothing intimate about preprinted cards written by unknown authors employed by card makers. This formality and distancing permitted a greater number of those wishing to console to send cards without awkwardly crossing social barriers. For example, Helen McDonough sent a card with lovely Easter lilies pictured on the cover to Florence Bankhead. The cover stated simply: "Thinking of You in Your Sorrow." Inside, a preprinted secular message required no further comments: "We sometimes bear things all alone When, if we only knew, The sympathy of those who care Would help – and comfort, too." By far, the most common card sentiment was a poem by James Whitcomb Riley. Outside, the card stated "He is only away" (or "She is only away" when appropriate). Inside, the full poem appeared:

> I cannot say, and I will not say
> That he is dead – He is just away!

[28] Edward R. Trapnell, "Health of City Better; Death Rate Declines," *Memphis Press-Scimitar* clipping, March 15, 1940, in Vital Statistics Folder, Memphis Public Library; Meta J. Crawford to Florence, September 18, 1940; Blanche Spain Sarner to Florence Bankhead, September 18, 1940; Ruby O'Neale to Florence Bankhead, September 17, 1940, all in Bankhead Papers.

> With a cheery smile and wave of the hand,
> He has wandered into an unknown land.
> And left us dreaming how very fair
> It needs must be, since he lingers there
> And you – O you, who the wildest yearn
> For the old-time step and the glad return, –
> Think of him faring on, as dear
> In the love of There as the love of Here;
> Think of him still as the same, I say
> He is not dead – he is just away!

"He is only away" appeared in many, many cards across the South. Because the deceased is not dead – he or she is only away on a trip – the card seemed appropriate for acquaintances or even strangers to send. By World War II, preprinted cards became ubiquitous. When newspapers announced a military death to the broader community, cards became ways to acknowledge the sacrifice without the expected intimacy between sender and recipient. Ben Espey's parents received dozens of these cards when he was reported missing and then deceased in April 1944. "In Sympathy" or "Sympathy," the cards read, and in most cases, only the sender's signature appeared on the inside. And they were convenient, offering a ready solution for those without the time or inclination to write a longer note. When a fellow soldier died in the war, George Maupin's mother suggested he simply send a card "if you haven't time to write much."[29]

World War II also forced substantial changes in the ways Southerners – and other Americans – wrote condolence notes. Nearly four times as many men died in World War II as had in World War I, and their deaths on distant European and South Pacific battlefields required Southerners to reassess the meaning of those deaths, particularly when they had occurred far from the family's view and without the immediacy of a funeral. (Most soldiers who died overseas were temporarily interred and then sent home between 1947 and 1952). In the 1920s, condolence notes had proclaimed the well-lived life of the deceased. In the 1940s, a young man who died in battle had not yet achieved that meaningful measure, and so the death itself came to be significant. Letter writers claimed that wartime deaths

[29] Preprinted note; Helen McDonough to Adelaide Bankhead, ca. September 1940, both in Bankhead Papers. For examples of preprinted cards, see Willie Newson McJilton to Florence Bankhead, ca. September 1940; and Sallie Robertson Frazier to Florence Bankhead, ca. September 1940, both in Bankhead Papers; Dora Oliver to Ben K. Espey, ca. March 1944, Balch Family Papers, Tennessee State Library and Archives; Julia Allen Russell Venturis to George Roy Maupin, April 9, 1943, North American Women's Letters and Diaries: Colonial to 1950, solomon.nwld.alexanderstreet.com.

washed sin from an evil world, struck a blow against dictators, and were heroic and noble no matter how the death occurred.[30]

In their condolence letters, politicians understood the importance of honoring young soldiers' deaths as noble and heroic. Memphis's Ed "Boss" Crump lost his youngest son, John, in a plane crash in May 1939, and he used his constituents' knowledge of his own loss when he wrote multiple Memphis families after their sons' and husbands' wartime deaths. To Theresa Galliani when her son, Julius, died in Germany in November 1944, Crump wrote that "The fact that he died a hero's death in the gigantic struggle for world freedom is a consoling thought." But Crump also employed his own loss: "I want you to know how deeply I sympathize with you and yours. Only those who themselves have experienced the loss of loved ones can plumb the depths of sorrow that is yours." A congressional staffer used a similar assessment of death when he comforted Mr. and Mrs. William Major of Virginia when their son, Ensign Charles Major, died in March 1942:

> There is the force of good countered by the forces of evil, but through all the conflicts of which life is made up there is no force so potent or more magnificent than the immovable force of a boy who knows right from wrong, and who cleaves to the right without compromise and unflinchingly risks his life that right may win. If this were not so God alone knows what would happen to this sorry world.[31]

Assigning meaning to a young man's death became more widespread, however, and was not the exclusive language of politicians. Writing to Billy Faulkner's parents, Tennessee State College's president, W. S. David, wrote,

> We were aware that with his background and rich heritage he was destined to reach great heights. This was especially evidenced by his outstanding achievements over such a short period of time. These achievements, together with the inspiration of his courageous life, will stand as a beacon to the youth of our race for generations to

[30] David Kennedy, *Freedom from Fear: The American People in Depression and War, 1929–1945* (New York: Oxford University Press, 1999); Carole Byerly, *Fever of War: The Influenza Epidemic in the U.S. Army during World War I* (New York: New York University Press, 2005).

[31] There are multiple examples of Crump letters to the bereaved. Most have the original newspaper clipping attached to the letter and, in some cases, a notation of a donation in the soldier's name to a local charity is also attached. See Ed Crump to Mrs. Theresa Galliani, December 8, 1944, Ed Crump Papers, microfilm, Memphis Public Library. For information on John Crump's death in a plane crash, see "E. H. Crump's Son, Pilot George Stokes, Reporter Ted Northington Die in Crash of Commercial Appeal Plane at Grenada," *Memphis Commercial Appeal*, May 3, 1939; unknown, on House of Representatives stationery, March 7, 1942, Charles Nance Major Papers, Virginia Historical Society.

come. He has stamped himself indelibly upon the age in which he has lived. He made an outstanding contribution toward world peace.

Beyond the fact that Billy had "fought bravely and brilliantly for the rights of his people and for the world peace which would ultimately mean so much to all mankind," George W. Gore Jr. assigned meaning to Billy's death in the advancement of civil rights: "despite the handicaps of race which he may have encountered, [Billy's accomplishments] stand out as a shining example of what the youth of the race can hope to attain through preparation and hard work." At Ben Clay Espey's death, the University of the South's Vice Chancellor's office reminded his parents of "the pride that is yours in having made such a costly sacrifice upon the altar of liberty. How we must strive with all our being to make this country the sort of land for which gallant young men like Ben have died to preserve for themselves, and for their children, and their children's children!"[32] In this case, the parents' own grief became a noble sacrifice to the war effort.

Condolence notes built relationships between families whose sons served together, drawing Southerners beyond region and into a larger American nation. Without regard to class, ethnicity, or region, the military combined young men from across the nation into units, creating what historian David Kennedy called the "mother and father of all melting pots." (Only race remained a barrier.) The ten Americans who staffed each B-24 plane, for example, could come from different states and different walks of life. Because crewmates swapped addresses with each other, soldiers could share information with their families when they lost comrades. In June 1944, Virginian Harold Leazer's plane went down. Four crew mates survived, but Leazer did not. Nearly every crewmate's mother wrote Mrs. Leazer to comfort her. Survivor Don Johnson's mother wrote from Minnesota that "my heart just ached for you and Mr. Leazer. I just can't express my sympathy in words to you both. My thoughts and prayers are with you." Several letters evinced some guilt that the writers' sons had survived while another's had died. But condolence cards allowed for the creation of an extended community of mourning that could last for years. Don Johnson, for example, sent Mrs. Leazer a Mother's Day card every year until her death.[33]

[32] W. S. David, President Tennessee A and I State College, to Reverend and Mrs. William J. Faulkner, Sr., ca. December 1944; George W. Gore, Jr., to Reverend and Mrs. William J. Faulkner, Sr., January 1, 1945, both in Faulkner Papers; Alex Guerry to Ben K. Espey, August 30, 1944, Balch Papers.

[33] Kennedy, *Freedom from Fear*, 712; Mrs. Charles Johnson to Mrs. Leazer, October 16, 1944, Harold Leazer Papers, Virginia Historical Society.

Although unit assignments did not cross the color line, sympathy did. The deaths of young black soldiers occasionally elicited white Southerners' condolences as they recognized that black parents had sacrificed as well. After Billy Faulkner was reported missing in action, Nashville mayor Thomas L. Cummings typed a condolence note to the Faulkners (in contrast to a handwritten one that would have implied a familiarity that was not acceptable in the Jim Crow South) that acknowledged their son's honorable service: "May your pride in his splendid record of service and the awards to him by his grateful Country, be a source of comfort to you in your anxiety."[34]

The preprinted card industry adapted to wartime soldiers missing in action (MIAs) and deaths as well. Cards were printed that declared on the exterior, "Because your loved one is missing," and inside expressed, "May all these anxious hours be filled with hope and courage too. Until the happy day arrives when good news comes to you." If the unhappy day should arrive, there were preprinted wartime death cards as well. One sent to the Faulkners read, "A Tribute to One who has served." Inside, the sentiment read: "What greater tribute could we offer than to say HE GAVE HIS LIFE FOR HIS COUNTRY." Such messages contributed to the "Americanization" of the South during World War II, explicitly reminding grieving Southerners that theirs was a national loss.[35] And those messages also implicitly recognized that black parents' sacrifices were not different from those of white parents who had lost sons.

Between the 1910s and the 1940s, condolence writing reflected the emergent modern South – a region that no longer relied exclusively on evangelical Christian language to express sympathy, embraced and employed the convenient preprinted cards of modern industry, and began to abandon its regional identity for a greater national character. Condolence letters evidenced shifts in language and content – even in the form of the sympathy note itself. But whether grappling with private losses or with a soldier's deaths, Southerners found comfort both in receiving condolences and in sending them. The gracious impulse to comfort remained constant. Responding to the news that Billy Faulkner had died, Reverend W. S. Ellington rejoiced that "it is just as near from Austria to

[34] Thomas L. Cummings to Reverend and Mrs. William J. Faulkner, Sr., November 24, 1944, Faulkner Papers.

[35] Reverend and Mrs. Julius C. Johnson to Reverend and Mrs. William J. Faulkner, Sr., ca. November 1944; Havens and Allan to Reverend and Mrs. William J. Faulkner, Sr., ca. December 1944, both in Faulkner Papers.

Heaven as it is from Nashville. Since you have a heroic son up there, it will seem more like home when you arrive."[36] Promised by ministers of a family reunion in heaven if not on earth, mourners were reminded by condolence literature of those assurances even as they struggled with grievous loss and the transformation of their South.

[36] Reverend W. S. Ellington to Reverend and Mrs. William J. Faulkner, Sr., December 26, 1944, Faulkner Papers.

10

"A Monument to Judge Lynch": Racial Violence, Symbolic Death, and Black Resistance in Jim Crow Mississippi

Jason Morgan Ward

"Mississippi must lead the world in the lynching of children," wrote Langston Hughes in 1955, days after white men tossed Emmett Till's battered corpse into a Mississippi bayou. Images of Till's bloated and disfigured face, framed between screaming headlines from Manhattan to Moscow, made him the most famous lynching victim in American history. Indeed, historians and activists alike cite Till's grisly murder as a catalyst for the civil rights campaigns of the 1950s and 1960s. But the Till lynching took Hughes back to another place – a rusty river bridge in Shubuta, Mississippi, where vigilantes had hung six black youths since the turn of the century.[1]

Even as African Americans mourned Emmett Till's death, Hughes reminded his readers of two other dead Mississippians. "Charlie Lang and Ernest Green," Hughes wrote, "were young Negro boys like Emmett Till, too, only fourteen years old, when they were lynched."[2] And like Till, Lang and Green met their deaths after allegedly "bothering" a white girl. In October 1942, vigilantes snatched both boys from the Clarke County jail, where they were being held on charges of attempted rape, and hanged them from a bridge near the small town of Shubuta. In the wake of the killings, a reporter for the Baltimore *Afro American* branded Mississippi's Hanging Bridge a "monument to 'Judge Lynch.'"[3] Like Hughes, Walter

[1] Langston Hughes, "Langston Hughes Wonders Why No Lynching Probes," *Chicago Defender*, October 1, 1955.

[2] Ibid.

[3] Walter Atkins, "Shubuta Bridge's Toll Stands at Six Lynch Victims, But Span Is Doomed," *Chicago Defender*, November 7, 1942.

Atkins recalled an earlier generation of lynching victims. Back in 1918, a mob hanged two brothers and two pregnant sisters from the same bridge. By the time Emmett Till became the nation's most famous lynching victim, the Hanging Bridge was already its most notorious lynching site.

When Langston Hughes invoked Ernest Green and Charlie Lang in 1955, he linked Emmett Till's death to a longer protest tradition of collective and symbolic mourning. As historians have noted, Till's lynching grabbed the world's attention largely because his mother insisted on an open-casket funeral. Mamie Till Bradley wanted "the world to see what they have done to my boy." Civil rights activists, recognizing the power of the press and the diplomatic liability of racial violence, desired the same thing. Although Till's murder received unprecedented attention, the representation and remembrance of lynching victims had fueled African-American protest for decades.[4] In moments of global war and domestic turmoil, civil rights activists and everyday people harnessed lynching's symbolic power at Mississippi's Hanging Bridge. And, like Mamie Till Bradley, earlier generations of black Southerners sacrificed burial customs, even the bodies themselves, in order to defy the lynching routine.[5]

Because whites repeatedly lynched at the Hanging Bridge, the site dramatized the dynamic interplay between racial violence and protest politics in the Jim Crow era, even as it confirmed the consistent brutalization of black bodies by white hands. This gory monument, and the generation separating the lynchings that occurred there, provides a rare opportunity to measure the increasing political clout and diplomatic leverage that civil rights activists wielded. Depictions of mob violence, and the response to them, highlight how the deployment of lynching imagery evolved from Jim Crow's heyday to the eve of its demise. As the site of repeat lynchings, the Hanging Bridge provides a singular lens through which to view this change.

4 Suzanne E. Smith, *To Serve the Living: Funeral Directors and the African American Way of Death* (Cambridge: Belknap Press, 2010), 124–25; Stephen J. Whitfield, *A Death in the Delta: The Story of Emmett Till* (New York: Free Press, 1988), 23. Karla FC Holloway, *Passed On: African American Mourning Stories* (Durham: Duke University Press, 2003).

5 "As important as the responses of black institutions and black elites to white violence were," W. Fitzhugh Brundage argues, "the resistance of unorganized and seemingly powerless blacks is of equal significance, especially in a region and at a time when only a small minority of blacks were either members of reform groups or participants in organized protest"; see "The Roar on the Other Side of Silence: Black Resistance and White Violence in the American South, 1880–1940," in *Under Sentence of Death: Lynching in the South*, ed. W. Fitzhugh Brundage (Chapel Hill: University of North Carolina Press, 1997), 271.

When activists and everyday people encountered the Hanging Bridge and its victims, they projected their hopes and frustrations onto this gory monument. They cheered signs of courage and defiance in the stories and images from Shubuta, but they simultaneously lamented local blacks' seeming acquiescence to white supremacy. In 1918, and again in 1942, black activists debated the efficacy of armed self-defense, the extent of "race militancy," and the vulnerability of white supremacy in the South's most remote corners. From the vantage point of World War II, they looked again to Mississippi for glimmers of progress and found ample evidence of ongoing repression and intransigence. In both eras, African Americans measured the promise and limits of their freedom struggle at the Hanging Bridge.

Walter White never believed the newspaper accounts coming out of Shubuta, Mississippi. By the waning weeks of 1918, the National Association for the Advancement of Colored People (NAACP) staffer had read the same details dozens of times – the "overpowered" jailer, the spontaneous and shadowy mob, the justifications for retributive white violence against supposed mortal threats from African Americans, the guilt of the victims, and the particulars of their offense. In this case, four black youths – two brothers and two sisters – had supposedly plotted to murder their employer, a "wealthy retired dentist" named E. L. Johnston. Several accounts alluded vaguely to the "trouble" that prompted Maggie Howze to conspire with her sister Alma and the Clark brothers, Major and Andrew, to kill their boss. The day after Johnston's mysterious death, all four youths swung from a nearby river bridge.[6]

Despite the predictable storyline, the Shubuta lynchings compelled White's attention. During the Atlanta native's first year working for the NAACP, the New York office rarely went a week without receiving at least one report of mob murder. But with four confirmed dead in Mississippi, the official wartime lynching count topped one hundred. The Shubuta mob, which struck five weeks after Armistice Day, heightened fears that the wartime violence would spill over into the postwar months. Black

[6] "Lynch Four Negroes; Two of Them Women," *New York Times*, December 21, 1918; "Mob Shackles Deputy Sheriff and Hangs 4 Negroes at Shubuta," *Laurel Leader*, December 21, 1918; "Jury Fails to Locate Guilty Mob Members," *Hattiesburg American*, December 23, 1918; "Four Negroes Met Death by Hanging at Hands of Unknown Parties Was Coroner's Verdict in Lynching Case," *Meridian Star*, clipping in Papers of the National Association for the Advancement of Colored People, microfilm. For mention of the "trouble" between Johnston and Maggie Howze, see "Bodies of Negroes Mobbed at Shubuta Cut from Bridge," *Memphis News Scimitar*, December 21, 1918; "Four Blacks Lynched at Shubuta, Miss.," *Memphis Commercial Appeal*, December 21, 1918, both clippings in Papers of the NAACP [microfilm].

newspapers contrasted the brutality in Mississippi with the soaring war rhetoric of freedom and democracy. "Is this the kind of democracy we have fought and suffered for," asked the *New York Call*, "and is this our reward for all that we have done?" The editor of the *St. Louis Argus*, one of the oldest black newspapers in the country, wondered if southern vigilantes were mobilizing to force returning veterans back into their prewar place. The newspaperman asked "When the black boys come marching home, what will be their reward for their true devotion to the Stars and Stripes?" Referring directly to the dead youths in Mississippi, he concluded, "Will it be lynchers' rope for them and their sisters?"[7]

Mississippi's official response to the Shubuta lynchings further discouraged and incensed African Americans. Governor Theodore Bilbo ignored the NAACP's request for an investigation. When a reporter asked Bilbo if he planned to respond to the NAACP's well-publicized telegram, the governor boasted, "I will tell them, in effect, to go to hell." Local officials and Mississippi newspapermen, although less combative, closed ranks to rationalize the vigilantes' actions and protect their anonymity. Despite the fact that the mob abducted the prisoners from the jail around 6:30 PM, reported the *Hattiesburg American*, "no hint of disorder was noticed." The *Laurel Leader* claimed that "the mob worked so quietly and swiftly that few citizens were aware of it." The mob, local papers assured their readers, had dispersed as quickly and quietly as it had materialized: "no further trouble is anticipated."[8]

Black activists and editors responded with protest telegrams and fiery editorials, but they lacked the on-the-ground facts that southern white papers routinely omitted. Noting white papers' allusions to "trouble" between the murdered dentist and his female employees, Baltimore newspaperman W. T. Andrews read between the lines. "Negro women have absolutely no protection from white monsters in the South," he editorialized, "and when they are violated and degraded by white men the only remedy is that which was used by Major Clark and resulted in his lynching by a mob." Predicting that an investigation "would reveal that there was

[7] "100 Lynchings Since the Beginning of World War," *St. Louis Argus*, December 27, 1918; "Our Black Brothers," *New York Call*, December 23, 1918; "The Reward for Devotion," *St. Louis Argus*, December 27, 1918; frame 1145, all in Papers of the NAACP [microfilm].

[8] "Jury Fails to Locate Guilty Mob Members," *Hattiesburg American*, December 23, 1918; "Governor of Mississippi Tells NAACP to Go to Hell," *Baltimore Daily Herald*, December 31, 1918; "Mob Binds Deputy; Hangs 4 Negroes," *Gulfport Daily Herald*, December 21, 1918; "Four Negroes Lynched by Mob at Shubuta; Two Women," *Jackson Daily News*, December 21, 1918, all in Papers of the NAACP [microfilm].

some facts that the lynchers desired to cover up," Andrews wrote the NAACP for assistance. By the time his letter arrived in New York, Walter White had already boarded a southbound train.[9]

Although White had worked for the NAACP for less than a year, he had quickly established himself as the secret weapon in the organization's antilynching crusade. Fair-skinned, blond-haired, and blue-eyed, the twenty-six-year-old field secretary had already passed as white on fact-finding missions to Tennessee and Georgia. His Atlanta upbringing and the skills he honed selling insurance helped him win the confidence of unsuspecting whites. During the Georgia trip, White sipped Coca-Cola while a white storeowner casually described how his neighbors had cut a fetus from Mary Turner's charred body and stomped it to death. Armed with such gruesome details, the fledgling NAACP spearheaded a national campaign against mob violence and served as a clearinghouse for the black press. Without Walter White's daring investigations, many brutal lynching stories would have never seen the light of day.[10]

On his trips southward, White juggled investigation with organization. He visited fledgling NAACP chapters in Chattanooga, Nashville, and New Orleans on his roundabout journey to southern Mississippi. After delivering "the best speech I have made" to a packed New Orleans auditorium, White signed up 102 new members on the spot. The next morning, a slight and unassuming traveling salesman ambled through Shubuta. Although "the white people would not talk very much about the matter," White pieced together the story with the help of a local black preacher and a cousin of the Howze sisters.[11]

The "wealthy retired dentist," White learned, was a philandering alcoholic who had abandoned his Mobile, Alabama, practice and moved back home to his father's farm. Johnston was very unpopular locally, White noted, "because of his general worthlessness and looseness with women." Many townspeople believed that Johnston had impregnated both Howze sisters and that this provoked a confrontation with the Clark brothers. The brothers, each of whom was courting one of the Howze sisters, had ample motive to kill Johnston. Several informants suggested otherwise, believing

[9] "Four Negroes, Two of Them Wmoen [sic], Lynched in Mississippi," *Baltimore Daily Herald*, December 23, 1918; W. T. Andrews to John R. Shillady, January 14, 1919, both in Papers of the NAACP [microfilm].

[10] Thomas Dyja, *Walter White: The Dilemma of Black Identity in America* (Chicago: Ivan R. Dee, 2008), 51–52; Kenneth Robert Janken, *Walter White: Mr. NAACP* (Chapel Hill: University of North Carolina Press, 2006), 32–33.

[11] Walter White to John R. Shillady, January 20, 1919, Papers of the NAACP [microfilm].

that a white man murdered Johnston for having an affair with his wife. Since Johnston's feud with his black workers was "common knowledge in the community," Walter reported, this white assassin "felt that he could kill the dentist safely and the blame would be put on the Negroes." When Johnston turned up dead, allegedly shot from ambush while milking a cow, a posse seized Major Clark and whisked him off to nearby Meridian. Clark confessed only after the police placed his testicles in a vise. Back in Clarke County, authorities rounded up Clark's brother and the Howze sisters on charges of a murder conspiracy. That night a mob seized the suspects from Shubuta's tiny jailhouse and hanged them from a nearby bridge.[12]

White's investigative report, titled "An Example of Democracy in Mississippi," juxtaposed America's lofty war aims with the brutal reality of the Shubuta lynchings. The gruesome details convinced White that the Shubuta lynchings were "more repulsive and horrible than the [Mary Turner lynching] in South Georgia last May." Like the Turner lynching, the Shubuta case involved pregnant women. But the youth of the victims, who White referred to as "Negro children," made the Shubuta killings that much more detestable.[13]

Despite the victims' youth and vulnerability, White intertwined a story of brutal repression with imagery of courage and resistance. Maggie Howze, he noted, loudly protested her innocence until a mob member clubbed her with a monkey wrench. The first blow knocked out her teeth, and the second cut "a long gash in which the side of a person's hands could be placed." When the mob tossed her over the railings, she twice caught herself and tried to pull her battered body back up. The next day, Maggie's cousin told White that mob members laughingly recounted how hard they had worked to kill "that big black Jersey woman." An informant told White that after the corpses had been cut down, the gravediggers saw movements in Alma Howze's abdomen. She would have given birth in just two weeks.[14]

White memorialized Maggie Howze's battered corpse as a symbol of resistance, but the conflict over the victims' burial suggested that others shared her defiant spirit. "Burial took place in a negro graveyard at the expense of the county," a local paper reported, after the victims' families refused to claim the bodies. Coverage of the killings in white-owned

[12] Walter F. White, "An Example of Democracy in Mississippi," typescript, 2, Papers of the NAACP [microfilm]; White to Shillady, January 20, 1919.

[13] Walter White to W. H. P. Freeman, February 7, 1919, Papers of the NAACP [microfilm]; White, "An Example of Democracy in Mississippi," 1.

[14] Ibid., 3.

newspapers interpreted this as a sign of lethargy rather than defiance. A Hattiesburg newspaperman noted "the laconic reply of the father of the Clarkes ... when asked by the authorities ... whether or not he cared to claim the bodies of his sons." Walter White challenged this self-serving narrative. Not only did the families decline to retrieve the bodies, but, as White put it, "the Negroes refused to allow them to be buried in the colored cemetery." White Southerners willfully misinterpreted African Americans' refusal to bury lynched bodies as a sign of meekness and apathy. But Walter White countered with an alternative interpretation – that African Americans in Shubuta forced local whites to shoulder responsibility for the lynchings and their aftermath. That the town's only undertaker was "freely said ... to have led the mob" only strengthened black resolve to take no part in the lynching's resolution. Left with four unclaimed corpses, Will Patton packed the bodies in cheap pine boxes and buried them just outside the white cemetery fence.[15]

White's exposé dramatized the depravity of white supremacy, the resilience of black Southerners, and the hypocrisy of American war rhetoric. Even as Woodrow Wilson and Allied leaders hashed out a peace treaty at Versailles, White urged the president to protect black life back home. "Ten thousand Leagues of Nations may be formed, and the leaders of thought through-out the world may talk of democracy until the end of time," White warned, "but as long as lawless mobs can willfully murder in cold blood ... as the Shubuta mob has done, the world is not a place made 'safe for democracy.'" White's stinging rhetoric and graphic imagery proved too much for sympathetic yet squeamish contacts in the white press. The managing editor of *The Nation* passed the article along to *The Independent*, whose editor requested revisions, White complained, "leaving out all horrible details." Indeed, even the NAACP cut out some of White's most searing passages.[16]

By the time *The Crisis* ran White's report in May 1919, the black press had new killings to investigate. Still, the Shubuta lynchings, which White deemed "the most atrocious affair of its kind ever known," punctuated the emergence of a national campaign for antilynching legislation. Just weeks

[15] "Jury Fails to Locate Guilty Mob Members," *Hattiesburg American*, December 23, 1918; White to Shillady, January 20, 1919.

[16] White, "An Example of Democracy In Mississippi," 4; H.R. Mussey to Walter White, February 24, 1919, Papers of the NAACP [microfilm]; editor, *The Dial*, to Walter White, March 13, 1919, Papers of the National Association for the Advancement of Colored People, Library of Congress, Washington, DC; "The Shubuta Lynchings," *The Crisis* 18 (May 1919): 25.

after White's trip to Shubuta, the NAACP published *Thirty Years of Lynching in the United States*. Sandwiched between a statistical summary and a sixty-page roster of 3,224 documented victims, a section entitled "The Story of One Hundred Lynchings" chronicled representative atrocities in narrative form. The final lynching "story" memorialized the Hanging Bridge's four young victims and closed with the image of an unborn child still moving inside a dead woman's womb.[17]

The publication of *Thirty Years of Lynching* built momentum for the NAACP's May 1919 Anti-Lynching Conference at New York City's Carnegie Hall. At this historic meeting, the imagery of the Hanging Bridge and its victims punctuated three decades of atrocities and the killing spree that accompanied the Great War. Conference planners hoped to have Mississippi-born Attorney General Thomas Gregory present the findings from Walter White's recent lynching investigations. Instead, in front of Gregory's successor A. Mitchell Palmer and 2,500 distinguished delegates from across the country, NAACP field secretary James Weldon Johnson recounted the Shubuta lynching story himself. "We need a little common honesty," he concluded, "This nation needs to humble itself before God. It needs to stop some of its loud boastings about humanity and democracy ... until it is able to throw the arm of protection around the weakest within its own borders."[18]

The imagery of the Hanging Bridge and its young victims punctuated a decisive moment in the emergence of the century's first nationally viable civil rights campaign.[19] At a crucial turning point in the history of lynching

[17] NAACP, *Thirty Years of Lynching in the United States, 1889–1918* (New York: NAACP, 1919), 27; Robert L. Zangrando, *The NAACP Crusade against Lynching, 1909–1950* (Philadelphia: Temple University Press, 1980), 48.

[18] "Suggestions Re: Anti-Lynching Conference – March 1919," 3; "Address Delivered by James Weldon Johnson, National Conference on Lynching, Carnegie Hall," May 5, 1919, both in Papers of the NAACP [microfilm]; Cameron McWhirter, *Red Summer: The Summer of 1919 and the Awakening of Black America* (New York: Henry Holt, 2011), 34–36.

[19] In his pioneering and authoritative study of the NAACP's antilynching campaign, Robert Zangrando contends that the crusade against mob violence "had an urgency, a public visibility, and a dramatic quality that no other civil rights activity quite matched"; see *The NAACP Crusade against Lynching*, 21. The antilynching drive unified an otherwise fractious black activist community, gained white sympathizers who would have balked at more direct assaults on the color line, and gained traction in Congress years before other legislative and legal campaigns. Although scholars have challenged the notion of a "long civil rights movement" that incorporates earlier racial reform campaigns into a broader timeline of black protest, the antilynching drive stands out as an early example of interracial, interregional mobilization in opposition to a particularly egregious civil rights abuse. For more on the "long civil rights movement" and its detractors, see Jacquelyn

and antilynching activism, the NAACP portrayed the Shubuta slayings as Mississippi's most notorious atrocity. In response, the state's white elites took unprecedented steps to distance themselves from the mob. Indeed, the head of the newly formed Mississippi Welfare League, founded ten days after the Shubuta lynchings, presided over a session of the Anti-Lynching Conference.[20]

Although some white elites professed a desire for racial goodwill, their immediate objective was to stem the dramatic exodus of black Mississippians to the urban North. Alongside imagery of tortured children and mutilated corpses, black editors evoked scenes of fleeing workers and rotting crops. "Is This an Invitation to Negroes to Move?" a New Orleans paper asked in the wake of the Shubuta lynchings. "We sincerely hope," the editorial continued, "that there will not be enough Negroes in Clarke County, Mississippi, to carry a pail of water two blocks, and that they will move out at the first opportunity."[21]

Hundreds of Clarke County residents had already seized that opportunity, and many more followed in the wake of the Hanging Bridge lynchings. No other corner of the Deep South illustrated more dramatically the link between racial slayings and black outmigration in the postwar months. "After the incidents at Shubuta I had only one obsession," one Clarke County native recalled: "That was to get up North to magic places like Chicago and New York, where I'd heard there was some freedom, and where white folks didn't shoot you, lynch you, and insult you every day." In a state that accounted for an estimated one-fourth of all southern black migrants during the 1910s, Clarke County outpaced its neighbors. The 1920 Census revealed a 30 percent drop in the county's black population – three times the rate for Mississippi as a whole.[22] Clarke County migrants

Dowd Hall, "The Long Civil Rights Movement and the Political Uses of the Past," *Journal of American History* 91 (2005): 1233–64; Sundiata Keita Cha-Jua and Clarence Lang, "The 'Long Movement' as Vampire: Temporal and Spatial Fallacies in Recent Black Freedom Studies," *Journal of African American History* 92 (spring 2007): 265–88.

20 Jack C. Wilson, the head of the Mississippi Welfare League, presided over the afternoon and evening sessions on May 6, 1919. His comments to the conference stressed the shame of lynching but also the white South's opposition to "social equality" and "radicalism"; see Wilson's addresses to the Anti-Lynching Conference, Papers of the NAACP [LOC].

21 "Is This an Invitation for Negroes to Move?" New Orleans *Southwestern Christian Advocate*, n.d.; "The Shubuta Lynching and a Query," New Orleans *Southwestern Christian Advocate*, n.d., both in Papers of the NAACP [microfilm].

22 James Yates, *From Mississippi to Madrid: Memoir of a Black American in the Abraham Lincoln Brigade* (Greensboro: Open Hand, 1989), 22–23; Stewart E. Tolnay and E. M. Beck, *A Festival of Violence: An Analysis of Southern Lynchings, 1882–1930* (Urbana: University of Illinois Press, 1995), 214.

joined the steady stream of Southerners who swelled the ranks of northern black voters and made tangible civil rights activists' estimations of their growing political clout.

By the time white vigilantes again executed black youth at the Hanging Bridge, lynching's opponents yielded unprecedented leverage. Despite an ominous spike during the 1930s, lynching declined dramatically after 1919 and never again returned to prewar rates. A coalition of civil rights groups and white liberals pressured northern Congressional leaders to repeatedly introduce federal antilynching bills in the 1920s and 1930s. A 1937 bill, which sailed through the House by a three-to-one vote, died only after a six-week filibuster by southern Senate Democrats. Although President Franklin D. Roosevelt refused to endorse such legislation for fear of alienating his southern base, the outbreak of World War II forced him to take concrete steps to eradicate mob violence. When a mob in Sikeston, Missouri, lynched Cleo Wright in January 1942, the President ordered the Federal Bureau of Investigation to dispatch agents to the scene.[23]

Eight months later, vigilantes snatched Ernest Green and Charlie Lang from the Clarke County jail and hanged them from the Shubuta bridge. Like Emmett Till thirteen years later, the two boys met their deaths after crossing paths with a young white woman. On a sunny afternoon in October 1942, they were rummaging for scrap by a highway bridge when fifteen-year-old Dorothy Martin came upon the boys on her way home from school. Her mother claimed that Dorothy ran home screaming after one of the boys tried to drag her under the bridge and rape her. When her father, a hard-drinking lumber mill worker, returned home from work, word of the incident had already spread through town. Within a few hours, a posse led by the local deputy and the girl's father had rounded up Green and Lang and hauled them off to the county jail in Quitman. Local authorities immediately charged the frightened boys with attempted rape, and county sheriff Lloyd McNeal maintained vehemently in later days that the boys had promptly pled guilty.[24]

[23] Dominic J. Capeci, Jr., *The Lynching of Cleo Wright* (Lexington: University Press of Kentucky, 1998). For an analysis of the federal government's changing response to lynching during the New Deal and World War II eras, see Christopher Waldrep, "National Policing, Lynching, and Constitutional Change," *Journal of Southern History* 74 (August 2008): 589–626.

[24] Enoc P. Waters, "Two Lynched Boys Were Ace Scrap Iron Collectors in Mississippi Town," *Chicago Defender*, March 6, 1943; Victor H. Bernstein, "Mississippi Laments Lynchings – But Doing Something About Them Is Another Matter," *PM*, October 28, 1942. White witnesses offered varying accounts of the alleged rape attempt, arrest, and

A few days later, a small gang of white men converged on the jailhouse just after midnight. Town marshal Fortner Dabbs claimed that a constable had phoned him and said he was delivering a prisoner. Phone records later revealed that no one had called him. When he arrived at the jail, Dabbs claimed, a shadowy gang of men threw a blanket over his head, locked him in a cell, and sped off into the night with the two terrified boys. The next morning, October 12, 1942, passersby discovered the bodies of Ernest Green and Charlie Lang hanging from the Shubuta bridge. Local authorities quickly cut down the bodies and loaded them onto a pulpwood truck. White townspeople surrounded the truck as it rolled to a stop in front of the post office, the uncovered corpses sprawled across the bed. Local African Americans avoided the spectacle and, as in 1918, refused to accept the bodies for burial. Left with no alternative, undertaker Will Patton once again packed lynching victims into wooden boxes and secured a black chain gang to bury the boys just outside the white cemetery.[25]

By the next morning, newspapers across the country announced the latest wartime lynching. In Washington, an official in the Justice Department's Civil Rights Division phoned the FBI after noticing "several news items appearing in the New York papers." Later that day, Assistant Attorney General Wendell Berge fired off a memo to FBI chief J. Edgar Hoover, reiterating President Roosevelt's wartime directive that lynching cases should be investigated promptly and prosecuted if possible. Alluding to the urgent need to quell domestic protests and counteract enemy propaganda, Berge stressed that "the results of the investigation should be made public in all instances." Hoover dutifully ordered the FBI's Jackson office to take "immediate action" and submit a report "within two weeks ... without fail."[26]

If the 1918 quadruple lynching at the Hanging Bridge stood out for its brutality, the age of the latest victims heightened federal anxiety and public disgust. In his memorandum to Hoover, Berge stressed that the Clarke

confession to the FBI; see John W. T. Falkner, IV, "Unknown Subjects: Lynching of Charles Lang ... and Ernest Green, Shubuta Mississippi," October 27, 1942, Records of the Federal Bureau of Investigation, National Archives and Records Administration, College Park, MD.

25 "Mississippi on Another Rampage; Two 14 Year Old Boys Lynched!!" *Chicago Defender*, October 17, 1942; Faulkner, "Lynching of Charles Lang ... and Ernest Green," 10; Waters, "Two Lynched Boys Were Ace Scrap Iron Collectors in Mississippi Town," 13; Gayle Graham Yates, *Life and Death in a Small Southern Town: Memories of Shubuta, Mississippi* (Baton Rouge: Louisiana State University Press, 2004), 37.

26 J. A. Cimperman to Mr. Mumford, October 13, 1942; Wendell Berge to J. Edgar Hoover, October 13, 1942; J. Edgar Hoover to SAC, Jackson, October 14, 1942, all in Records of the FBI.

County lynchings "deserve special attention in view of the extreme youth of the victims." Although the first reports of the lynchings lacked the details that northern reporters and FBI investigators would later uncover, none failed to mention the boys' ages. The day the story broke, the liberal-left New York daily *PM* denounced the "Kid-Lynchers" in Mississippi. "When a race-mad mob of morons lynches a couple of adolescents," the editor declared, "one begins to wonder if even a colored infant in its crib is immune from the perverted wrath of such sorry specimens."[27]

Protest letters and telegrams emphasized the victims' youth as well. In 1918, Walter White had lamented the lynching of "Negro children" at Mississippi's Hanging Bridge. Twenty-four years later, now the NAACP's executive secretary, Walter White again underscored the victims' youth. "We protest this lynching, as we have protested all those that have gone before," the NAACP declared in a telegram to President Roosevelt, "but we are more shocked and outraged, as we are sure every decent American must be, at the thought that anywhere in our land in 1942 could be found a mob which would hang two boys barely in their teens." In Mississippi, the victims' youth provided the cautious black press with an outlet for condemning white brutality. In Meridian, just forty miles north of the Hanging Bridge, the *Weekly Echo* used the word "children" nine times in a brief but poignant editorial. "I wonder," the editor concluded, "if they called for mother?"[28]

Invocations of youth and motherhood appeared most frequently in protest letters and telegrams from black women. Young Women's Christian Association leaders from Youngstown, Ohio, questioned how the United States could "continue to talk about democracy for all peoples wherever they may be, when ... fourteen year old children ... are denied every aspect of liberty and human rights and are subjected to the brutality of a lynch mob?" Thanks to a coordinated effort by the Indiana State Federation of Colored Women's Clubs, the White House and the Justice Department received numerous letters and petitions demanding justice "as Mothers, who are giving our sons, husbands and fathers to our Country." A Gary, Indiana, woman whose son "volunteered to give his life if necessary to fight for Democracy," asked Roosevelt, "Must we make such supreme sacrifices and yet have our children lynched for no apparent reason?" In a

[27] Wendell Berge to J. Edgar Hoover, October 13, 1942, Records of the FBI; Albert Deutsch, "Kid-Lynchers," *PM*, October 13, 1942.

[28] "Ask Roosevelt to Condemn Lynchers," October 16, 1942, Papers of the NAACP [microfilm]; "Two Negro Children Lynched at the Age of 14," *Meridian Weekly Echo*, October 16, 1942.

petition that dramatized how northward migration had reshaped the struggle against mob violence, the female members of Chicago's "Natchez Social and Civic Club" protested the lynching of two "mere boys" in their native state: "We are willing that our Sons go over there and die, and we want Justice here."[29]

Both in 1918 and 1942, the rhetoric and imagery of motherhood informed the public's response to the Hanging Bridge lynchings. In 1918, the mutilation and murder of two soon-to-be mothers stood out from dozens of other atrocities committed in that era. In 1942, the mother was no longer the victim but rather the agent of mobilization and retribution. Thirteen years later, these legacies of grief and protest collided in Mamie Till Bradley's decision to make her son's corpse a galvanizing symbol for the civil rights movement.[30] The lynchings at Mississippi's Hanging Bridge show that the roots of this discourse ran deep and developed through decades of struggle against mob violence. In 1942, the victims' youth threw into bold relief black mothers' resolve and resonance.

Emphasis on the boys' age softened Mississippi leaders' characteristic defiance. Even as the *Meridian Star* blamed the racial turmoil in nearby Clarke County on civil rights activists and their "vote-hungry" political allies, the editor condemned the "inexcusable brutality" on behalf of all "decent" Mississippians. "The outrage, in and of itself, is bad enough," the editor lamented, "But the element of youth harks back to semi-savagery." Widespread attention to the victims' youth clearly bothered Clarke County's sheriff as well. "First off," he informed a northern reporter, "the papers got the ages wrong, sayin' they were 14 .... You better put it down ... they were maybe 16 to 18." Several county officials also challenged the boys' ages in interviews with FBI agents, who dutifully confirmed their birth dates – Green was indeed fourteen and Lang had only recently turned fifteen – through Mississippi's Bureau of Vital Statistics. After an enterprising local tire dealer sold snapshots of the corpses to a wire service, several northern publications

[29] The Woman's Club, Belmont Branch YWCA to J. Edgar Hoover, October 30, 1942, Records of the FBI; Lena Harris, et al., to Franklin D. Roosevelt, October 22, 1942; Mrs. John A. Bolden to Franklin D. Roosevelt, October 19, 1942; Natchez Social and Civic Club, Chicago to Hon. Francis Biddle, November 8, 1942, all in Civil Rights Division, Department of Justice Records, National Archives and Records Administration.

[30] Other scholars have explored how the politics of motherhood, particularly in the Emmett Till case, shaped responses to racial violence. As historian Ruth Feldstein demonstrated, Till's mother Mamie Bradley "was central to the politicization of her son's murder"; see "'I Wanted the World to See': Race, Gender, and Constructions of Motherhood in the Death of Emmett Till," in *Not June Cleaver: Women and Gender in Postwar America, 1945–1960*, ed. Joanne Meyerowitz (Philadelphia: Temple University Press, 1994), 266.

decided to let their readers judge for themselves. Two weeks after blasting Clarke County's "Kid-Lynchers," New York's *PM* published a photograph of the dead boys sprawled across a truck bed. Nooses still gripped their necks. "Ordinarily we don't print this kind of horror picture," noted the editor, "But this time we are trying to drive home a lesson – and we think this picture will help."[31]

In the wake of the latest Shubuta lynching, the press – white and black – demonstrated a greater willingness to depict mob violence in graphic detail. Lynching's opponents increasingly relied on photographic imagery after the turn of the twentieth century, yet practical and political changes set the 1942 lynchings apart. By the 1930s, advances in photographic technology and transmission made the printing and distribution of such graphic images simpler. Furthermore, sympathetic white editors were no longer as squeamish as they had been when Walter White submitted his account of the 1918 Hanging Bridge lynchings. By World War II, photographs of racial violence served the dual purpose of "news and propaganda" for civil rights sympathizers and the public at large.[32]

Black newspapers across the country published the postmortem photograph of Ernest Green and Charlie Lang. In Baltimore, the *Afro-American* ran the image under the heading, "After Miss. Mob Took Law in Own Hands." At the Baltimore city jail, the warden ordered the picture cut out because he feared that the image might provoke a riot. Across the country, a *Los Angeles Sentinel* subscriber clipped out the picture and sent it to the White House. "We saw this photograph in the *Sentinel*," the reader reported, "These happenings are the reasons our boys resent fighting for our country."[33]

From prison wardens to the president, government officials recognized the demoralizing and potentially destructive consequences of lynching imagery. Likewise, African Americans deployed the images tangibly as well as symbolically. Printed images catalyzed black protest and provided

[31] "The Bitter Fruit," *Meridian Star*, October 13, 1942; Bernstein, "Mississippi Laments Lynchings – But Doing Something about Them Is Another Matter," 2. The sheriff, county attorney, and the justice of the peace all questioned the boys' ages in interviews with FBI agents; see Falkner, "Lynching of Charles Lang ... and Ernest Green," 8, 18, 23, 49.

[32] Amy Louise Wood, *Lynching and Spectacle: Witnessing Racial Violence in America, 1890–1940* (Chapel Hill: University of North Carolina Press, 2009), 193–95; Bernstein, "Mississippi Laments Lynchings – But Doing Something about Them Is Another Matter," 2.

[33] "Jail Warden Censors Mob Victims' Picture," Baltimore *Afro-American*, October 31, 1942; "An American Citizen" to Franklin D. Roosevelt, October 30, 1942, Department of Justice Papers.

irrefutable proof of racist brutality down South. When African Americans clipped photographs of the boys' corpses from newspapers and sent them to the White House or the Justice Department, they offered evidence for federal prosecution.

Before and after the photograph hit the presses, black journalists juxtaposed images of lynched children with denunciations of fascist aggression. The *New Amsterdam News*, a black New York weekly, opted to run an editorial cartoon that depicted the two boys hanging from a bridge and a jackbooted Nazi saluting from below. Graphic and rhetorical parallels between mob violence and Axis atrocities abounded in black newspaper coverage of the Hanging Bridge lynchings. In the wake of Pearl Harbor, the black press had launched a "Double Victory" campaign – victory over fascism abroad and racial discrimination at home. Eighteen months later, the Hanging Bridge lynchings dramatized the stakes of "Double V" for journalists, activists, and everyday Americans.[34] See Figure 7.

Southern racial conservatives recognized Double Victory's symbolic power and attempted to undercut criticism with their own Axis analogies. Even as he condemned mob violence, Governor Paul B. Johnson warned Mississippians that shadowy Axis agents were sowing seeds of racial strife. "There are some disturbing elements at work now which have in mind only one purpose," the governor declared, "that of aiding the Axis powers seeking to create unrest and unhappiness." Following the governor's lead, the *Meridian Star* suggested that the racial agitators who goaded white Mississippians into vigilantism had "An (Axis?) Axe to Grind." For Mississippi's white elite, mob violence did not represent a pillar of Jim Crow but rather an inevitable response to any attempt to dismantle it. Thus, they deemed racial reformers as culpable as lynchers and as dangerous as Nazi saboteurs. "The root of present evil, as Gov. Johnson suggests,

[34] "Answer to the Poll Tax," *New York Amsterdam Star-News*, October 17, 1942. For a broader discussion of the "Double V" campaign and the politics of wartime protest, see Richard Dalfiume, "The 'Forgotten Years' of the Negro Revolution," *Journal of American History* 55 (June 1968): 90–106; Harvard Sitkoff, "Racial Militancy and Interracial Violence in the Second World War," *Journal of American History* 58 (December 1971): 661–81; Neil A. Wynn, *The Afro-American and the Second World War* (New York: Holmes and Meier, 1976). For a critical reassessment of the impact of the "Double V" campaign and the success of the wartime civil rights movement, see Lee Finkle, "Conservative Aims of Militant Rhetoric: Black Protest during World War II," *Journal of American History* 60 (December 1973): 692–713. For a survey of recent critical scholarship on the relationship between World War II and black protest, see Kevin M. Kruse and Stephen G.N. Tuck, eds., *Fog of War: The Second World War and the Civil Rights Movement* (New York: Oxford University Press, 2012).

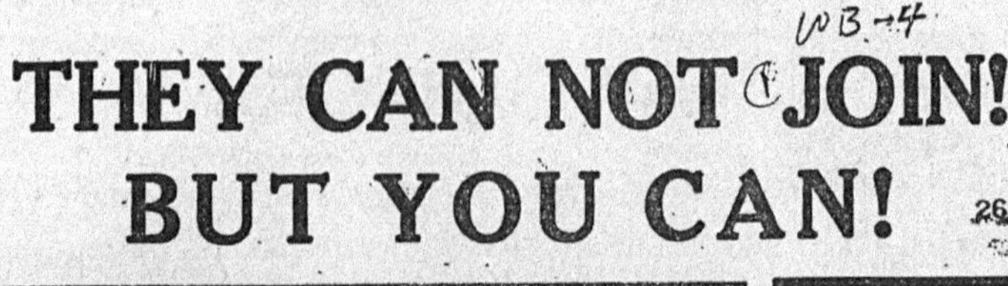

For The Past 34 Years The N. A. A. C. P. Has Been On The Firing Line Fighting Our Battles Against Racial Discrimination, Segregation, and Disfranchisement.

The New Orleans Branch Is Now Conducting A Campaign For 10,000 Members. Will You Be One Of Them? Join Now. Don't Wait For Someone To Call On You For A Membership . . . Mail or Bring It To Our Branch Headquarters, At 4134 Willow Street or 810 No. Claiborne Avenue.

The Campaign Ends May 9, 1943.

Memberships:
$1.00; $2.50; $5
$25.00; $100.0

Pictured above are Charles Lang, left, and Ernest Green, two 14-year old Mississippi boys who were lynched near Shubuta, October 11, 1942.

JOIN TODAY!!

Ask Your Neighbor T Join — Work For The Cause

Williams Printing Service — 930 N. Claiborne Ave.

FIGURE 7. Photograph of the boys' bodies, taken by a local white man after they were cut down from the bridge and carried into town, sparked black outrage and fueled wartime organizing. The New Orleans branch of the NAACP plastered the image on recruitment fliers during its wartime drive for ten thousand members. Source: "They Can Not Join! But You Can! Join Today!!" recruitment flyer, New Orleans NAACP, late 1942, reproduced in Louisiana Joint Legislative Committee, *Subversion in Racial Unrest: An Outline of a Strategic Weapon to Destroy the Governments of Louisiana and the United States*, 2 parts (Baton Rouge: Joint Legislative Committee, 1957), pt. 2: 265.

smacks of the Mein Kampf of Hitlerdom," the *Star* concluded; "At least, our current distemper follows the pattern of Nazi technique: 'Divide and conquer.'"[35]

This white supremacist version of "Double V" could not compete with the gory evidence emanating from Clarke County. In 1942, graphic lynching imagery reached more Americans than Walter White's 1918 investigative report. Yet, the return to the Hanging Bridge echoed many of the themes that activists and journalists had emphasized twenty-four years before. Like their counterparts a quarter century earlier, those who covered the 1942 lynchings emphasized not only the manner of death but also the treatment of the bodies. Claiming to have "The Real Story" on the lynchings, black journalist J. Don Davis cited "unconfirmed" but "reliable" reports that the lynchers had castrated the boys. NAACP youth director Madison Jones, who talked to relatives of the boys while on a recruiting swing though Mississippi, reported to White that both boys had been mutilated with pliers and that one had a screwdriver rammed down his throat. The photographs of the dead boys neither confirmed nor refuted the claims of torture. Nevertheless, investigators and everyday people drew from swirling rumors and a past replete with brutal lynching stories as they passed along details from Mississippi's Hanging Bridge. At the same time, they projected their own fears onto the boys' battered corpses. As in 1918, some read into those bodies stories of resistance. A black wire service reported that one boy had a bullet wound in his back: "This, they say, came about when the helpless child displayed the slow but rising new spirit that is gripping the Mississippi Negro." When the boy "steadfastly refused to help in his own death" by jumping from the railing, the report concluded, the lynchers shot him.[36]

As civil rights activists crisscrossed the South in a wartime organizing blitz and debated the extent of "race militancy" among rural blacks, signs of everyday defiance held enormous symbolic power. Like Walter White's earlier investigation, the divergent accounts of the 1942

[35] "Biddle Orders Probe Lynchings in Mississippi," *Meridian Star*, October 20, 1942; "An (Axis?) to Grind?" *Meridian Star*, October 20, 1942. For a broader discussion of southern whites' rhetorical and strategic resistance to the wartime civil rights campaign, see Jason Morgan Ward, "'A War for States' Rights': The White Supremacist Vision of Double Victory," in Kruse and Tuck, eds., *Fog of War*, 126–44.

[36] J. Don Davis, "Here's Real Story of Lynching of Children," Baltimore *Afro-American*, October 31, 1942; Madison Jones to Walter White, November 7, 1942, Papers of the NAACP [microfilm].

lynchings emphasized white sadism and black resistance. African Americans refused to retrieve and bury the bodies, just as they had in 1918. This time, journalists framed grassroots resistance in "Double V" terms. A black newswire reporter cheered the "defiant refusal" as "their protest" against "Hitlerian savagry." The same account praised a black employee of the white undertaker who reportedly vowed to "quit or die" before he would retrieve the bodies from the bridge. The report characterized black defiance as a collective show of strength and resolve. "Assuming an 'it was your dirty work, now remove it' attitude," reporter J. Jon Davis claimed, "the mill workers, soil tillers, and railroad employees mustered up courage ... and vehemently declined permission to bury the boys in a colored cemetery." Echoing this sentiment, a reporter from the *Chicago Defender* concluded, "They're learning to be proud ... they refused to bury their dead."[37]

The boys' parents cited poverty and fear, rather than protest, as their reason for leaving the bodies in the hands of white authorities. When questioned by white FBI agents shortly after her son's murder, Mentora Green claimed that she could not afford to bury her son. Charlie Lang's father caught a glimpse of his dead son when the truck first rolled into town, but he refused to set foot in Patton's Undertaking Establishment. Lang believed that "Mr. Will" had led another mob, and he feared that he might be its next victim.[38]

Whether or not these families embodied the defiant spirit that civil rights proponents celebrated, both refused to play along with a paternalistic charade. With their sons' bodies lying in a funeral parlor run by an alleged lynch mob leader, the white community's complicity could not have been more glaring. The agonizing decision to leave the corpses to be hastily boxed and unceremoniously buried reveals that black Mississippians resisted white attempts to wash their hands of lynched boys' blood.

While activists, journalists, and everyday citizens deployed the symbolic power of bodies and burial, others invoked the imagery of Mississippi's most infamous lynching site. Walter Atkins of the *Chicago Defender* branded the Hanging Bridge a "monument to 'white supremacy'" and an "altar to 'Judge Lynch.'" Other articles focused on

[37] Enoc Waters, "Waters Finds Rural Areas Lag behind Cities in Race Militancy," *Chicago Defender*, May 15, 1943; Davis, "Here's Real Story of Lynching of Children," 1; Atkins, "Shubuta Bridge's Toll Stands at Six Lynch Victims," 2.

[38] Faulkner, "Lynching of Charles Lang ... and Ernest Green," 43–45.

the victims and the crimes committed, but Atkins's commentary centered on the "rickety old span" that racked up six victims across two generations. As a monument, the bridge served to shore up white power and deter black resistance. As an altar, the structure served as a site "to offer as sacrifices" those who threatened that order in any way. The Shubuta bridge, Atkins declared, "is a symbol of the South as much as magnolia blossoms and mint juleps." Yet, the river flowing beneath the bridge symbolized something entirely different. While the Chickasawhay flowed gently, Atkins concluded, "even some of the old timers see a flood coming, a long overdue flood that will smash and sweep away Shubuta bridge and all it stands for." Invoking the ever-present imagery of the "Double V," Atkins traced that flood back to "a storm brewed in Berlin."[39]

The river flowing beneath the Hanging Bridge symbolized something entirely different to fellow *Chicago Defender* contributor Langston Hughes. For the poet laureate of the wartime civil rights movement, the muddy Chickasawhay represented the hatred and repression endured by southern blacks. In "The Bitter River," a poem dedicated to the memory of Ernest Green and Charlie Lang, Hughes lamented the murky water, tasting of "blood and clay" that drowned black dreams and choked out black life. That brown sludge reflected "no stars," Hughes wrote, only the "bars" of the looming bridge's long shadow. Behind those bars, Hughes saw the Scottsboro boys, union organizers, "the voteless share-cropper," and a "soldier thrown from a Jim Crow bus." The bars evoked imagery culled from wartime headlines and generations of racial abuse. After alluding to wrongly imprisoned southern blacks, Hughes likened the shadowy bars to "my grandfather's back with its ladder of scars."[40]

Hughes's mournful poem offered none of Atkins's redemptive imagery or retributive metaphors. Still, for Hughes, as for many who protested the Hanging Bridge lynchings, grief and despair fueled protest politics. Hughes published "The Bitter River" in *Jim Crow's Last Stand*, a 1943 pamphlet dedicated to the black freedom struggle. If "The Bitter River" catalogued discrimination and abuse seemingly without end, the booklet's title poem predicted Jim Crow's imminent demise. "Pearl Harbor put Jim Crow on

39 Atkins, "Shubuta Bridge's Toll Stands at Six Lynch Victims," 1.

40 Langston Hughes, *The Collected Poems of Langston Hughes*, ed. Arnold Rampersad, 1st Vintage Classics ed. (New York: Vintage, 1994), 242–44.

the Run," Hughes declared; "That Crow can't fight for Democracy/And be the same old Crow he used to be."[41]

While Hughes grieved Shubuta's dead youth in angry and despairing verse, the poet embraced the same geopolitical calculus that drove the "Double V" rhetoric of the black press and filtered down to everyday freedom fighters. As an NAACP Youth council president from Oakland, California, informed President Roosevelt, "These incidents though happening in Mississippi have international implications and we may rest assured that the Chinese coolie, the native of India, and every Burmese under the control of Japan is better informed of these atrocities than are the people of the neighbor counties."[42]

Despite national attention and diplomatic liabilities, no one ever stood trial for the lynchings of Ernest Green and Charlie Lang. By the time FBI agents rolled through town, they had another lynching to investigate in nearby Laurel.[43] But in Green's and Lang's deaths, the black press searched not only for symbolic resistance but also for divine retribution. A few weeks after the lynching, Shubuta's deputy sheriff fell ill. "They ended up tying him in bed," remembered a Shubuta native, where he reportedly clutched his throat and begged, "Take Ernest and Charlie off of me!" The family swore the white doctor and black maid to secrecy, but the story leaked out. "And so," the *Chicago Defender* concluded, "a law higher than that of man … defied the southern custom of 'unable to recognize the guilty parties.'"[44] Although cold comfort to the victims' families, the fact that such stories circulated months after the lynchings

[41] Langston Hughes, "Jim Crow's Last Stand," Baltimore *Afro-American*, October 24, 1942. The Baltimore *Afro-American* published the poem less than two weeks after Ernest Green and Charlie Lang were lynched. The pamphlet of the same name, which also included "The Bitter River," appeared the following summer; see Hughes, *Jim Crow's Last Stand* (New York: Negro Publication Society of America, 1943).

[42] Thomas L. Berkley to President Roosevelt, November 13, 1942, Department of Justice Papers.

[43] The lynching of Howard Wash on October 17, 1942, in Laurel, Mississippi, marked a watershed moment in federal lynching investigation and prosecution. Unlike in Clarke County, FBI agents gathered enough evidence to secure grand jury indictments against mob leaders and the complicit jailer. The trial jury refused to convict, but the promise of the Wash case distracted federal prosecutors from the Hanging Bridge lynchings; see Waldrep, "National Policing, Lynching, and Constitutional Change," 616–21; idem, *African American Confront Lynching: Strategies of Resistance from the Civil War to the Civil Rights Era* (New York: Rowman and Littlefield, 2009), 88.

[44] Waters, "Ignorance and War Hysteria," 13; "Miss. Lyncher's Conscience Talks on His Death Bed," *Chicago Defender*, July 10, 1943.

suggests how closely black observers connected the boys' fate to an imminent triumph over Jim Crow and Judge Lynch.

As the modern civil rights movement gained steam in the war's wake, the Hanging Bridge continued to cast a long shadow. Although Emmett Till's death garnered unprecedented international attention due to multiple factors, from his mother's courageous decision to display his disfigured face to the Cold War contest for hearts and minds, the tradition of making meaning from racial violence and murdered bodies reached back into earlier generations.

In two eras of world war and domestic turmoil, black responses to Mississippi's Hanging Bridge and its young victims dramatize how grief and protest operated in tandem throughout the black freedom struggle. By publicizing the horrors of mob murders, activists and everyday observers redeployed imagery meant to subdue and silence. In the process, the Hanging Bridge's utility as a symbol of white control contended with its potential to spark black protest. During decades when brutal repression isolated black Southerners from organized protest movements, racial violence spurred interaction between elite activists and rural people. In 1918 and 1942, the lynching of black youth at Mississippi's Hanging Bridge accelerated campaigns against racial discrimination. In both cases, civil rights activists deployed images of death and the dead to wield newfound political and diplomatic leverage. At the same time, rural black Southerners rejected white duplicity, sacrificed cherished burial customs, and kept alive stories of resistance. They invoked the dead, and they defied death.

11

Reframing the Indian Dead: Removal-Era Cherokee Graves and the Changing Landscape of Southern Memory

Andrew Denson

In November 1910, the Daughters of the American Revolution (DAR) placed a monument at the grave site of Cherokee warrior Junaluska in Robbinsville, North Carolina. An iron tablet bolted to a rough boulder, it honored Junaluska's service to the United States in the Creek War of 1813–1814. During those years, several hundred Cherokees joined militia troops led by Andrew Jackson in a campaign to destroy the nativist Creek movement known as the Red Sticks. At the war's climactic battle, tradition holds, Junaluska rescued Jackson from certain death by killing a Creek warrior who had assaulted the general. The DAR memorial invoked this legend and noted that "for his bravery and faithfulness," the state of North Carolina made Junaluska a citizen and gave him land in Graham County in the years after the United States forced the majority of Cherokees to remove to the West.[1]

If you visit Junaluska's grave today, you will still find the DAR marker, but you will encounter another monument as well. In the 1990s, Cherokees from the nearby Snowbird community led an effort to create a new memorial and persuade the government of the Eastern Band of Cherokee Nation to purchase the land where the old warrior lies. Around the grave they placed seven additional markers describing Junaluska's life in greater detail and emphasizing his determination to remain in what became Western North Carolina. In particular, they brought Junaluska into the history of Cherokee removal, highlighting his role as a resistance leader. Captured in 1838 and started on the journey westward, he and his brother Wachacha led about fifty Cherokees in an escape attempt, abandoning their detachment and

[1] "Junaluska," *Daughters of the American Revolution Magazine* 39 (July 1911): 64–66.

heading back toward the mountains. Although Wachacha and others made it home, Junaluska was retaken and forced on the long journey to Indian Territory. Within a few years, he returned, walking back to the southern highlands and reversing the Trail of Tears. Only then did whites in North Carolina decide that his "faithfulness" to the United States merited citizenship and the gift of a small portion of the Cherokees' stolen homeland.[2]

Placed together, the two memorials engage in mute debate over the meaning of Junaluska's life and the place of this particular Indian man in American and Cherokee history. The Daughters' monument is both a gesture of respect and an act of possession. It draws Junaluska into the history of the United States, but only on terms that emphasize American nationalism and white munificence. Junaluska becomes an agent of the empire he and other Cherokees resisted. The newer memorial attempts to revise the old by repatriating Junaluska. It works to restore his reputation as a Cherokee who served his own people, regardless of what he might have done for Andrew Jackson. Yet, neither story manages to dominate the site. Instead, they stand in awkward tension, the grave's meaning left open and unresolved.

The dead occupy a central place in the public memory of Cherokee removal. Popular depictions of the Trail of Tears often dwell on the thousands of Cherokee people who perished either in captivity while awaiting migration or during the exodus to present-day Oklahoma, and removal-era Cherokee graves have become significant sites of commemoration. Some of these graves display multiple layers of memory, different markers placed at varying periods offering clashing stories of the dead. The memorials reveal conflicts over how to include Native Americans in public narratives of American and Indian history, and, like the Junaluska Memorial, they often resist resolution. Recalling their own development, they invite us to consider the malleable nature and basic instability of public memory. They also suggest that human graves possess a distinct power to inspire historical interpretation. As tangible objects linking the past and present, graves work on the living, compelling them to try to make sense of the dead.

This essay examines the histories of three Cherokee graves, moving from east to west along the Trail of Tears. It treats these marked historical graves as dynamic sites, places where memorials interpret the past in

[2] Brett Riggs and Barbara Duncan, *Cherokee Heritage Trails Guide* (Chapel Hill: University of North Carolina Press, 2003), 118–23; interpretive markers, Junaluska Memorial and Museum, Robbinsville, NC.

complex and shifting ways.[3] A human grave is a relatively static physical thing. When it inspires memorialization, however, it becomes active. Individuals and communities express their identities through the site, whereas commemoration itself can shape the identities of those engaged in public memory work. The living animate the dead, using the grave to communicate their conceptions of the past and present. Once commemorated, moreover, the site can draw new rounds of memorialization, particularly as social and political conditions change over time and as new actors encounter old memorials. Not all commemorated graves announce their complex histories. In fact, many acts of public commemoration work to suppress previous interpretations in the interest of correcting the historical record or presenting an authentic image of the past. When historic grave sites do hint at their own development, however, they provide distinctly rich opportunities to explore the process of public memory. At the grave sites along the Trail of Tears, monuments not only recall Cherokee removal, but speak eloquently of Southerners' ongoing and contentious efforts to interpret the Indian past.

The story of Cherokee removal is familiar enough that only a brief synopsis is necessary here. Removal was the early nineteenth-century policy of compelling eastern Indian tribes to exchange their lands for territory west of the Mississippi River. After decades of piecemeal treaties allowing gradual American expansion, removal sought to open the entire East to non-Indian settlement as rapidly as possible while eliminating the presence of independent Indian nations within the borders of established states.[4]

Although federal authorities applied the policy to a host of Indian peoples, the Cherokee Nation – located within the present-day borders of North Carolina, Tennessee, Georgia, and Alabama – became the most significant test of the removal campaign. By the 1820s, the Cherokees had gained a public reputation as a "civilized tribe" due to the willingness of

[3] Communications scholar Marita Sturken calls memorialization a "technology of memory." Sturken uses this term to capture the ways in which memorials and monuments actively represent and interpret the past rather than merely contain it. Technologies of memory, she writes, are "not vessels of memory in which memory passively resides so much as objects through which memories are shared, produced, and given meaning"; Marita Sturken, *Tangled Memories: The Vietnam War, the AIDS Epidemic, and the Politics of Remembering* (Berkeley: University of California Press, 1997), 9.

[4] Francis Paul Prucha, *The Great Father: The United States Government and the American Indians* (Lincoln: University of Nebraska Press, 1984), 183–200; Ronald N. Satz, "Rhetoric vs. Reality: The Indian Policy of Andrew Jackson," in *Cherokee Removal: Before and After*, ed. William L. Anderson (Athens: University of Georgia Press, 1991), 29–54.

some members to adopt Euro-American economic practices and cultural forms. For some white Americans, Cherokee "civilization" proved that Indians and non-Indians could coexist in the East, and removal opponents frequently pointed to the tribe as evidence of the policy's illogic and brutality. During this same period, moreover, Cherokees developed a body of written law and a constitutional government by which they defined themselves as an independent nation. This government provided a strong official voice of opposition as federal authorities and American states pressed the tribe to relocate.[5]

Beginning in 1828, the state of Georgia passed a series of laws designed to take possession of Cherokee territory and compel tribal leaders to negotiate a removal treaty. Georgia extended its jurisdiction over tribal lands, outlawed the Cherokee government, and declared Cherokee laws invalid. These acts violated federal law and the Cherokees' treaties with the United States, but President Andrew Jackson, a longtime advocate of Indian removal, declined to intervene. Cherokee leaders responded by petitioning Congress while mounting a press campaign against removal with the help of sympathetic Euro-Americans. They also brought their battle to the American judicial system, hiring lawyers and contesting the Georgia laws in two landmark Supreme Court cases: *Cherokee Nation v. Georgia* (1831) and *Worcester v. Georgia* (1832). In the second, the Court ruled against the state and recognized the Cherokees as a distinct political community to which Georgia's laws could not apply. This victory proved shallow because Jackson continued to refuse to act, insisting that the tribe must end its opposition and make a removal treaty.[6]

In the wake of Jackson's refusal to enforce the *Worcester* decision, some Cherokee leaders began to argue that removal was now inevitable and that the tribal government must consent to negotiations and make the best treaty possible. Although most Cherokees, led by Principal Chief John Ross, disagreed, federal commissioners moved to negotiate a treaty with the pro-removal minority. In late 1835, this "Treaty Party," as it came to be known, signed the Treaty of New Echota by which the Cherokees sold their territory in the East and promised to migrate within two years of the

[5] Prucha, *Great Father*, 200–208; Theda Perdue and Michael Green, *The Cherokee Nation and the Trail of Tears* (New York: Penguin, 2007), 20–41; William G. McLoughlin, *Cherokee Renascence in the New Republic* (Princeton: Princeton University Press, 1986), 277–311, 388–410.

[6] Prucha, *Great Father*, 191–94; Perdue and Green, *Cherokee Nation and Trail of Tears*, 57–89; McLoughlin, *Cherokee Renascence*, 411–47; Jill Norgren, *The Cherokee Cases: The Confrontation of Law and Politics* (New York: McGraw-Hill, 1996), 49–62, 98–122.

agreement's ratification. Ross and his allies condemned the treaty and urged their Euro-American supporters to do likewise. Even after the Senate narrowly approved the agreement in the spring of 1836, the Cherokee majority refused to consider removal. In May 1838, when the two-year deadline passed, federal troops entered the Cherokee Nation and began to carry out removal by force. They established a network of military posts where they gathered groups of Cherokees before marching them to camps in southeastern Tennessee. As it became clear that removal was truly unavoidable, Ross asked that his people be permitted to oversee their own relocation. Some Cherokees migrated by river, but most traveled overland, a journey occupying several months during the winter of 1838–1839. The majority followed a route that led from the Chattanooga region northwest through Nashville and into Kentucky. Crossing the Ohio River, they moved through the southern tip of Illinois, crossed the Mississippi River, and then traversed southern Missouri, finally turning south to arrive in the new Cherokee territory in present-day eastern Oklahoma. The first detachment to travel this "northern route" left in late August 1838 and arrived the following January. The final detachment, departing in October 1838, arrived in late March.[7]

Cherokees suffered terribly during this forced migration, and most historians concur that around four thousand died as a result of removal. Even before the journey began, crowding and poor sanitation in the holding camps in southeastern Tennessee led to widespread sickness and numerous deaths. At one camp in late July, an army doctor speculated that as many as five hundred Cherokees were ill out of approximately sixteen hundred prisoners. He reported: "Their children were sick with whooping cough and dysentery before they left their homes and were traveled here through the heat labouring under those afflictions. A considerable number . . . have died since they came here, refusing to take medicine or to have anything done for them." Conditions scarcely improved as Cherokees began traveling westward, and in every detachment, disease, exposure, and exhaustion took Cherokee lives. "We found the road literally filled with the procession about three miles in length," a correspondent for the *New York Observer* wrote, describing a detachment in Kentucky. "The sick and feeble were carried in wagons . . . a great many ride on

[7] Perdue and Green, *Cherokee Nation and the Trail of Tears*, 94–113, 123–35; Thurman Wilkins, *Cherokee Tragedy: The Ridge Family and the Decimation of a People*, rev. ed. (Norman: University of Oklahoma, 1996), 236–41, 264–90; Duane King, *The Cherokee Trail of Tears* (Portland: Graphic Arts, 2008), 89–136, 170–72.

horseback and multitudes go on foot. Even aged females, apparently nearly ready to drop into the grave, were traveling with heavy burdens attached to the back, on the sometimes frozen ground, and sometimes muddy streets, with no covering for the feet except what nature had given them." This detachment, he reported, "buried fourteen or fifteen at every stopping place."[8]

An even worse stage of the journey lay ahead on the roads between the Ohio and Mississippi Rivers in southern Illinois. Ice in the rivers prevented the ferries from operating, and Cherokee detachments had to pause in some cases for several weeks as they waited for opportunities to cross. Daniel Butrick, a white missionary who accompanied the Cherokees, described the result: "One detachment stopped at the Ohio River, two at the Mississippi, one four miles this side, one 18 miles and one 3 miles behind us. In all these detachments comprising about 8,000 souls, there is now a vast amount of sickness, and many deaths. Six have died within a short time in Major Brown's company and in this detachment of Mr. Taylor's – there are [Cherokees] affected with sickness in almost every tent and yet all are houseless and homeless in a strange land and in a cold region exposed to weather almost unknown in their native country." Later, reflecting on the Cherokee ordeal, Butrick wrote, "O what a sweeping wind has gone over, and carried its thousands into the grave, while thousands of others have been tortured and scarcely survive.... For what crime then was this whole Nation doomed to this perpetual death?"[9]

The harrowing scenes Butrick described while traveling the northern route represented only a portion of the Cherokee removal experience. Some Cherokees left voluntarily in the years between the treaty and the arrival of American troops, and a community of "Old Settler" Cherokees

[8] L.H. Jordan to Lyde, July 22, 1838, Correspondence Pertaining to Cherokee Removal, National Archives, Washington DC; *New York Observer*, January 26, 1839, quoted in King, *Cherokee Trail of Tears*, 102–03. It is unclear how many Cherokees died as a result of removal. The pioneering anthropologist James Mooney, writing around the turn of the twentieth century, put the number at four thousand, and most subsequent writers have followed his example. Yet Mooney never explained how he arrived at this number, and he may have relied on a single estimate made by Elizur Butler, a white missionary and physician who joined the Cherokees on the journey westward; see Mooney, *History, Myths, and Sacred Formulas of the Cherokees* (1891; reprint, Asheville: Bright Mountain Books, 1992). For a further discussion of this demographic issue, see Russell Thornton, *The Cherokees: A Population History* (Lincoln: University of Nebraska Press, 1990), 73–76.

[9] Daniel S. Butrick, *The Journal of Rev. Daniel S. Butrick, May 19, 1838–April 1, 1839: Cherokee Removal* (Park Hill: Trail of Tears Association, Oklahoma Chapter, 1998), 52.

already existed in the West as a result of migrations earlier in the nineteenth century. Moreover, a substantial number of Cherokees avoided removal altogether, either by eluding capture or by securing permission to stay in the East. About eleven hundred remained in Western North Carolina, and this population became the nucleus of the Eastern Band of Cherokee Nation, which emerged as a distinct tribal community in the mid-nineteenth century.[10] The northern route, however, provided the enduring image of the removal era – that of a wronged people exiled from their homeland and forced on a long sorrowful passage through deadly conditions. This journey of "perpetual death" was the conception of removal white Southerners retained and then drew into public memory.

With most Cherokees safely expelled from the region, white Southerners could remember them as romantic victims. Popular writing in the South in the decades following removal often voiced laments for departing Native Americans. Historians and novelists celebrated resistance leaders like the Seminole Osceola or the Creek William Weatherford, expressing regret that American progress required the defeat of such brave warriors. Other writers painted sympathetic pictures of Indians leaving the southeast, conveying their suffering and their sorrow at the loss of their homes. These works seldom questioned the necessity of Indian removal. On the contrary, they suggested that the disappearance of Native Americans was inevitable, a belief that absolved whites of any guilt over Indian dispossession. By end of the nineteenth century, southern culture had relegated Native Americans to the region's past and to myth. Absent from the modern South, as far as most whites were concerned, Indians became suitable subjects of memorialization.[11]

The modern South has witnessed three waves of public history commemorations related to Cherokee removal. In the early twentieth century, local heritage groups in historically Cherokee places memorialized a host of removal-era individuals and events. As the Junaluska Memorial exemplifies,

[10] Perdue and Green, *Cherokee Nation and the Trail of Tears*, 117–23; King, *Cherokee Trail of Tears*, 47–88, 139–57; William G. McLoughlin, *After the Trail of Tears: The Cherokees' Struggle for Sovereignty, 1839–1880* (Chapel Hill: University of North Carolina Press, 1993), 4–5; Morris L. Wardell, *A Political History of the Cherokee Nation, 1838–1907*, rev. ed. (Norman: University of Oklahoma Press, 1977), 4–8; John R. Finger, *The Eastern Band of Cherokees, 1819–1900* (Knoxville: University of Tennessee Press, 1984), 20–29.

[11] Joel W. Martin, "'My Grandmother Was a Cherokee Princess': Representations of Indians in Southern History," in *Dressing in Feathers: The Construction of the Indian in American Culture*, ed. S. Elizabeth Bird (Boulder: Westview Press, 1996), 134–42. See also Steven Conn, *History's Shadow: Native Americans and Historical Consciousness in the Nineteenth Century* (Chicago: University of Chicago Press, 2004).

local chapters of the DAR were particularly active in this work.[12] These efforts merged with the heritage boom of the 1930s, spurring further commemoration, especially in communities that hoped to benefit from tourism related to the creation of the Great Smoky Mountains National Park. Tourist festivals in places like Asheville, North Carolina, and Knoxville, Tennessee, began to feature historical pageants that included the Trail of Tears. The Eastern Band of Cherokees also staged a pageant as part of its annual Fall Fair. In the late 1930s, the removal story even found its way into a federally sponsored event, when organizers of a week-long Civil War commemoration in Chattanooga decided to set aside one full day to mark the centennial of the Trail of Tears.[13]

These early commemorations set the stage for more substantial public history work in the decades following World War II. In the 1950s and early 1960s, communities in northern Georgia restored a removal-era Cherokee plantation house and one of John Ross's homes, while the state rebuilt a portion of the Cherokee capital at New Echota, advertising it as one of its premier historic attractions. During this same time, white civic leaders in North Carolina joined Eastern Band Cherokees in founding the Cherokee Historical Association, best known for producing the long-running outdoor drama *Unto These Hills* and for building the Museum of the Cherokee Indian. Tennesseans, meanwhile, set up numerous markers to Cherokee history and began to develop the Red Clay historic site where Cherokees held their final national councils in the East. Throughout the 1950s and 1960s, the Civil War remained the dominant subject of southern public memory, but Cherokee history received significant attention.[14]

[12] Martha Lynn Fuquay Cummings and Ida Garrett Herod Smothers, *Historical Markers Placed by the Tennessee Society Daughters of the American Revolution* (Knoxville: Tennessee Valley Publishing, 2007), 4–5, 413–18, 422–23, 439, 490. In Tennessee, for instance, DAR chapters placed markers to John Ross and the removal-era Cherokee leader John Walker, Jr. while staging several rounds of commemoration at the site of the Brainerd Mission, a removal-era mission and school near present-day Chattanooga.

[13] *Asheville Citizen*, June 2, 4, and 24, 1931; Edith Russell, "The Spell of the Smokies," 1933, Edith Harrington Papers, Southern Historical Collection, University of North Carolina, Chapel Hill; "The Spirit of the Great Smokies," October 1935, General Library, Kansas State Historical Society, Topeka; Program, Cherokee Indian Fair, October 1935, Bureau of Indian Affairs, Cherokee Agency, General Records, National Archives-Southeast, Morrow, GA; "National Chickamauga Celebration," September 1938, Local History Department, Chattanooga Public Library, Chattanooga, TN; *Chattanooga Daily Times*, September 21, 22, and 23, 1938.

[14] *Calhoun* (Georgia) *Times*, May 28, October 22, and November 12, 1953; January 1 and 7, 1954, February 2 and December 29 1956; November 7, 1957; September 4, 1958; *Atlanta*

Finally, in recent decades, the South has experienced a third and even greater wave of removal commemoration, encouraged by the participation of the federal government. In 1987, Congress approved the creation of the Trail of Tears National Historic Trail, designating a heritage corridor along the northern migration route. This act has inspired a vast amount of research and public history work related to removal. States and local communities have developed historic sites along the national trail, while the National Park Service (NPS) has certified automobile routes retracing the Cherokees' journey west. Since the mid-1990s, a voluntary organization known as the Trail of Tears Association has conducted research on removal while working to protect sites related to the trail. Although most association members are non-Indians, the organization includes Cherokees and other tribal citizens and consults with tribal authorities. The trail itself has grown over the years, as communities overlooked in the original act have sought to include their Cherokee history in the national trail system. In 2009, Congress approved a bill to expand the national trail to include two additional overland routes traveled by Cherokees during removal, along with trail sections in several states representing the roads used during the military round-up.[15] This work on the national trail, which continues unabated today, has made Cherokee removal one of the most thoroughly commemorated episodes from the American Indian past. The recent projects, however, have not erased the marks left by earlier memorialization.

Constitution, April 20, 1954; *Atlanta Journal and Constitution*, September 18, 1955; Gertrude McDaris Ruskin, *John Ross, Chief of an Eagle Race* (Decatur: Gertrude Ruskin, 1963); James Corn to Penelope Allen, January 30, 1950, Corn correspondence, William Snell Papers, Cleveland Public Library, Cleveland, TN; *Chattanooga Times*, January 19, 1961; *Cleveland* (TN) *Daily Banner*, September 26, 1979; *Tennessee Historical Markers*, 8th ed. (Nashville: Tennessee Historical Commission, 1996), 24, 152–53, 155, 162–64; John Finger, *Cherokee Americans: The Eastern Band of Cherokees in the Twentieth Century* (Lincoln: University of Nebraska Press, 1991), 114–17, 138–39; Tiya Miles, "'Showplace of the Cherokee Nation': Race and the Making of a Southern House Museum," *Public Historian* 33 (fall 2011), 11–34.

15 "To Amend the National Trails System Act to Designate the Trail of Tears as a National Historic Trail," Public Law 100–192, 1987; "Places to Go," Trail of Tears National Trail, National Park Service, www.nps.gov/trte/planyourvisit/placestogo.htm; "Plan Your Visit," Trail of Tears National Historic Trail, National Park Service, www.nps.gov/trte/planyourvisit; Trail of Tears Association, nationaltota.org; Duane King, "Wamp, Berry Lead Trail of Tears Legislation Effort," *Trail News* 7 (August 2005): 1, 3; "President Signs Bill Expanding Trail of Tears," *Trail News* 11 (June 2009): 1. For state and local commemoration efforts, see the "State Chapter News" columns in *Trail News*, the Trail of Tears Association newsletter, available on the NPS website, www.nps.gov/trte/parkmgmt/newsletter.htm.

The fact that removal has inspired several distinct waves of commemoration means that today some Cherokee sites display multiple layers of public memory. Take, for example, the grave site of Nancy Ward in Polk County, Tennessee. Born in the 1730s at Chota on the Little Tennessee River, Ward played a significant role in late eighteenth- and early nineteenth-century Cherokee political life. In the Revolutionary era, she advocated peace between Cherokees and Euro-American settlers and, according to tradition, warned early Tennessee white settlements of an impending Cherokee attack in 1776. On several occasions, she helped prevent the execution of white captives, acts that reflected both her desire for peace and her authority as a respected Cherokee woman. Toward the end of her life, she argued against removal, leading a group of women who urged the Cherokee National Council to reject further land sales and to resist American pressure to migrate and resettle in the West. She died in the early 1820s, before the Trail of Tears, and was buried near present-day Benton, Tennessee.[16]

A century later, a DAR chapter from Chattanooga placed a monument at her grave. In fact, the Daughters responsible for the marker called themselves the "Nancy Ward Chapter," which hints at the status they accorded this particular Cherokee woman. In eastern Tennessee, the DAR's most important objects of reverence were the early settlers whom Ward was said to have alerted to danger at the start of the Revolution. The Daughters viewed these "Overmountain Men" as the founders of the state, and they never tired of celebrating their contributions to the War of Independence. In 1780, militia from those early settlements secured the patriot victory at the Battle of Kings Mountain, which helped to blunt the British campaign to regain control of the southern colonies. Appalachian whites subsequently remembered that battle as a major turning point of the Revolution. Without the mountain militia, they reasoned, the British might have reconquered the South, eliminating the conditions that led to the Continental Army's victory at Yorktown the following year. Without that triumph, in turn, the United States might never have gained its independence. In the Daughters' view, Nancy Ward's warning at the start of the Revolution made her an ally of the early settlers and thus a powerful actor in the state's most sacred historical drama. Like Junaluska, Ward was a brave and faithful supporter of revered American ancestors. As the

[16] Theda Perdue, *Cherokee Women: Gender and Culture Change, 1700–1835* (Lincoln: University of Nebraska Press, 1998), 54, 92, 100–101; Robert J. Conley, *The Cherokee Nation: A History* (Albuquerque: University of New Mexico Press, 2005), 68–69.

inscription on the grave site monument explained, Ward was "the Pocahontas of Tennessee" and "the constant friend of the American pioneer."[17]

The DAR's narrative about Ward obscured much of the context for her life and actions during the Revolutionary era. Most of the Cherokees who participated in the Revolutionary War fought on the side of the British. Like many eastern Indians, they viewed the war as an opportunity to end colonial Americans' encroachment on tribal lands and to push back the frontier of white settlement. They allied with the British as part of a long struggle to protect their homes and independence, and consequently, the Overmountain Men became some of the Cherokees' worst enemies. Tennessee militia participated in immensely destructive raids on Cherokee towns during the war, while Cherokee warriors assaulted the early Tennessee settlements on several occasions. The fighting proved disastrous for the tribe, laying waste to much of the Cherokee country.[18]

In DAR commemoration, however, most of this history disappeared, supplanted by the story of one Cherokee woman's heroism, having the effect of making Euro-American domination seem welcome and inevitable. As they had Junaluska, the Daughters defined Ward as a willing agent of the American empire that displaced the Cherokee Nation at the time of removal. Separating her actions from the context of Cherokee politics and culture, they reduced her to the role of the loyal Indian helper who recognized the superiority of the coming Euro-American civilization and welcomed its rise. White communities had long used memorialization at patriot graves as a means of consecrating the landscape, an act that reinforced Euro-American possession of formerly Indian places. At sites like Nancy Ward's grave, the Daughters took this process a step further. They drew particular Native people into the ranks of revered patriots and honored them in ways that made Indian dispossession seem natural and benign. At the dedication of the Ward monument, the DAR embellished this theme by inviting a Cherokee man to participate in the ceremony. Esia Kolunaheskie "spoke in broken English of his tribe," a local newspaper

[17] "Work of the Chapters," *Daughters of the American Revolution Magazine* 59 (October 1925): 638, 646; *Tennessee State History of the Daughters of the American Revolution* (Knoxville, TN: S.B. Newman and Company, 1930), 154–60; Cummings and Smothers, *Historical Markers Placed by the Tennessee Society Daughters of the American Revolution*, 425, 476.

[18] Conley, *Cherokee Nation*, 57–60, 64–68; Collin G. Calloway, *The American Revolution in Indian Country: Crisis and Diversity in Native American Communities* (New York: Cambridge University Press, 1995), 182–212.

reported, and he recalled the unveiling of the Junaluska memorial a decade earlier. "This stolid old Indian," the reporter wrote, "usually not given to emotion, was deeply moved, and the sight of his tears was a very unusual one to most of those present." White communities' commemorations of the Cherokee past, it seems, benefited from the inclusion of Native Americans who could acknowledge the commemorators' efforts to honor Indian ancestors. Participants in the dedication rites, but seldom their authors, Cherokee witnesses served to confirm the dominant society's power over Indian lands, Indian memories, and the Indian dead.[19]

Since the 1920s, Ward's grave site has witnessed three additional phases of commemoration. In the 1950s, the state of Tennessee improved a nearby highway and placed a roadside marker indicating the grave's location. Members of the Nancy Ward Chapter of the DAR proposed this marker and suggested the text, which echoed the earlier memorial. It named Ward "a loyal friend of white settlers" and referred to her rescue of captive pioneers. It also noted that Ward was "credited with the introduction of milk cows and many improvements in homemaking into the Cherokee economy." The new sign amplified the narrative broadcast by the older monument, reasserting the Daughters' preferred understanding of Ward as the Pocahontas of Tennessee: an acculturated Native woman and an agent of the dominant white society.[20]

Later, in the 1990s, a group called the Tennessee Overhill Heritage Association began a more significant reworking of the site. Launched with the help of the National Trust for Historic Preservation, the association was dedicated to cultivating heritage tourism in the southeastern corner of the state. From its founding in 1990, it identified the region's Cherokee heritage as a particularly valuable resource for tourism, as suggested by the selection of the name "Overhill," a historical term for the Cherokee towns in eastern Tennessee. At the Ward grave site, the Tennessee

[19] *Cleveland Daily Banner*, October 26, 1923; "Work of the Chapters," 646. For the consecration of patriot graves, see Matthew Dennis, "Patriotic Remains: Bones of Contention in the Early Republic," in *Mortal Remains: Death in Early America*, ed. Nancy Isenberg and Andrew Burstein (Philadelphia: University of Pennsylvania Press, 2003), 136–48. Historian Jean O'Brien refers to this kind of interpretation of the Indian past as a "replacement narrative"; see *Firsting and Lasting: Writing Indians out of Existence in New England* (Minneapolis: University of Minnesota Press, 2010), 55–57.

[20] "Nancy Ward," roadside marker, Tennessee Highway Commission; Marion Wells to Francis Warfield, May 10, 1949 and Francis Warfield to Marion Wells, May 13, 1949, both in Nancy Ward (Polk County), historical marker files, Tennessee Historical Commission, Tennessee State Library and Archives, Nashville. A handwritten note in this file indicates that the marker, although first proposed in 1949, was erected in 1959.

Overhill Heritage Association improved the walkways approaching the grave and added new signage that offered a portrayal of Ward in line with modern academic literature on the Cherokees. The new markers placed Ward in the traditional role of a Cherokee Beloved Woman, a position of social power and political influence, and they mention her opposition to removal. Like the reinterpretations at Junaluska's grave, the new markers at Ward's grave attempted to return her to the history of her own people. They also suggest that the memory of Ward as the protector of white settlers is more myth than fact.[21]

Finally, visitors themselves have contributed further commemorative content by leaving gifts at the grave. They have tied strips of brightly colored cloth, along with small bundles of cornmeal and tobacco, to the iron fence that encloses the grave and in the tree that shades it. Such offerings have become commonplace at historic Native American graves as expressions of respect for the Indian dead and as tokens of prayer at the grave site. Although there is nothing particularly Cherokee about this activity, it reflects a broader pan-Indian practice. For the people who leave them, the offerings may represent an effort to reassert Nancy Ward's Native American identity, or perhaps the gifts are expressions of the visitors' own sense of Indianness. If nothing else, the offerings illustrate visitors' ongoing participation in the site, suggesting a continual endowment of new memories in this already recontextualized grave.[22]

The history of the Nancy Ward grave site illustrates a significant shift in the culture of American public memory. In the early twentieth century, memorialization took the promotion of national unity as its primary goal. Monuments cultivated emotional bonds between diverse local publics and the nation by reminding viewers of their communities' participation in great national events like the Revolution or the Civil War. In recent decades, this focus on national unity has diminished, and contemporary memorials tend to reflect more specific group identities while emphasizing conflict and injustice in the American past.[23] The Nancy Ward grave site

21 "Nancy Ward," interpretive marker, Nancy Ward grave site; Tennessee Overhill Heritage Association, tennesseeoverhill.com; Riggs and Duncan, *Cherokee Heritage Trails Guidebook*, 266–70; Linda Caldwell (Tennessee Overhill Heritage Association), personal communication, March 19, 2012, in possession of the author.

22 Riggs and Duncan, *Cherokee Heritage Trails Guidebook*, 266–70.

23 As American Studies scholar Erika Doss writes, "contemporary American commemoration is increasingly disposed to individual memories and personal grievances, to representations of tragedy and trauma, and to the social and political agendas of a diffuse body of rights-bearing citizens"; see *Memorial Mania: Public Feeling in America* (Chicago: University of Chicago Press, 2010), 26–37, 47–48.

reflects this transformation. The original DAR memorial placed Ward in the story of Tennessee's founding, which was, in turn, a narrative of the Revolution and the forging of the American nation. In the Daughters' hands, Ward became an Indian founding mother. The newer commemoration draws Ward back into Cherokee history while invoking the memory of removal. It affirms her specifically Cherokee identity and reminds visitors of the trauma of Indian dispossession. Pausing at the grave, one glimpses not only Ward's history but an important element of the history of modern American commemoration.

With its accretion of memorial artifacts, meanwhile, the grave site offers a striking example of commemoration's inherent tendency toward multiplicity. Public monuments often attempt to express a single view of a historical subject, presenting their chosen message as consensual and excluding competing narratives. In practice, however, they seldom achieve this level of authority. Instead, they provide common memorial spaces that visitors then invest with a variety of different, often competing conceptions of the past. They contain *collected* memories, rather than express a single *collective* memory. When examining a memorial, it can be difficult to recover this sense of diversity and competition because monuments generally present themselves as unified works of public art. Nancy Ward's grave site, however, displays its collection: it tells the visitor that different people have ascribed varying meanings to Ward's life, and thus it demonstrates how a memorial site, once designated as significant, can attract multiple narratives. The Beloved Woman jostles against the Pocahontas of Tennessee, and the resulting incongruity defeats any attempt at coherent interpretation. For some visitors, this inconsistency may render the site a less successful example of public history. Yet, it makes the grave a very good illustration of one process of public memory.[24]

When Tennessee residents marked Nancy Ward's grave, they commemorated the Indian history of a place that had once been part of the Cherokee Nation. Farther west along the Trail, the presence of removal-era dead encouraged other white communities to find Cherokee history in places only briefly influenced by the tribe. Hopkinsville, Kentucky, for instance, played a relatively small role in the Trail of Tears story. Cherokee detachments rested there and resupplied while traveling the northern land route from Tennessee to Indian Territory in late 1838. In the 1980s, however,

[24] This distinction between "collected" and "collective" memory comes from art historian James Young's work on Holocaust memorials; see *The Texture of Memory: Holocaust Memorials and Meaning* (New Haven: Yale University Press, 1993), xi.

residents of Hopkinsville organized one of most substantial removal commemorations in the South, and the presence of Cherokee graves enabled that effort. Two prominent Cherokee leaders, White Path and Fly Smith, died while camped near Hopkinsville, and their people buried them near the Little River, a short distance from town. Over the decades following removal, the white community retained a public memory of those particular deaths that helped to remind them, in turn, that thousands of Cherokees had once passed through their area. Local histories generally highlighted the fact that this section of Kentucky was the final resting place of prominent Cherokee "chiefs," and, as one writer noted in the 1880s, "many can point out the spot where these noble red men sleep their last, long sleep."[25] In the twentieth century, the town expanded to encompass the land that residents identified as the site of the burials, but the graves themselves remained undisturbed. White landowners cared for the site informally and, in the process, helped to perpetuate the memory of Cherokee visitors and the Trail of Tears.[26]

In the 1980s, that memory became a focus of public commemoration through the efforts of a white Kentuckian named Beverly Baker who ran a book-keeping business in Hopkinsville with her husband, Walter, while also working in local advertising and public relations. In the latter pursuit, she participated in efforts during the mid-1980s to promote tourism in the region, and this interest in tourism apparently drew her attention to the Trail of Tears. In December 1985, Baker read a newspaper story explaining that the NPS was considering adding one or more of the Cherokee removal routes to the national historic trails system. This chance discovery gave her the idea of developing a removal-themed historic site at Hopkinsville. Like many residents, she remembered that exiled Cherokees had traveled through this part of Kentucky, and she knew about the "chiefs'" graves. Moreover, her husband's family claimed to be of Cherokee descent, and this may have provided Baker with a particular stake in the Native American past. A Trail of Tears historic site, she concluded, would illustrate a distinct feature of local history while encouraging tourists to visit. And perhaps the NPS would provide some of the

[25] William Henry Perrin, *The Counties of Christian and Trigg, Kentucky: Historical and Biographical* (Chicago: F. A. Battey, 1884), 38; Charles Mayfield Meacham, *A History of Christian County, Kentucky: From Oxcart to Airplane* (Nashville: Marshall and Bruce, 1930), 63–65; Grant Foreman, *Indian Removal: The Emigration of the Five Civilized Tribes of Indians* (Norman: University of Oklahoma Press, 1935), 303.

[26] *New York Times*, December 21, 1987.

money to create it. As Baker later wrote in a letter to her Congressman, "If there are plans for a 'Trail of Tears' Museum, why not in Hopkinsville?"[27]

Baker brought her idea to the attention of the local tourism commission while securing the endorsement of the city and county governments. Other residents joined in the effort, and together they wrote letters to the state government, Congress, and the NPS making the case that Hopkinsville should be the site of a memorial and interpretive center for the Trail of Tears. Although the NPS proved unable to provide money for the construction of museums, Baker and her allies formed a nonprofit "Trail of Tears Commission" and began raising funds. They secured a donation of the land that contained the grave sites, along with several acres of adjacent property, and they bought a log cabin to serve as the interpretive center. With the help of Michael Abram, a physician and art collector who ran a gallery in Cherokee, North Carolina, they created a museum exhibit that included historical objects, craft items, and contemporary Native American art. The commission also began to stage annual powwows at the site, which served both as fund-raisers and as a way to publicize the project. The result of all this work was the Trail of Tears Commemorative Park, which today features the log cabin museum, markers recounting the removal story, and two life-sized bronze statues depicting the Cherokee leaders whose graves form the focal point of the commemoration.[28] See Figure 8.

Baker and her allies, however, did more than develop the local attraction; they played a very significant role in securing the establishment of the Trail of Tears National Historic Trail. Recognizing that the national project could only help their local commemoration, they organized a public relations campaign aimed at convincing Congress and the NPS to complete the work of designating a national trail memorializing Cherokee removal. To help with this effort, they enlisted Hopkinsville school

[27] Beverly Baker to Carroll Hubbard, February 27, 1986, Beverly Baker Collection, Sequoyah National Research Center, University of Arkansas at Little Rock; Beverly Baker, "Baker Recounts Early Efforts for Recognition of Trail of Tears," *Trail News* 6 (February 2005): 1, 4; "Historical Data – Trail of Tears Commission, Inc.," in scrapbook, Kentucky Chapter, Trail of Tears Association, Hopkinsville, KY.

[28] "Historical Data-Trail of Tears Commission, Inc."; Program, Park Dedication, May 14, 1988, in scrapbook, Kentucky Chapter, Trail of Tears Association; Beverly Baker to Wendell Ford, August 12, 1987; Beverly Baker to Robert E. Thompson, July 5, 1988, both in Beverly Baker Collection; Press Release, 1992, Beverly Baker Collection; *Kentucky New Era*, September 16 and 26 and October 8, 1987; May 3, 1988; September 20, 1989; "Video Tour – Trail of Tears Park and Museum," n.d., Trail of Tears Commemorative Park. When completed, the museum included both the Cherokee-themed exhibit and a "western room" featuring art and craft items from a variety of other tribal communities. This room was meant to represent the variety of Native Americans who participated in the annual powwow.

FIGURE 8. Statues of White Path and Fly Smith, Trail of Tears Commemorative Park. Taken by and in possession of the author.

children and their teachers. More than five hundred middle-school students wrote letters to Congress in support of the national trail proposal as part of special history lessons on the Cherokees and the Trail of Tears. Baker and the other adults, meanwhile, cultivated the local media and convinced Kentucky Senator Wendell Ford to introduce the bill adding the Trail of Tears to the national historic trail system. When that bill became law in late 1987, Hopkinsville was one of four specific locations identified as sites related to Cherokee removal.[29] Most likely, Congress would have eventually approved the national trail, with or without the Kentuckians' efforts. The NPS had recommended designation of the Trail of Tears in its feasibility studies, and there were other constituencies supporting the idea. But Baker and her allies provided the immediate stimulus for the inclusion of the removal route in the trail system. In doing so, they ensured that Hopkinsville would figure prominently in the national effort to remember Cherokee removal.[30]

[29] Baker, "Baker Recounts Early Efforts," 1, 4; Beverly Baker to Leon Roberts, July 28, 1986; Beverly Baker to Senator Mitch McConnell, October 2, 1986, both in Beverly Baker Collection; Senate Report 100–461 (to accompany S. 578), Committee on Interior and Insular Affairs, December 1, 1987, 100 Cong., 1 sess., US Serial 13842, 2.

[30] *Trail of Tears Final National Trail Study* (Washington: Department of Interior, 1986), vi, sec. 2: 5–6, sec. 3: 1–2, sec. 11: 1–2, app. D: 4.

This commemorative work had the effect of greatly amplifying connections between Cherokee history and the town and its surrounding region. As residents promoted the local memorial and the national trail, their sense of the Cherokees' significance to the area grew, a process Baker's correspondence illustrates quite vividly. Her initial letters exploring the memorial idea simply noted that the Cherokee migration route passed through Hopkinsville and that White Path and Fly Smith were buried there. As the work continued, however, she began to argue that the Cherokees "played an important part in the history of this area" and that "many lives here were touched by that forced march."[31] Later, in discussing the school children's letter-writing campaign, she suggested that students should emphasize that the Trail of Tears "bears strong historical significance to western Kentucky." She also encouraged them to note that "many area citizens" like her husband could claim Cherokee descent. The idea of the memorial, in other words, led Baker to reinvent the historical character of her home place, finding a more pronounced Indian identity for the predominantly white southern town. At Hopkinsville, a non-Indian community enlarged its own role in Cherokee history while shaping a national project that today represents one of the most extensive efforts at recognizing the Indian past ever mounted by the federal government.[32]

Two graves lay at the heart of that process. At Hopkinsville, the presence of the removal graves and local residents' awareness of the dead created room for the Cherokee removal story within local memory. When national institutions displayed an interest in that story, residents remade the grave site, transforming it from a small cemetery into a substantial monument. In doing so, they moved the Cherokee story to the center of their town's public historical identity. The local commemoration then contributed to the national effort to memorialize removal, which in turn opened the prospect that other sites along the trail might be similarly transformed. The graves of White Path and Fly Smith made much of this possible by first anchoring the Cherokee story in a non-Indian place.

A similar series of developments occurred still farther along the Trail of Tears at a place called Moccasin Springs, in southeast Missouri. Here, one encounters perhaps the strangest of the recontextualized Cherokee graves. Located about ten miles north of Cape Girardeau, this area witnessed a

[31] Beverly Baker to Carroll Hubbard, February 27, 1986, and Beverly Baker to Ray Emmanuel, May 23, 1986, both in Beverly Baker Collection.

[32] Beverly Baker to Leon Roberts, July 28, 1986, and Beverly Baker to Jane Adams and Clyde Wallace, August 28, 1986, both in Beverly Baker Collection.

particularly terrible phase of the Cherokee journey along the northern route – the protracted winter crossing of the Mississippi River. Removal detachments reached the Mississippi during freezing weather, forcing many Cherokees to wait for conditions on the river to allow the operation of ferries. Packed together in camps on both banks, Cherokees suffered from exposure and disease, and scores perished as they waited for the journey to resume. The area around Moccasin Springs, then, became the final resting place for a great many of the removal dead.[33]

Like the people of Hopkinsville, local residents of Moccasin Springs remembered that Cherokees had passed that way and that some had died, and they elected to care for a particular Cherokee tomb. In this case, however, it was not the burial of a prominent leader like White Path, but the grave of a young woman whose name they recalled as "Otahki." In local memory, she was the daughter of Jesse Bushyhead, a Baptist minister and politically prominent Cherokee who led one of the detachments that crossed the river at Moccasin Springs. An especially beloved member of her party, she had "done much good toward cheering her people on the weary march," according to a 1962 account. Like Nancy Ward and Pocahontas, she played the role of a dutiful Indian woman, although in this case she supported her own exiled people rather than white settlers. She died shortly after crossing the Mississippi, having contracted pneumonia in camp, and her family buried her about a mile from the ferry landing. For a time, a wooden cross marked her grave, and when a brush fire destroyed that monument, local residents replaced it with a mound of stones and, still later, a cross made of iron. In the 1940s, Girl Scouts in Cape Girardeau adopted the name Otahki for their troop, an act that echoed the DAR's creation of a Nancy Ward Chapter in Tennessee. The Girl Scouts also placed a small additional marker at the site. For more than a century, white residents maintained this one grave and, with it, a particular memory of Cherokee removal.[34]

In the 1950s, civic leaders in Cape Girardeau mounted a campaign to establish a state park at Moccasin Springs, amplifying the Otahki memory which, in turn, influenced the historical character of the place the park

[33] Foreman, *Indian Removal*, 308; Mooney, *History, Myths, and Sacred Formulas of the Cherokees*, 132–33; King, *The Cherokee Trail of Tears*, 111–12, 130–31.

[34] (Jackson) *Missouri Cash-Book*, August 22, 1935; (Cape Girardeau) *Southeast Missourian*, October 10, 1962; (Kennett, Missouri) *Democrat*, January 5, 1962; Laura Hinkebein (Otahki Girl Scouts, Inc.), personal communication, June 29, 2004, in possession of author; Marie W. Exler, *Tears of the Trail* (Cape Girardeau: Southeast Missouri University, 2000), 9; Joan Gilbert, *The Trail of Tears across Missouri* (Columbia: University of Missouri Press, 1996), 57–59.

preserved. Initially, the campaign appears to have had little to do with history or commemoration. Residents simply wanted to create a camping and recreation area, making use of a scenic and relatively undeveloped stretch of land along the river to draw visitors. Their work fit with larger efforts in the South to capitalize on America's mid-century boom in automobile tourism. Once Cape residents decided that the place was special, however, they began to find cultural as well as natural assets in the landscape, and the memory of Otahki and removal quickly came to the fore. In promoting their plan, they chose to emphasize that Moccasin Springs was not only a beautiful spot but the setting for tragic historical events, personified by the young woman buried by the river. They made the area's fleeting role in the Cherokee removal story one of the main justifications for preserving the place, and Moccasin Springs became part of the South's substantial postwar wave of removal commemoration. They even named the park for the Trail of Tears. Thus, a memory of the Cherokee past fixed on the landscape by Otahki's grave became central to this non-Indian community's avowed historical identity. This corner of Missouri, hundreds of miles from either North Carolina or Oklahoma, became a Cherokee place.[35]

Missouri officially opened its Trail of Tears State Park in the spring of 1962, and one of the highlights of that first season was the dedication of a new monument at the grave. Erected by the Cape Girardeau Rotary Club, it consisted of a bronze tablet set in a stone slab and sheltered within a pagoda-like structure made of iron and concrete. The tablet told of Otahki's death during the Cherokees' "forced exodus" to Indian Territory, identifying her as a "princess" and Jesse Bushyhead as a "chief." At the dedication, a crowd of five hundred listened as Missouri legislator and jurist Rush Limbaugh (grandfather of the radio personality) recounted the Cherokee removal story and described the development of the park. Oklahoma Supreme Court Justice N. B. Johnson, a citizen of the Cherokee Nation, elaborated on the history of the Trail of Tears, thanking Missourians for preserving the memory of this "foul blot" on American history. With this ceremony, local residents and the state government completed the sanctification of the grave. It became a

[35] Minutes for February 5 and August 6 1954; May 4, 1956; July 1, 1957, State Parks Board, Archives, Division of Parks, Recreation, and Historic Sites, Missouri Department of Natural Resources, Jefferson City; Report on the Master Plan for the Trail of Tears State Park, July 1957, Archives, Division of Parks, Recreation, and Historic Sites; *Southeast Missourian*, January 13 and 14, March 24, 1956.

FIGURE 9. Dedication in May 1962 of the Princess Otahki Memorial in the Trail of Tears State Park, Jackson, Missouri.
Source: Photograph. Courtesy of (Cape Girardeau) *Southeast Missourian*, May 27, 1962.

"shrine," as a local newspaper described it, set apart in the landscape as a place suitable for visitors' moral contemplation.[36] See Figure 9.

There was a problem, however, with all of this activity: Otahki, it seems, never existed. A host of Bushyhead descendants attended the dedication, and others visited in the years that followed, but none of them could recall a young woman named "Otahki." Jesse Bushyhead, as far as anyone could determine, had not lost a daughter on the Trail of Tears. In fact, his wife delivered a baby girl not long after the Mississippi crossing, and the minister commemorated her place of birth in her name, Eliza Missouri Bushyhead. Although other young women, including a sister of Jesse Bushyhead, died during this stage of the journey, the person enshrined in

[36] Program, Dedication Ceremony, Princess Otahki Memorial, May 27, 1962, Archives, Division of Parks, Recreation, and Historic Sites; *Southeast Missourian*, October 11, 1961; May 28 and 29, 1962. For the sanctification of sites of violence or tragedy, see Kenneth E. Foote, *Shadowed Ground: America's Landscapes of Violence and Tragedy*, rev. ed. (Austin: University of Texas Press, 2003), 8–16.

local memory had never lived. By the time park officials realized this, the story of the princess had literally been set in stone – marked, dedicated, and sanctified. It could not be erased without offending the local community that had worked so hard to preserve Otahki's memory.[37]

Instead, the story and monument were recontextualized, like Nancy Ward's grave and those of White Path and Fly Smith. Park personnel began to treat the Otahki story as a legend and to suggest to visitors that they view the grave site memorial as a tribute to all of the Cherokees who died during removal. Although park records do not indicate precisely when this shift occurred, an interpretive plan written in 1980 suggests that staff members were presenting Otahki as fiction rather than fact. The park then reworked the monument itself after the NPS included the site on the Trail of Tears National Historic Trail. In 2001, park personnel installed new signage at the grave, unveiled during a conference of the Trail of Tears Association. They placed the signs on the approach to the 1962 monument, so that visitors would encounter the new memory just before they met the old. The signs referred to Otahki as a "local legend" and explained that "princess" was merely a title of respect conferred by whites. The signage suggested, meanwhile, that the person buried in the grave was Jesse Bushyhead's sister, although the evidence for this identification was more circumstantial than the signs implied. Bushyhead's sister had, in fact, perished during removal, but there was no way to prove that her death had initiated the Otahki story in local memory.

Finally, park officials identified the site as the "Bushyhead Memorial," drawing attention away from the name Otahki, the origins of which had always been unclear. They did not remove the older monument, however, or in any way change its problematic text. Officials chose to respect the local community's original conception of the site, allowing the Otahki story to coexist with the narratives told by the new signs. Those signs attempted to correct elements of the local memory, but even today, the story of the Cherokee princess remains a powerful presence. The Otahki monument from the early 1960s is larger than the new signs and more visually striking, and it occupies the very center of the site, the tomb. Park personnel may call the site the Bushyhead Memorial, but it remains

[37] Booker Rucker to Brick Autry and Thomas Holloway, July 27, 1992, Archives, Division of Parks, Recreation, and Historic Sites; Jesse Bushyhead to Duane H. King, December 12, 1993, King Research Collection, Archives, Museum of the Cherokee Indian, Cherokee, NC; Carolyn Thomas Foreman, "Aunt Eliza of Tahlequah," *Chronicles of Oklahoma* 9 (March 1931): 43–55.

Otahki's grave. As a result, the site presents another uneasy conversation between clashing public memories: the romantic legend of the dying princess grating against the more recent interpretation.[38]

"Monuments seem to remember everything but their own past," art historian James Young has written.[39] Frozen and apparently timeless, they refuse to divulge the conditions that prompted their own creation. The sites described here, however, do remember. In their layers of commemoration, they exhibit at least a portion of their individual histories. The Nancy Ward grave site tells of its origins as a tribute to the "Pocahontas of Tennessee," while Otahki's shrine hints at the process whereby a section of southeast Missouri became a Cherokee place. By gesturing toward their individual pasts, these three monuments call attention to their own constructed natures, reminding us that histories continually change, even those written in stone. The monuments encourage this awareness, in part through their inconsistency. Although the newer memorials revise the stories told by the old, they never fully accomplish the revision. The older monuments retain some of their authority as long as they are present, and consequently the meaning of the graves remains open. Standing at these sites, one experiences the incompleteness and pliable character of public memory.

Removal graves, meanwhile, illustrate the particular power the dead can confer upon sites of memory. In Hopkinsville and at Moccasin Springs, residents' awareness of Cherokee graves played an essential role in commemoration. The dead encouraged the public identification of these places with Cherokee history by rooting the removal story in the landscape, and they led some members of these communities to consider the moral significance of the Trail of Tears. Sites of violence and tragedy can act on communities, encouraging public examination of the past. To set this work in motion, however, the sites require tangible evidence of their violent histories. Graves provide such evidence, promoting an awareness of past human suffering that encourages historical reflection. A landscape visibly marked by the dead demands interpretation from the living.[40]

38 "Heritage Interpretation Conceptual Plan," February 27, 1980; Larry Grantham to H. G. Riggs, May 29, 1991; Booker Rucker to Brick Autry and Thomas Holloway, July 27, 1992, all in Archives, Division of Parks, Recreation, and Historic Sites; Jesse Bushyhead to Duane H. King, December 12, 1993, King Research Collection; "Bushyhead Memorial," interpretive sign, Trail of Tears State Park.

39 Young, *Texture of Memory*, 14.

40 As cultural geographer Kenneth Foote has written, "the evidence of violence left behind often pressures people, almost involuntarily, to begin debate over meaning"; Foote, *Shadowed Ground*, 5.

Several of these acts of public interpretation took place within tourism development, and it is worth considering the relationship between tourism and the dead. At Hopkinsville and Moccasin Springs, tourism promoters sought distinctive elements of local history to market to visitors. The presence of Cherokee graves helped them define the removal story as part of their local heritage and thus craft a narrative they could offer to tourists. They took possession of the Indian dead, making Cherokee history their own. The graves made that history salient while providing a concrete focus for tourism-oriented commemoration. An awareness of the dead, meanwhile, may have also provided a more tangible experience of the removal story for visitors. Cherokee suffering forms one of the major themes of the public memory of the Trail of Tears. At a removal grave, tourists encounter a physical artifact of that suffering and of the harm caused by removal's injustice. The grave renders the historical episode more perceptible and real, even when, as in the case of Otahki, the person commemorated never actually existed. Scholars have long argued that tourists leave home in search of authentic experiences separate from their normal, day-to-day lives.[41] If this is true, the presence of the dead may contribute to that sense of authenticity.

Finally, these complex monuments remind us that some histories and some lives are better told with their incongruities left intact. They provide an argument for the value of contradiction in public history. Consider again Junaluska's grave in the mountains of North Carolina. Surely, some of the Cherokees who created the new monument preferred to remove the DAR's tablet, replacing it and erasing its embarrassing colonial narrative. By leaving it in place, however, they created a richer site of memory and a more thorough testament to the dead man at its center. Junaluska was a Cherokee patriot who resisted removal, a man who sought to ensure that some of his people would persist in the Cherokee homeland; and Junaluska was a warrior for the United States, an ally of Andrew Jackson, and the recipient of North Carolina's bounty. Today, the grave site holds those memories in tension. It allows one to hear the dissonance of its multiple narrative, and, in so doing, it communicates more about Junaluska's life and about the history of the South than could one memory or the other alone.

[41] Dean MacCannell, *The Tourist: A New Theory of the Leisure Class* (New York: Shocken Books, 1976), 2, 14–16, 91–107; John Urry, *The Tourist Gaze* (1990; reprint, London: Sage, 2002), 2–3, 9–15. For a critique of the focus on authenticity, see Edward M. Bruner, *Culture on Tour: Ethnographies of Travel* (Chicago: University of Chicago Press, 2002), 4–7.

Index

Lightning Source UK Ltd.
Milton Keynes UK
UKHW04f0302011018
329669UK00001B/107/P